Reggae on CD

Lloyd Bradley is a classically trained chef, one time DBC Radio and club deejay, owned and operated the Dark Star soul sound system during the 1970s; was part of the Parliament-Funkadelic on the *Uncle Jam Wants You* tour; sings lead and background vocals on Bootsy's *Sweatband* album; used to write Delbert Wilkins monologues for Lenny Henry; was a former contributor to *Blues and Soul*, *Black Music & Jaxx Review*, *NME*, *Q Magazine*, *The Independent*, and *The Independent on Sunday*. He currently writes for *The Guardian* and *The Voice*, compiles *Classic Funk* albums for mastercuts and, with Ian Dewhirst, occasionally rocks the house at The Jazz Cafe in Camden Town.

Reggae on CD

THE ESSENTIAL GUIDE

Lloyd Bradley

KYLE CATHIE LIMITED

First published in Great Britain in 1996 by
Kyle Cathie Limited
20 Vauxhall Bridge Road, London SW1V 2SA

ISBN 1 85626

A Cataloguing in Publication record for this title is available
from the British Library.

Typeset by SX Composing DTP, Essex.
Printed by Cox & Wyman, Berkshire.

CONTENTS

ACKNOWLEDGEMENTS

Without reggae music there'd be a big hole in music. And an even bigger hole in *my* music. Whether one book is enough to cover it all is debatable, but I hope this one comes somewhere near it. All credit, all praise and much, much respect is due to the producers, the singers, the players of instruments, the deejays and the sound system operators.

Inspiration: Spinners; The Railway Hotel, Harrow; Bluesville; The Cobweb; Sir George HiFi; Weasel's; The JBs FC; Rodigan; Tommy Vance; Paul's Records, Finsbury Park; Musik City, Dalston; Dennis Bovell; the Carnival before they stopped sound systems setting up under the flyover; Ron Shillingford; and hanging outside Sunshine Records in Turnpike Lane.

Most of all though: Cheddie, who used to drive me mad with reggae; Lepke, Dr Watt, Chuckie, Dr Martin and The Rankin' Miss P – the original DBC crew who made me appreciate a whole spectrum of it; and Steve Barrow, who made so much of it available.

Big thanks to: Murray 'Jah Fish' Elias, Liz Greader, Bob Harding, Hedge, Gaylene Martin, Quentin Scott, Tom Terrell and, last but certainly not least, Ballard.

Bigger thanks to: Kyle, Catherine and Beverley, who proved themselves to be as ridiculously patient and understanding as they were ludicrously good-tempered. And Emma, who probably would've been if she'd had to.

But the biggest thanks of all to: Keith and Wayne at Daddy Kool Records, London's premier reggae retailer (12 Berwick Street, London W1V 3RG; 0171 437 3535), who put themselves out way beyond the bounds of friendship.

Five on the black hand side for Stanley, Kester, Kenny, Kevin, Percy, Overton, Ronald, George, The Capelli Crew and Simon Hills. And much more than that for Diana, George and Elissa.

IN MEMORY OF DUKE REID, KING TUBBY, BOB MARLEY AND KEITH HUDSON

A Personal Selection

What follows, in diplomatically alphabetical order, is a selection of twenty of my favourite reggae albums available on CD. While each has got into the list only by being something very special in its own right, they all provide a gateway into more specialist areas of this thing we call reggae. In other words, it's not quite an instant reggae collection but it'll be a step in the right direction. (As indicated by the page numbers, each is looked at in greater detail later in the book.)

The Abyssinians: *Satta Massa Gana*; Heartbeat HBCD190
Probably the best, most consistent example of roots reggae harmonizing available on CD. (*See page 178*)

Aswad: *Showcase*; Island IMCD57
Further proof that UK reggae could be far more inventive than its Jamaican counterpart, as the Lions Of Ladbroke Grove stir jazz/funk and soul into their roots. (*See page 186*)

Buju Banton: *'Til Shiloh*; Loose Cannon 524 135-2
A stunning example of life after dancehall, this revives traditional values of melody and righteousness in an entirely modern digital setting. (*See page 320*)

Beenie Man: *Blessed*; Island Jamaica IJCD 3005
Dancehall's current champion, blending righteous Rasta sentiment with the hardest, sparsest rhythms, capturing the flavour and excitement of post-gun lyric ragga. (*See page 321*)

Big Youth: *Screaming Target*; Trojan CDTRL61
One of the first roots deejays, Youth's melodic toasting was as vibrant and as joyously self-celebratory as it was original. (*See page 190*)

Dennis Brown: *Wolves And Leopards*; Blue Moon CDBM046
The most seductive voice in reggae, at what was the peak of his powers. The best original album of cool roots and smoove lovers' rock. (*See page 198*)

Burning Spear: *Social Living*; Blood And Fire BAFCD004
A singer who summed up Rasta reggae with his rich, smokey tones, hazy, horn-loaded mixes and 100 per cent cultural lyrics. (*See page 204-205*)

The Congos: *Heart Of The Congos*; Blood And Fire BAFCD009
Classic Jamaican three-part harmony given the Rasta vibe, and produced by Lee 'Scratch' Perry to stunning, mellow dub effect. (*See page 211*)

Joe Gibbs: *African Dub Chapter Three And Four*; Rocky One Records RGCD024
The peak of the legendary *African Dub* series, in which Gibbs and engineer Errol Thompson show exactly how far a tune can be deconstructed and still rock you as hard as the original cut. (*See page 225-226*)

King Tubby: *Dub Gone Crazy – The Evolution Of Dub At King Tubby's 1975-1979*; Blood And Fire BAFCD002
King Tubby was a dub genius, and these twelve tracks bear witness to that as they show his repertoire of manipulation, fading and phasing to stunning effect. (*See page 299*)

Luciano: *Where There Is Life*; Island Jamaica IJCD3001
In a world dominated by deejays, this modern-day roots singer brings a sense of swing and genuine upfulness to the dancehall, without sacrificing any of the excitement. (*See page 343*)

Bob Marley: *Songs Of Freedom*; Tuff Gong TGCBX1
With its numerous previously unreleased tracks, this four-CD, handsomely packaged, informatively bookleted A-Z of Bob Marley is as valuable to a long-time devotee as it is to a novice. (*See page 252*)

Augustus Pablo: *King Tubby Meets The Rockers From Uptown*; Sanachie MESSCD1007
Pablo's up-tempo rockers' rhythms, melodica melodies and 'East Of The River Nile' sound were a major part of roots reggae. This album gives it a riotous King Tubby dub mix. (*See page 271*)

Lee Perry: *Reggae Greats*; Mango 162 539 792-2
Ten wonderfully warm examples of Lee Perry's genius, as he applies his cool roots techniques and *sans frontières* approach to the mixing desk to eight different artists as diverse as Junior Murvin, The Heptones and Prince Jazzbo. (*See page 278*)

Steel Pulse: *Handsworth Revolution*; Mango RRCD24
This debut album shows astonishing breadth of approach within reggae's boundaries, and the band never really bettered it. (*See page 291*)

U-Roy: *Your Ace From Space*; Trojan CDTRL359
The first toaster to make it big on record, U-Roy always had a sense of joy at what he was doing. This is most of his original work with Duke Reid, setting his lively style over some cool rock steady rhythms. (*See page 157*)

Various Artists: Ba Ba Boom – Classic Rock Steady And Reggae 1967-1972; Trojan CDTRL265
A collection of classic Duke Reid recordings, showing how rock steady eased its way into reggae. (*See page 72-78*)

Various Artists: *Big Blunts – Twelve Smokin' Reggae Hits*; Tommy Boy TBCD1077
Cutting across twenty years of reggae – from U-Roy to Ninjaman – this concerns itself with hymns to the herb, and I can't work out why there aren't more albums like it. (*See page 357*)

Various Artists: *Respect To Studio One*; Heartbeat HBCD181/182
The pick of Coxsone's catalogue, from the ska days right up through roots to his early dancehall experiments. Contains The Heptones' 'Pretty Looks Isn't All'. (*See page 106*)

Various Artists: *Tougher Than Tough – The Story Of Jamaican Music*; Mango IBXCD1
Ninety-five tracks, taking you on a journey from the pre-ska 'Oh Carolina' to a dancehall version of the same song nearly thirty-five years later, and visiting practically every important Jamaican tune along the way. (*See page 168*)

INTRODUCTION

Reggae on CD? *Reggae* on CD? Don't be absurd.
When you come out with it like that, it just doesn't seem natural. Almost a cultural contradiction, in fact. Reggae is all about *singles*. Trojan, Bluebeat, Bamboo, Pressure Beat, Pyramid, Pama, Attack, Upsetter and so on. And when you had more than just Saturday job money to spend, singles meant fresh-from-Jamaica pre-release items, with plain paper covers, no centres and even less information on the label. Singles that came at you first in a sound system dance or in the cramped confines of Musik City in Ridley Road, Dalston, or Paul's in Finsbury Park, or Desmond's Hip City in Brixton. In each case you would have *felt* them as much as heard them. The bass boomed out of speakers so big you could raise a family in them and thumped you firmly in the guts. Reggae in its intended environment would show such a total lack of respect for the sonic range that anything that wasn't driving those eighteen-inch woofers would be forced through high-frequency horn units capable of only the absolute top of the treble. A couple of two-bob bits Sellotaped to the turntable arm's headshell would be the only concession to increased fidelity.

Not exactly intermodulated, twin-processor, 24-bitstream, oversampled digital clarity, is it?

And the only way to measure your reggae collection was by the size of your box. Your box full of seven-inch singles that is. Singles that always seemed slightly thicker than their main-stream counterparts; with labels fixed somewhere near the centre. A bit of dreadlock pressed into the groove would be held

1

up as a badge of authenticity – hell, even a B-side was an optional extra.

All of which tends not to equate reggae for domestic consumption with the sleek, shiny sophistication of your Compact Disc. Indeed, it wasn't so long ago that the notion of reggae on an LP was a bit much to deal with. With the exception of *Prince Buster Live On Tour*, that is, which, even as early as 1968, kids far bigger and hipper than you carried about with them in the most ostentatiously casual way as possible. But largely, like pre-Isaac Hayes/Norman Whitfield soul music, reggae artists' long-playing offerings stood or fell by how many existing/potential hit singles they had on them. And this meant, as saleable propositions, they often shot themselves in the foot, for the people most likely to buy them would already own several tracks. The only reggae albums anyone took at all seriously were compilation sets: the *Tighten Up* series – fourteen shillings and sixpence for a dozen or so of the most recent reggae hits – *Club Ska '67*, *Club Reggae*, and so on. And they were *collections of singles*.

However – and this would be typical of reggae's 'on the down beat' approach to life – the reasons the music never lent itself to the LP are precisely the reasons why it works so well on CD. Because, quite simply, you can collect a lot more singles on the one CD than you can on twelve inches of vinyl. Check it. The more album-oriented mainstream act feels the need to extend the usual forty-five minutes of an LP to well over an hour to fill the average CD. Which often results in at least twenty minutes of music you could (should?) live without. Reggae-style means you'll finish up with half a dozen more killer tunes. In fact, you could almost say that reggae on CD is so spot on a proposition that, in many cases, it will eclipse rock as The Reason CD Was Invented.

All of this, of course, only applies if your name's not Lee Perry or Augustus Pablo. In their case, something on the 'conceptular' side of innovative would be taken as read. The longer player is then the only format that could do their work justice – work that has a centric thread, with themes, moods and musical ideas that need to be stretched out to be fully appreciated. Thus, and this would be another nod in the direction of the digital revolution, the Longer it Plays the better.

But these two artists, and the legendary dub master King

Tubby, are exceptions rather than the rule. Reggae was always instant in its relationship between player and audience. It is a mass-participation event, with the emphasis on the mass, as far removed as anybody could get from the sadly solitary notion of sitting about listening to records over headphones, nodding to oneself and murmuring how 'brilliant' it all is. Indeed, progressive rock and its slipstream seemed to bypass Jamaica more or less completely. From day one, back in the late fifties, reggae's direction was dictated by the people it was aimed at. And all those people ever wanted when it came to VFM (Value From Music) was to move their bodies.

Ska, rock steady, reggae – the indigenous Jamaican music industry – grew up out of Kingston ghetto dances. It was the deejays and sound system operators who were the earliest record producers, cutting the sides and initiating musical changes in direct response to their crowds' demands. Being able to road test their musical ideas instantly meant that when they did take the lead it was only ever to where the dancers wanted to go.

Thus it came to make sense to serve reggae up in an easy-access, self-contained, almost self-celebratory fashion. The whole purpose of which being to provide three minutes of excitement and enjoyment on a dance floor: shuffling, stepping, skanking, rocking, holding up a girl, or just plain showing off. And in ram-packed blues dances in north London in the early-seventies, it wouldn't have made sense any other way. An aspect that, more than twenty years later, hasn't changed at all. It's still all about that vital three minutes.

The successful performers understood this too. After all, they were often alarmingly youthful and only one step removed from being in the audience themselves. It was this perpetual stream of hopefuls looking for a route out of poverty that kept reggae close to its ghetto roots. A situation perpetuated by the fact that, until very recently, it was nigh on impossible to get rich from reggae, so its practitioners were never able to stray too far from the source. In fact, reggae has remained more or less the exclusive property of the black Jamaican bloodline for thirty-odd years. Take the most expensive American or British session musicians and none of them could ever play reggae that will genuinely move a crowd from the dark sides of Kingston or Harlesden.

But then again, what we're dealing with here is the cultural rather than strictly musical. If you grew up in the 'wrong' part of Kingston or its unofficial colonies – Stoke Newington, Hornsey, Willesden, Peckham, Handsworth and the like – reggae was a vital part of life. It was also, quite naturally, a reflection of that life. In much the same way that Trinidad's calypso kept its people, both at home and abroad, informed with local news and views, so Jamaica's musical output quickly earned its nickname of 'the ghetto's newspaper'. From ska onwards, just by buying records and hanging out at sound systems, kids in coldest Dalston could keep informed of such JA occurrences as the sustained ghetto violence and rioting that were the rude boy wars in the early sixties, the Rasta revolution, gun court justice, election shenanigans, economic decline or the rise of the posses. Of course it would never be as fact-checked accurate as, say, the international pages of *The Times*, but it was always going to have a better bassline. Likewise it was always going to be an up-to-the-minute source of the latest yard slang or style affectations. In short, reggae has always been inseparable from its environment. It could never, ever, be anything other than an expression of where it came from. This is a music with genuine soul.

Soul that lives on – literally – thanks to CD and its revisiting of past glories and an accessible cataloguing of all things present. The reggae industry, both in the UK and Jamaica, embraced Compact Disc technology somewhat belatedly. But what was lacking in punctuality has been more than made up for in enthusiasm, and reggae on CD is currently one of the fastest growing areas in the music business. It is an activity that is based more in the past than in the present, as back in the day there was just so much reggae about. During the fifties and sixties the producers ruled the business, there was no such thing as royalties, and the closest most artists got to a recording contract was a few dollar bills for cutting a record. Thus the only way to make ends meet was to cut an awful lot of them. Or, as became almost regulation in the seventies, you set up your own studio, so that you could make as much music as you liked, when you liked.

All these factors led to a situation whereby Jamaica – with a population half the size of London's – boasted more record labels than the entire UK. Most of these labels were so precariously financed, however, that they didn't last too long, so much of this vast output has long since disappeared. But, happily, it's precisely these hard-to-get-hold-of gems that are now coming out on CD, both as repackaged compilations or as original albums.

The CD drive really began at the start of the 1990s, with a few tentative CD collections that were more the compiler's labour of love than a serious commercial proposition. But these early CDs were very well received, and seemed to trigger a tidal wave of nostalgia – which, naturally enough, stimulated supply. With quality rising as rapidly as quantity, today a CD reggae reissue is such a big deal that only the very best need apply. The presentation and track-listing standards set by such revival market leaders as Blood And Fire, Rewind Selecta and Island's Reggae Refreshers would put most big time labels to shame.

Now add this rapidly escalating back catalogue to a new generation of reggae performers and producers who may be entirely digital-friendly, but have never managed to remove themselves from the high-output-singles format – thoroughly modern reggae that still takes the idea of albums little further than a string of recent, highly desirable, fast turnover collections, with titles like *Romantic Ragga*, *Boglemania* and *Dancehall Killers*. When Keith Stone at specialist London reggae shop Daddy Kool talks about labels' CD catalogues being 'current this afternoon, but probably completely different by lunchtime tomorrow', he's only half joking.

As with *Soul On CD* (Kyle Cathie Ltd, £10.99), the rules of inclusion for this book are very straightforward. Does the act in question have a worthwhile CD on the shelves at the time of writing? If the answer is yes then they're in. (Except for a very select few, who are there because they *ought* to have a CD on offer.) 'Worthwhile' means: Has said disc in some way contributed to reggae as a whole other than just selling by the bucketload?

The yardstick is all to do with *soul*. That certain vibrant something that connects all the best reggae to its roots as a modern day-black folk music. A dark mixture of hope, happiness, love and a sense of community, steeped in 400 years of sufferation but as capable as any other genre of enjoying a pointless knees-up or looking to, er, capture the gal. It doesn't matter if the folk making it are from Trenchtown, Tottenham or Brooklyn either they're all branches of the same spiritual tree.

Spirit that Bob Marley had on tap. As did Duke Reid, Coxsone and Prince Buster. Likewise the dub masters Lee Perry, King Tubby, Keith Hudson and Augustus Pablo. So, too, do singers such as Burning Spear, Gregory Isaacs, The Mighty Diamonds and Sugar Minott. Or, deejay style, U-Roy, Big Youth, Jazzbo and Prince Far-I. Then as well as these old-timers there's the new blood: Bobby Digital, Garnett Silk, Buju, Tiger, Capleton, Steely and Cleevie, Chaka Demus, Pliers, Spanner Banner, Spragga Benz and Shaggy. Spirit so strong the music has survived and thrived for nearly forty years without deviating too far from its essence. A crossing of chronological and geographical boundaries illustrated with circular efficiency by the tune 'Oh Carolina': a hit for the acoustic Folkes Brothers in Jamaica in 1958, and a worldwide smash in 1993 for the New York raggamuffin Shaggy. Although both renditions are utterly different, noticeably they're both exactly the same.

Once more, as with *Soul On CD*, forget all that dreadful old tosh about CDs not being 'the real thing' – that bizarre conversational twilight zone in which people try to claim that this new, sparkling computer-controlled presentation of the music is, somehow, not nearly as desirable as seven inches of scratched-up, warping, fuzzy-sounding vinyl. It's almost as if the 'realness' – whatever that means – of a piece of music increases in direct relation to the age of your copy and in inverse proportion to its condition. Or that a tune will only have any bearing on anything if it's been commercially unavailable for about twenty years. As if artistic value is in some way linked to fiscal value.

My aim in life, probably the aim of most music fans for that matter, is to have as much music as I can – i.e. as much as my wife and my bank manager will let me – going back as far as I can, and to be able belatedly to catch up, through re-releases, with anything I might have missed. I want it sounding as close as possible to how it was played at the recording session too, not deteriorating with the passing of years or number of plays. And it'll help if it's in a handy-sized format that'll work in my car, in my office, in my living room, on the beach or on the bus. If CD satisfies all the above conditions – which it does – then it's got my vote. Period.

You don't even need to think too hard to realize CD is nothing more than reggae deserves.

NOTE:
This book is divided into four sections – Ska and Rock Steady, Reggae, Roots Reggae, and Dancehall – each one covering a specific phase of the music's development as it progressed out of an approximation of American R&B into the thoroughly modern, technology-friendly sound it is today. A few artists made significant contributions in more than one genre, and the symbol ↦ at the end of an entry denotes there is more on this artist later in the book.

Because so many reggae CDs are collections of singles or re-compiled original albums with additional tracks or alternate mixes, I have not given the release date with the catalogue number. This date would refer to when the CD was *put together* – and as in most cases this is later than 1990, the figure is irrelevant.

IN THE BEGINNING THERE WAS SKA

It's almost impossible to say who 'invented' reggae, or when, exactly. But the chain of events can be traced back to around the second half of the 1940s when the sound systems became an integral part of black Jamaican culture. A kind of monster cousin of the latter day British mobile disco, these earthquake capability rigs were put together using imported American equipment. The sound system operators would play open-air dances on the areas outside Kingston nightclubs that were known as 'lawns'. Or they'd simply set up on a street corner, using the attractions of the music to sell jerk chicken, curry goat or beer to an enthusiastic crowd. And back then the music they played was strictly fresh-off-the-boat-from-the-USA R&B. Far more raucous than anything that was heard on Jamaican radio. In fact, the wilder the better.

For people who couldn't afford radios, and to whom admission to the more formal night spots was not available – i.e. the West Kingston slum dwellers or 'sufferahs' – the sound systems became the heart of the community. Not just a dance, but a hang-out, a meeting place, an information exchange and a singles bar. By the middle of the next decade there were so many outfits operating on that side of the tracks that rivalry between them was intense – sometimes a matter of life and death – and it was the exclusivity of your tunes that kept you in front of the pack. As the American styles changed, so the supply of new R&B started to dry up, and in the search for obscure, never-been-heard-in-Jamaica records, soundmen (sound system operators) were having to go further and further inland from their traditional hunting grounds of Miami, New Orleans and New

York – which was fast becoming more trouble and expense than it was worth.

From the 1930s onwards Jamaica's dispossessed had produced some marvellous musicians, and the big swing bands of the cruise ship and hotel lounges of the newly established tourist industry, as well as America's jazz orchestras, had offered a genuine employment opportunity. And one in which race was not an immediate disadvantage. But as the 1950s unfolded, so the swing era was over, leaving a huge pool of players, notably horn men, kicking their heels in Kingston. It was only a matter of time before enterprising soundmen tapped into their own community's wealth of talent and began recording their own music. By the end of the 1950s, a large proportion of the records being played on such sounds as Sir Coxsone Down Beat, Duke Reid The Trojan, Tom The Great Sebastian and Count Boysie were 'Made In Jamaica'. Usually instrumental to allow the sound system deejay to scat his own vocals over the top, and recorded in crude local studios by a floating group of session men, the Rhythm & Blues stompers were one-off acetates, strictly for use by the soundman who produced the record, i.e. paid the bills.

Although the sound system operators had a thriving trade in these tunes amongst themselves, it wasn't until several years later that records were mass-produced for sale to the public. Curiously, in spite of the audience enthusiasm at sound system dances, the soundmen didn't believe anybody would be interested enough in the music to pay money to take it home. Any sales there were were largely confined to the ghettos, as the uptown types tended to view anything that came out of the slums as intrinsically inferior. What that meant, though, was that right from the start Jamaican music was made in direct response to what the ghetto people wanted, with the people who were putting it together coming from the self-same community. And as sound system crowds weren't slow in showing displeasure, the soundmen soon knew when they'd got it wrong. Music by the masses for the masses thus shaped itself as an exact reflection of the sufferahs' lives, hopes and culture. Something which, forty years later, still hasn't changed.

What did change, however, was the beat. Once the fledgling Jamaican music scene detached its R&B from its American roots, it set about customizing it with a gusto. The accent was shifted towards the down beat and the piano was favoured over the organ, which kept the whole balance far more staccato. At this point there were no electric basses on the island and the stand-up model produced a less aggressive bassline. And with crisply syncopated guitar chords augmenting the rhythm section, the horns had much more space for some wild soloing. This all combined to create the shuffling style of Jamaican Boogie, which may have been very recognizable as an R&B derivative but was only a short step away from the ska of the early 1960s, which in turn was the first truly Jamaican music to reach the outside world.

This upbeat style was true to the mood of the people as the island enjoyed relative economic prosperity in the run up to independence. On August 5 1962, when the Union Jack was finally replaced by the green, black and gold of the new Jamaican flag, a wave of optimism washed over the ghettoes. It was all going to be so simple – now that colonialism, the linger-ing vestiges of slavery, had been banished and Jamaicans were left to run t'ings for themselves, everything was going to be all right. The horn-driven, raucous, largely self-celebratory ska was, most importantly, something unique to the island, and therefore the ideal theme music for an emerging nation.

It crossed the Atlantic too. During the first half of the sixties, as emigrant Jamaicans established themselves in the UK, the best way to deal with the social alienation, and the equally hos-tile weather conditions presented by the Mother Country was to create a piece of West Kingston in Handsworth or Brixton or Moss Side or wherever. Blues dances, shebeens and house par-ties brought sound system culture and the fresh ska beat to Britain in a big way. Jamaican bands and artists toured regu-larly, a network of shops specializing in imported records flour-ished and legitimate nightclubs began to cater to this new clientele who, as working-class British kids began to pick up on their new neighbours' rhythms, were no longer exclusively ex-pat West Indians. Naturally enough, shrewder operators within the community began licensing tunes for British release, estab-lishing a UK reggae industry as early as 1962, which without any help from chart placings or BBC radio was regularly shifting tens of thousands of the more popular titles.

Meanwhile, back home, the main musical protagonists – Duke Reid, Clement 'Coxsone' Dodd and Prince Buster – by now owned their own studios and were turning out music at an astonishing rate (musicians, paid by the recording, were keen to cut as many sides as possible). But the main effect of this prolifigacy and lack of studio-hire bills was they had much more scope to experiment. It was only a matter of time before the beat shifted again.

A couple of years on from Independence Day, and the brave new dawn the politicians had promised simply wasn't happening. In fact many – i.e. the poor – were far worse off than they had been under colonial rule. A great number of British businesses had simply packed up and gone home, leaving the new government to encourage American involvement. Which is where the economy went badly astray. The heavy US investment in the island's tourism and bauxite industries resulted in an appalling outside exploitation of Jamaica's natural resources – ensuing corporate structures held an enormous vacuum cleaner over Jamaica and hoovered a large proportion of prospective wealth out of the country and across the ocean to America. Naturally the slums of West Kingston felt the pinch as there was less money to spend on public works, municipal services and welfare, but this time the rural areas were badly hit too. While farms were being bought up by multi-national corporations looking to mine the bauxite-rich red dirt, European beet sugar was killing one of the island's biggest agricultural export markets, the sugar trade. The knock-on effect was that rural people flooded into the capital, looking for jobs that weren't there and hoping to live in houses that didn't exist. Over-crowding and mass unemployment led to the rude boy era, several years of riots and urban unrest caused by gangs of disaffected teenagers, whose code of belligerence and violence escalated into armed warfare.

One thing hadn't changed though: the sound systems still remained the focus of their communities. And they demanded the deejays play less carefree music than the necessarily exuberant ska beat. The result was rock steady – slower, tenser, internalized by the dancers to a far greater degree. Looking back on it now, musicians and producers will see rock steady as an artistic translation of the frustration felt by the ghetto youths – remember, so many artists were West Kingston teenagers just like their audience. Rock steady changed the face of Jamaican music, by putting less emphasis on large horn choruses, making far more use of the organ and bringing up the bass to drive the rhythm now that the piano was being phased out.

As the sixties progressed and the rude boy era faded into history – put down by a combination of authority crackdowns and ordinary people who weren't going to take it any more – so the producers subtly began to speed up the beat . . .

Laurel Aitken

(Born 1928; Cuba; singer)
Probably best known in mainstream circles as a cultural icon to the first wave of British skinheads, there was always much more to Laurel Aitken than such unsubtle boot-boy jolly-ups as 'Skinhead Train'. In the late 1950s his records were a text book study of how that new, indigenous Jamaican music called ska emerged from its R&B cocoon. His semi-crooning vocal style was used as an effective counterpoint to the increasingly customized US-style arrangements. It was quite literally bounced off the backing tracks and deftly served to highlight the downbeat emphasis.

As a teenager, Aitken earned a good living from the island's Tourist Commission, singing dockside calypso to visitors disembarking the cruise liners at Kingston Harbour, while in the evening, under the name 'El Cubano', he fronted R&B bands in the downtown clubs. He was nothing if not versatile, and such adaptability of approach undoubtedly played a part in an early recording career that reads like a series of 'firsts'. His single 'Boogie Rock' was the first home-grown record to make it into the newly established Jamaican Broadcasting Corporation charts in 1959. The next year his 'Boogie In My Bones' became Chris Blackwell's first production success. Aitken's cuts 'Mighty Redeemer', 'Zion' and 'What A Weeping' were among the first openly Rasta recordings, and he was part of the initial wave of ska musicians to leave Jamaica in response to a combination of police persecution of dreadlock sympathizers and (what they saw as) limited career opportunities.

In 1960, Aitken, JACKIE EDWARDS and Owen Grey, the three most influential Jamaican singers at that time, had all decamped to England, where it was Aitken's dynamic stage performance that was vital in establishing the music in the UK. Hence the skinhead connection, in spite of the fact that he actually devoted far more vinyl to his own people with numbers like 'Haile Selassie', 'Deliverance Will Come' and 'Suffering Still'. These socio/politically slanted records became another reggae milestone as the first songs to be officially condemned for political content when the record company's UK manufacturers refused to handle them because of their subject matter (they had to be pressed in Holland for import into Britain).

Aitken progressed to become one of the most important players – both as a performer and a producer – on the UK reggae scene. He produced for Pama and Trojan, giving UK hits to Winston Groovey, Tiger, and King Horror, as well as himself. King Horror, whose ultra-rude reggae is the mainstay of the old *Loch Ness Monster* album, cut some of the very few UK-recorded reggae records that made it big in Jamaica back then.

But none of this was enough to keep Laurel Aitken up with trends as they evolved beyond blue beat and ska into the 1970s, when the rhythm as well as the philosophy turned dread. Although the 2-Tone craze of the late 1970s briefly rekindled interest in a busily self-promoting Aitken, and there have been sporadic indie releases – usually sponsored by his original ska fans – he has for the last decade or so been more or less invisible. Mind you, he is nearly seventy so we've really got no right to expect him still to be shuffling at that age.

Godfather Of Ska; Gaz's Rockin' Blues CDGNZ009

An excellent collection of mid-period Aitken, cutting across labels and producers, presenting the less frantic, almost meditative ska at which he excelled. And, as it goes from 1962 to 1966, it takes in a lot of rock steady too. The set covers Aitken's sphere of interest from the profane to the profound, with the political nestling somewhere in between – included are 'Jenny Jenny', 'Propaganda', 'Street Of Glory', 'Coconut Water' and 'Shake'. The singer spent so much of his time in the UK during this period – where these tunes came out on such Melodisc subsidiaries as Blue Beat, Ska Beat, Rio and Giant, and also Chris Blackwell's fledgling Island label – he did much to advance this the cause of Jamaican music over here. This is one of the very few compilations that collects what amounts to reggae's advance invasion force – a kind of scouting mission – and should be valued as such.

ALSO RECOMMENDED:

The Early Days Of Blue Beat, Ska And Reggae; Reprive BRMCD025

Less sharply focused than *Godfather*, and shifting through the different styles tends to show up how he was much more at home with rock steady than anything else.

SEE ALSO:

Aitken's better known tracks can be found on the following Various Artists compilations: *The Trojan Story Volume One* (Trojan CDTAL100); *Scandal Ska* (Island CID9929).

Roland Alphonso

(Born mid-1930s; Clarendon, Jamaica; saxophonist)
'Pheeeonix City . . . ba ba baaa da dum ba ba baaa da dum . . .'
Getting on towards the end of the 1960s, at your better educated club, it was still common practice for a deejay to kick up the tempo with a run of ska beat classics. And 'Phoenix City', with those opening words stretched out long enough for the crowd to join in, was one of two favourite opening tracks. It was Roland Alphonso's sax that powered the cut, just as he fronted such ska classics as 'Green Door', 'Feeling Fine', 'El Pussy Cat' and – in keeping with a Jamaican trend for covering cinema and TV themes – ska versions of 'From Russia With Love' and 'James Bond'.

Like so many of his horn-honking peers, Alphonso was an Alpha Boys Catholic School graduate (see THE SKATALITES) and a former jazz and R&B player. But he escaped the drudgery of knocking out cheesy cover versions to American tourists in the island's swank hotels when, in 1959, he teamed up with

15

COXSONE DODD as musical director and sax man for the producer's first, pre-Studio One, house band Clue J and His Blues Blasters. It's Alphonso's sax on THEOLONIUS BECKFORD's pioneering 'Easy Snappin''. Four years later, Alphonso was a founder member of The Skatalites, and it's said that one of the reasons the band broke up after only two years together was the mutual antagonism between Alphonso and his fellow saxophonist TOMMY MCCOOK. It was also reported that this rivalry was fuelled by Dodd's playing the two horn men off against each other, greatly favouring his long-time associate. What is fact, though, is that as the group was splitting up, Dodd immediately employed Alphonso and keyboard player Jackie Mittoo to form the nucleus of his ever-fluctuating house bands named The Soul Brothers, The Soul Vendors (re-named specifically for a UK tour in 1967, backing KEN BOOTHE and ALTON ELLIS, as a reference to the novelty hit 'Peanut Vendor'), The Sound Dimension, The Brentford Rockers, The Brentford Disco Set (the studio was in Brentford Road, Kingston) and, for one thankfully brief period, The Underground Vegetables.

Although Coxsone remained loyal to his long-time confederate – he released two Roland Alphonso LPs in the mid-1970s – like so many others from this embryonic period of Jamaican music, Alphonso never survived beyond rock steady. His last known musical output was a none-too-successful album recorded for Wackies (the famous reggae label and studio) in New York in 1985.

There is an import CD in existence entitled *Roland Alphonso – Reggae Sax*, featuring Jah Jerry and comprising rock steady and early reggae, but although it comes highly recommended it's proved impossible to track down. Meanwhile, the two most readily available Various Artists compilations with the cream of Roland Alphonso-led numbers are *Ska Bonanza – The Studio One Ska Years* (Heartbeat CDHB86/87) and *Original Club Ska – Studio One's Authentic Jamaican Beat* (Heartbeat CDHB55). The former, a twin CD set, has some real gems on offer, including 'Bongo Tango', 'Old Fowl Ska' and Don Drummond and Roland Alphonso's 'Roll On Sweet Don (Heaven And Hell)'. The latter features Alphonso taking the lead in front of The Soul Vendors for a scorching cut of 'From Russia With Love'.

And Roland Alphonso in almost equally full effect can be found on the following:

20 Film And Stage Classics Jamaican Style; Trojan CDTRL 319
Shufflin' On Bond Street – Jamaican R&B and Ska Instrumentals; Trojan CDTRL275
Club Ska 67; Mango IMCD53
Intensified – Original Ska 1962-1966; Mango IMCD51
Blow Mr Hornsman – Instrumental Reggae 1968-1975; Trojan CDTRL257
In **The Soul Vendors:** *Musical Fever 1967-1968*; Trojan CDTRL408
In **The Skatalites:** *The Birth Of Ska*; Trojan CDTRL274

Theolonius Beckford

(Born 1935; Kingston, Jamaica; pianist/singer)
By comparison with many Jamaican musicians, Beckford entered the business late – he was at the almost pensionable age of twenty before he bought a piano, and spent two years learning how to play it before he ever got paid to do so. However, once he was working, Beckford's lazy way with the ivories proved a crucial factor in the Birth Of Ska As We Know It.

Like any other working musician on the island at that time, Beckford was playing the local approximation of swing and R&B, most notably as part of Cluett Johnson's Blues Blasters. It was this group who, as COXSONE DODD's band, were among the market leaders in the slowed down R&B often referred to as 'Jamaican Boogie'. This was where the downbeat emphasis really began to take hold: while the keyboard retained R&B's stabbing syncopation on every beat, it combined with drums that were reversing the American style by stressing the first and third beats. During the producer's first session at Federal Studios in 1959, the combination of Johnson's sleepy bass and Beckford's lead piano created 'Easy Snappin'', a sound system sensation and huge national hit. After widespread imitation, a style was born.

Although he formed his own label and had a couple of minor hits, Beckford's stature never again matched his influence and the bulk of his later work was as a session player for Dodd, DUKE REID, PRINCE BUSTER and CLANCY ECCLEs.

'Easy Snappin'' can be found on *Tougher Than Tough – The Story Of Jamaican Music* (four-CD set); Mango IBXCD1

Ken Boothe

(Born 1948; Trenchtown, Jamaica; singer)
Ken Boothe used to be called the Wilson Pickett of reggae, but really, if ever there was a Sam Cooke of Jamaican Music, he was it. Good looking, with a delivery very close to the US soul singers of the 1960s in its passionate smoove with frequent flashes of fire, he was a pin-up for the island's female teenagers long before he made it to his twenties. At age fifteen, COXSONE teamed him up with the not-a-great-deal-older STRANGER COLE – Stranger and Ken – for a series of ska beat duets, the best known of which were 'World's Fair' and 'All Your Friends'. But the Boothe Smooth never really came into its own until the tempo slowed down to rock steady during the second half of the decade. Again with Dodd, he racked up a series of Jamaican hits (among them 'Just Another Girl', 'The Train Is Coming' and 'Moving Away'), while his big sellers 'Say You' and 'Freedom Street' were for SONIA POTTINGER and LESLIE KONG respectively. It was in the early 1970s that Boothe moved on again, to be produced by Lloyd Charmers, but by then the beat had changed once more. ••

*The Ken Boothe Collection – Eighteen Classic Songs; Trojan CDTRL249

This thoroughly worthwhile Ken Boothe compilation mostly concerns itself with the singer's later work, thus is looked at in detail elsewhere (pages 110-111). But it does include one track from the era described above – 'Freedom Street', produced by Leslie Kong. At the time of writing, this is about the only example of Ken Boothe singing ska that exists on CD. However, a thoroughly abbreviated selection of his rock steady work can be glimpsed on the following compilations:

Put On Your Best Dress – Sonia Pottinger's Rock Steady 1967-1968;
Attack ATCD109
Tougher Than Tough – The Story Of Jamaican Music (four-CD set);
Mango; IBXCD1
Ska Bonanza – The Studio One Ska Years; Heartbeat CDHB86/87
By himself and with **Stranger Cole**: *Respect To Studio One*;
Heartbeat CDHB181
With **Stranger Cole**: *Ska Bonanza – The Studio One Ska Years*;
Heartbeat CDHB86/87
With **Roy Shirley:** *Monkey Ska*; Trojan CDTRL 323

Prince Buster

(Born Cecil Bustamante Campbell, 1938; Kingston, Jamaica;
band leader/producer/singer)
Mr Ska? He probably was, as far as a couple of generations of
white working-class UK youngsters were concerned – namely
the mods and their immediate predecessors the skinheads. As
the Prince's name was then kept alive through to the 1980s with
musical tributes from Midlands 2-Tone outfits such as The
Specials and Selecter, and also Camden Town's 'nutty boys'
Madness, it'll be Prince Buster's exuberant brand of ska that will
find its way into the average student union disco.

So Prince Buster has been able to continue to make money off
what he produced more than thirty years ago. It is one of the rare
occasions (rare in the music business in general, almost non-
existent in reggae) when an artist gets exactly what he or she
deserves. Prince Buster's importance in the story of Jamaican
music cannot be overstated. He's the third side of the holy trinity of producers – COXSONE and DUKE REID are the others –
who can truthfully be credited with shaping ska out of the US-
derivative music immediately preceding it.

The tune with which Buster made his mark on the fledgling JA
scene was his production of The Folkes Brothers' 'Oh Carolina'.
The track came out of Buster's first ever session as a producer,
for his own newly formed record label Voice Of The People, and
was made in the cramped one-overhead-mic, one-track recording facility at the Kingston radio station Radio Jamaica
Rediffusion. In spite of such a rudimentary studio, and his lack

of previous experience running a recording session, it still wasn't altogether surprising that 'Oh Carolina' was such a huge hit. This was several months on from Coxsone's groundbreaking 'Easy Snappin'', and Buster had taken this new approach to higher levels. While he followed fashion with the accent on the second and fourth beat by having his guitarist stress the afterbeat, he shifted the overall feel further away from American R&B and into Jamaican cultural heritage with a drum pattern noticeably removed from straight 4/4.

As a producer Prince Buster wanted to bring a feel to the music that expressed how he felt about himself as a black Jamaican. He wanted something both musically unique and socially relevant, which reflected the lasting impression that Marcus Garvey's 'Back To Africa' ideology had on Kingston's growing numbers of dispossessed. He achieved his aim by employing Rasta drummer Count Ossie and his group of four Burru skinsmen to provide the back beat. Although Ossie was initially sceptical that the recording industry would want to have anything to do with his famously dread posse, he liked Buster's sentiments. Together they created a sound that was entirely fresh, yet obviously of Jamaica. And when the people took to it as Prince Buster felt sure they would, it became both culturally valid *and* commercially viable.

Although this was Prince Buster's first foray into production, he was in no way a newcomer to the music business. A promising semi-professional boxer in his teens, he'd supplement his income from scrapping in the Kingston boxing booths as a minder/foot soldier for Coxsone's Down Beat sound system. So intense was the rivalry between Kingston's soundmen that if you couldn't mash another operator's reputation with an exclusive tune, you'd mash his equipment or his patrons with your henchmen. Buster still carries the scars from his days as a Coxsone heavy. An incident that may have influenced his decision to quit came one night at the end of the 1950s when LEE PERRY, then a Down Beat deejay, was knocked out in a fight: according to Buster, Dodd and his men vanished, leaving him to fight off the rival gang single-handed before slinging the unconscious Perry over his shoulder and getting away to safety.

But being around one of the island's top sound systems meant Buster both understood the record business and appreciated its financial potential. He founded his own Voice Of The People sound system in 1959 (which quickly became serious competition for the big two), and then, under the same name, the record label and a record shop. His Orange Street HQ, The World Famous Record Shack, was established a couple of years later.

As a music business entrepreneur, Buster spotted and was keen to exploit his music's overseas potential. In the UK he struck a deal with the black music licensing label Melodisc to issue his work on the specialist Blue Beat imprint – hence the generic name – and in spite of BBC Radio virtually ignoring the music, Buster succeeded way beyond Britain's Jamaican community. A supercharged appearance on the mod-friendly TV programme *Ready, Steady, Go!* turned him into a cult figure, and by taking his wild stage show beyond such obvious venues as Paddington's Q Club, The Marquee, The Ska Bar in Woolwich and Brixton's Ram Jam Club, to theatres in places like Norwich, Basingstoke, Oldham and Cambridge, he ensured lasting success in this country.

Back home, too, Buster operated with intelligence and integrity. His record labels – The Voice Of The People, Wild Bells and Record Shack – cut a succession of hits with artists such as Millie Small, Owen Grey, THE MAYTALS and THE SKATAL-ITES. And as an entrepreneur, he controlled jukeboxes in Kingston as well as running his own shops.

Buster was also a glowing example of a black business man whose success hadn't affected his sense of self. When DERRICK MORGAN, a close friend of his, recorded the song 'Shake A Leg' with Chinese/Jamaican producer LESLIE KONG, the Prince was furious at what he felt amounted to his friend selling out his own race. Buster recorded a single, 'Black Head Chinee Man', lampooning Morgan with lines like 'Do you prefer the Chinee man to your fellow black man?'.

Prince Buster also knew when to call it a day. Although he carried on producing into the 1970s, success was only sporadic and he was among the first to realize that his future was now his past. Which is why Prince Buster is so comprehensively represented on CD, as he devotes time and energy to repackaging his old hits and licensing them to yet another generation of ska fans. And he's still reaping the rewards. Once again, it's no more than he deserves.

With the exception of *Fabulous Greatest Hits* and *The Original Golden Hits*, all the albums below are reissues of Blue Beat originals. Each one is a collection of singles in perfect illustration of how ska and rock steady were never intended for an albums market. Even the themed sets here are made up of bunches of self-contained songs – it just happens that several of them share their subject matter.

*Big Five; SKA MSTCD3
*She Was A Rough Rider; SKA MSTCD2

Big Five and, to a degree, *She Was A Rough Rider* are living, breathing (panting?) proof that Yellowman, Shabba Ranks and the like didn't invent slackness. To sing about, er, gal, in as graphic a way as the morals of the day will allow has long been part of Caribbean musical tradition – just check through calypso's back catalogue. 'Big Five', the homage to nookie that inspired that string of 1970s rudeness by Londoner Alex Hughes (aka Judge Dread – another Busterism), is merely a starting point for twelve tracks that progress briskly downhill to such delights as 'Kinky Griner', 'Bald Head Pum Pum', 'Fishy Fishy' and 'Wash The Pum Pum'. Although they're nursery rhymes compared with what's on offer post-ragga, I can vividly remember the cleverness involved in getting some of these tracks played at school dances – most teachers didn't have a clue, while you could've powered the national grid off the blushes from the well-brought-up West Indian girls.

She Was A Rough Rider at least mixes the sex tunes up with such self-explanatory righteousness as 'Taxation' and 'Hypocrites', while sweet love songs take over with covers of soul songs 'Dreams To Remember' and 'You Send Me' and 'Closer Together'. It's an oft-needed reminder that ska was much more than a one-trick pony, and worth the price of admission for the title track, a genuine classic, and written by one Eddy Grant. And he always seemed such a nice boy.

*Judge Dread Rock Steady; SKA MSTCD4

This is Buster's wrath at the black-on-black violence being wreaked in Kingston's ghettos by the rude boys. Judge Dread was the Prince's creation, a cartoon alter ego meting out the kind of uncompromising justice he felt the rude boys deserved. Sentences of a hundred, five hundred, hell, a thousand years fell like rain at the drop of his gavel. And forget leave to appeal, even approaching the bench was a risky proposition – it wasn't unheard of for Judge Dread to send a barrister down the steps for a century or so. As ever, Buster was in tune with what the people really wanted. Although the enormous number of records glorifying the rudies might seem to indicate there was widespread support for their ways, there were a great deal more respectable ghetto folk who were sick of living under seige in their own neighbourhoods. It's not unlike the situation in South Central Los Angeles in the 1990s: the sheer volume of gangsta rap records presents a distorted picture of local attitudes.

Buster was in tune with what was required musically too. Most of these tunes were cut towards the middle of the 1960s, and by now Prince Buster was slowing down to accommodate the notion of rock steady along with his more perceptive peers. Proving there was always more to the Prince than frantic happy hour ska.

Prince Buster On Tour; SKA MSTCD1

Exactly what it says it is. Cut on a UK tour in 1967, and without the benefit of what is coyly called 'post production', this is ska at its rawest, most irreverent best. The show moves through 'Al Capone', 'Madness', '007', 'Take It Easy' and 'Sound And Pressure', celebrating the full range of Buster's music. And, revisiting this set nearly thirty years later, it's become blindingly obvious why the original Blue Beat pressing of this LP was such a desirable underarm accessory at my school.

Fabulous Greatest Hits; Sequel NEXCD253

A far more comprehensive collection than the album of the same name it replaced a couple of years ago. While this has got everything its predecessor had – 'Madness', 'Al Capone', 'Ghost Dance', 'Judge Dread', 'Earthquake' and 'Take It Easy' – its two dozen tracks also manage to include 'Black Head Chinee Man', 'Hard Man Fe Dead' and '30 Pieces Of Silver', all of which were

23

part of Buster's musical feud with Derrick Morgan. Oddly, it doesn't include 'Barrister Pardon', but really things are much too far down the road marked 'F-U-N' for anybody to complain about that.

Prince Buster's Record Shack Presents The Original Golden Hits Volume One; Prince Buster PBCD9

Issued on the Prince's own label from his Orange Street head-quarters, this is a little diamond. Along with such well-known numbers as 'Madness', 'They Got To Come' and 'Enjoy Yourself', this has got 'Time Longer Than Rope', 'Over And Over', 'Wash Wash' and 'Blackhead Chinee Man'.

SEE ALSO:

'Oh Carolina' is featured on *Tougher Than Tough – The Story Of Jamaican Music* (four-CD set); Mango IBXCD1

The Clarendonians

(Ernest Wilson, Peter Austin; both born late 1940s; Clarendon, Jamaica; singers)
In much the same way as The Jackson Five were to become a direct representation of their own audience – same age, same background, same sensibilities and so on – The Clarendonians were Studio One's take on the youthful rude boy sub-culture of early 1960s Kingston. Barely into their teens when COXSONE signed them up after a string of local talent contest wins, they were good-looking, sweet-voiced and, by all accounts, stroppy little sods. In other words, perfect to interpret such hymns to rudie life as 'Be Bop Boy', 'Rudie Bam Bam' and 'Rudie Gone A Jail', in a way that would appeal to both boys and girls. And Coxsone knew his market, too, because to keep the harmonies as fresh-faced as possible, a seven-year-old FREDDIE MCGRE-GOR was added to the studio line-up. Even though he had to stand on a chair to be heard on the overhead mic.

During the first half of the 1960s, The Clarendonians were ska personified, in attitude, age, music and appearance. Their popu-larity mushroomed as Coxsone milked them for all they were worth, cutting the threesome as a trio, as solo artists, or in all permutations of duets. Indeed their only serious singing rivals for the hearts and minds of young urban Jamaica was Coxsone's other rudie-type hopefuls THE WAILING WAILERS.

The Clarendonians disbanded during the second half of the decade, and while to this day Wilson maintains a modest success rate, it was only McGregor who fulfilled their early promise and went on to stardom on an international level.

At present, the only CD examples of The Clarendonians in action can be found on:

Rudies All Round; Trojan CDTRL332
Dance Crasher – Ska To Rock Steady; Trojan CDTRL260
Original Club Ska – Studio One's Authentic Jamaican Beat; Heartbeat CDHB55

Jimmy Cliff

(Born James Chambers, 1948; Somerton, Jamaica; singer)
If sheer hard work and just plain wanting it bad enough were all it took to make something come about, then Jimmy Cliff's name would have been the international metaphor for reggae music that BOB MARLEY's eventually became. This isn't, of course, to take anything away from the Tuff Gong, but there was a time when Marley would do practically anything to avoid leaving Jamaica. Yet since virtually day one, Cliff has laboured to promote reggae overseas – both through his music and his cult status movie *The Harder They Come*. Maybe 'laboured' ought to be taken literally too: during the late 1960s in Jamaica, the then fledgling roots reggae industry was already judging itself by its own blackness, while Cliff, resident in London, was cutting sides with the likes of Madeline Bell and Mott The Hoople, and assuming the role of token black act on largely hippified rock sampler albums. Although any attempts to take the music beyond its immediately visible horizons has to be, broadly speaking, a good thing, there are limits. And it's not unfair to say that this singer's lamentable cover version of Procul Harum's 'Whiter Shade Of Pale' crosses them.

Jimmy Cliff's *sans frontières* approach to reggae began relatively early in his career. A tailor's son, he came to Kingston at the age of twelve to stay with relatives and to break into the music business. Arriving during boomtime 1960, he soon began cutting singles for sound system use, trying to disguise his lack of years by singing ska in contrivedly gruff tones. But he didn't progress beyond the town's second division outfits – nothing on the scale of Down Beat or The Trojan. During the next year he was taken on by LESLIE KONG, the result of a move on Cliff's part that showed ingenuity way beyond his tender age. Kong and his three brothers ran a combined record shop and ice-cream parlour called Beverley's. It was well known that Leslie Kong wanted to expand vertically within the music business into making his own records. Cliff wrote a song entitled 'Dearest Beverly', breezed into the shop and sung it a cappella. The three brothers laughed, but Leslie rushed him down to the Federal recording studio, and it became the first release on his Beverley's record label.

Although the song wasn't an enormous success, for the next two years the teenager was one of Kong's resident ska singers. And he did well there – notably with other opportunistic lyrical content: 'Hurricane Hattie' concerned itself with a storm that did much damage in Jamaica, while 'Miss Jamaica' was an unashamed hymn to the newly inaugurated JA beauty pageant. Cliff even made enough of a name for himself to get on the musical party, featuring Millie Small and PRINCE BUSTER, going to the World's Fair in New York in 1964. This was promoted by record producer/politician Edward Seaga and musician/businessman BYRON LEE as a way of presenting Jamaica's newly established art form as a viable export proposition. It didn't. Or at least not on the scale intended. But it sort of worked for Cliff, as he was spotted by Chris Blackwell, signed up and sent to London.

It was at this time that Blackwell was elbowing his company into the mainstream UK rock market, and Cliff managed to get himself shoved in there with it. Although most of his output during that time was singularly undistinguished, it saw the singer safely through the rock steady era and into the next development of Jamaican music. ♦♦

'Miss Jamaica' can be found on *Tougher Than Tough – The Story Of Jamaican Music* (four-CD set, Mango IBXCD1), while the single 'Hard Road To Travel', a serious slice of 1967 rock steady, is featured on *Reggae Greats* (Mango RRCD22) and *Jimmy Cliff* (Trojan CDTRL16). These are about the only examples of early-Cliff to have made it on to CD. The latter two albums, both (very similar) greatest hits compilations, will be featured in more detail on page XXX.

Stranger Cole

(Born Winston Cole, mid-1940s; Kingston, Jamaica; singer)
When DUKE REID returned to the recording studio in 1962, it was for Stranger Cole's ska beat single 'Rough And Tough'. An enormous Jamaican hit, it kicked off a run of success for Reid that, for the rest of the decade, meant he had few serious rivals. It was really none too surprising that this easy-action tune was such a monster, either. Ska had firmly established itself by then, but the style's frantic musical structure meant that every now and again dance crowds would need a rest. The Stranger's laid-back-to-almost-horizontal delivery stood out from the pack with exactly that cool counterpoint. During three years with Reid – plus a bit of freelancing for Duke's biggest shuffle beat rivals, PRINCE BUSTER and COXSONE – Cole established himself as one of the island's premier vocalists, with such stand-out tunes as 'Stranger At The Door', 'We Are Rolling' and 'Run Joe', plus a few duets, notably with Patsy Todd and KEN BOOTHE, and his uncredited co-vocalising (his is the ultra-relaxed voice) on Eric Morris's massive 'Penny Reel O'.

Of course, such an understated vocal approach made Cole a natural for the slowed down tempos of rock steady. He worked with SONIA POTTINGER, BUNNY LEE and JOE GIBBS – even going on to produce himself – and tunes like 'Bangarang', 'Tell It To Me' and 'Just Like A River' kept him in the Jamaican charts until he emigrated to Canada in the early 1970s. It's a mark of Stranger Cole's importance in the early days of Jamaican music that he continues to make a good living touring expatriate communities. It's just a pity that the more recently recorded output can't quite respark that old flame.

A compilation LP, *The First Ten Years Of Stranger Cole*, was released on his own label towards the end of the 1970s, but that has long since vanished and, for some reason, the big hits from his early years have never been re-collected. So while a good cross-section can be found on the compilation CDs listed below, it's not much more than a taster.

Intensified – Original Ska 1962-1966; Mango IMCD51
More Intensified – Original Ska Volume Two 1963-1967; Mango IMCD52
In duet with **Ken Boothe:** *Ska Bonanza – The Studio One Ska Years*; Heartbeat CDHB86/87
Jumping With Mr Lee – 1967-1968; Trojan CDTRL270
Rudies All Round; Trojan CDTRL332
The Trojan Story Volume One; Trojan CDTAL100
Dance Crasher – Ska To Rock Steady; Trojan CDTRL260
Adults Only, Volume Two; Trojan CDTRL308
Put On Your Best Dress – Sonia Pottinger's Rock Steady 1967-1968; Attack ATCD109

Desmond Dekker

(Born Desmond Dacres, 1942; Kingston, Jamaica; singer)
If, during the second half of the 1960s, rock steady in the UK had one dominating image, it was that of the tiny Desmond Dekker on *Top Of The Pops*, in a dapper suit, doing a neat little dance and twisting up his body as he screwed his falsetto voice out of the side of his mouth. 'Dem a weep, dem a wail/A sha-a-a-nty town'. Never mind he went on to become a skinhead hero, or even a genuine property-of-the-mainstream pop star, Desmond Dekker's success was something rather marvellous to a young black British audience. Incredibly important because, exciting as it was, ska really belonged to our mums and dads, but this new beat was entirely up for grabs. And with its Caribbean roots it was somehow much more 'ours' than the music coming over courtesy of Stax, Atlantic and Tamla Motown.

Dekker worked this Jamaican-ness too. His songs were folk tales of ghetto life seen from both sides of the law: '007 (Shanty Town)' was a rudie anthem, as were his domestic hits 'Rudie Got Soul' and 'Rude Boy Train'; while 'The Israelites' and 'Problems' concerned themselves with the everyday pressures on those trying to make an honest living. And he sang in an uncompromising patois/ghetto slang that provoked a million baffled discussions and attempts at explanation from English deejays and, er, pop-pickers. But the significance of such colloquialisms at the top of the British charts was enormous. At my school at least. It gave us a massive infusion of cool, as if this was some sort of secret language to which we held the key. Suddenly, West Indian was the thing to be and you'd have a seemingly endless stream of white kids coming up to you asking what the hell Desmond Dekker was on about. You could tell them anything – anything at all – and they'd go away looking pleased with themselves.

Maybe Dekker's understanding of what ordinary working people wanted came about because he actually used to be one. Unlike so many reggae stars who, from adolescence onwards, had made music their full-time occupation, Dekker had a job well into his teens. He was a welder (apprenticed to the same firm as BOB MARLEY), who was always singing in the workshop, apparently fancying himself as an island version of Nat King Cole or Sam Cooke. At the start of the 1960s, nagging from his workmates pushed him into auditioning for COXSONE and DUKE REID. Amazingly, both producers turned him down. It was the far less prestigious LESLIE KONG who recognized his talent and signed him to Beverley's in 1963. There he changed his name to the more marketing-friendly Dekker, and the run of hits began: 'Honour Your Father And Your Mother', a number 1 hit in Jamaica, kicked off domestic success that took him easily through ska to rock steady as the next rhythm pattern proved just right for his high-pitched tones. Teamed up with Kong, and backed by the sweet harmonizing of The Aces (initially it was THE MAYTALS, another Kong act), Dekker racked up a string of hits that included over twenty domestic chart-toppers and, in 1967, second place in the island's prestigious Unity Song Festival (a kind of Caribbean, entirely credible, Eurovision Song Contest).

It was in that same year that Dekker moved from merely selling records to becoming something of a cultural figurehead. The hot rock steady '007 (Shanty Town)' so perfectly captured the mood of a period when, as a reaction to the perpetual armed confrontation between rude boys and the authorities, bulldozers were sent in to raze the corrugated tin shanty towns of West

Kingston. Such a move affected far more than merely the lawless and, amid the rioting, so great was the tension that even the respectable folk began to identify with the confrontational sub-culture. As deejay DENNIS ALCAPONE, a young resident of the area at the time, puts it, 'The rude boy thing just burst right open. Then when he came with "007" it was the icing on the cake – it was an era *fe real!*' The tune went as far as the UK Top 20.

In 1969, as that thoroughly modern development, reggae, boomed in the UK, Desmond Dekker crossed the Atlantic. ↦

King Of Ska; Trojan CDTRL292

Desmond Dekker's early years, or a selection of those pre-'Shanty Town' Jamaican recordings that didn't come over here at the time. 'King Of Ska', 'Wise Man', 'Maggie', 'Archawawa' and so on. Whether it was because the style was several years on by the time these tunes were made (between 1963 and 1966), and thus well into its evolution, or whether it was a matter of accom-modating Dekker's voice, Kong's ska beat productions are a lot smoother than much of what was going on around him. This isn't to say it's any less exciting. In fact, it's all too rare for the ska beat built round multi-part harmony vocals to have survived on to CD, and it's a rather welcome change of approach from the dedicatedly frantic instrumentals. Fact fans may be interested to know that although these were largely Dekker's own composi-tions, much of their musical style can be put down to session pianist THEOLONIUS BECKFORD's arrangements.

The Best Of Desmond Dekker; Music Club International MCCD115

Although firmly rooted in the later period, this attractive great-est hits package has the nous to go back past '007 (Shanty Town)' to 'King Of Ska', 'Problems', 'Rudie Got Soul' and 'Archawawa'.

Desmond Dekker And The Aces – Officially Live And Rare; Trojan CDTRD404

Cut in Camden Town's Dingwalls in the mid-1980s, this is a blistering example of the old guy still cutting it. The recording manages to catch so much atmosphere from the cramped, sweaty club that you can almost feel the dance floor heaving. As expected, the tracklisting reads like the Desmond Dekker Hit Parade.

SEE ALSO:

The Trojan Story; Trojan CDTRS402
More Intensified – Original Ska Volume Two 1963-1967; Mango IMCD52

Clement 'Coxsone' Dodd

(Born Clement Seymour Dodd, early 1930s; Kingston, Jamaica; producer/songwriter)
It's impossible to imagine what sort of state Jamaican music would be in today if Clement Seymour Dodd had stuck to his original occupation as a sugar cane cutter on the plantations in the southern states of America. Indeed, had he stayed in the fields or simply chilled out in between the six-month-long work contracts (US immigration laws meant immigrant workers had to leave the country every six months), Jamaican music would probably have remained American music; i.e. whatever the notoriously conservative broadcasting systems felt was suitable for the masses.

By the end of the 1960s, when the music's identity was complete and it was accepted internationally as 'reggae', 'Coxsone' was at the cutting edge of this new presentation – both artistically and technically – with some of the new style's most exciting producers and performers having served apprenticeships at his Studio One. Prior to that, it was his way with a rhythm track that played a major part in the simmering down of ska to rock steady. Just as, as a producer and songwriter, he had been a prime force in creating ska out of R&B in the first place – THEOLONIUS BECKFORD's 'Easy Snappin'' was a Dodd tune. And back even further: Sir Coxsone's Down Beat sound system may not have been the first mobile lawn dance set-up, but by the mid-1950s it was simply the best. DUKE REID's Trojan Sound was the only operation that could give it any trouble.

In other words, as far as the development and popularisation of Jamaican music goes, Clement Dodd's significance is such that it'll be taken as read by anybody with the remotest appreciation of pre-digital reggae. For those less enlightened souls it would be best to compare his importance to Berry Gordy's standing in 1960s soul. An analogy underlined by the fact that as producers first, both men created instantly recognizable sounds: Coxsone's, whether applied to ska, rock steady or roots reggae, was always a luxuriantly warm, soft-edged presentation that seemed to round off the sharp angles which the music's necessarily syncopated approach could involve. It had a depth of arrangement creating layers that flowed across each other with such consummate skill that his music assumed a sometimes genuinely startling 3D-ness. It's entirely understandable why, just as people would once go into record shops and feel secure enough simply to ask for 'the new Tamla Motown singles' – Coxsone's Studio One label became a reggae sub-section in itself. It remains the most collectable of Jamaican imprints, with original pressings of early singles and classic albums now changing hands at very silly prices.

It was at the start of the 1950s that the adolescent Dodd hung around Kingston's very early sound systems as a 'box boy' – one of the small army of youths who helped maintain, transport and set up the cliff faces of loudspeakers necessary to a top-drawer sound system. His fascination with music had pushed him into such employment, but it wasn't ever going to break any pay barriers. Hence the cane cutting. These overseas trips were never an end in themselves, more a means to realizing a dream. From the first time Coxsone went away he would come back with pieces of equipment to build his own system, along with US R&B records to play on it, all bought in the States with money earned on the plantations.

By the middle of the decade, Clement Seymour Dodd was calling himself Coxsone, Sir Coxsone or Scorcher, and his Down Beat sound system was using the best possible equipment to see off any serious competition as it became the island's number one. At this time the sound systems had only American records, and whoever had the best of these had the biggest crowds at their dances. The competition to find the latest, the rarest, the wildest, was so intense that operators would travel to Miami or New Orleans to search out choice cuts, while trading with visiting American sailors at Kingston dock could become as frantic as a busy day on the Stock Exchange floor.

By the end of the 1950s, though, the styles were changing in America and the supply of raw R&B records was drying up. In 1959, to keep Down Beat on the cutting edge, Coxsone, like other sound men, turned to producing his own music on one-off acetates – among his first recordings was the seminal 'Easy Snappin'' by Theolonius Beckford. But Coxsone's real contribution didn't come until 1963 when he opened his own studio, The Jamaican Recording and Publishing Studio, in Brentford Road, Kingston. Or, as it was known to anybody who worked there, Studio One.

As one of the island's top sound system operators – by this point, he owned several rigs which he would send out manned by his 'apprentice' deejays – recording for Coxsone meant automatic high-level exposure. But in newly independent Jamaica an additional plus point for his operation was that Studio One was the first recording set-up owned by a black man. The combination of a guaranteed audience, an empathy with the ordinary people, and not having to pay for studio time, gave Coxsone *carte blanche* to experiment. With the aid of the best musicians and highly talented arrangers and other producers, he developed the uniquely mellow Studio One sound that, in itself, was a key factor in the onset of rock steady and, later, reggae. Although established Jamaican artists flocked to Coxsone and such a music-friendly environment – ironic really, as opening the studio and starting the eponymous record label were, primarily, business decisions – one of the reasons Studio One pushed forward stylistically was Coxsone's keenness to involve new, young artists and take up their ideas. There were audition sessions every Sunday at Brentford Road, when the queues of fresh-faced hopefuls would stretch for several blocks.

During this first period of Coxsone's career, his production roster read like a who's who (past and future) of Jamaican music. Backed by studio bands that included an ever-evolving upper stratum of Jamaica's session players (see THE SKATALITES), such acts as THE WAILERS, THE MAYTALS, JOHN HOLT, KEN BOOTHE, Marcia Griffiths, DELROY WILSON, STRANGER COLE, FREDDIE MCGREGOR, SLIM SMITH and BOB ANDY all cut sides under his guidance. While such influential producers and deejays as LEE PERRY, Jackie Mittoo, King Stitt, DENNIS ALCAPONE, Count Matchuki, NINEY THE OBSERVER and even PRINCE BUSTER all apprenticed either on Coxsone's sound or in his studio. ••

The following compilations will give the best tasters of what all the fuss is about, and provide a list of names who have Coxsone-produced albums on their back catalogues. With the exception of *Musical Fever 1967-1968*, each of the CDs listed below moves through Coxsone's musical development into roots reggae and dancehall, thus making them particularly attractive as they accurately illustrate how the Clement Dodd 'feel' for music was much greater than any one style.

*Ska Bonanza – The Studio One Ska Years; Heartbeat CDHB86/87

DISC ONE: **The Skatalites,** Nimble Foot Ska; **The Skatalites,** Spred Satin; **Ken Boothe and Stranger Cole,** Arta Bella; **Roland Alphonso and The Soul Vendors,** Streets Of Gold; **Rita Marley Anderson and The Wailers,** A De Pon Dem; **The Skatalites,** Black Sunday; **Cornell Campbell,** Don't Want Your Loving; **Roland Alphonso,** Old Fowl Ska; **Eric 'Monty' Morris,** Enna Bella; **Owen Grey With Clue J and His Blues Blasters,** Jezebel; **Frank Anderson and Tommy McCook,** Always On A Sunday; **Lee Perry,** Sugar Bag; **Lester Sterling, Johnnie Moore and Tommy McCook;** Settle Down; **The Checkmates,** Turn Me On; **Bunny and Skitter,** When The Well Runs Dry; **Frank Anderson and Tommy McCook,** Wheel And Turn; **Cecil Lloyd and Roland Alphonso,** Oceans 11; **The Jiving Juniors,** Over The River; **Alton Ellis and Eddie Perkins With Aubrey Adams and The Dew Droppers,** My Heaven; **Roland Alphonso and Carroll McLaughlin,** Set Back (Just Cool); **Chuck Josephs and Dobby Dobson With Aubrey Adams,** Du Du Wap; **Don Drummond and His Group,** Don Cosmic.

DISC TWO: **Don Drummond,** Man In The Street; **The Wailing Wailers,** Simmer Down; **Toots and The Maytals,** Shining Light; **Jackie Opel,** Push Wood; **Andy and Joey,** Wonder No More; **Roland Alphonso,** Bongo Tango; **Roland Alphonso,** Sucu Sucu; **Roland Alphonso,** 20.75; **The Gaylads,** Stop Making Love; **Bob**

Marley and The Wailers, How Many Times (Do You Remember); **Don Drummond and Roland Alphonso,** Roll On Sweet Don (Heaven And Hell); **Jackie Opel,** Sit Down Servant; **Bob Marley and The Wailers,** Go Jimmy Go; **Aubrey Adams and Rico Rodriguez,** Stew, Peas and Cornflakes; **Derrick Harriot,** Answer Me My Darling; **Clancy Eccles With Hersang and The City Slickers,** River Jordan; **Clue J and His Blues Blasters,** Salt Lane Shuffle; **The Charmers,** Jeannie Girl; **Lascelles Perkins With Clue J and His Blues Blasters,** Lonely Moments.

*Original Club Ska – Studio One's Authentic Jamaican Beat; Heartbeat CDHB55

Roland Alphonso and The Skatalites, Magic Star; **The Wailers,** Ska Jerk; **Jeff Dixon With Alton Ellis,** Yakety Yak; **Roland Alphonso and The Soul Vendors,** From Russia With Love; **The Clarendonians,** Do It Right; **Roland Alphonso and The Skatalites,** Ball Of Fire; **The Gaylads,** Stop Making Love; **Roland Alphonso and The Skatalites,** Timothy; **The Mellolarks,** Romantic Dance; **The Skatalites,** Phoenix City; **Delroy Wilson,** Dancing Time; **Jackie Mittoo,** Dancing Groove; **The Skatalites,** Guns Of Navarone; **The Bassies,** Take Me To The Door.

*Musical Fever 1967–1968; Trojan CDTRL408

DISC ONE: **Winston and Robin,** Bad Mind Grudgeful; **Bennet and Dennis,** Puppy Love; **Cannon and The Soul Vendors,** Bad Treatment; **Bumps Oakley,** Get A Lick; **The Sultans,** Hip Hugger; **Jacob Miller,** Let Me Love You; **The Termites,** Push Up; **Winston and Robin,** Wailing Time; **Eric Frater,** Venus; **Marshall Williams,** Norwegian Wood; **The Soul Vendors,** Love Me Girl; **Winston Holness,** You Shouldn't Be The One.

DISC TWO: **Jackie and The Soul Vendors,** Ram Jam; **The Octaves,** You Gonna Lose; **The Soul Vendors,** Get With It; **The Viceroys,** Fat Fish; **Jackie and The Soul Vendors,** Grooving; **Zoot Sims,** Grooving; **The Soul Vendors,** Soul Junction; **Slim and The Freedom Singers,** Mercy Mercy; **Jackie and The Soul Vendors,** Baba Boom; **The Viceroys,** Love And Unity; **Bob and**

Ty, I Don't Mind; **Lester Sterling,** Zigaloo; **Barrington Spence,** Contemplating Mind; **Ed Nangle,** Good Girl; **The Enforcers,** Musical Fever; **Lester Sterling,** Wiser Than Solomon.

*The Best Of Studio One; Heartbeat HBCD07

The Cables, Baby Why; **The Termites,** My Last Love; **Marcia Griffiths,** Melody Life; **Alton Ellis,** Can I Change My Mind; **Johnny Osbourne,** Jah Promises; **Michegan And Smiley,** Rub-a-Dub Style; **Dennis Brown,** Impossible; **The Heptones,** Party Time; **Larry Marshall,** Throw Mi Corn; **Slim Smith,** Born To Love; **The Gladiators,** Roots Natty; **Sugar Minott,** Oh, Mr DC.

*Best Of Studio One Volume Two; Heartbeat HB14

Carlton and His Shoes, Love Me Forever; **The Paragons,** Danger In Your Eyes; **Culture,** Behold The Land; **The Bassies,** Big Mistake; **Willie Williams,** Armageddon Time; **The Lone Ranger,** Love Bump; **Norma Frazier,** First Cut Is The Deepest; **Delroy Wilson and Slim Smith,** Look Who Is Back Again; **The Ethiopians,** Open The Gate; **Bob Andy,** Desperate Love; **John Holt,** I Don't Want To See You Cry; **Sound Dimension,** Full Up.

*Respect To Studio One; Heartbeat CDHB181

DISC ONE: Intro: The Sound Of Young Jamaica Radio Show – Saturday 18 July 1970, by **MC Winston 'The Whip' Williams; The Heptones,** Pretty Looks Isn't All; **General Smiley and Papa Michegan,** Nice Up The Dance; **Marcia Griffiths,** Melody Life; **The Brentford All Stars,** Throw Mi Corn; **Slim Smith,** I'll Never Let You Go; **Delroy Wilson,** Run Run; **Carlton And The Shoes,** Love Me For Ever; **Dennis Alcapone,** Forever Version; **Jackie Mittoo,** Wire Higher; **The Cables,** What Kind Of World; **Larry Marshall,** Nanny Goat; **Burning Spear,** Fire Down Below; **The Termites,** Have Mercy Mr Percy; **Freddie McKay,** Picture On The Wall; **Horace Andy,** Skylarking; **Sugar Minott,** Vanity.

DISC TWO: **Alton and Hortense Ellis,** Breaking Up Is Hard To Do; **Sound Dimension** Psychedelic Rock (Rockfort Rock); **Ken Boothe,** Moving Away; **Lee Perry,** Don't Blame The Baldhead;

Freddie McGregor, Bobby Babylon; **The Viceroys,** Ya Ho; **Johnny Osbourne,** Sing Jay Style; **Willie Williams,** Armaggedon Time; **Lone Ranger,** Natty Dread On The Go; **John Holt,** Strange Things; **Roland Alphonso and The Skatalites,** Timothy; **The Wailers,** Simmer Down; **Ken Boothe and Stranger Cole,** Artibella; **The Skatalites,** I Should Have Known Better; **Lee Perry,** Chicken Scratch; **Don Drummond and Roland Alphonso,** Roll On Sweet Don.

There are a dozen or so other compilation CDs easily available on import. As the whole point about Studio One was the unique – and uniquely continuous – feel that ran through each release, if these are to your taste then the others won't let you down either. Expect to pay up to £15 per disc, but do shop around if asked for a great deal more, as most specialist reggae outlets will carry a decent selection.

Don Drummond

(Born 1933; Kingston, Jamaica; trombonist)
If you looked in the dictionary under 'a shocking waste of a talent' you'd find a picture of Don Drummond. Or at least you ought to, though it was through no fault of his own.

Even among the quality of brass players that came out of Alpha Boys' Catholic School, or lined up next to him inn THE SKATALITES, Drummond was a giant. Such was his ability and understanding of how music works, he was taken on as a teacher when he left the school at the end of the 1940s. But that was only his day job. By night, Drummond and his 'bone were carving a career for themselves on the Kingston nightclub scene, swinging with the big bands, big time. By the mid-1950s he'd established himself as one of the island's top jazz players, indeed RICO would then (and still does) describe Don Drummond as the best trombonist Jamaica ever produced. Naturally he was in enormous demand when the recording boom began – in fact, the evolution from R&B to ska was as much down to him and the other first-class players who wanted to experiment, as it was to the producers.

This was one of the reasons why Don Drummond and the

Jamaican studio system of the 1960s never really got on. He felt his musical skills and talent were being exploited for piece rate. Even though DUKE REID and COXSONE would both feature him as a named artist – which did get him more in terms of cash and kudos – this was the exception rather than the rule, and mostly his informal arranging work or ad-libbed solos went uncredited (and unpaid). His sense of frustration was huge, and having to keep it contained for fear of being branded a trouble-maker (and so losing work) contributed to mental problems that would put him into a sanitarium for increasing stretches of time. During this period – the early 1960s – Drummond became a devout Rastafarian and reports were that the faith's fierce black pride was manifesting itself in him as a hatred of white people: the stories of the mentally declining Drummond smiling serenely at all and sundry are laced with tales of his spitting at white people on the street.

Eventually he snapped. In 1965, using his pocket knife, and apparently without motive, he stabbed to death his long-time girlfriend, Margarita. He gave himself up to the police instantly and was committed to a secure hospital, where he died in 1969. Just as the music he had so much to do with inventing was going large, and was obviously evolving into the proudly black art form he would have wanted it to be.

The Best Of Don Drummond; Studio One SOCD9008
Memorial; Lagoon LG1203

Both of these albums will give you a good idea of why it was that British jazz legend George Shearing once described Don Drummond as among the best five trombone players in the world. The two sets share a few titles – 'Music Is My Occupation', 'Silver Dollar' and 'Cool Smoke' – and feature mostly The Skatalites in one form or another. But there are two crucial differences: the former is Coxsone – produced at Studio One; the latter had Duke Reid at the controls at Treasure Isle. It's a wonderful way of directly comparing the two producer's approaches: Coxsone looking for subtlety, whereas the Duke clearly considers excitement the main objective.

ALSO RECOMMENDED:

Greatest Hits; Treasure Isle TICD004
The Best Of Don Drummond; Studio One SOCD9008

Like the above-mentioned discs, these contrast Reid's and Dodd's approaches during the same period. And although both sets are very very good, the track selection on the previous two is noticeably superior.

A selection of Drummond-credited tracks can be found on the following compilations, while, as a founder member of The Skatalites, it's his distinctive blowing that can be heard on much of their work.
Ska Bonanza – The Studio One Ska Years; Heartbeat CDHB86/87
Music Is My Occupation – Ska Instrumentals 1962-1965; Trojan CDTRL259
Dance Crasher – Ska To Rock Steady; Trojan CDTRL260
The Trojan Story Volume One; Trojan CDTAL100
Intensified – Original Ska 1962–1966; Mango IMCD51
More Intensified – Original Ska Volume Two 1963–1967; Mango IMCD52
Monkey Ska; Trojan CDTRL323

Jackie Edwards

(Born Wilfred Edwards, 1938; Kingston, Jamaica; singer)
The original Cool Ruler? Certainly some would have it that way. Indeed, there's no denying the man had the silver tones and a worryingly smoove way with a ballad to make sure that Jamaican R&B, ska and early rock steady journeyed down lovers' lane once in a while. *But was he really ever anything much more than another Jamaican Nat King Cole wannabe?* Of course he was. He made his contribution to Jamaican music as Chris Blackwell's right-hand man at the setting-up of Island Records in London in 1962. It's a well-known fact of the Island Story that Blackwell distributed his records off the back seat of his Mini, but less talked about is how the majority of them found their way into the shops thanks to Jackie Edwards and the buses that run up and down the Edgware Road.

Edwards was far more important than a delivery service though. He was vital to Blackwell's exploration of London's black communities – the ear to the streets, so to speak – and was sufficiently talented as a songwriter to be able to compose for this particular market. Edwards recorded too, often cutting tunes with Millie Small as Jackie and Millie.

What enabled Edwards to succeed in this area was an understanding of British pop music and how it was accepted by the West Indian communities over here, and thus how it should affect reggae music aimed at that audience. That same understanding was to become an end in itself when, in 1966, Jackie Edwards wrote two songs for The Spencer Davis Group, one of the growing stable of rock artists that were becoming Chris Blackwell's main concern. 'Keep On Running' and 'Somebody Help Me' became huge international hits, greatly boosting the credibility of Jamaican musicians on a worldwide scale.

Jackie Edwards continued recording throughout the 1970s and 1980s – to little other than specialist market success – and died in 1992.

Paradise; Trojan CDTRL344

A couple of dozen examples of why Edwards was such a highly regarded lurrrve man – oozing through the changing styles on sheer schmaltz, but projecting enough sense of actually meaning it to keep it this side of wet. *Just* – Remarkably, his own highly listenable take on 'Keep On Running' isn't one of them.

Alton Ellis

(Born 1944; Kingston, Jamaica; singer)
When rock steady rolled around, Alton Ellis was a STAR. In the dancehalls and house parties during the second half of the 1960s, when guys wanted to go on the serious pull – as in couldn't afford to fail – Alton Ellis would be slipped on to the turntable. 'Slipped' being the operative word, as nothing Ellis ever put his name to was anything other than e-e-easy. He sung with a feeling and honest emotion that was matched only by his church-influenced way of swooping in and around a melody.

In spite of starting out with COXSONE in the early 1960s, he came to prominence in 1966 with a tune cut for DUKE REID entitled 'Girl I've Got A Date'. Its enormous success more or less instantly established Reid as the man in charge of the new, cooler post-ska style and, in Ellis's own words, 'took him past Coxsone for the first time'. The record remained a Trojan sound system favourite for a couple of years and did wonders for Ellis too: star status that was soon consolidated when he used his success to try to cool down the rude boy situation in Kingston by issuing such socially concerned tunes as 'Cry Tough', 'Dance Crasher', 'Harder And Harder' and 'Blackman's Pride'. He then ensured his place in the history books by writing and recording 'Get Ready, Rock Steady', which is universally acknowledged as the first use of the term. Indeed, over the next four or five years Alton Ellis was so big he was able to oscillate between arch rivals Dodd and Reid. Recording either by himself or with his sister as Alton and Hortense Ellis, or with Eddy Perkins as Alton and Eddy, he cut himself a niche as one of the island's top vocalists.

The change from rock steady to early reggae appeared to suit Ellis as comfortably as the slowing down from ska some years before – the almost universally regarded best single artist albums of the period, *Sunday Coming* and *Mr Soul Of Jamaica*, are both by Ellis.

He earned a particular place in UK reggae's heart, too, when he capitalized on the success of his records by touring with The Soul Vendors. It was regulation for the former dancer to send the women in the crowds wild with some particularly 'wine up' moves. And to think, all this from a man who, on one of his first public appearances – a big deal talent contest in 1960 – sang a straight cover of 'Begin The Beguine'. That he won with such a song ought to tell you something.

Alton Ellis never seemed to fulfil his reggae potential though. In spite of the 1972 sound system perennial 'It's Too late To Turn Back Now' (one that mums seemed particularly keen on, and another record that would get a crowd joining in a chorus) and a couple of roots-ish hits for Lloyd Daley around the same time, the singer's best days were by now behind him. It seemed odd at the time, as Ellis's voice appeared ideally suited for the style. Totally hacked off with the reggae industry and its cavalier attitude to business, he left Jamaica for the UK in 1972, believing that to go back and reimmerse himself in that system would have been pointless. Unfortunately, his career took a nosedive and virtually nothing was heard from him until Althea and Donna scored a UK number 1 in 1978 with 'Uptown Top Ranking', which was based on his Studio One rock steady classic 'I'm Still In Love'. And no, it's not known if he got paid for this usage.

The Legendary Alton Ellis; Attack ATCD012

The best of the earlier Treasure Isle sessions, and a fully comprehensive example of Ellis's enormous range of subject matter. We get the consciousness of 'Cry Tough', 'Going Back To Africa', 'Blackman's Pride' and 'Dance Crasher', the lurrrrve power of 'Remember That Sunday', the mild psychedelia – done rock steady style! – of a cover of 'It's Your Thing' and the barely concealed lewdness of 'Mini Skirt'. It's while enjoying this freedom that Ellis is really given the chance to stretch out and demonstrate the enormous breadth of his voice. A truly special set of songs.

The Best Of Alton Ellis; Studio One SOCD8019

That this has 'Sitting In The Park' on it ought to be enough, but the CD version of this old Studio One collection stretches to Ellis's first big hit for the label, 'Muriel', plus three of the songs he wrote for Pearl, his wife of the time and one true love – 'Pearl', 'I'm Still In Love' and 'Girl I Have A Date'. The fact that the last of these is a Duke Reid production, a record that reigned supreme on the Trojan sound system for the best part of two years, is a further inducement, as the album has the good sense to cut across both labels to present the genuine best of Alton Ellis. Also included are a few of the soul covers that were so predominant as rock steady moved away from rude boy anthems to concentrate on love songs. The pick of the list here is 'Knock On Wood'.

Sunday Coming; Studio One PSOCD3423

As I said before, this is one of the best early reggae albums made.

Largely because a fair amount of care seems to have been put into the track selection and running order – i.e. it's not just a couple of hits and a dozen or so also-rans. It has a real flow to it. And, of course, a bunch of tunes of incredibly high quality. As well as the sound system classic of a title track, there's 'Wide Awake In A Dream', 'You Make Me So Happy', 'Alton's Groove' and 'Your Heart Is Gonna'. Plus the obligatory soul covers 'These Eyes' and 'What Does It Take', which each lose nothing in the transition from Junior Walker's sax to Alton Ellis's croon.

ALSO RECOMMENDED:

25th Silver Jubilee; Skynote SKYCD46

To celebrate his quarter of a century in the business, this is a series of re-recordings of some of his best tracks. 'I'm Still In Love', 'Blackman's Pride', 'Girl I've Got A Date', 'Too Late To Turn Back Now', 'Get Ready, Rock Steady', 'Only Sixteen', 'And I Love Her' and 'Fattie Fattie' among them. As you can imagine, with those titles and Ellis's voice the disc has its moments, but it's far from first division.

*Alton and Hortense Ellis: *Alton and Hortense Ellis*; Heartbeat CDHB64

A compilation of individual numbers (there's only one duet) from the Ellis siblings, all Coxsone-produced, that tends to concentrate more on a later period. However, the cool rock steady of 'Willow Tree' and 'Can I Change My Mind', plus the deep soul 'Cry Together', show that Hortense Ellis is one of the great forgotten talents of Jamaican music.

'Girl I've Got A Date' can be found on *Tougher Than Tough – The Story Of Jamaican Music* (four-CD set, Mango IBXCD1). While 'Get Ready, Rock Steady' is on *The Trojan Story*; (Trojan CDTRS402). The big shame, though, is that the most wonderful album from those Bond Street sessions, *Mr Soul Of Jamaica*, is not available on British CD release.

SEE ALSO:

Ba Ba Boom – Classic Rock Steady And Reggae 1967–1972; Trojan CDTRL265

20 Film And Stage Classics Jamaican Style; Trojan CDTRL 319
Rudies All Round; Trojan CDTRL332
Ska Bonanza – The Studio One Ska Years; Heartbeat CDHB86/87
With **Jeff Dixon**: *Original Club Ska – Studio One's Authentic Jamaican Beat*; Heartbeat CDHB55
Cultural Things; Lagoon LG21011

The Ethiopians

(Leonard 'Sparrow' Dillon, born 1945, Portland, Jamaica; Stephen Taylor, born 1944, St Mary, Jamaica; Aston Morris, born 1944; Portland, Jamaica; vocal trio)
This trio/duo (Morris left early into their career, to return years later after Taylor was killed in a car crash) were a vivid example of the kind of righteousness/rudeness combination that could exist within Jamaican music. With their sharp suits and equally well-tailored harmonies they were as much a part of the rudie scene as their easy action rock steady-ish songs – 'I'm Gonna Take Over Now' summed up their tuffer than tuff attitude, while 'Last Train To Skaville' is probably the best known example. Yet, as their name might suggest, they were converts to the Rasta faith, and it was this group who gave the world that enduring, much-versioned sufferation classic 'The Whip'. Any apparent schizophrenia was no big deal – much like US R&B's sex and sanctity crossover.

What did matter, though, was The Ethiopians' plaintive singing. The harmonies were made sweeter in the early days at Studio One when their backing vocalists were PETER TOSH and BUNNY WAILER, a combination that was perfect for songs that covered all manner of social and racial injustice, from slavery through colonialism to post-independence disappointment. But it was the group's ability to create these outspoken, for-the-people songs over bang-up-to-date rhythms, with whatever producer they were working for – DODD, REID, SONIA POTTINGER, JJ Johnson to name but four – that kept them at the sharp end of Jamaican vocalizing while rock steady osmosed into reggae.

Although their hit percentage slowed down to a virtual standstill as the 1970s got underway, they continued to perform and record in much the same style. Until, by the middle of the decade, a new breed of Rasta took over and they seemed to fit in all over again. At the very end of the 1970s, first Dillon and Morris, then Dillon as a solo artist, released the deeply dread albums *Slave Call* and *Open The Gates Of Zion*. Neither was particularly successful commercially, but they remain two vivid examples of what the group were still capable of. Since then the only significant Ethiopians action has been the updating and re-releasing of the better known bits of their back catalogue.

The Original Reggae Hitsound; Trojan CDTRL228

Probably the best Ethiopians collection. Although post-Studio One, thus minus 'Owe Me No Pay Me', 'Dun Dead Already' and 'Free Man', it covers the 1967 to 1971 period, i.e. the group's real glory years. It's a seminal rock steady selection: 'The Whip', 'Train To Skaville' and 'Engine 54' at one end, with 'Everything Crash', 'The Selah', 'Hong Kong Flu' and 'Gun Man' from the later years. Then, of course, the other side of The Ethiopians' subject matter is adequately represented with the classic 'Woman A Capture Man'. The only notable omission is 'Reggae Hit The Town', which crops up on *Tougher Than Tough – The Story Of Jamaican Music* (four-CD set; Mango IBXCD1).

ALSO RECOMMENDED:

Let's Ska And Rock Steady; Creole JMC200103
The World Goes Ska; Trojan CDTRL312

Collections focusing more on the band's earlier efforts, and although marginally interesting – especially the latter to the more committed ska collector – all the best tunes are on *The Original Reggae Hitsound*.

Slave Call; Heartbeat HBCD56

NINEY THE OBSERVER's rhythms (he produced this 1977 set) should always be worth the time out of your schedule, and although this isn't one of his most interesting albums, for Ethiopian completists it neatly tops off the group's history.

Owners Fi De Yard; Heartbeat CDHB127

Duke Reid recordings, made in the period immediately following the *Hitsound* years.

SEE ALSO:

More Intensified – Original Ska Volume Two 1963–67; Mango IMCD52
Ska Spectacular Volume One; Charly CPCD8021
Ska Spectacular Volume Two; Charly CPCD8022
Rock Steady Rave; Charly CPCD8023
Dance Crasher – Ska To Rock Steady; Trojan CDTRL260
Tougher Than Tough – The Story Of Jamaican Music (four-CD set); Mango IBXCD1
Cultural Things; Lagoon LG21011

Derrick Harriot

(Born 1942; Kingston, Jamaica; singer/songwriter/producer)
Derrick Harriot is one of Jamaican music's great survivors, having participated in and, in many cases, actively chivvied along every phase of the development from R&B-based boogie to fast-toasting dancehall. Harriot now owns a record store in Kingston, occasionally performs, and makes the living he deserves by astutely exploiting the rights to his own marvellous and marvellously comprehensive back catalogue – which is very much A Good Thing. Harriot's contribution has always been far greater than reggae history would have it, and if he weren't preserving his work for posterity himself it might well have got lost along the way.

Harriot's musical life began as half of the adolescent duo Sang and Harriot with Claudie Sang. The two sound-system – obsessed school friends did well in the local theatres – on the same bills as KEN BOOTHE, JIMMY CLIFF and DELROY WILSON. In 1957 they got to cut a demo tune, 'Lollipop Girl', a pre-skabeat shuffle, and this one cut took them to both COXSONE and DUKE REID. Dodd had acquired it from the small sound system the pair had sold it to, while Reid heard it on Down Beat and was so impressed he coerced a Dodd employee into letting him borrow it to make a duplicate. Apparently the two men came to blows when Coxsone discovered Duke was playing a Down Beat 'exclusive'! But whatever came about, it was enough to keep the sixteen-year-old Harriot, with his new group The Jiving Juniors, recording for both men, until the 1960s rolled around and he started his own label.

Always a natural crooner, Harriot and the group rode the ska boom out recording their own productions in New York. By using American musicians they attained a smooth soulful sound, not enormously removed from the rock 'n' roll ballads of the day that commanded an enormous Jamaican radio audience.

However, the rock steady style was tailormade for Harriot's silky tones. Back in Jamaica, using a succession of different studios and Boris Gardiner as an arranger, he cut some of the best ever rock steady for his own labels, Crystal and Move 'N' Groove. It was at this point he put together his Crystalites backing band – the nucleus of the next wave of musicians who were to have a massive influence as the music crossed into reggae. Then, as success raised his profile, his labels built up a formidable roster of rock steady naturals: ERIC DONALDSON, Nicky Thomas, Junior Smith (who would later change his name to JUNIOR MURVIN), Rudy Mills and Keith 'N' Tex all benefited greatly from Derrick Harriot's innate understanding of smoove. ⬥⬥

*The Sensational Derrick Harriot Sings Jamaican Rock Steady Reggae; Jamaican Gold JMC200213

That this disc has 'Riding For A Fall' on it should be enough to ensure desirability. A supersmoove example of what it took to make a brilliant rock steady love song: a crisp mid-tempo beat; the bass pushing rather than driving the melody; and enough syrup poured over the vocal track to make sure it oozes its way through the ram-packed blues dance. What's going on around 'Riding' is more or less the best of the man they called The Chariot. While it demonstrates Harriot's brilliant handling of the new styles of the 1960s, this set is also an early showing of how, at the lighter end, Jamaican music had an enormous appetite for rearranged covers of US soul hits – a habit that continued through the next decade. Best examples here are the early-reggae version of The Temptations' 'Message From A Black Man' and the ska-to-rock steady treatment of 'The Girl's Alright With Me' and 'You Really Got A Hold On Me'. And, to prove he could write for himself too, we have the sublime 'Long Time' and 'I'm Not Begging', each one among the most intricately arranged and musically sophisticated rock steady ever made.

*From Chariot's Vaults: 16 Rock Steady Hits; Jamaican Gold JMC200214

Exactly what it says, each one produced (and many written) by Derrick Harriot, featuring such front men as Lloyd and Glen, Rudy Mills, Noel Brown, Keith and Tex, Junior Soul (another aka for the man soon to be called Junior Murvin) and David Anthony. It's one of the best cross-sections of lively, melodically intricate rock steady, and although Harriot's honey-dripping tones are missed at times, a big band that includes Lyn Taitt, Boris Gardiner, Bobby Ellis, Gladdy Anderson and Val Bennett tends to make amends.

*Derrick Harriot And Friends: *Step Softly – Rock Steady and Reggae, 1965–1972*; Trojan CDTRL267

Harriot's golden years, from his early post-ska period ('The Jerk' and 'Mama Didn't Lie'), through the rock steady balladeering that made his name as a producer (Bobby Ellis's 'Step Softly', THE PARAGONS' 'Lonely And Blue' and Keith and Tex's 'Stop That Train'), right up to his always very tuneful dabblings in roots reggae (I-ROY's 'Tougher Than Tough' and GLEN BROWN's 'Love I'). Arranged like this, it's easy to see the natural progressions in Harriot's work and how staying up with the way things changed kept him on top for the best part of a decade.

ALSO RECOMMENDED:

*Derrick Harriot and The Jiving Juniors: *The Donkey Years 1961–1965*; Jamaican Gold JMC200212

The early days, which are very much about R&B crooning, as

any indigenous Jamaican music was in the embryonic stages. A good example of where it all started.

SEE ALSO:

Monkey Ska; Trojan CDTRL323
As part of **The Jiving Juniors** and **solo**: *Ska Bonanza – The Studio One Ska Years*; Heartbeat CDHB 86/87

The Heptones

(Leroy Sibbles, born 1949, Kingston, Jamaica; Earl Morgan, born 1945, Kingston, Jamaica; Barry Llewelyn, born 1947, Kingston, Jamaica; vocal group)
The name was originally meant to have been The Hep Ones, as in the American teenage jargon of the early 1960s, but it was soon corrupted into something far more original. Fittingly so, too. This trio were, if not the founding fathers of rock steady harmonizing, then certainly the market leaders – the one the others imitated. Witness 'Pretty Looks Isn't All'. Masterly, intricately intertwined three-part harmonies, with such substance to them you could wrap yourself up in them, and an all-round expressiveness that puts many of the big-monied American soul outfits of the time to shame. Yet all the while it drives itself with such a joyous verve that, over twenty-five years later, in original fashion, it'll still rock a house.

Coached by neighbours THE PIONEERS, the group attempted to make an impression back in 1965 with a bizarre interpretation of *The William Tell Overture* with lyrics about gunmen. Thankfully, though, this was all forgotten by the next year when COXSONE signed them up. Studio One's stylistic warmth was tailormade for The Heptones' harmonics, and Coxsone's skill coaxed a further layer out of their sound that seemed to give it a fourth dimension. Built on Sibbles's swooping, infinitely flexible alto, the sheer class of this lead and the attention to fine detail in the vocal arrangement meant every subtle nuance showed up. To such a degree, the notion of the midtempo ballad was expanded, widthways, to limits that had previously not seemed possible. Thanks to The Heptones, the Jamaican vocal trio was lacking nothing that might have been found in Detroit or Chicago: 'Party Time', 'Only Sixteen', 'Baby', 'Triple Girl', 'I Hold The Handle', 'Fattie Fattie' (their first big hit, in late 1966), 'A Change Has Got To Come' and, of course, 'Pretty Looks Isn't All'. To name but a few.

As rock steady carried the swing, Brentford Road was undoubtedly where this group ought to be – check out the almost spooky musical/vocal empathy in 'Pretty Looks Isn't All' as that trombone 'ba ba da da da daa daa ba ba daaa' sets up the singing. It was an environment in which Sibbles grew into a songwriter – both words and music – of astonishing ability. One of the reasons why these songs have stood the test of time, with so many people 'reinterpreting' them, is simply because they're brilliantly written, from the bassline upwards. And the most surprising thing about 'Pretty Looks', to bring that one up yet again, is that Sibbles *didn't* write it, Llewelyn did. So the song-writing talent ran deeper still.

However, this marriage made in heaven of The Heptones and Studio One wasn't one that would last. ⟶

The Heptones; Studio One SOCD9002

A straight CD reissue of The Heptones' first Studio One album of 1968, and a short sharp lesson in why this group commanded the respect it did. Even at this very early stage, their harmonizing was achingly smooth – it was then far more a threesome than a lead singer and two others – and Sibbles was writing killer songs. This set is based on that big, banned hit 'Fattie Fattie', but eases right along to include 'Only Sixteen', 'The Best Things In Life', 'Cry Baby Cry', 'Tripe Girl', 'I've Got A Feeling' and 'Get In The Groove'.

SEE ALSO:

The Best Of Studio One; Heartbeat HBCD07
Respect To Studio One; Heartbeat CDHB181 (the compilation that got 'Pretty Looks Isn't All')

Justin Hines and The Dominoes

(Hines (sometimes spelt Hinds) born 1943, St Anns, Jamaica;

Dennis Sinclair; Junior Dixon; vocal group)
Loyalty – be it to a particular studio, record label, producer or
backing band – has never been a prominent feature of early
Jamaican music. Handshake contracts, no copyright laws and
somebody always ready to offer you a few dollars more meant
it was an option rather than a prerequisite. Which makes Hines's
allegiance to DUKE REID for more than ten years a remarkable,
if not unique, state of affairs. But it was one that was repaid in
full, for between 1963 and 1969 the group enjoyed an enormous
run of success, bookended by their first recording, 'Carry Go
Bring Come', to a new rock steady version of it five years later.
And what was so surprising about their rich vocal presentations
was that they sang in unison rather than harmonizing, relying
on Hines's impassioned tenor to carry them through. This trio
made an enormous contribution to the establishment of Duke
Reid and Treasure Isle as a force to be reckoned with.

But much of Justin Hines and The Dominoes' appeal was
down to the combination of influences that manifested themselves in their writing and performance. Hines himself was a
huge R&B fan – the group's name was his tribute to Fats Domino
– which showed in his early work. Thus, even with its ska direction, his music slotted in alongside the existing, R&B-based
Jamaican boogie. It probably helped get Duke Reid's attention
too, as the producer's sound system made its name with
imported New Orleans R&B. It was Hines's obviously church
roots that gave the vocal arrangements their depth, while his
rural background enabled him to write and put across lyrical
messages in a way that touched a nerve in many many
Jamaicans. Remember, in the early 1960s there were far more
people living in the country than the cities, yet the music business was entirely Kingston-based and increasingly urban-ori-
ented, so anything with rural appeal was seized upon. The
group leader's open Rasta faith put him slightly ahead of the
pack during that post-independence period when, although this
proud black religion was mushrooming, relatively few performers had 'come out'.

However, as the music moved into the 1970s and internationally marketed reggae became the order of the day, Hines had
difficulty keeping up with trends. The hits rapidly dried up.
After Reid's death in 1975, he recorded for Jack Ruby and

SONIA POTTINGER, and tried his luck in the USA, but never repeated the ska and rock steady success he had at Treasure Isle.

Ska Uprising; Trojan CDTRL314

Going up to the late 1960s and covering their time as Duke Reid's premier ska/rock steady singers, these twenty tracks give the best flavour of what this trio was all about. Just a few bars of the original version of that raucous Rasta-influenced classic 'Carry Go Bring Come' is enough to see why this first recording was also their first hit. Then, as we progress through more spiritual ska – 'Mighty Redeemer', 'Botheration' and 'Teach The Youth' – to the original LOVERS' ROCK style of 'Here I Stand', with the very best in backing from the TOMMY MCCOOK-led SKATALITES, this album shapes up as a shining example of what made Duke Reid's label so special. Likewise, as the trio eases into rock steady – 'On A Saturday Night', 'Save A Bread', 'Once A Man Twice A Child', the rock steady re-recording of 'Carry Go Bring Come' and the seminal 'The Higher The Monkey Climbs' – they vividly present one of the best surviving examples of the music. This would be when rock steady hadn't slowed down too much, but was already creating some cleverly shaded, three-dimensional situations because it wasn't so well established that people were afraid to experiment. Although this disc doesn't stretch itself quite as far as 'King Samuel', 'The Ark' and 'Jump Out Of The Frying Pan', what it has got is good enough for these tracks not to be (too badly) missed.

ALSO RECOMMENDED:

Early Recordings; Heartbeat LG21017

Fourteen tracks on this one – all drawn from the above, with the most glaring omissions being the second cut of 'This Carry Go Bring Come' and 'Rub Up Push Up'. But still, it's not too bad a substitute.

This Carry Go Bring Come; Heartbeat CDHB 24

Another permutation of most of *Ska Uprising*, but with both the ska and the rock steady treatments of the title track, plus

'Botheration', 'Cheer Up', 'If It's Fine' and 'Penny Reel'.

SEE ALSO

Intensified – Original Ska 1962–1966; Mango IMCD51
Club Ska 67; Mango IMCD53
The Birth Of Ska; Trojan CDTRL274
Ba Ba Boom – Classic Rock Steady And Reggae 1967–1972; Trojan CDTRL265
It's Rockin' Time – Duke Reid's Rock Steady 1967–1968; Trojan CDTRL279
Cultural Things; Lagoon LG21011

Pat Kelly

(Born 1949; Kingston, Jamaica; singer)
For a while, back when the 1960s were rolling into the 1970s, the name Pat Kelly was synonymous with silkily smooth rock steady singing. Mums had copies of his records, while the next generation knew that one of the best chances of grabbing a gal at a dance was when the singer's 1969 hit 'How Long Will It Take' was dropped. An attraction that lasted for two or three years after the record was made. Cut for BUNNY LEE, it was the island's biggest tune of that year, and when strings were added on UK release it was the first record of its kind to use such an orchestral approach. Indeed, this extra sweetening so boosted Kelly's honeyed croon that the record was a huge success in certain parts of the UK and the singer was offered a deal – reportedly £20,000 – to sign to The Beatles' record company, Apple. This was around the same time that the Fabs signed soul star Billy Preston. But the deal with Kelly came to nothing as his UK record company opted to hold him to his contract.

Remarkably, Kelly's involvement with music came about through the technical rather than the creative. On returning to Jamaica in 1967 after studying electronics in the USA, he found work as a studio engineer in the country's mushrooming recording industry and, naturally enough, it wasn't long before his soulful falsetto was noticed. Indeed, that very same year, Kelly took over as lead singer in THE TECHNIQUES, after SLIM SMITH left to go solo. Kelly seemed made for the job too. At

DUKE REID's, the group cut a series of hits in a classic rock steady–style, the biggest being 'You Don't Care' and 'Queen Majesty' – both adaptations of Impressions songs. Such choices were hardly surprising: not only were The Impressions huge on Jamaican radio at the time, but The Techniques' church-rooted arrangements were not dissimilar and Kelly's voice is, in many ways, very close to Curtis Mayfield's, the Chicago group's then lead singer. In fact, when Kelly went solo with producer Bunny Lee during the next year, he continued to cover Curtis Mayfield songs.

Although Kelly enjoyed a series of hits, including 'Somebody's Baby' and 'Dark End Of The Street' (re-recorded as 'Little Boy Blue'), after 'How Long Will It Take' in 1969 things seemed to go cold. Perhaps the changing styles had overtaken him, or maybe leaving Bunny Lee had an adverse effect, but recording became sporadic. Instead he devoted much time to a return to engineering. The only noticeable recording success since the 1960s was 'Talk About Love' in 1972.

True Devotion; Rhino RNCD2113

A collection of the best Duke Reid moments, many of them solo cuts of tunes originally recorded with The Uniques. The fact that the CD kicks off with 'Queen Majesty' and moves right along with 'Loving Pauper' and 'You Don't Care' ought to be enough to convince any malingerers. Which means such superb rock steady as 'Better Get Ready', 'Last Chance' and 'You'll Never Get Away' is quite a bonus.

Portrait Of A Living Legend; Angel ANGD21

The era when Phil Pratt produced Pat Kelly. By which time, rock steady had more or less completed its osmosis into reggae but Kelly was hanging back and, as a result, delivered some brilliant material. And although this manages to avoid the huge JA hit 'Talk About Love', it does include 'On Top Of The World', 'Losing My Baby', seven minutes of 'The Winner' and 'Summer In Jamaica'.

SEE ALSO:

Tougher Than Tough – The Story Of Jamaican Music (four-CD set)
Mango IBXCD1
Jumping With Mr Lee – 1967–1968; Trojan CDTRL270

Leslie Kong

(Born 1933; Kingston, Jamaica; producer)
A Chinese-Jamaican, Leslie Kong was the subject of open scorn
from his black music business peers – the best known example
being PRINCE BUSTER's 'Black Head Chinee Man', aimed at
DERRICK MORGAN when the singer left Buster to record for
Kong (see page 21). But far more significantly, Leslie Kong was
one of the first producers to come into the business with a view
to making records for retail rather than to play on his sound
system. He wanted something different from a record, which
might explain why he seemed more open to change than others.
It was largely Kong (together with BUNNY LEE) who broke the
REID/DODD domination of the first half of the 1960s, and was
then instrumental in establishing reggae as a force to be reckoned with as it came out of rock steady. And this was after he
played the major role in kick-starting the careers of three of
Jamaica's biggest stars.

Kong had a hankering for the music business for some time
before he got into it – it's said that when he worked in a Kingston
restaurant he used to fix it so Morgan and other musicians ate
free just so he would be able to talk to them about studios and
music. Thus, when he and his three brothers opened their own
ice-cream parlour Beverley's, he insisted that part of the floor
space be given over to selling records. And it might have
stopped there if JIMMY CLIFF hadn't had the wit to write a song
called 'Dearest Beverly'. In 1962, that song and another Cliff-
penned number 'Hurricane Hattie' (musical homage to the
storm that had recently hit South America) became the first
releases on the hastily formed Beverley's label.

After turning Jimmy Cliff's career around, Kong took on a
singing welder who had been rejected by both Reid and
Coxsone. At Beverley's, DESMOND DEKKER went on to

become one of the era's biggest stars. When another youth-on-the make, one of Dekker's welding workmates, came to Kong looking for a break Kong cut three tunes with him. 'One Cup Of Coffee', 'Judge Not' and 'Terror' became the first recordings by one Robert Nesta Marley.

Although he didn't hold on to BOB MARLEY through the ska and rock steady 1960s, Leslie Kong did more than hold his own. Through artists like Derrick Morgan, The Spanishtonians, Dekker, Cliff, STRANGER COLE and JOE HIGGS, his calmer, more melodic ska was exactly right to osmose into rock steady. It must be remembered that Kong – who didn't operate a sound system – wasn't looking to make records that would keep a crowd hyped all night, he was after the sort of music they'd want to take home. However, Kong's real mark on the Jamaican music scene was yet to be made. ↦

Currently, *Leslie Kong – The Best Of Beverley's*, a compilation set which includes examples of this period, is available only on vinyl. It is hoped it will come out on CD sometime soon, but in the meantime the following feature early Kong:
Any Desmond Dekker compilation, or compilations featuring Desmond Dekker.
Bob Marley: *Songs Of Freedom* (four-CD set); Tuff Gong TGCBX1
Tougher Than Tough – The Story Of Jamaican Music (four-CD set); Mango IBXCD1
Rudies All Round; Trojan CDTRL332
More Intensified – Original Ska Volume Two 1963–1967; Mango IMCD52
Intensified – Original Ska 1962–1966; Mango IMCD51

Bunny 'Striker' Lee

(Born Edward Lee, 1941; Kingston, Jamaica; producer)
Ask anybody who ever met Bunny Lee what he was like and the replies will be laced with such descriptions as 'lovely', 'decent', or even 'benevolent'. Certainly not the sort of words you'd expect to hear in the same sentences as the names of old-time reggae producers. But while Bunny Lee, or 'Striker' as he's frequently known, worked to support a huge extended family, he

was also something of a Godfather figure in his local community. People would come to him with their problems and he was frequently bailing his fellow citizens either out of debt or the police station. He was, by all accounts, a thoroughly nice fellow.

Bunny Lee's entrance into the music business wasn't exactly par for the course, either. For a start, it came relatively late in his life – he was twenty-one years old. When his friend, the successful singer DERRICK MORGAN introduced him to DUKE REID in 1962, it was to utilize Lee's affable personality as a record plugger, convincing local radio stations that they should be airing Treasure Isle releases. This was a career that clearly suited Lee as he continued this service for several labels after he left Reid's. At the same time, by playing on the contacts he was making, he was building a name for himself as a music business 'Mr Fixit', introducing musicians, singers and producers to each other and putting together bands for studio sessions. It was Striker who teamed up singer Roy Shirley, producer JOE GIBBS and the musicians (Gladdy Anderson, Lyn Taitt, Joe Isaacs and Bryan Atkinson) who cut 'Hold Them' in 1966, which is widely acclaimed as the first ever rock steady tune.

Bunny Lee didn't actually produce his first record ('Listen To The Music' by Lloyd Jackson) until 1967. By the end of that year, though, he had a string of hits behind him. While he may not have been directly responsible for the invention of rock steady, Lee seemed to understand it to such a degree that his presentation took it to a new level. He was the man behind such hardy perennial-type rhythms as 'Love And Devotion' and 'Hold You Jack', and the careers of vocalists like PAT KELLY, Roy Shirley, Ken Parker and STRANGER COLE owe him a great debt.

But where Lee truly made his mark on rock steady was in exploiting Jamaica's keenness for US vocal groups. He recognized how vocal-friendly this new far-more-melodic style was, and concentrated on harmony-singing outfits like The Uniques and The Sensations, who both fronted an incredibly successful series of sweetly crooned rock steady records for the producer. 'Girls Like Dirt', 'Long Time Me No See You Girl', 'Love And Devotion' and 'The Beautitude' are just a few.

By the end of the 1960s, Bunny Lee was already one of the island's most successful producers. Then, when the change came to reggae, he seemed to move up a gear. ❧

***Jumping With Mr Lee – 1967–1968;* Trojan CDTRL270

The Sensations, Long Time Me No See You Girl; **The Uniques,** Love And Devotion; **Val Bennett And The Bunny Lee Allstars,** Jumping With Mr Lee; **Lester Sterling And Winston 'Stranger' Cole,** Bangarang; **Pat Kelly,** Little Boy Blue; **The Uniques,** Story Of Love; **Ken Parker,** A Change Is Gonna Come; **Val Bennett,** Jumping With Val; **The Uniques,** Girls Like Dirt; **Lester Sterling,** Tribute To King Scratch; **Pat Kelly,** Somebody's Baby; **Vin Gordon,** Sounds And Soul; **The Uniques,** My Conversation; **Lester Stirling,** Sir Lee's Whip; **Slim Smith and The Uniques,** The Beatitude.

This is the only dedicated CD collection of Bunny Lee productions from this period available at the moment. But that doesn't really matter as it's got all the crucial tunes. It shows both Lee's silky approach to these smoother rhythms, and how he took an almost gospel slant on singing – solo as well as harmonics.

SEE ALSO:

Tougher Than Tough – The Story Of Jamaican Music (four-CD set); Mango IBXCD1

Byron Lee

(Born 1935; Clarendon, Jamaica; bass player/singer/producer) Although Byron Lee will often be rounded on by reggae regulars, both back then and now, for being too 'uptown', and for cutting tunes strictly for tourists, it would be grossly unfair to dismiss him. Indeed, it was his poppier, more accessible approach that went a long way to advancing the cause of indigenous Jamaican music.

A professional musician since his late-teens, and a band leader since the mid-1950s, Lee learned his trade playing US Top 40 cover versions and gentle Jamaican R&B to entertain Americans in the swankier hotels.

But essentially he was a businessman. At the end of the 1950s, when ska had come about, Byron Lee correctly perceived it as a Kingston-based experience, and realized that outside of that city's sound systems it was impossible to hear too much of it.

After all, there was no ska record industry as such then, Jamaican radio stations were deeply conservative and existed to serve the middle classes, and thus loath to play this 'ghetto music'. So as early as 1961 he established a promotions company with the express intention of taking his band and other ska artists on regular road trips around the country, putting on dances in the remote towns and villages. In doing so, he quite deliberately smoothed the music out a bit, to widen its appeal. This seemed to do the trick and much of ska's early nationwide popularity can be attributed to him.

Byron Lee saw the potential for ska on an international stage too. Perhaps running a travel firm and promotions company that brought in American artists had something to do with this. It was Lee's band, The Dragonaires, who were selected by the Jamaican government to perform at the World's Fair in New York in 1964, as backing band to artists like Millie Small and JIMMY CLIFF. (This still enrages other musicians active at the time, who claim that this particular outfit was chosen because they were establishment-approved, and therefore could never represent the real deal ghetto-bred soul of ska.) The venture was to promote the music as a Jamaican cultural export, and Lee saw it as an opportunity to do business with Atlantic Records – he recorded an album for them and signed a Caribbean distribution deal for their products. While his LP (like the World's Fair shows) wasn't too successful, it had at least established the notion of an alternative to calypso in the minds of the rest of the world.

Oh and by the way, before this, during the very early 1960s, Lee brought in an electric bass guitar and bass amp from the USA. The first of their kind on the island, their usage pushed the bassline to the front of the mix – in much the same way they did to US R&B – and changed the shape of Jamaican music for ever.

In the 1970s, roots reggae never really fitted into Byron Lee's game plan, and he devoted increasing time to his many business interests. Performing less, he set up his own recording studio which was hired out far more often than he produced acts there. More recently, his band of young musicians has specialized in soca (soul/calypso), touring abroad and putting on shows at home. But this seems more of a hobby, for Byron Lee has, for a long time, been one of reggae's relatively few millionaires.

The Best Of Ska; Jamaican Gold JMC200104
The Best Of Ska Volume Two; Jamaican Gold JMC200105
The Best Of Ska Volume Three; Jamaican Gold JMC200106

Three selections of covers of popular hits of the early to mid-1960s, and although none of this will rank at the more exciting end of reggae's past – indeed, downright cheesy might be a better description – it exists for a purpose. Which is to appeal to people who might have dipped a toe into the music at their hotel's Welcome Barbecue while on a North Coast holiday. And if what was intended as a vacation souvenir convinces the listener to go a bit deeper and search out something with a higher roots factor, then who are we to complain? (Likewise, there are a number of Byron Lee titles on the Jamaican Gold series that approach reggae in exactly the same way.)

The Maytals

(Frederick 'Toots' Hibbert; Nathaniel McCarthy; Henry Gordon; all born mid-1940s; Kingston, Jamaica; vocal trio)
Nobody who's seen the film classic *The Harder They Come* will ever forget The Maytals. Grouped round a microphone, bawling out 'Sweet And Dandy' with harmonies so impassioned it was impossible not to join in. Indeed, such was their trademark gusto it wasn't unusual for them literally to sing their throats ragged looking for that higher level of soul. But long before their later LESLIE KONG-produced reggae, The Maytals were a pretty nifty ska act.

Formed in 1961, they were ideally placed to get in on the new craze, because their powerful vocal style was able to compete with the horn-driven raucousness going on behind them. And, understandably, they were in huge demand, firstly cutting sides for COXSONE at Studio One, then moving on to PRINCE BUSTER, and by the middle of the decade, working with BYRON LEE. They also freelanced all over town under such names as The Vikings, The Royals and The Flames – although this was often the result of producers making up different names to print on the record's label, and thus remove the inconvenience of paying the group any royalties.

The Maytals quickly became one of the top vocal groups in the business, and maintained this position thanks to a number of high-profile events. They were among the first to promote the notion of the Caribbean/American black population as the lost tribe of Israel with 'Six And Seven Books Of Moses'; they took the competition between studios to a new level when they left Coxsone for Prince Buster (they released 'Broadway Jungle', a single that was a none-too-veiled reference to Dodd's set up, with an even more confrontational track, 'Dog War', on the other side); in 1965 they topped both Jamaican charts with the same song, 'Daddy', a feat that had never before been achieved; then in 1966 they won the annual Jamaican Festival Song Competition with 'Bam Bam'.

Unfortunately, that same year, Hibbert was jailed for eighteen months after he was caught with a bag of ganja. The other two waited for him to come out, but by the time they got back into studio the music had changed drastically. The Maytals, however, were far from finished. ↦

Sensational Ska Explosion; Jamaican Gold JMC200112

This was recorded between 1964 and 1965, after The Maytals had left both Coxsone and Prince Buster, and is the best of their Byron Lee productions. As a result, the music isn't perhaps as fiery as it might be, but there's very little anybody can do to keep the irrepressible Mr Hibbert and chums down. This is vocal ska at its best, with the trio's gospel-rooted roof-raising approach to harmonizing communicating the very essence of the music. The CD is a straight lift of the original 1965 LP, *The Sensational Maytals*, with eight alternative takes added. As well as the two huge Jamaican hits, 'Daddy' and 'It's You' – one extra cut of the former and two of the latter – there's four versions of 'Never You Change', plus three of 'What's On Your Mind'.

SEE ALSO:

Do The Reggae 1966–1970; Attack CDAT103
Reggae Greats; Island IMCD38
Although both of these feature 'Bam Bam', along with a couple of other late-model ska tunes, they are really a representation of The Maytals' later work.

Ska Bonanza – The Studio One Ska Years; Heartbeat CDHB86/87
Tougher Than Tough – The Story Of Jamaican Music (four-CD set);
Mango IBXCD1

Tommy McCook

(Born 1932; Kingston, Jamaica; saxophonist/band leader)
There's a verse in LORD CREATOR's bawdy ska classic 'Big
Bamboo' where the vocalist rhymes 'Tommy McCook is at my
side/He blow him sax so don't run and hide/He blow him sax
with a nice sweet tone/But his bamboo is as big as his saxophone'. Whether or not this last statement is true is not in the
public domain! The rhyme is there to 'big up' Tommy McCook
in the most spectacular manner – which is no less than this most
venerable of sidemen deserved, as his is one of the largest names
in ska, rock steady and, later, reggae. He was the original
SKATALITE, the founding member of The Supersonics,
featured soloist with THE AGGROVATORS, The Revolutionaries and The Professionals, and the musical arranger for
many a classic track from DUKE REID, COXSONE, JOE GIBBS
and BUNNY LEE – in fact the term 'sideman' really does
Tommy McCook an enormous disservice.

Another graduate of the Alpha Boys' Catholic School, the
teenage McCook put his theory into practice when he played
big-band jazz around Kingston's upmarket dancehalls, on cruise
ships and, later, in the Bahamas. It was while he was earning a
considerable reputation in these environments that he took
every opportunity to hang out at COUNT OSSIE's Rasta camps,
studying their approach. By the time he came home for good in
the early 1960s, spiritual understanding and enthusiasm for an
indigenous music were as keen as his technical skills. So it was
natural that he was at the heart of the music as it developed from
R&B into ska.

The Skatalites – it was McCook who thought up the name
with reference to 1963's Soviet space shot – came about as a
result of the desire of both himself and mento recording artist
Lord Tanamo (who produced live shows in Kingston) to formalize the floating pool of local musical talent into a recognized
unit. They correctly believed this would vastly increase their

negotiating clout. Such a degree of labour organization was something of a first for the embryonic recording industry. It was very successful though, as The Skatalites and the group's direct descendant, the exclusively Duke Reid Supersonics, provided backing for nearly every important record made in Jamaica during the mid-1960s. During this period McCook not only handled a lot of arrangement chores for producers more concerned with putting the singer in front of the microphone, but he also developed as a writer of note – 'Music Is My Occupation', 'Silver Dollar', 'Yard Broom' and 'Thunderball' all flowed from his pen.

Such was Tommy McCook's ranking in Jamaican music that he has never truly been overtaken. Even when reggae arrived and with it, initially, far fewer hornlines, the chances he would be in there somewhere when horn parts were required . Through the 1970s and into the next decade he played a big part in such vital house bands as Bunny Lee's Aggrovators, Joe Gibbs's Professionals and Channel One's Revolutionaries.

Although he went into a bit of a trough in the dancehall-crazy late 1980s, McCook never retired, and now, as the roots – or 'real' reggae – revival gathers pace, so his workload, both as a stage and studio musician, is increasing once more.

Tommy McCook and The Supersonics: Down On Bond Street; Trojan CDTRL326

Post-Skatalite Duke Reid productions that move into rock steady and thus give an excellent example of the man's range and how the music was changing. He takes lead on tunes like 'Tommy's Rock Steady', 'Real Cool', 'Moody Ska', 'Music Is My Occupation' and 'Down On Bond Street', while letting his jazz roots show through on 'The Yellow Basket (A Tisket A Tasket)' and 'Soul Serenade'.

When discussing this period, it would be far quicker to list the tracks Tommy McCook didn't play on, so the best thing to do is to check down the players' credits on any early reggae albums. In fact, right up to the second half of the 1980s, even outside the groups mentioned in his entry, he'll figure on an enormous proportion of the classier reggae records. However, apart from the abovementioned and Tommy McCook and The Skatalites' *The*

Birth Of Ska (featured under Skatalites, page XX), he can be found fronting various ensembles on the following compilations:

Ska Bonanza – The Studio One Ska Years; Heartbeat CDHB 86/87 (this album contains a couple of particularly hard-to-find permutations of McCook and other featured names – with Lester Sterling and Johnnie Moore, and with Frank Anderson).

Monkey Ska; Trojan CDTRL323

Music Is My Occupation – Ska Instrumentals 1962–1965; Trojan CDTRL259

It's Rockin' Time – Duke Reid's Rock Steady 1967–1968; Trojan CDTRL279

Shufflin' On Bond Street – Jamaican R&B and Ska Instrumentals; Trojan CDTRL275

Cultural Things; Lagoon LG21011

Real Cool Rock Steady – Gems From The Treasure Isle; Trojan CDTRL206

The Melodians

(Brent Dowe, born 1948, Kingston, Jamaica; Tony Brevett; Trevor McNaughton; Robert Cogle; vocal trio)
Yes, this is the only four-piece trio in the history of music! Cogle was a fully-fledged Melodian throughout their career, but he didn't sing, he just contributed to the writing and arranging. To say 'just' is to make it sound as if his contribution wasn't very important, which is far from the case. Not only were The Melodians responsible for a string of rock steady and early reggae classics – 'Swing And Dine', 'Too Young To Fall In Love' and 'Sweet Sensation' among them – but they also wrote what was to become one of the biggest ever selling pop songs in the UK, 'Rivers Of Babylon'.

The group came together as teenage friends in the very early 1960s, determined to become part of the wave of Impressions-style Jamaican vocal groups as it began to gain momentum. They built up a huge following by continued success in the local talent shows, but the only recording they did prior to 1967 was a few sides at Studio One that disappeared without trace. Which was strange, as the group's harmonizing was exactly right for the new, mellower approach Jamaican music was taking. Firstly they were tight, but instead of just locking together they oozed all over each other with no gaps or sharp edges. Then they hooked up with, in succession, DUKE REID and SONIA POT-TINGER and for three years the flow of hits was simply unstop-pable: 'You Don't Need Me', 'I Will Get Along', 'Come On Little Girl', 'I Caught You', 'Little Nut Tree' and the all-time celebra-tory rock steady celebration 'Swing And Dine'. By the time The Melodians took up with LESLIE KONG at the end of the decade, their name had become a byword for Jamaican love songs.

At Beverley's, things only got better. As well as 'Sweet Sensation' and 'Rivers Of Babylon', the three singers enjoyed considerable local success as solo performers – Brent Dowe, in particular. And probably would have continued doing so for a lot longer than the turn of the decade had Leslie Kong not passed away in 1971. After spending the next couple of years moving around nearly every big-name studio in town – except COXSONE'S – trying to recapture the old Melodian magic, the group split in 1973. Dowe and Brevett, as solo artists and devout Rastafarians, went on to notch up a few hits in the mid-1970s – notable are 'Down Here In Babylon' and 'Deh Pon De Wicked'.

Today the trio are back together again and live comfortably in Kingston, earning a good living as mainstays of the growing revival scene, and selling a lot of records (re-recordings of their old hits) in Japan.

The Melodians Rock It With You; Mango 162539635-2

This is the Leslie Kong era, and as such is built on 'Sweet Sensation' and 'Rivers Of Babylon'. But there's much more than that to it, like 'Too Young To Fall In Love', 'Walking In The Rain', 'Give Thanks And Praise', 'Rock It With Me' and 'I Don't Love You'. This album is also a very good indicator of Leslie Kong's real contribution to Jamaican music, as it shows the change from straight rock steady to reggae and how an integral part of this development took place at Beverley's.

ALSO RECOMMENDED:

There is an import CD called *Swing And Dine*, consisting of ear-lier Melodians material, and including the classic tracks from the

Treasure Isle and Tip Top vaults. However, it proved impossible to track down.

SEE ALSO:

Put On Your Best Dress – Sonia Pottinger's Rock Steady 1967–1968; Attack ATCD109
Ba Ba Boom – Classic Rock Steady And Reggae 1967–1972; Trojan CDTRL265
Real Cool Rock Steady – Gems From The Treasure Isle; Trojan CDTRL206
Tougher Than Tough – The Story Of Jamaican Music (four-CD set); Mango IBXCD1

Derrick Morgan

(Born 1939; Stewarton, Jamaica; singer)
Derrick Morgan's claim to fame is that he is the man who *didn't* discover BOB MARLEY. On the surface, a far from unique state of affairs, but made remarkable as a matter of sheer bad luck. Morgan was chief talent scout for LESLIE KONG's Beverley's label. But the youthful Marley came looking for a deal on Morgan's day off, and so his second-in-charge, JIMMY CLIFF, takes the credit for introducing reggae's biggest star to the recording business.

But Derrick Morgan still has plenty to feel proud of. He was part of Jamaican music before it had a name or a true identity, recording R&B and JA Boogie for sound system use from 1958 onwards. It was his cool, naturally rhythmic – rather than over-melodious – voice that proved ideal on top of a shuffle beat, and after working with PRINCE BUSTER he moved to Beverley's where his hit sound momentum built to such a point that in 1961 he had seven records in the Jamaican Top 10. The biggest of which, the very aptly titled 'Housewives' Choice', was one of the most requested records on Jamaican radio around that time. (His best remembered record was still to come, though.)

Post-independence, Derrick Morgan took to the new ska style like a needle to a groove and cut 'Forward March', a celebratory slice of musical optimism that was taken up as something of an unofficial national anthem for the newly created nation.

Prince Buster had never been too happy about his one-time good friend deserting to go to work with the Chinese Kong, but it wasn't until 'Forward March' came out that he declared open war. The Prince claimed that Morgan's hit had ripped off one of his tunes, and cut 'Black Head Chinee Man' as a none-too-subtle dig at Morgan and his new employer. Morgan replied with 'Blazing Fire', and the tit-for-tat recordings went on for the best part of a year. The feud was impossible to escape if you lived in West Kingston and stands as a good example of how the sound systems always meant more to life than just a mobile disco.

Derrick Morgan survived through rock steady, by moderating his passion and building up a considerable fan base in the UK, thanks to frequent touring, some recording with Georgie Fame and a dress code – sharp mohair suits plus the regulation pork-pie hat – that appealed to the skinheads of the time. But with a couple of exceptions, notably 'Greedy Gal' and 'Moon Hop', he never repeated the sustained success of previous years. Although he still performs occasionally, failing eyesight has meant this is, sadly, infrequent.

I Am The Ruler; Trojan CDTRL300

A selection of early Leslie Kong productions that runs from 'Housewives' Choice' and 'Forward March' through some of the shots Morgan took at Prince Buster – 'No Raise No Praise', 'I Am The Ruler' and 'Blazing Fire' – to the far less frantic likes of 'Gypsy Woman' (were there any early Jamaican acts who *didn't* cover this song?) and 'I Found A Queen'. While *I Am The Ruler* provides an excellent cross-section of what Derrick Morgan was all about, there are a few holes: such big hits as 'Be Still' and 'Travel On', not to mention 'Shake A Leg', one of the original ska tunes. Perhaps they're being saved for *Volume Two*.

SEE ALSO:

Tougher Than Tough – The Story Of Jamaican Music (four-CD set); Mango IBXCD1 (as a solo act and in tandem with Patsy)

The Paragons

(John Holt, born 1947, Kingston, Jamaica; Tyrone Evans; Howard Barrett; vocal group)

It's hard to imagine what a vocal group containing both JOHN HOLT and BOB ANDY would have to do to improve itself, but, rather remarkably, The Paragons' finest hours did not happen until the latter – an original member of the group – left. At around the same time, they settled with DUKE REID to become an integral part of the warm, laid back sounds he was developing into rock steady.

The Paragons began as a quartet at the very start of the 1960s. Holt replaced original lead singer Leroy Stamp in 1964 and they had sporadic success with COXSONE during that year – so sporadic in fact that in 1965 Andy felt he'd do better as a solo artist. The following year the threesome moved to Reid's Treasure Isle, where the cooler approach was exactly the right showcase for arrangements consisting of Holt's lush tenor on top of powerful harmonies from Evans and Barrett.

During the second half of the decade, the group became Jamaica's most consistently successful singing act – they even had a few hits on Studio One, once the beat had slowed down there too. Tunes like 'My Best Girl Wears My Crown', 'Wear You To The Ball', 'When The Lights Are Low' and 'Happy Go Lucky Girl' came to epitomize the new style of Jamaican love song. The Paragons were a far clearer reflection of the island's own people than the previous smooch role model Nat King Cole could ever hope to be, and the group ruled the dancehalls until the beat changed up once more to reggae.

The Paragons split in 1970, as Evans and Barrett moved to North America. Although John Holt went on to become one of the new style's most important singers, it would have been wonderful to have heard The Paragons, in their entirety, in action in the LOVERS' ROCK of the second half of the 1970s.

My Best Girl Wears My Crown; Trojan CDTRL299

As near to a Paragons' Greatest Hits as you're ever likely to get. Apart from the title track, this album is stuffed to the gills with seventeen of the finest, smoovest mostly Duke Reidest rock steady harmonics. Alongside 'My Best Girl Wears My Crown', there's 'Wear You To The Ball', 'The Tide Is High', 'On The Beach', 'Island In The Sun', 'Happy Go Lucky Girl', 'Riding High On A Windy Day', 'Only A Smile' and 'When The Lights Are Low'. Or, in other words, every Paragons track you're ever likely to want.

SEE ALSO:

Real Cool Rock steady – Gems From The Treasure Isle; Trojan CDTRL206
Tougher Than Tough – The Story Of Jamaican Music (four-CD set); Mango IBXCD1

Lee 'Scratch' Perry

(Born Rainsford Perry, 1936; Hanover, Jamaica; producer/engineer/singer/genius)
That Lee Perry is one of reggae's few true geniuses isn't really open to question. During the next phase of the music's development, Scratch, or – as he is also known – The Upsetter, essentially redefined the boundaries. Several times. But all that will be dealt with in future chapters (see pages 145-150, and 274-281). Even before the ska-to-rock steady era, Perry's presence was manifesting itself as COXSONE's right-hand man.

As far back as the mid-1950s, when the Down Beat sound system was carrying the swing, Lee Perry was very much part of it as one of Coxsone's record spotters – a combination quality controller cum detective, responsible for judging which US R&B records should be played, then physically tracking down copies. By this time, Dodd owned more than one sound system, and Perry would operate (i.e. work the controls) on one of the secondary Down Beat rigs. A crucial job for all concerned.

While this functioned as a nursery slope for the sonic experimentation that, in twenty years' time, would become Perry's trademark as a producer, these adventures in sound played such an important part in Down Beat's success that by the start of the next decade Coxsone had virtually handed the whole operation over to him. It was around this time that Perry acquired the nickname 'Scratch' – while working the sound, he'd get so carried away he'd perform a dance that looked just like a chicken scratching in the farmyard dirt. But life could be physically hazardous too. Perry was not a big man (before Scratch, he was known as 'Little' Perry) and during the frequent attacks by rivals on Coxsone dances, he would, as operator, be the equipment's last line of defence. On more than one occasion he had to be carried home.

Perry remained a vital player after Coxsone set up his recording operation too. In the R&B and boogie late 1950s, he acted as A&R man, auditioning hopefuls, arranging musicians and coaching singers. Then, as ska took over, he accepted production duties for several acts and developed into quite a writer. DELROY WILSON, THE MAYTALS and ERROL DUNKLEY were among those to benefit from the Lee Perry touch.

He began singing too, recording a string of averagely successful Studio One ska tunes. But his raucous vocal style (another latter-day calling card) was always something of a specialist taste. He'd crop up on other people's records too, most notably those by his apparent sworn enemy PRINCE BUSTER – it has long been a feature of the Jamaican music scene that musical rivals are firm friends away from their respective studios.

Not so when Lee Perry and Coxsone Dodd fell out in 1966, though. Perry believed that Dodd was deliberately holding him back as a producer, and stormed out to work with a series of record men – JOE GIBBS and CLANCY ECCLES among them. He also recorded a few musical attacks on his former employer. But really, leaving Coxsone at that time was about the best thing Perry could have done. The beat was changing and he was now free to change with it as he shifted into his Upsetter phase.➤➤

Chicken Scratch; Heartbeat HB53
The Upsetter And The Beat; Heartbeat HB59

Both these collections of Perry's early Studio One recordings are currently available on import only in the UK. Either will be worth it for the Lee Perry completist to search out, though. Backed first by THE SKATALITES then The Soul Vendors, they are a collection of lively ska and solid rock steady covering Perry's three subject-matter obsessions – other producers, social injustice and sexual shenanigans. Expect to find such tunes as

'Chicken Scratch', 'Doctor Dick', 'Give Me Justice' and 'Help The Weak'.

SEE ALSO:

Respect To Studio One; Heartbeat CDHB181
Ska Bonanza – The Studio One Ska Years; Heartbeat CDHB 86/87
Solid Gold From The Vault, Volume Three; Trojan CDTRL295

Sonia Pottinger

(Born 1943; Kingston, Jamaica; producer)
The Jamaican music industry has never exactly been a hotbed of equal opportunities, so women in charge of themselves were never too plentiful. Women in charge of other people though – i.e. men – was virtually unheard of. And a woman who had arrived at reggae via country and western would be even less common than that.

But Sonia Pottinger was an exceptional woman. During the 1960s she ran a Kingston record shop, thus witnessed the sharp end of the Jamaican music boom and got into it by recording a C&W song (her favourite music) with Joe White in 1966. Sloppy country tunes had a huge audience in Jamaica at that time, as they found favour on the radio playlists, and the massive hit that followed encouraged her to continue. However, as the now-fashionable rock steady was, in many ways, just another approach to balladeering, she opted for that. And got such a handle on it that Sonia Pottinger's Gayfeet and Tip Top labels (the latter named after her record shop) brought a fresh, love's-young-dream aspect to it, while her natural toughness ensured it never spilled over into out-and-out slush.

From this period, her best-known work is THE ETHIOPIANS' 'The Whip', but the same group also cut 'Train To Glory' and 'Stay Loose Mama' for her. Other landmark tunes include 'Swing And Dine' (THE MELODIANS), 'Tell It To Me' (STRANGER COLE) and 'ABC Rock Steady' and 'Hard To Confess' (The Gaylads). In the early 1970s Pottinger bought DUKE REID's Treasure Isle studio to expand her production empire, but in spite of work with a series of roots favourites, she never repeated her success of the previous decade.

Put On Your Best Dress – Sonia Pottinger's Rock Steady 1967–1968; Attack ATCD109

The Conquerors, What A Agony; **The Valentines,** Blam Blam Fever; **Al and The Vibrators,** Move Up; **Monty Morris,** Play It Cool; **The Melodians,** Swing And Dine; **Johnny and The Attractions,** Young Wings Can Fly; **Patsy And The Count Ossie Band,** Pata Pata Rock Steady; **The Valentines,** All In One; **Monty Morris,** Put On Your Best Dress; **Stranger Cole and Patsy,** Tell It To Me; **The Gaylads,** Hard To Confess; **The Conquerors,** Won't You Come Home; **The Melodians,** Little Nut Tree; **Charlie Ace,** Creation Version; **The Gaylads,** I Need Your Loving; **Ken Boothe,** Say You.

Even though this collection manages to omit 'The Whip', it's got 'Swing And Dine' and 'Hard To Confess', and is Pottinger at her coolest, rocking steadiest best.

ALSO RECOMMENDED:

Musical Feast 1967–1970; Heartbeat CDHB84

While this is still excellent, it continues a little later than the previous compilation and is thus slightly less focused. As the other one seems to have had first pick of the tunes, really this is for completists only.

Treasure Isle Meets Tip Top; Sonic SONCD0047

A thumb through Duke Reid's back catalogue, put together on Tip Top when Pottinger took over Treasure Isle after the Duke died in 1974.

Duke Reid

(Born Arthur Reid, 1915; Kingston, Jamaica; producer)
When this man ran his sound system during the 1950s and 1960s, he called himself Duke Reid the Trojan. The name was actually taken from the model of Bedford truck in which he used to haul his rig around Kingston. But it was, in fact, a staggeringly appropriate moniker as Duke Reid was a genuine giant of

Jamaican music. Yet his name isn't nearly as recognizable as it should be. While most casual fans of early reggae will have heard of such tunes as 'Wear You To The Ball', 'Queen Majesty', 'Carry Go Bring Come' and 'Guns Fever', it will really only be the specialist who can instantly connect these records as Treasure Isle productions by Duke Reid. For some reason his corporate identity never endured in the same way as Studio One; therefore Reid never became as forceful a brand name as COXSONE DODD. All the more remarkable when you consider that at one point Reid and Dodd between them practically *were* the Jamaican music business. And Reid's involvement went back way before such an industry even existed.

As owner of the Treasure Isle Liquor Store, back in the early 1950s, Reid sponsored, and fronted, the radio show Treasure Isle Time, as much to indulge his passion for American R&B as to promote his already thriving business. As the decade progressed, the sound system became a natural extension of this, growing in importance as Reid, by now leaving his wife to run the shop, made regular trips to the US to hunt out the sort of tunes that would trump his arch rival Dodd's Down Beat. It was at this time that Reid turned his hand to producing his own records – one of the very first Jamaicans to do so – and at the end of the 1950s he cut a few Jamaican Boogie/R&B sides. These would have greatly boosted his sound system credibility, but this was before there was a Jamaican record industry as such and so outlay couldn't be recouped on sales. So Reid more or less abandoned the recording studio, preferring to stick with import sounds.

Until 1962, that is. It was then, as the indigenous sound of ska carried the swing at Jamaica's lawn dances, that Duke Reid got back into recording. Big style. He assembled a crew of local musicians including DON DRUMMOND, TOMMY MCCOOK, Jackie Mittoo, Baba Brooks, ROLAND ALPHONSO and Lloyd Brevett and, kicking off with STRANGER COLE's 'Rough And Tough', cut a stream of ska beat hits on his three newly formed labels, Treasure Isle, Duke Reid and Duchess. Over the next four years Reid's ska spectacular included the best work by ALTON ELLIS, THE TECHNIQUES, JUSTIN HINES, THE SKATALITES, DON DRUMMOND, Frank Anderson and Stranger and Patsy.

Primarily, these records were to service his sound system: his musicians would work into the night, and at around two in the morning Reid would arrive at a Trojan dance with acetates literally hot off the presses. He soon began releasing the more acute crowd-pleasers and swiftly parlayed this into a profitable business. One made all the more lucrative by keeping artist payments to an absolute minimum – Reid would pay a flat rate of between ten shillings and one pound ten shillings per player per side. As so much of Reid's early music was recorded in one take, using one overhead mic, it wasn't unusual for musicians to cut a dozen sides per session. Singers arriving with their own compositions would also be paid a flat fee for their work. Royalties? *In Jamaica in the early 1960s*? You might as well have been talking a foreign language.

It was Reid's legendary toughness that maintained such an exploitative system. Prior to joining his wife in the liquor store, he had spent ten years as a policeman on some of Kingston's meanest streets, and once in the music business he would make payments from the pouch of cash he wore around his neck, discouraging contract negotiation with a clearly visible brace of pistols and bandoleers of ammunition.

Such ruthlessness extended to his sound system operation too. He used contacts made during his years as a policeman to recruit some of the baddest of the ghetto badmen – and women – and formed a security team that was far more aggressive than the name might suggest. Apart from merely protecting Trojan dances, they would disrupt the opposition's by storming the lawns and laying out punters, as they proceeded to trash the equipment. His thugs gave the term 'sound clash' a whole new, quite literal, meaning. And once again, thanks to Reid's police contacts, the authorities seldom took any action. Talk to anybody who followed Coxsone's sound system during that time, and their stories will be laced with episodes of violence at the hands of Reid's soldiers. Many a small operation went out of business in the face of perpetual intimidation.

Against such a background of violence, it's perhaps understandable that Duke Reid really made his name as a record producer in the rock steady years, which were also known as The Rude Boy Era. But Reid's success was due as much to his love of melody and soul and his natural musical sensibilities. As made obvious by his *Treasure Isle Time* radio show, he was an expert on US R&B, and from 1966 onwards sought to apply the same sense of musical/lyrical narrative to the new Jamaican style. He quite simply revolutionized the music. Utilizing such a hugely talented musical arranger as guitarist Ernest Ranglin, and the Tommy McCook-led Supersonics for backing, he established a passionate, soulful approach that was dripping with sophistication, but which never forgot that its primary function was to make the people *dance*. With rock steady classics like 'Wear You To The Ball', 'Cry Tough', 'Rock Steady', 'Carry Go Bring Come', 'The Things You Say You Love', 'Queen Majesty' and 'Love Is Not A Gamble', Duke Reid proved unequivocally that Jamaican music had come of age.

He rode this wave until it finally broke at the end of the 1960s. When the reggae vibe took over, Reid seemed at odds with the change and it seemed he was getting left behind. As it turned out, the Duke was far from finished. ↝

The following compilations represent the very best cross-sections of Duke Reid's Treasure Isle productions from the ska and rock steady days. Compiled by reggae scholar and archivist Steve Barrow, they are themed and ordered to provide a perfect introduction to the music, while at the same time contain enough surprises to satisfy the veteran.

*Music Is My Occupation – Ska Instrumentals 1962–1965;
Trojan CDTRL259

Tommy McCook, Magic, Twelve Minutes To Go, Strolling In, Apanga, Yard Broom; **Tommy McCook and The Skatalites,** Silver Dollar; **Tommy McCook and Don Drummond,** Music Is My Occupation; **Baba Brooks,** Vitamin A, River Bank Pts 1 and 2, Guns Fever; **Don Drummond,** Musical Store Room, Green Island, Eastern Standard Time, Don De Lion; **Baba Brooks and Don Drummond,** Dr Decker.

*It's Rockin' Time – Duke Reid's Rock Steady 1967–1968;
Trojan CDTRL279

Lloyd and Glen, Jezebel; **Eric 'Monty' Morris,** If I Didn't Love You; **Justin Hines and The Dominoes,** Fight Too Much; **Tommy**

McCook and The Supersonics, Indian Love Call; **Phyllis Dillon,** It's Rocking Time; **The Techniques,** Day-O; **The Conquerors,** I Fall In Love; **Tommy McCook and The Supersonics,** Jam Session; **Phyllis Dillon,** Things Of The Past; **The Conquerors,** Lonely Street; **The Techniques,** Drink Wine; **Tommy McCook and The Supersonics,** Train To Ska-thedral; **The Three Tops,** The Sound Of Music; **The Melodians,** I Know Just How She Feels; **The Silvertones,** Slow And Easy; **Lynn Taitt with Tommy McCook And The Supersonics,** Spanish Eyes.

*Ba Ba Boom – Classic Rock Steady And Reggae 1967–1972; Trojan CDTRL265

The Jamaicans, Ba Ba Boom; **The Paragons,** Only A Smile; **The Three Tops,** Do It Right; **Justin Hines And The Dominoes,** Carry Go Bring Come; **The Techniques,** I'm In The Mood For Love; **Alton Ellis,** Willow Tree; **The Paragons,** My Best Girl; **The Gladiators,** Sweet Soul Music; **Alton Ellis,** Breaking Up; **The Tennors,** Hopeful Village; **The Termites,** Love Up Kiss Up; **Justin Hines And The Dominoes,** Botheration; **John Holt and Joya Landis,** I'll Be Lonely; **Phyllis Dillon,** Midnight Confession; **The Tennors,** Weather Report; **The Melodians,** Passion Love.

*Shufflin' On Bond Street – Jamaican R&B and Ska Instrumentals; Trojan CDTRL275

The Baba Brooks Band, Watermelon Man, Country Town, Rain Fall, Western Flyer, Froggy, Mad World; **Drumbago's Orchestra,** Duck Soup; **Roland Alphonso,** Green Door, Blackberry Brandy; **Duke Reid Group,** What Makes Honey, Joker, The Rude Boy; **Tommy McCook and The Supersonics,** Thunderball; **Tommy McCook and The Skatalites,** Cotton Tree, Nuclear Weapon; **Lynn Taitt and The Boys,** Storm Warning.

*The Birth Of Ska; Trojan CDTRL274

Justin Hines and The Dominoes, Carry Go Bring Come, Strongman Sampson; **Baba Brooks,** River Bank, Musical

Communion, When I Call Your Name; **Roland Alphonso,** Feeling Fine; **Justin Hines and The Dominoes with The Skatalite Band,** Over The River, Corner Stone; **Owen and Leon Silvera and The Skatalite Band,** Next Door Neighbour; **Stranger and Patsy with Baba Brooks and His Band,** Yeah Yeah Baby; **The Skatalite Band,** Hog In A Cocoa; **Frank Anderson and The Skatalite Band,** Musical Store Room.

Not compiled by Steve Barrow, but far too good to overlook:

Cultural Things; Lagoon LG21011

The Tennors, Ride Your Donkey; **Dennis Alcapone and Hopeton Lewis,** Judgement Day; **The Ethiopians,** Rub It Down; **The Conquerors,** Lonely Street; **The Techniques,** Travelling Man; **Justin Hines and The Dominoes,** Mighty Redeemer; **The Tennors,** Hopeful Village; **Errol Dunkley,** Girl You Cried; **The Ethiopians,** Mother's Tender Care; **Tommy McCook and The Supersonics,** Marbrouk; **Justin Hines and The Dominoes,** It's Love You Need; **The Tennors,** Weather Report; **Alton Ellis and U-Roy,** Behold; Natural Youth, Jungle Skank.

Real Cool Rock steady – Gems From The Treasure Isle; Trojan CDTRL206

Alton Ellis, Rock Steady; **The Melodians,** You Don't Need Me; **Tommy McCook and The Supersonics,** Marbrouk; **Phyllis Dillon,** Love Was All I Had; **The Techniques,** You Don't Care; **Dennis Alcapone,** This Great Woggie; **Dennis Alcapone,** No. 1 Station; **Ken Parker,** True True True; **Tommy McCook,** Soul For Sale; **The Tree Tops,** It's Raining; **The Paragons,** Only A Smile; **U-Roy,** Flashing My Whip.

The great thing about these two compilations is that they're relatively late in this period, and thus excellent pointers to how the Duke adapted to the beat that was changing to beyond rock steady, and to the creeping influence of dread within the music scene.

Duke Reid productions will be found on virtually any multi-label compilation from the era – see Various Artists (pages

91-99) – so it's best simply to check the records' tracklistings. Elsewhere, albums by The Ethiopians, Justin Hines and The Paragons are among Duke Reid's finest work.

The Skatalites

(Founded 1963; session band supreme)

As reading just about every other entry in this section will tell you, The Skatalites were the number one session band in Jamaica during the first half of the 1960s. They were formed in 1963 by Joe Gordon, a local mento/calypsonian, who used to perform and record under the name Lord Tanamo. As mento and calypso made up the bulk of Jamaican record production pre-R&B, Gordon had good studio contacts by the time the style changed, and he was soon in frequent demand to supply musicians for sessions. For a fee, of course. He would draw from the pool of players who had made names for themselves playing jazz or big-band swing, regularly recruiting the same crew, among which was sax man TOMMY MCCOOK, who suggested the idea of formalizing the group. This was as much for the creative advantages of a stabilized line-up as for the financial gain of collective bargaining, because McCook quite correctly believed that if one tight unit evolved it would provide the ideal musical framework to experiment. The name came about when Gordon suggested 'Satellite' – after that year's Soviet space launch – and immediately, in true Jamaican play-with-words fashion, McCook corrupted it to 'Skatalite'.

The original line-up was: Tommy McCook, lead tenor sax; ROLAND ALPHONSO, tenor sax; Lester Sterling, alto sax; DON DRUMMOND, trombone; Johnny 'Dizzy' Moore, trumpet; Jah Jerry/Harold McKenzie, guitars; Jackie Mittoo, piano; Lloyd Brevette, bass; Lloyd Knibbs, drums; and Lord Tanamo/Tony DaCosta, vocals. It was the vocalists who were vital in establishing the group as an act in their own right rather than merely a posse of musical hired guns. The Skatalites immediately set out playing club and theatre dates – some they put on themselves – and recording under the group name, with or without a featured front man. But it was in the studio that they played a huge part in shaping Jamaican music of the day:

whereas other keyboard players began to switch to the organ, Mittoo stuck with the piano, which contributed greatly to the rhythmic drive; and it was their monstrously horn-heavy line-up that made the notion of the scorching ska instrumental so attractive a prospect.

However, this wild solo-ing was far more educated than many might imagine. Jamaica has turned out what seems like a disproportionately large number of superlative brass players thanks to the Alpha Boys' Catholic School in Kingston. A kind of reform school, it ran a strict regime and the only way to earn respite from the endless round of chores was to volunteer for the school band, which was always weighted well towards the brass section. Being in the orchestra was far from a skive, however; it involved taking formal lessons, learning the theory and developing an understanding of music, plus coming to grips with classical pieces before any kind of improvization was allowed. McCook, Don Drummond, Lester Sterling, Roland Alphonso, RICO Rodriguez, Leroy 'Horsemouth' Wallace, Vin Gordon and Bobby Ellis were all Alpha graduates.

Although there are very few Jamaican singers The Skatalites have not backed, the bulk of their work was done for, unsurprisingly, DODD and REID, with a significant amount for the Yap Brothers' Top Deck Records. But the group only stayed together two years, falling apart in late 1965 to a background of in-fighting. It's widely believed that the producers engineered internal stress by capitalizing on personality clashes and playing members off against each other – notably McCook and Alphonso. McCook formed The Supersonics and worked for Duke Reid (they are the backing on so many of the Treasure Isle rock steady classics), while Alphonso, together with Jackie Mittoo, became The Soul Vendors, the mainstay of Studio One's backing for the rest of the decade.

*Tommy McCook and The Skatalites: *The Birth Of Ska*; Trojan CDTRL274

The 'Tommy McCook and The' tag is perhaps a little misleading here, for although McCook would have handled much of the musical arranging, on various tracks the band are led by trumpeter Baba Brooks, sax man Roland Alphonso, or vocalists such as STRANGER COLE or JUSTIN HINES. Not that this detracts from anything, as these Duke Reid numbers are all very much about the band. As the sleeve notes say, 'the power and beauty and joy of the earth ... that rhythm deep inside is truly Jamaican.'

ALSO RECOMMENDED:

*Lord Tanamo With The Skatalites: *In The Mood For Ska*; Trojan CDTRL313

Tanamo was the nearest thing The Skatalites had to a regular vocalist, and even he wasn't exactly regular until the 1980s when he toured with the reformed group as they revisited some of their finest ska beat sides. He's a shouter of sufficient gusto not to be intimidated by the band's power, so they can blow their lungs out here. And it's interesting for featuring a few of the less frantic numbers, reminding us all that it was also a beautifully subtle music form.

Credited Skatalites tunes can be found on just about every ska compilation album – see the Various Artists section on pages 91-99. On other albums made around this time, even if it doesn't say the name the chances are it's the same musicans playing. Once more, it's best to check the sleeve notes.

Slim Smith

(Born Keith Smith, 1947; Kingston, Jamaica; singer)
One of *the* great rock steady singers, Slim Smith's top-of-the scale delivery underlined the style's obsession with The Impressions as it was very similar to Curtis Mayfield's in its balance of ease and urgency – much like PAT KELLY, who replaced him in THE TECHNIQUES. Yet Slim Smith's career was never the easiest of affairs.

He was one of the original members of The Techniques in 1962, and still a member two years later when STRANGER COLE introduced them to DUKE REID. But after a year and several hits, including 'Little Do You Know', Smith thought he'd do better on his own – in Canada! The album he recorded up there failed dismally, and he was soon back in Jamaica and in the studio with both PRINCE BUSTER and COXSONE DODD. At this time things were going well for Smith, and, mostly on Studio One, he cut a series of smoove classics, including 'Never Let Go' which has been 'versioned' (the same rhythm used as the basis for numerous different songs) nearly five hundred times, more than a few of which have got into the Jamaican charts. Then, curiously, in 1967 he opted for the security of a group again and re-formed The Uniques, this time with Martin Riley and Lloyd Charmers. Under the guidance of producer BUNNY LEE they harmonized their way to a string of entirely Impressions-like rock steady classics, including a cover of 'Gypsy Woman'.

The group made one great album – *Absolutely The Uniques* – before Smith opted to go solo again. A factor in this decision may have been that a number of Uniques records had found their way into the shops credited to Slim Smith only. He stayed with Bunny Lee and, although he remained successful, little of what he did during this period came close to the first record this new pairing produced: 'Everybody Needs Love' (1969) still stands today as a genre great. Sadly though, to a background of increasing mental problems, Smith was admitted to Bellevue Hospital in 1972, where he committed suicide within a year.

*The Best Of Slim Smith and The Uniques (1967–1969); Trojan CDTRL340

This three-handed environment is probably the best way to appreciate Slim Smith's sweet falsetto, as the gospel/R&B-rooted Jamaican vocal trios were an art form in themselves. Largely produced by Bunny Lee, who had a marvellous under-standing of what was by now being called soul singing, this set's tracklisting reads like a roll-call of vocal group rock steady at its very best: 'Girls Like Dirt', 'Love And Devotion', 'The Beatitude (Blessed Are The Meek)', 'My Conversation', 'Let Me Go Girl' and so on. Naturally, there's a large number of cover versions – 'That's The Way Love Is', 'Build My World Around You' and, of course, 'Gypsy Woman' among them – but such originators as The Tams, The Temptations and Smokey and The Miracles weren't that far away from The Uniques in approach, so it's a very happy marriage.

This collection has the added bonus of including a number of the self-productions the group recorded for their own Tramp label – 'Watch This Sound', 'You'll Lose A Precious Love' and 'Out Of Love'.

ALSO RECOMMENDED:

20 Super Hits; Sonic Sounds SON004

The best of the Bunny Lee cuts, but nothing from other producers.

Rain From The Skies; Trojan CDTRL 303

Again mixing up Smith by himself with his work with The Uniques. While Smith's voice will always be worth the price of admission, and this set contains 'My Conversation', 'Stand Up And Fight', 'Sitting In The Park' and the title track, it isn't even close to the artist's best work.

Born To Love; Heartbeat HBCD3501

Compiled from the solo sessions Smith did with Coxsone during 1966 and 1967; while this features 'Rougher Yet', 'I'll Be Around', 'I've Got Your Number' and 'Born To Love', it's really one for collectors only.

Currently in existence is an album produced and mixed by Bunny Lee and Rupie Edwards called *My Conversation* and consisting entirely of different cuts of the 'My Conversation' rhythm. Lee had for some time been advancing the cause of versioning and many Uniques songs formed the basis of Jamaican hits for years to come, but in the late 1960s this was the first LP to take such an approach. So why hasn't somebody reissued it on CD?

SEE ALSO:

Various Artists: *Jumping With Mr Lee*; Trojan CDTRL270
Tougher Than Tough – The Story Of Jamaican Music; Mango IBXCD1

The Techniques

(Winston Riley, Slim Smith, Frankie White; all born Kingston, Jamaica; vocal trio)

Put together by Riley in 1962 as an R&B/ska trio, once the group had hooked up with DUKE REID in 1964 – STRANGER COLE had spotted them on a talent show's bill and took them to Treasure Isle – the group became a virtual nursery slope for vocal stars of the future: Lloyd Charmers, PAT KELLY, Lloyd Parkes, Freddy Waite and Dave Barker all served their time as Techniques before the group finally broke up at the end of the 1970s. Although they had a few hits with the original line-up, it wasn't until SLIM SMITH left in 1966 and Pat Kelly took over that things really began happening. This wasn't because Kelly was so much better, but simply because the style was changing to a groove that so much better suited their silky, US-style harmonising.

During the next couple of years the hits flowed like a river: 'Queen Majesty', 'You'll Want Me Back' (both covers of Impressions songs), 'Run Come Celebrate', 'I Wish It Would Rain' (a Motown classic for The Temptations), 'It's Your Love' and 'I'm In The Mood'. It was copy-book rock steady. And even changes of personnel or producer – they left Duke Reid in 1968 – couldn't faze them. 'Love Is Not A Gamble', 'Travelling Man', 'Lonely Man', 'What Am I To Do' and 'Go Find Yourself A Fool' were all big hits, the latter two featuring Pat Kelly who, among the bewildering number of line-up changes, returned to reclaim lead vocals in 1969 having left two years previously. But like the Jamaican trios in general, they were very much 'of the day', and the coming of reggae rather left them behind.

*Run Come Celebrate – Their Greatest Reggae Hits; Heartbeat HBCD121

There's no chance of this set falling foul of the Trades Descriptions Act. It is exactly what it says it is, taking the best from the Duke Reid years, and then going on to the hits Winston Riley produced for them on their own label. It's got everything you want, and very little you don't.

SEE ALSO:

Cultural Things; Lagoon LG21011
Classic Rock Steady and Reggae 1967–1972; Trojan CDTRL265
Tougher Than Tough – The Story Of Jamaican Music; Mango IBXCD1

The Termites

(Lloyd Parkes, born 1949, Walton, Jamaica; Wentworth Vernal, born 1945, Kingston, Jamaica; vocal duo)
The rock steady duo was a comparatively rare commodity, because harmonies were so rooted in the US-based three-part style that many arrangers found it impossible to construct them any other way. However, if The Termites were anything to judge two-handed rock steady vocals by, this is a great loss to the music. So named because insects of that ilk had attacked the piano the pair used to rehearse on, the duo came together when Parkes, an accomplished bass player and member of The Invincibles band (other personnel included SLY DUNBAR and Ansell Collins), teamed up with Vernal to do some singing together in the clubs. They got on so well they decided to formalize the arrangement, at which point COXSONE signed them as an act. They cut one album for Studio One in 1968, before Parkes joined THE TECHNIQUES and Vernal faded from view. The album has since become one of the most sought after pressings of the era.

Do The Rock Steady; Heartbeat CDHB3506

It's easy to hear why, too. There may only be two of them, but Parkes and Venal make up for it with a passion and gusto that pushes the style beyond the usual limits – nobody is ever going to call these two old-time shouters 'smoove'. But that's the attraction: plenty of fire and a splash of mad, robust humour, making it the perfect earthy anecdote to what was going on around them in the genre. The music drives it hard too, with more horns than you might expect in 1968 and the sort of punchy bottom end you ought to get when a bass player is doing the writing. This is the whole original album – 'Do The Rock Steady', 'Have Mercy Mr Percy', 'Beach Boy' and 'My Last Love' are included, plus an extended mix of their biggest hit, 'Heartaches', and the additional track 'Mommy Didn't Know'.

The Wailers

(Bob Marley, born 1945, St Anns, Jamaica; Peter Tosh, born Winston McIntosh, 1944, Westmoreland, Jamaica; Bunny Wailer, born Neville O'Riley Livingston, 1947, Kingston, Jamaica; vocal trio)

It's difficult to imagine where reggae would be, in terms of internationalism, if The Wailers hadn't happened. Courtesy of buckets of charisma, seriously good music and the most astute marketing, by the middle of the 1970s they were the biggest reggae band ever. By the 1980s their leader and founder BOB MARLEY was revered all over the globe, and in most countries they remain a byword for Jamaican music and culture. Years before that, though, were their Trenchtown ska beat beginnings and some of the best tunes to come out of the area at the time.

Marley and Livingston were friends from adolescence – after coming to Kingston, Marley's mother had set up house with Livingston's father – but it was Bob Marley by himself who cut the first records. As a music-obsessed sixteen-year-old he did three tracks for Leslie Kong – 'Terror', 'One Cup Of Coffee' and 'Judge Not' – which came out on two singles in 1962, but he felt he was being exploited by the producer and didn't go back. Yes, even at that tender age, Bob Marley had a highly developed sense of what was right and what was not.

The group came about in the next year, thanks to JOE HIGGS, a singer of considerable distinction and something of a ghetto philanthropist, who held free singing classes outside his house as his contribution to keeping the local youth out of trouble. As music was one of the most obvious ways out of poverty, he figured it would give them something to aim for and, as a devout Rasta, he reckoned on it improving their spiritual well-being too. In Marley's case it would seem he had a point.

At Higgs's yard, Marley and Livingston hooked up with another local lad, who owned a real guitar as opposed from the tin can and bamboo home-made jobs. His name was Peter Tosh. Together with three more regulars at these tutorials – the strong-voiced Junior Braithwaite, Beverly Kelso and Cherry Smith to augment the high end – they formed a group. Originally it was called The Teenagers, but was soon changed to The Wailing Wailers, in recognition of their sufferah status and probably as a result of Higgs's consciousness-raising.

Higgs had an enormous influence on the group's musical abilities too. He singled them out for special tuition, working on their harmonizing and teaching them how to structure songs formally, while his good friend, professional drummer Alvin Patterson, introduced them to the rudimentary theories of rhythm. Before the end of 1963, Higgs considered the group good enough to recommend them to Studio One, and under COXSONE's guidance The Wailing Wailers were an instant smash. They had enormous success in the baptism of fire that were the talent shows held in West Kingston's theatres, and the following they'd built up saw to it that their first release for Dodd was a smash hit. 'Simmer Down' (1963) stayed at Number 1 in Jamaica for several weeks, and went on to sell over 60,000 copies.

In many ways this wasn't too surprising. The group's stage success had a lot to do with the amount of hard work they put into their presentation: crisp stage suits from day one and carefully rehearsed dance routines (*à la* US doo-wop acts). Crowds would regularly be dazzled with an ultra-flashy display from Marley himself, who could cut a wicked rug – when he was recording for Leslie Kong, it was believed he had more potential as a dancer than as a singer. But what really clinched it with the hard-to-impress ghetto audiences was the total mutual identification. Although music was always viewed as an escape route from those surroundings, The Wailing Wailers were very aware of their situation and right from the start were determined their lyrics should reflect it and try to address the issues of the day. They were, after all, no more than teenage rude boys themselves, as at home on the street corner as on the stage; they just wore better suits. 'Simmer Down' was an appeal to the area's warring gangs to cool it, while other songs cut for Dodd included such self-explanatory titles as 'Jailhouse', 'Holligan' (sic), 'Good Good Rudie' and 'Let Him Go (Rudie Get Bail)'. The majority of the lyrics were written by Bob Marley, who, barely out of his teens, was already a bona fide man of the people.

Naturally enough, The Wailers – they'd soon dropped the 'Wailing' – were right at home with rock steady, considered to be the rude boy rhythm, and by the end of 1965 were about the biggest, most consistent vocal group on the island, rarely out of the charts. Then two months into 1966, it all seemed to fall apart: Kelso, Smith and Braithwaite had split; and Bob, who was now married and had a child to support, had done the unthinkable – he'd left the music business to get a proper job in a factory. In Wilmington, Delaware, USA.

This sabbatical, with his mother and her new husband, lasted a mere six months, though. And when Marley returned to Jamaica he was more determined than ever to make a success of his musical career. The Wailers reformed as a trio – they didn't have to regain their audience, as Coxsone had such a backlog of their material he'd maintained a hard-working release schedule throughout the year. But by this time they wanted to stretch themselves more in terms of what their music could achieve, and felt their relationship with Dodd was passing its sell-by date. A mutual consideration, it appears, as the producer was working harder on his new rock steady-friendly acts such as THE HEPTONES and ALTON ELLIS. Lacking the capital to make their own label – Wail 'N' Soul 'M – pay, and with a repu-tation among producers as difficult to deal with – i.e. they stood up for themselves – The Wailers ended up back at Leslie Kong's. Although the group was satisfied with the resulting releases – 'Soul Captive', 'Caution' and 'Freedom Train' among them – without Coxsone's clout they didn't sell well.

Midway through 1969, Bob Marley returned to his mother in the USA, and a job in the Chrysler car factory. But his heart was-n't in it. He came home at the end of the summer, when the group got together with another disgruntled ex-Coxsone employee LEE PERRY. A new phase in the career of Bob Marley and The Wailers was about to begin. ➤➤

The Wailing Wailers; Studio One SOCD 001

From the Miracles-esque skinny mohair suit cover shot, to the occasional presence of Beverly Kelso, Junior Braithwaite and

Cherry Smith, to the backing by THE SKATALITES and The Soul Brothers, this CD presents the original Wailers at their absolute best. A sample of the group as they started off with Coxsone in the mid-1960s, this is a collection that provides a fascinating snapshot of the Jamaican music industry of the day. Firstly, there's the R&B trio approach to their phrasing, like a less sophisticated Impressions, that was par for the course among the early ska singers. The material is part of this US-influenced theme too – 'Ska Jerk' being a thinly disguised version of Junior Walker's 'Shotgun', and much of it follows the US preoccupation with love ballads. It's here, with numbers like 'It Hurts To Be Alone', 'How Many Times' and 'I Need You', that Marley's reputation as a modern-day romantic poet took root. Then, of course, there's that ska standard – the Jamaicanized cabaretesque cover version of what was already distinctly cheesy. It's worth the price of this disc to hear The Wailers steaming through a shuffle beat reading of 'What's New Pussycat?', confusingly titled 'When The Well Runs Dry'. But what really counts is the group's already developed sense of social concern. It shines through on numbers like 'Simmer Down' and 'Rude Boy', but really kicks in with the later, Lee Perry-produced tunes, early versions of 'Kaya', '400 Years', 'Soul Rebel' and 'Duppy Conqueror' among them.

As regards the performances, although lovingly tutored by Joe Higgs on the very early material, their harmonising is still a little raw in places. But this in no way detracts; indeed it accurately sets them up as from the same streets as their intended audience. Besides, what they lack in polish they make up for in gusto.

There are a couple more selections of Studio One material available on import CD, both, a touch confusingly, entitled *The Wailing Wailers* and with very similar cover shots. They are really only for completists or at least A-Level Wailers students, as, like the Devil, this one has all the best tunes.

In The Beginning; Trojan CDTRL 221

The best of the Leslie Kong-produced sides of the late 1960s/early 1970s, plus a sprinkling of Perry and a couple courtesy of Johnny Nash, all of which adds up to a much neglected

Wailers period. But the music was never nearly as bad as people tend to assume. Prime cuts here are 'Soul Shakedown Party', 'Caution', 'Stop That Train', 'Jah Is Mighty' and 'Turn Me Loose'.

Songs Of Freedom; Tuff Gong TGCDBX1

A four-CD set that has so far sold over a million and remains second only to the Led Zeppelin remasters as the best-selling CD box. It's the first disc that concerns us here, taking twenty-four tracks from Bob's first solo recordings through The Wailers' work with Dodd and Kong and, ending up with Lee Perry and 'Mr Brown' from 1970. As with the rest of the set, the track selection here is faultless and provides superb representation of the group at that time. A useful Marley jumping-in point. ↦

ALSO RECOMMENDED:

Birth Of A Legend; Pickwick 9825882

A relatively small compilation that takes tracks from different early labels, but serves to titillate rather than satisfy.

SEE ALSO:

Tougher Than Tough – The Story Of Jamaican Music; Mango IBXCD1
Ska Bonanza – The Studio One Ska Years; Heartbeat CDHB 86/87
Respect To Studio One; Heartbeat CDHB 181/182

Delroy Wilson

(Born 1948; Kingston, Jamaica; singer)
Another of Kingston's child prodigies, Delroy Wilson was doing his bit in the theatre talent shows while his years were still in single figures. His yet-to-break, untutored voice proved exactly right for the emergence of ska – high-pitched and raucous – so once he'd reached the almost pensionable age of fourteen, Coxsone took him into the studio. His debut tune was entitled 'If I Had A Beautiful Body', which seems an remarkably apt choice for a lad yet to reach puberty. However, a year later he was

enjoying his first hit as he became the studio's – or more specifically LEE PERRY's – frontline weapon in attacking the recently
departed PRINCE BUSTER. That record, 'Joe Liges', told of the
fictitious character of the title who had forgotten where he'd
come from and had now sold out the people who'd helped him
get started. Other Studio One singles of the same sentiment followed and, entertaining and musically correct as they were –
several were hits – ultimately the tunes meant more to the music
business than to the general public. But, in the mid-1960s, just as
it was starting to look like Delroy Wilson was heading up a blind
alley, rock steady happened.

By now, his voice had matured into a rich, almost seasoned
croon (well, he had been singing for nearly a decade) and the
less frantic style was the perfect vehicle. Between 1965 and 1969
Wilson remained with Dodd to develop into one of the genre's
most popular singers, with hits such as 'Riding For A Fall', 'I Am
Not A King', 'True Believer', 'Get Ready' and 'Won't You Come
Home'. Success that continued after his move to first BUNNY
LEE and then SONIA POTTINGER at the end of the decade,
considerably aided by the Jamaican predilection for covering US
soul hits, as his way with a song involved many similar phrasings – most notable in this department were Wilson's big-selling
cuts of 'Dancing Mood' (The Tams), 'Get Ready' (The Temptations), 'Put Yourself In My Place' (The Elgins) and 'This Old
Heart Of Mine' (The Isley Brothers).

It was during this time that Wilson built up a strong following
in the UK, with frequent touring and releases on the Blue Beat
and Black Swan Labels. But his biggest contributions to reggae
history were yet to come. ⁕

The Best Of Delroy Wilson; Heartbeat CDHB3507

Twelve Studio One tracks, each a huge Jamaican hit and a sound
system favourite here in the UK. Delroy oozes his way through
'Riding For A Fall', six minutes of 'Run Run', 'Someone's Gonna
Cry', 'True Believer', 'Run For Your Life' and five and a half
minutes of 'Conquer Me'. It makes his passing that much more
regrettable.

Greatest Hits; Creole JMC200102

Going right back the Studio One days with 'Rain From The Skies', 'Never Will Conquer Me' and 'Riding For A Fall', through Bunny Lee's 'This Old Heart Of Mine' and right up to 'Cool Operator' his second success with that producer. Although this hasn't got 'Better Must Come', it's still an excellent snapshot of the singer's early career. Worth it for 'I'm In A Dancing Mood' alone.

SEE ALSO:

Respect To Studio One; Heartbeat CDHB181/182
Tougher Than Tough – The Story Of Jamaican Music; Mango IBXCD1

VARIOUS ARTISTS

20 Film And Stage Classics Jamaican Style; Trojan CDTRL 319

The Trenton Spence Orchestra, People Will Say We're In Love; **Lloyd Clark,** Summertime; **The Skatalites,** Guns Of Navarone; **Carlos Malcolm and The Afro Caribs,** Bonanza Ska; **The Soul Brothers,** A Shot In The Dark; **Roland Alphonso,** From Russia With Love; **Tommy McCook and The Supersonics,** Dr Zhivago; **Lyn Taitt and The Jets,** To Sir With Love; **The Silvertones,** Old Man River; **Tommy McCook and The Supersonics,** Get Me To The Church On Time; **Richard Ace,** Hang 'Em High; **Slim Smith,** Zip A Dee Doo Dah; **Winston Wright,** The Magnificent Seven; **Pat Satchmo,** Hello Dolly; **Lloyd Charmers,** Theme From A Summer Place; **Pat Kelly,** Try To Remember; **The Chosen Few,** Theme From Shaft, I'm In The Mood For Love; **Alton Ellis,** Moon River, There's No Business Like Show Business.

Back in Kingston in the 1950s and 1960s, if you weren't in the dancehall the cinema was the place to be. The Jamaican love of American films of the era, notably the classic Westerns, is legendary and translated itself into the rude boys' shoot-'em-up antics as they attempted to emulate what they saw on the silver screen. This album is an eclectic homage to that enthusiasm, but it's probably more valuable as a curio than as a serious addition to your record collection, as, quite simply, it's far too varied. While it'll give you such vibrant ska classics as 'Guns Of Navarone' and 'Bonanza Ska' (one of the most popular Jamaican TV shows of the era, although it was never a true depiction of life in the wild west), it also dips more than toe into the nation's other love of the day – schmaltzy show tunes. Hence such pure cornball as 'Hello Dolly', 'Zip A Dee Doo Dah' and 'There's No Business Like Showbusiness'. Although The Chosen Few's 'I'm In The Mood For Love' became the basis for a few classic versions.

Dance Crasher – Ska To Rock Steady; Trojan CDTRL260

Lord Creator, Big Bamboo; **The Skatalites,** Latin Goes Ska; **The Maytals,** Hallelujah; **Don Drummond,** Garden Of Love; **Stranger Cole,** Rough And Tough; **The Skatalites,** Beardman Ska; **Peter Tosh and The Wailers,** Shame And Scandal, **The Skatalites,** Street Corner; **Carlos Malcolm and The Afro Caribs,** Bonanza Ska; **Alton Ellis and The Flames,** Dance Crasher; **Don Drummond,** Let George Do It; **The Clarendonians,** Rudie Bam Bam; **Tommy McCook and The Supersonics,** Ska Jam; **Lee Perry and The Soulettes,** Doctor Dick; **The Skatalites,** Ball Of Fire; **The Ethiopians,** Owe Me No Pay Me; **Baba Brooks and Band,** Independence Ska; **The Rulers,** Don't Be A Rude Boy.

Compiled by Steve Barrow, this superb selection of Duke Reid productions recorded between 1963 and 1965, proves a deft illustration of how the music changed.

The Trojan Story Volume One; Trojan CDTAL100

Laurel Aitken, Bartender; **Derrick Morgan,** Fat Man; **Eric Morris,** Humpty Dumpty; **Derrick and Patsy,** Housewives' Choice; **Jimmy Cliff,** Miss Jamaica; **Kentrick Patrick,** Don't Stay Out Too Late; **Jackie Edwards,** Tell Me Darling; **Stranger Cole,** Rough And Tough; **Kentrick Patrick,** Man To Man; **Stranger Cole,** Uno Dos Tres; **Don Drummond and The Skatalites,** Confucious; The Mellow Larks, Time To Pray (Alleluia); **The**

Blues Busters, Soon You'll Be Gone; **Lord Tanamo,** I'm In The Mood For Ska; **The Riots,** Yeah Yeah; **Don Drummond,** Man In The Street; **Baba Brooks,** One Eyed Giant; **Honeyboy Martin,** Dreader Than Dread; **Owen Grey,** Darling Patricia; **Joe White,** Every Night; **The Astronauts,** Syncopate; **The Clarendonians,** Rules Of Life; **Slim Smith,** The New Boss; **George and Winston,** Keep The Pressure On; **Roy Shirley,** Musical Train; **The Techniques,** Oh Baby; **Sir Lord Comic,** The Great Wuga Wuga; **Dandy Livingstone,** A Message To You Rudy; **The Ethiopians,** Train To Skaville; **The Three Tops,** It's Raining; **The Ethiopians,** The Whip; **Desmond Dekker,** Pretty Africa; **Alton Ellis,** Get Ready Rock Steady; **Baba Brooks,** Kingsize; **Evan and Jerry,** Rock Steady Train; **Sugar Simon,** King Without A Throne; **Phyllis Dillon,** Perfidia; **Derrick Morgan,** Do The Beng Beng; **Lynn Taitt,** Way Of Life; **The Tennors,** Got To Get You Off My Mind; **The Supersonics,** Second Fiddle; **The Maytals,** Do The Reggay; **The Pioneers,** Mama Look; **The Maytals,** Pressure Drop; **The Slickers,** Nana; **The Maytones,** Black And White; **The Charmers,** Rasta Never Fails.

At one point, in the UK in the 1960s, the Trojan Story was the Reggae Story, as 75 per cent of all Jamaican music issued in Britain was coming out on either that famous orange and white label or one of its subsidiaries such as Pressure Beat, Upsetter or Songbird. This is some of the best moments of the earliest contents of their vaults, going from the JA Boogie of 'Bartender' through to the modern reggae sounds of 'Black And White'. This disc probably represents the only available release of many of these tracks. Understandably, there is a Duke Reid bias – originally the British company had an exclusive deal with Reid for the UK rights to Treasure Isle recordings and the corporate name was chosen in recognition of the Duke's mighty sound system.

Rudies All Round (Rude Boy Records 1966–1967); Trojan CDTRL332

The Rulers, Don't Be A Rude Boy; **The Spanishtonians,** Rudie Gets Plenty; **Alton Ellis,** The Preacher; **The Valentines,** Blam Blam Fever; **Rio Grande,** Soldier Take Over; **Bobby Aitken,**

Curfew; **The Rulers,** Copasetic; **The Clarendonians,** Rudie Bam Bam; **Derrick Morgan,** Cool Off Rudies; **Winston and George,** Denham Town; **Stranger Cole,** Drop The Rachet; **Alton Ellis,** Blessings Of Love; **Desmond Dekker,** Rude Boy Train; **The Overtakers,** Beware; **Joe White,** Rudies All Round; **The Pioneers,** Rudies Are The Greatest; **The Valentines,** Stop The Violence; **The Tartans,** What Can I Say; **Derrick Morgan,** Judge Dread In Court; **Lee Perry and The Sensations,** Set Them Free.

The dates of the selections are significant, as it was during the exceptionally hot summer of 1966 that the rude boy 'situation' in Kingston – indeed all over Jamaica – got out of hand. Between July and September there were numerous rudie-related slayings in the capital and in October the government declared a state of emergency: soldiers took to the streets of certain parts of Kingston, preventing citywide movement, and a 10 p.m. to 6 a.m. curfew was enforced. These are some of the many rude boy songs, both pro and anti, that were recorded during that period. And to think the recent wave of ragga deejays believe they thought this stuff up!

Depth Charge; Lagoon LG21071

The Ethiopians, Pirate; **Tommy McCook and The Soul Syndicate,** Depth Charge; **Justin Hines,** Hey Mama; Stranger Cole, Crying Every Night; **Eddie Ford,** Guess This Riddle/ Riddle Dub; **John Holt,** Ali Baba; **The Gladiators,** You Were To Be; **Justin Hines,** Fight Too Much; **The Willows,** Ah So; **The Mello Lads,** Chatty Chatty Mouth; **Lloyd Robinson,** Fire Fire; **The Ethiopians,** Rub It Down; **The Gladiators,** Sweet Soul Music.

All recorded between 1967 and 1971, this is late-model rock steady, showing clearly how it was osmosing into reggae. Indeed, in some cases how it had already done so.

Monkey Ska; Trojan CDTRL323

Derrick Harriot, Monkey Ska; **The Dreamletts,** Ready Now; **Don Drummond,** Vat Seven; **Chucky and Dobby,** I Don't Need Your Love; **The Hals,** Don't Throw It Away; **Tommy McCook and The Supersonics,** Out Of Space; **Clancy Eccles,** Sammy No

Dread; **The Techniques,** I'm So In Love With You; **Los Cabelleros Orchestra,** Make Yourself Comfortable; **Horrell and Dawkins,** Cling To Me; **Clue and Naomi,** Open The Door; **The Soul Brothers,** Live Wire; **Bonny,** The Seed You Sow; **The Silvertones,** True Confessions; **The Blues Blenders,** Girl Next Door; **Baba Brooks,** Jam Session; **Lee Perry,** What A Good Woodman; **Lyn Taitt and The Comets,** Tender Loving Care; **Roy Shirley and Ken Boothe,** Paradise; **The Granville Williams Orchestra,** Third Man Theme.

You shouldn't let the unfortunate title put you off. This collection really does contain some rarities and, better than that, rarities that deserve to be heard.

Solid Gold From The Vaults Volume Two; Trojan CDTRL293

The Soul Brothers, Train To Skaville; **The Wailing Wailers,** Ska Jerk; **Don Drummond and The Skatalites,** Coolie Boy; **The Monarchs,** Sauce And Tea; **The Baba Brooks Band, Lyn Taitt and The Jets,** Seven Guns Alive; **The Maytals,** Treating Me Bad; **Bob Marley and The Wailers,** I Stand Predominant; **Tommy McCook,** Out Of Space; **The Observers,** Lightening And Thunder; **Dennis Alcapone and John Holt,** Togetherness; Dennis **Alcapone,** Blessed Are The Meek; **Sir Harry,** Butto Down; **Prince Buster Allstars,** Smooth; **George Ferris,** With Every Dream; **Herman Chin Loy,** Invasion.

Rock Steady Rave; Charly CPCD8023

Delroy Wilson, I'm In A Dancing Mood, This Old Heart Of Mine, Rain From The Skies, I'm In The Mood For Love; **Bob Marley and The Wailers,** Put It On; **Hopeton Lewis,** Take It Easy; **The Jamaicans,** Ba Ba Boom; **The Ethiopians,** You Got The Dough, Long Time Now; **Byron Lee and The Dragonaires,** Rock Steady, Musical Pressure, Girl I've Got A Date, Bend Down Low, 007 (Shanty Town), Shoo Be Doo.

Let's Ska Again; Charly CDCHARLY203

The Ska Boys, Let's Dance Again, **Hoot To Skaville,** You Got To

Move; **The Maroons,** Struggling Man; **The Prophets,** The Scorcher; **The Cimarons,** Kung Fu Fighting; **Des All Stars,** Skaing South; **U-Roy,** Hat Trick; **The Deltones,** I'll Take You There; **Pat Rodhen,** Reggae Woman; **Freddie Notes,** Night Food; **Dizzy Ranks,** Do It; **Laurel Aitken,** It's Too Late.

*Scandal Ska; Island CID9929

Don Drummond, Scandal; **Bob Marley,** Judge Not; **Desmond Dekker,** Honour Your Father And Your Mother; **Jimmy Cliff,** Miss Jamaica; **Laurel Aitken,** Love Me Baby; **Cornell Campbell,** Turn Down Date; **Ernest Raglin,** Exodus; **Roy and Millie,** We'll Meet; **Skitter,** Mr Kruschev; **King Edwards,** Russian Roulette; **Theolonius Beckford,** Now That You're Dead; **Lloyd Clark,** Girls Rush, Japanese Girls; **Kenrick Patrick,** Beyond; **Roland Alphonso,** Christine Keeler; **Basil Gabbidon,** Get On The Ball.

*Intensified – Original Ska 1962–1966; Mango IMCD51

Roland Alphonso, El Pussy Cat; **Eric Morris,** Solomon Grundie; **Baba Brooks,** Teenage Ska; **The Charms,** Carry Go Bring Come; **Baba Brooks,** Duck Soup; **Shenley Duffus,** Rukumbine; **Don Drummond and Drumbago,** Stampede; **The Skatalites,** Independent Anniversary Ska; **The Maytals,** John and James; **Tommy McCook,** Rocket Ship; **Stranger Cole,** We Are Rolling; **Roland Alphonso,** James Bond; **Derrick and Patsy,** Housewives' Choice; **Don Drummond,** University Goes Ska; **Eric Morris,** Penny Reel; **Justin Hines,** The Higher The Monkey Climbs.

*More Intensified – Original Ska Volume Two 1963–1967; Mango IMCD52

The Maytals as The Vikings, Six And Seven Books Of Moses; **The Skatalites,** Dr Kildare; **Lord Brynner And The Sheiks,** Congo War; **Marguerita,** Woman Come; **Don Drummond,** Man In The Street; **Eric Morris,** What A Man Doeth; **Roland Al And The Soul Brothers,** Miss Ska-Culation; **Stranger Cole,** Run Joe; **The Skatalites,** Sucu-Sucu; **Roland Al And The Soul Brothers,** Dr Ring A Ding; **Sir Lord Comic,** The Great Wuga Wuga; **The**

Skatalites, Dick Tracy; **Desmond Dekker And the Four Aces,** Mount Zion; **The Soul Brothers,** Marcus Junior; **The Ethiopians,** Last Train To Skaville.

Both volumes of Intensified – Original Ska are Steve Barrow-compiled, and here he has managed to surpass his own excruciatingly high standards. Both (although more so the second disc) contain some recordings it's unlikely anybody outside a very select few has even heard of, let alone owns! But, as would be expected, they're put together in an imaginative, completely user-friendly fashion. These two come highly recommended to the more advanced ska collector.

*Tougher Than Tough – Rude Boy Ska, Rock Steady And Reggae; Trojan CDTRL304

The Soul Brothers, Lawless Street; **The Clarendonians,** Rude Boy Gone Jail; **The Heptones,** Gunmen Coming To Town; **Desmond Dekker and The Aces,** Rudy Got Soul; **Derrick Morgan,** Tougher Than Tough; **Dandy,** Rudy (A Message To You); **Derrick Morgan,** Court Dismiss; **Desmond Dekker and The Aces,** 007 (Shanty Town); **Honey Boy Martin,** Dreader Than Dread; **Jackie Edwards,** On The Run With A Gun; **Boris Gardiner and Love People,** Scarface; **The Slickers,** Johnny Too Bad; **The Starlites,** You're A Wanted Man; **The Untouchables,** Cool Down; **Jackie Edwards,** Johnny Gunman; **Dennis Alcapone,** Al Capone's Guns Don't Argue; **The Slickers,** You Can't Win; **Andy Capp,** The Law.

More rudie soundtrack, not to be confused with the Island box set of the same name – see below. This has its own merits as one of the few places you'll find Jackie Edwards's gunman tracks or The Heptones' rude boy classic 'Gunmen Coming To Town'.

*Club Ska 67; Mango IMCD53

The Skatalites, Guns Of Navarone; **Roland Alphonso,** Phoenix City; **Desmond Dekker,** Shanty Town; **The Flames,** Broadway Jungle; **Roy Richards,** Contact; **Baba Brooks,** Guns Fever; **Justin Hines,** Rub Up Push Up; **Delroy Wilson,** Dancing Mood; **The Gaylads,** Stop Making Love; **Rita Marley,** Pied Piper; **The Soul**

Brothers, Lawless Street; **Sir Lord Comic,** Ska-ing West; **The Rulers,** Copasetic.

At the time (1967, of course) this was an absolutely vital album to own. Everybody who was anybody would have one tucked under their arm at any available opportunity. And quite rightly so – after nearly thirty years, its excitement has in no way diminished.

*Ska Boogie – Jamaican R&B, The Dawn Of Ska; Sequel NEXCD254

Laurel Aitken and Hyacinth, Baron Twist and His Knights, You Got Me Rocking; **Owen Grey,** Millie Girl; **Duke Reid and His Group,** Pink Lane Shuffle; **Keith and Enid,** Worried Over You; **Lloyd Clarke,** Parapinto Boogie; **The Jiving Juniors,** I Wanna Love; **Derrick Morgan,** Shake A Leg; **Eric Morris,** Humpty Dumpty; **The Bubbles,** The Wasp; **Owen Grey and Buster's Group,** On The Beach; **Prince Buster,** Open Up Bartender; **Al T Joe,** Slow Boat; **Bobby Aitken,** Never Never; **Busters All Stars,** South Virginia; **Rudy and Sketto,** Hush Baby; **The Folkes Brothers and Count Ossie,** Oh Carolina; Errol Dixon, Midnight Train.

As the title would suggest, this is very early stuff – more like a week or so before the actual dawn, as the most modern tune on it is 'Oh Carolina', which is pretty much acknowledged as one of the two original ska records. And as such, as the listener is taken on a journey through some rollicking Caribbean R&B, this album becomes a thoroughly entertaining musical history lesson.

*Ska Spectacular Volume One; Charly CPCD8021

The Maytals, It's You, Never You Change, If You Act This Way, It's No Use, You Make Me Feel The Way I Do, What's On Your Mind; **The Blues Busters,** Wings Of A Dove, Donna, I Don't Know; **The Ethiopians,** Engine '54, Train To Skaville; **Byron Lee and The Dragonaires,** Sammy Dead, Oil In My Lamp, Jamaican Ska.

*Ska Spectacular Volume Two; Charly CPCD8022

The Maytals, Daddy, My New Name, Fever, She Will Never Let

Me Down, I Know, Tell Me The Reason; **The Blues Busters,** Soon You'll Be Gone, Baby What You Want Me To Do; Shame And Scandal, Love Me Forever; **The Ethiopians,** Train To Glory, Come On Now; **Byron Lee and The Dragonaires,** Simmer Down, Soul Ska.

*Tougher Than Tough – The Story Of Jamaican Music; Mango ICDBX1

The Folkes Brothers, Oh Carolina; **Laurel Aitken,** Boogie In My Bones; **Owen Grey,** Midnight Track; **Theolonius Beckford,** Easy Snappin'; **Derrick and Patsy,** Housewives' Choice; **Derrick Morgan,** Forward March; **Jimmy Cliff,** Miss Jamaica; **Millie Small,** My Boy Lollipop; **The Maytals,** Six And Seven Books Of Moses; **The Wailers,** Simmer Down; **Don Drummond,** Man In The Street; **Justin Hines and The Dominoes,** Carry Go Bring Come; **The Skatalites,** Guns Of Navarone; **Prince Buster,** Al Capone, Hard Man Fe Dead; **Derrick Morgan,** Tougher Than Tough; **Alton Ellis,** Girl I've Got A Date; **The Paragons,** Happy Go Lucky Girl; **Delroy Wilson,** I'm In A Dancing Mood; **Ken Boothe,** The Train Is Coming; **Hopeton Lewis,** Take It Easy; **The Jamaicans,** Ba Ba Boom; **Desmond Dekker,** 007 (Shanty Town); **Bob Andy,** I've Got To Go Back Home; **The Techniques,** Queen Majesty; **Dobby Dobson,** Loving Pauper; **Phyllis Dillon,** Don't Stay Away.

This is the first disc of a four-CD box set, and covers the period from 1958 to 1967. And the title doesn't lie, the set genuinely does tell the story of Jamaican music from when it first achieved its own identity up until 1993 (when the set came out). The sheer comprehensiveness of the Steve Barrow-selected tracklisting for this disc should give some indication of how good it is. What it doesn't let you in on though is the magnificence of the packaging. Included in the stylish 'digipack' is a comprehensive, fascinatingly illustrated, gloriously designed book telling the story in words, with each of the 95 tracks being discussed individually to provide some background and so vividly bring to life the history as it unfolds. It'll set you back about fifty quid, but as an instant reggae collection it's worth much more than that. ♦♦

2

IN AN INTERNATIONAL STYLE

A t the end of the 1960s, the United Kingdom was the biggest single market for Jamaican music. Just as the urban mods had adopted ska as part of their preferred listening, so their spiritual and sartorial descendants, the original skinheads, were taking to the next wave of music from the island. Given the notions of the ultra-right, openly racist politics associated with skinhead culture in the 1990s, it seems remarkable that, twenty-five years ago, similarly attired boot boys were one of the largest black music consumer groups in the country – skinheads took to the pre-street funk soul of Stax, Tamla (as Motown was then referred to) and Atlantic as well as Jamaican-originated sounds. And it was the latter that was perhaps the most obvious choice.

Skinheads were working-class white kids who were growing up on estates next to the newly arrived or born-over-here black kids. The two groups attended the same schools, played in the same football teams, went to the same church hall/youth club discos – supplying their own 45s for the occasion – chased the same girls (in London in the late-1960s/early 1970s, well brought up West Indian girls weren't allowed out after dark) and shared the same approach to crisp street fashion. Derrick Morgan's pork-pie hat was a forerunner of the skinhead's stingy brim 'trilbies'; Desmond Dekker's halfmast trousers were echoed in the white kids' abbreviated Levis Sta-Prest; tonik mohair had been in vogue in West Kingston for years; and the Jamaican rude boy fashion for suits with very long jackets was translated into the deep-vented, single-breasted Crombie-style overcoats, complete with carefully arranged red silk hand-

101

kerchief in the breast pocket. Even if the two cultures didn't always like each other *en masse*, there was an enormous mutual respect – remember, there had been more than a few black mods.

And by this time the music was being called reggae. A new generation of producers and musicians had picked up the tempo and the rock steady rhythm had been superseded by a newer, tougher beat. Much of this was because the rude boy era was over, and producers and performers deliberately wanted to distance themselves from any lingering aspects of it, but once again the direction also seems to have been influenced by what was happening in America. In much the same way as ex-R&B US soul music was busily reinventing itself as street funk, Jamaican studios were taking an equally hard-kicking approach. The bass and drums were now the engine room of any tune that hoped to succeed – electric bass guitars were by then standard issue – while the guitar and organ were being approached from a far more percussive point of view. Horns as lead instruments were being used less and less, whereas pin-point, multi-part brass riffing became yet another rhythmic device.

Indeed, the only real continuation from the previous era was the sweet singing – both in harmony or as a solo proposition. But any vocalizing was by now being supplemented by an entirely new development: deejay toasting. Entirely new to vinyl, that is. Once again, this was simply a commercially available representation of what had been taking place on the sound systems for more than ten years. Since the 1950s, deejays had been enhancing the music they played by scatting over the top, whipping the crowd into a frenzy as they celebrated both themselves and the sound system. Not long after operators like Reid and Coxsone began cutting their own records, when two-track recording was widely available, it became a trend to cut separate versions of tunes leaving out the singing, to allow the more inventive deejays room to perform. An early incarnation of dub. The dancehall popularity of these spontaneous vocal sessions was such that it made perfect sense to sell them on the B-sides of certain records. And then, by natural progression, the better toasters – U-Roy and Dennis Alcapone were the first two of note – became accepted as stars in their own right.

Reggae came into being in 1968, but as you'd expect it's all a bit murky as to who was the originator. Producer Clancy Eccles maintains he came up with the term as a corruption of 'streggae', Kingstonian slang for a woman of no or low morals. Then Lee Perry will happily tell you that his self-produced, anti-Coxsone hit of the same year, 'People Funny Boy', was the first reggae single. Needless to say this 'fact' is hotly disputed by more than one other artist. Yet the first record to use the word in the title was Toots and The Maytals' 'Do The Reggay' (sic). So pick the bones out of that!

Not that origins seemed to matter too much in the UK, where companies like Trojan and Pama were selling enormous quantities of the style. A lot of reggae was being recorded with one eye on the British market – Leslie Kong paid particular attention to what the UK audience wanted, and his jaunty poppy style was rewarded with a string of big sellers. And with this lucrative new outlet in mind, once master tapes came across the Atlantic they'd be sweetened for greater pop chart appeal, usually by adding a string section. This became a widespread practice after the UK success of Pat Kelly's 'How Long Will It Take', the first tune to be treated in this way. It was also something that carried back to Jamaica, giving rise to a whole subtext of reggae-based JA pop that often nodded towards the Country and Western music that remained a firm favourite with radio programmers and large, er, respectable sections of the public – artists like John Holt, Ken Boothe and Nicky Thomas did very well out of covers of songs more associated with the likes of Jim Reeves, Pat Boone and Kris Kristofferson.

Back in the UK, though, in spite of virtually no radio support, it wasn't unusual for titles to sell upwards of 50,000. But as so much of this action would take place in specialist outlets rather than chart return shops, during its first couple of years reggae was woefully under-represented on the Top 40 and assumed almost underground status. Interestingly, reggae producers and record companies didn't seem to care – positively revelled in it, in fact. While Jamaican music always had its earthy side – bawdy mento, ska and rock steady songs were far from unheard of – this new wave wholeheartedly embraced musical rudeness. Songs like 'Wreck A Pum Pum', 'Bang Bang Lulu', 'Barbwire', 'Fattie Fattie' and the record that needs no introduction or explanation, Max Romeo's Top 10 'Wet Dream', were enormous hits with both black and white kids. There was a secret language of *rudeness* – I can still remember taking an album called *Loch Ness Monster* to a school disco and watching the knowing looks and outright sniggering that went on when its codedly obscene classics were played.

Such was the momentum, though – 'Wet Dream', for instance, had sold close on 300,000 – that as the 1960s became the 1970s so reggae had to spill into the mainstream. For the first few years of the new decade, records by the likes of Desmond Dekker, Greyhound, The Pioneers, Nicky Thomas, John Holt and Bob and Marcia were virtually fixtures in the UK charts – Ken Boothe's 'Everything I Own' was one of 1974's Top 10 biggest-selling singles, having shifted just over a million units. Reggae had reached the music fan to become a fully paid-up pop style.

Yet it was reviled by critics and rock album buyers. Having ridden out the skinhead tag, it was now being seen as (or should that be 'written off as'?) music by simpletons for simpletons, rather than as a genuine folk music with a pedigree as valid as the blues. Your post-hippie progressive rock fan wanted something deep and meaningful, and reggae presented itself as deliberately lightweight. Even when there was a message, songs such as 'Young, Gifted And Black' or 'Black And White' were couched in terms as uncomplicated as possible. And anything they might have achieved in the social comment department would be swiftly nullified by the deluge of overly melodious middle-market-orientated offerings. *Ras Records Presents A Reggae Christmas . . . The Sounds Of The Seventies Reggae Style . . . Fab! 16 Reggae Beatles Classics* . . . not so much Easy Listening as Cheesy Listening.

In short, just a couple of years on from its golden period, reggae was having a bit of a credibility crisis. Outside its own highly marginalized fanbase it was perceived as having no third dimension – no spiritual or intellectual depth and precious little musical worth. A bit of a non-music.

But this was all about to change. While the skinhead fashion and pop reggae sounds were burning themselves out in the UK, back at the root, in Jamaica, the music was once again reinventing itself.

This time Rastafari was the guiding force . . .

Dennis Alcapone

(Born Dennis Smith, 1948; Clarendon, Jamaica; deejay)

Today, twenty-five years later, Dennis Alcapone is probably the most under-appreciated talent in the whole deejay school. He was the second toasting artist to make an impact on record in the very early 1970s, following U-ROY's lead. But unlike so many others at the time he was never merely a U-Roy imitator; from day one he had a softer, more melodic style of his own. He enjoyed a substantial run of hits with DUKE REID and BUNNY LEE, then in 1972 won Jamaica's prestigious annual deejay competition.

But Dennis Alcapone's timing was all wrong. Although doing a great deal to establish the style, he couldn't claim fame as the first vinyl-ized toaster. While his style was spot on for the post-rock steady, lighter-side-of-reggae grooves, the popularity and relevance of such a musical mood didn't last very long. As the new wave of roots reggae deejays swept all before them, anybody who wasn't keeping up – i.e. locksing up – was confined to the past without so much as a backward glance. In 1973 he moved to the UK, just as reggae was slipping from prominence as a preferred pop style, yet the punky reggae party was still a few years off. As a result, Dennis Alcapone does not enjoy the same legend as, say, BIG YOUTH, DILLINGER or Tappa Zukie. Which is far less than this enormously talented man deserves.

As a music mad teenager, Dennis Alcapone's most vivid memories involve hanging out at sound system dances, marvelling at the vocal dexterity of guys like Matchuki, King Stitt, Cuttings, Prince Buster and U-Roy himself. As you'd expect, it was only a matter of time before he took up the microphone. Before the end of the 1960s Alcapone was rocking the crowd as co-founder of the El Paso sound system, which finished the decade as one of Kingston's top-flight outfits, largely due to the deejay's innovative approach. Other than U-Roy, Alcapone was about the only toaster at that time to be constructing lyrics and phrasings to complement the tune itself and to interact with any existing vocals, rather than simply ego-tripping out on the rhythm or filling in the gaps in the singing. He always saw deejay music as something to be taken seriously, and so approached what he did with all the consideration of a singer, writing lyrics of great quality and attention to detail. But he was still as spontaneous and boastingly self-celebratory as he needed to be. All of which went a long way to getting what was essentially a dancehall style accepted on the radio and in the record shops.

Taking his vibrant, witty sounds into the studio was another natural progression. In 1970 Alcapone had kicked off a recording career that, during the next three years, would produce over 200 singles, three albums and make him a constant fixture in the Jamaican charts. He cut for COXSONE, Prince Buster, KEITH HUDSON, Duke Reid, LEE PERRY and Bunny Lee – the only big name from this period he didn't work with was CLANCY ECCLES – and rocked versions of everything from classic Treasure Isle and Studio One rock steady through early roots sounds to the reggae of the day. His subject matter ranged from the romantic to the raucous and the political to the preposterous, but everything sounded as if it was as much fun for him as it was for us. 'Musical Alphabet', 'Wake Up Jamaica', 'Ripe Cherry', 'Mosquito One', 'It Must Come', 'Rock To The Beat', 'My Voice Is Insured For Half A Million Dollars' and 'Alpha and Omega' are just a small portion of Dennis Alcapone's magnificent musical legacy.

He decamped to the UK in 1973 – 'I was on tour there, I met a girl and just kind of never got around to going home!' – and while he still performed regularly, his recording became sporadic. However, the good news is that the current wave of deejay music and the revisiting of the roots of reggae have combined to put Dennis Alcapone back in fashion. These days he's playing some big shows in Jamaica, overseeing future representation of his back catalogue, plus preparing to cut some new sides. And even at nearly fifty years old he still sounds as sharp as ever.

Unfortunately, all that is available on CD from this giant of Jamaican music are three frustratingly hard to find import sets: *Universal Rockers* (on the RAS label); *Guns Don't Argue* (Jamaican Gold JMC200115) and *Forever Version* (Heartbeat HBCD 3505). They are, respectively, a compilation, a Bunny Lee-produced 1971 set and, from the same year, a collection of his best from Studio One. It's unlikely any of them will disappoint – the latter two are worth it for the title tracks alone – it's just a matter of finding them. However, Trojan have a totally brilliant Steve

Barrow-compiled collection on the catalogue, *My Voice Is Insured For Half A Million Dollars*, but at present they see fit to stock it on vinyl. Somebody have a word. Please.

Meanwhile, enough Dennis Alcapone to keep you going – for a little while at least – can be found on:

Keep On Coming Through The Door – Jamaican Deejay Music 1969-1973; Trojan CDTRL255

Keith Hudson and Friends: *Studio Kinda Cloudy*; Trojan CDTRL258

Tougher Than Tough – The Story Of Jamaican Music; Mango IBXCD1

Respect To Studio One; Heartbeat HBCD 181/182

Solid Gold From the Vaults Volume Two; Trojan CDTRL293

Bob and Marcia

(Born Keith Anderson, 1944, Kingston, Jamaica; Marcia Griffiths, born 1954, Kingston, Jamaica; vocal duo)

Remember Bob and Marcia on *Top Of The Pops*, dressed like extras from those disco scenes in *The Persuaders!* , topped off with entirely improbable afros and doing that dancing for which you have to point backwards with your thumbs? Then you've probably had a few problems equating those Bob Andy and Marcia Griffiths with the completely righteous, musically correct Bob Andy and Marcia Griffiths, the artists they became. Unsurprisingly, so did they. Even though they scored a UK number 5 hit in April 1970 with 'Young Gifted And Black', and followed it up the next year when 'Pied Piper' got to number 11, it wasn't what you'd call a happy experience.

Each of them had enjoyed a career before that: Andy was an original PARAGON and became a songwriter/singer/arranger of huge acclaim at Studio One; while Griffiths was in front of the microphone cutting ska and rock steady tracks for COXSONE from the age of ten – among them was 'Feel Like Jumping', a big hit on both sides of the Atlantic. It was at Brentford Road, after Andy had supervised some sessions for Griffiths, that it occurred to him they'd work well as a duo. 'Young, Gifted And Black' (a cover of the Nina Simone post-Civil Rights anthem) was recorded for HARRY J in late 1969. The couple's dissatisfaction

107

with what happened next epitomizes so much that was wrong with the reggae business. The track was released in the UK on the Pama label and sold about three copies. Trojan then licensed the tune, dubbed a full string orchestra on to it, and had the hit. Although Bob Andy, a gifted producer himself, didn't object too much to this, what he wasn't keen on was having to act the pop part on tour in the UK – as a devout follower of Rastafari he believed such a presentation decimated the song's lyrical message. And on top of all that, while the record sold into the six-figure bracket, all he and Marcia got were the initial session fees.

The twosome recorded some successful Jamaican releases about that time, but after 'Pied Piper' (Andy's own production of a UK pop hit for Crispin St Peters in 1966) received much the same treatment as 'Gifted', the pair split up. Bob Andy returned to production, writing and low-profile performing, and Marcia cut a few sides for SONIA POTTINGER before becoming one of BOB MARLEY's permanent backing vocalists The I-Threes. More recently she has been recording as a solo artist, experimenting with dancehall styles and rap/reggae crossover, but nothing of any great note.

Really Together; I-Anka AV003CD

Not by any stretch of the imagination is this classic Bob and Marcia. It's caught between two ideas – pop appeal and roots credibility – and ends up fulfilling neither with any degree of conviction. It's probably a far better idea to stick to the hits as they surface on Various Artist compilations. That said, there are a couple of kicking rhythm tracks on this: 'Call Me Dub' and 'Really Together Dub'.

Marcia Griffiths: *Put A Little Love In Your Heart*; Trojan CDTRL325

A CD reissue of Marcia's *Sweet Bitter Love* album, but with extra tracks ('When Will I See You Again' and 'I Just Don't Want To Be Lonely' among them) plus both Bob and Marcia's hits and a few more US soul tunes they covered ('Put A Little Love In Your Heart' and 'We've Got To Get Ourselves Back Together', for instance). While it's pretty inoffensive, it's unlikely to ring any bells with too many serious reggae collectors.

In the meantime, one or the other or both of Bob and Marcia's hits can be found on:
Tougher Than Tough – The Story Of Jamaican Music; Mango IBXCD1
The Roots Of Reggae; Music Club MCBX003
Reggae Classics Volume Three; Trojan CDTRL256
Celebration: The Best Of Reggae – 25 Years Of Trojan Records; Quality QTVCD010

Marcia by herself features on:
Respect To Studio One; Heartbeat HBCD 181/182
Reggae Classics Volume Four; Trojan CDTRL284

Ken Boothe

➡ It was during this period that Ken Boothe became a bona fide pop star, both in the UK and Jamaica. When he hooked up with Lloyd Charmers (1970/71), reggae was firmly in fashion and the Boothe Smooth found a natural home as the style increasingly lent itself to soulful, lovers' rock sounds. His boyish looks and easy-going charm did him no harm, either! Ken Boothe had youth appeal – the girls loved him and his overly sentimental way; the guys figured than any system that played a lot of Ken Boothe would attract the women. He also crossed over to the 'mums and dads', who appreciated the tunefulness and conventional artistry involved. Indeed, it was this that did a lot to impress on the Jamaican middle classes that reggae was a valid musical form and not just some sort of ghetto racket – it seems its credentials needed to be reaffirmed after every new development.

But Ken Boothe was no uptown patsy. While he may not have had locks on his head, he had his priorities in the right place and showed as much with his choice of material. Amid his reggae-fied covers of US soul hits – a common enough carry-on among this end of the reggae spectrum – Boothe included such songs as Syl Johnson's 'Is It Because I'm Black?', BOB MARLEY's 'African

Lady' and his own 'Black, Gold and Green'. But whatever mark
the singer may have made on a nationalistic level, it was all just
a warm-up for his two monster hits.

The first was 'Everything I Own', a cover of Bread's soft rock
hit, and it was obvious it was going to be massive back at the
beginning of 1974 when the London soul sound systems were
playing it on pre-release. So little reggae was played at soul
dances back then – a bit of GREGORY ISAACS and DENNIS
BROWN, and a splash of JOHN HOLT – that the tunes had to be
special. When I went to New York for the first time, in April that
year, Brooklyn clubs were easing it in amongst Al Green and
Marvin Gaye. And when Trojan finally put it out in the UK
during the summer, it was more than ready to cross over from
the sound systems to the mainstream. In November the record
was number 1 for three weeks, and finished up as the ninth best-
selling British single, with figures just nudging a million. Boothe
followed it up almost immediately with 'Crying Over You',
which reached number 11.

Then Ken Boothe simply faded away. The swing towards
roots music is the most likely explanation for this, as it left very
little space for his pop leanings or even his subtle declarations of
black pride. Ironically, because so many of his tunes had such
strong melodies they became favourite backing tracks for deejays – unsurprisingly, 'Everything I Own' was one of the most
versioned records of its day.

The Ken Boothe Collection; Trojan CDTRL249

Eighteen Lloyd Charmers productions from the first half of the
1970. The point of sale here is that 'Everything I Own' and
'Crying Over You' are both present and correct. However, there's
much more to it than just those two. As well as a recut of his own
composition 'Freedom Street', there are covers of 'Ain't No
Sunshine', 'Walk Away From Love' and 'Let's Get It On', none of
which is in the remotest bit cheesy, as Boothe's rich baritone
allows you and the gal you're dancing with to wallow in the sort
of lurrrve power you'd normally expect from Barry White. This
is the beginnings of LOVER'S ROCK (see pages 245-247), when it
had a real sense of its own style. Hell, this man even turns 'Speak
Softly Love (Love Theme From The Godfather)' into a killer.

'Everything I Own' features on:
Tougher Than Tough – The Story Of Jamaican Music; Mango IBXCD1
The Roots Of Reggae; Music Club MCBX003
Reggae Classics Volume Three; Trojan CDTRL256

'Crying Over You' can be found on:
Reggae Attack; Attack CDAT113
20 Reggae Blockbusters; Trojan CDTRL176

Jimmy Cliff

➻ Jimmy Cliff arrived at reggae a couple of years late. He'd spent most of the second half of the 1960s living in London and flirting with the rock scene there, only to reintroduce himself to Jamaican music via Brazil. That's right, where the nuts come from. In 1968 he represented Jamaica in an international music festival down there, and the Brazilians took to him to such a degree that he stayed on after the competition to become one of the country's most popular entertainers (Jimmy Cliff remains a star in Brazil to this day). But his new audience weren't too keen on soul, underground rock or British-style pop: what they wanted was *reggae*, which meant he had to write some. Among his compositions were 'Wonderful World, Beautiful People' and 'Vietnam', plus a rearrangement of Cat Stevens' 'Wild World', each one a sizeable international hit.

It was the shot in the arm he'd been waiting for. Once back in Jamaica, initially with LESLIE KONG, but this time co-producing, before taking charge of himself, Jimmy Cliff put out a succession of near-perfect popular reggae records. 'Pop' would be entirely the wrong word for them, as, although they made the most of reggae's newly acquired rhythmic accessibility, they were far more lyrically thoughtful and structurally complex than anything else going on around them. Songs like 'Sitting In Limbo', 'Struggling Man' and 'Many Rivers To Cross' quite deservedly became instant classics on both sides of the specialist/mainstream divide.

But what cemented Cliff's place in reggae history was an event that was probably the single most important factor in breaking roots reggae to the world outside Jamaica: the monumental movie *The Harder They Come*. Originally asked to write the soundtrack, Cliff ended up starring in the film as Ivan, the country boy turned singer turned anti-establishment gunman – a sort of sharply dressed Jamaican Robin Hood. He couldn't have been given a more credibility-restoring role. The film was like a guided tour of sufferah culture: all aspects of life in the Jamaica the tourists don't see was here – Rastafari, the ganja trade, ghetto rude boy-ism, political corruption, and an insider's view of the Kingston music business fed into a tale of intrigue, excitement and razor-edged ghetto humour. Plus an entirely three-dimensional view of the roots movement, with some dynamite tunes thrown in for good measure. For black kids – of all nationalities – growing up in London, it was like a touchstone to a world we knew existed but were unlikely to see for ourselves, a world in which we ran t'ings ourselves, and therefore had an absolute logic to it. As with *Shaft* a couple of years earlier, anybody in my area who'd seen *The Harder They Come* walked with a bit of a spring in their step the next day. For the white people it was just as important: it was an honest, enjoyable primer to what was going on somewhere else. The *real deal*, nothing ersatz or deliberately flavoured in anticipation of a wider audience. And it was rightly appreciated for being so. *The Harder They Come* is still a regular at late-night screenings all over the world.

Not so Jimmy Cliff, unfortunately. Instead of capitalizing on this success, he spent the next few years moving from major record company to major record company, each one failing to get the most – or indeed anything very much – out of a talent that could combine a wonderful, urgent back-a-yard churchy delivery with brilliant song-writing and an international way of looking at things. In Africa and South America his work with local musicians and rhythm patterns has kept him the biggest foreign star in some countries, but in the UK or Jamaica it's unlikely too many people are waiting for the next album.

Meanwhile, after extending his acting career in *Bongo Man* and the Steven Segal action adventure *Marked For Death*, he is currently putting the finishing touches to his own script for *The Harder They Come Part Two*. Maybe this can repeat the impact of the original, and in so doing restore Jimmy Cliff to his rightful place among the still active reggae greats.

*Various Artists: *The Harder They Come Original Soundtrack*; Mango RRCD1

Jimmy Cliff, You Can Get It If You Really Want; Many Rivers To Cross; The Harder They Come; Sitting In Limbo; **Scotty**, Draw Your Brakes; **The Melodians**, Rivers Of Babylon; **The Slickers**, Johnny Too Bad; **The Maytals**, Sweet And Dandy; **Desmond Dekker**, Shanty Town; **The Maytals**, Pressure Drop.

Although this is, strictly speaking, a Various Artists release, it's so closely associated with Jimmy Cliff that this is the logical place for it. It is also one of the greatest film soundtrack albums ever put together – without question. Even if you haven't seen the film, just playing though this sequence of tunes reflects the hopes and fears of Kingston's ghetto communities with unerring accuracy, and so sums up exactly what was happening in reggae as it progressed into roots and culture. On a purely Value For Music level, it's worth the price just to hear THE MAYTALS bawling out 'Sweet And Dandy' or Cliff's less frantic version of 'You Can Get It If You Really Want', a song he wrote but which DESMOND DEKKER made famous. And hey, it's impossible to own too many copies of 'Johnny Too Bad' or the original 'Rivers Of Babylon'.

*The Best Of Jimmy Cliff; Mango CIDD6

This is the *mid*-period Jimmy Cliff set. As well as all the hits, it's got a few of the less readily available numbers: 'Another Cycle', 'Keep Your Eye On The Sparrow', 'I'm No Immigrant', and so on. You know, the best of the rest. In fact all that's missing is 'Bongo Man'.

ALSO RECOMMENDED:

*Reggae Greats; Mango RRCD22
*Jimmy Cliff; Trojan CDTRL16

These two are like lesser versions of The Best Of. There is little to choose between them in terms of tracklisting – perhaps the Mango offering has a slight edge – and although either may make a perfectly acceptable substitute for *The Best Of*, it won't quite be all the Jimmy Cliff you want.

*Unlimited; Trojan CDTRJ100

An odd collection of middle-period reggae-ish recordings, most notable for the obvious struggles Cliff was having trying to balance the traditional Jamaican sufferah sentiments with his new global perspective. Thus tunes have hard-hitting titles like 'Poor Slave', 'Oh Jamaica', 'Black Queen' and 'Rip Off', but come over as half-hearted pop songs.

SEE ALSO:

Tougher Than Tough – The Story Of Jamaican Music; Mango IBXCD1
Reggae Attack; Attack CDAT113
20 Reggae Classics Volume One; Trojan CDTRL222

There are several later Jimmy Cliff CDs on offer – *The Power And The Glory*, *Hanging Fire*, *Cliffhanger* and *Breakout* among them – but the music they feature is almost unrecognizable from the incendiary, meditative stuff of the early years.

Lord Creator

(Born Kentrick Patrick, early 1940s; Trinidad; singer)
One of the most remarkable things about reggae is its unwavering ability to take on the most mawkish of songs, put them over in a way that's so wet you could wring it out, and still walk away with credibility fully intact. Witness lovers' rock, most of Gregory Isaacs' output and those cover versions of soul songs that were all the rage twenty years ago. But nothing was more dopily sentimental than Lord Creator's 1969 hit 'Kingston Town'. Written by Lord Creator himself and produced by CLANCY ECCLES, it had the lot: an lively drum intro; a perkily textbook reggae beat; a hint of steel pan; lyrics that could have been written by the Jamaica Tourist Authority – 'Stars shine so bright/But they're fading at the dawn/There is magic in Ki-i-i-ngston town'; and Lord Creator's honey-throated crooning that kind of oozed its way over the groove to such a degree you felt you had to give the record a wipe every now and again. The sort of stuff that was crying out for a poolside welcoming party at an upmarket Kingston hotel. But we loved it. It's a cut that can still

be dropped on a roomful of thirty-somethings and have them singing along while they oh-so-slowly wine up their waists.

Curiously, Lord Creator wasn't even Jamaican. He'd come over from Trinidad in the second half of the 1950s to take advantage of the island's booming music industry and made his mark with straight calypso and mento – not too surprising really, given his chosen name. A still available example of Creator at his native art form is the ludicrously bawdy, and self-explanatory, 'Big Bamboo'. Although he had an entirely successful career in front of the R&B big bands of the time, which continued into ska (his Independent Jamaica was the first release on Chris Blackwell's Island Records in 1962, plus he recorded regularly for COXSONE, DUKE REID and Randy's) and rock steady, Lord Creator's isn't a name that is readily associated with the music's early days. Strange really, because thanks to tunes like 'Don't Stay Out Late', 'Man To Man', 'I'm Holding On' and 'Little Princess', he was one of Jamaica's biggest stars during the early 1960s. Just not internationally.

But international success didn't come until about five years later, when the likes of DESMOND DEKKER, Nicky Thomas and BOB AND MARCIA had introduced the idea of reggae as a global pop music. When 'Kingston Town' hit – it sold tens of thousands in the UK without ever showing up in the charts – Lord Creator was virtually destitute in that same city. Happily, Eccles had the artist on a points deal rather than a flat payment and the royalties involved put Lord Creator back on his feet.

During the mid-1980s he returned to Trinidad, where he lives today, presumably off his share of UB40's enormous-selling version of the tune. A cover both he and Clancy Eccles endorsed when they appeared in the Birmingham group's video.

There are no Lord Creator albums available on CD, but 'Kingston Town' can be found on:
Dance Crasher – Ska To Rock Steady; Trojan CDTRL260
Nice An' Ruff – A Crucial Brew Of Roots, Dub And Rockers; Music Club MCCD 092

Desmond Dekker

➡ By the time Desmond Dekker acquired a UK postcode in 1969, he was already big on these shores. But all this was about to change. In the April of that year he became, officially, *enormous* when 'The Israelites' got to number 1 in the pop charts, the first ever reggae record to do so. The follow up, 'It Mek' (an updated version of an old rock steady tune) went Top 10, and the one after that, 'Problems', sold well even if it didn't make it into the mainstream charts. This all conspired to mean Dekker finished the year as the sixth best-selling male vocalist in Britain, ahead of Cliff Richard and Peter Sarstedt. Further to that, he took 'The Israelites' into the US Top 10, a unique achievement for a Jamaican artist.

'The Israelites' marked the beginning of a run of reggae in the UK charts that lasted nearly five years, but it was Dekker who actually kick-started this state of affairs. By moving here to capitalize on his earlier efforts, he gigged practically non-stop – both club dates and concerts, to core audiences and to increasing numbers of white skinheads – and, as a thoroughly entertaining performer so made the idea of reggae seem like far more fun than it might have been. Combine this with producer LESLIE KONG's acute commercial sensibilities and it was only a matter of time before the mainstream pop crowds took notice. When 'The Israelites' came out in the UK, it had already been a club and sound system favourite for some time, meaning that demand had built up over several months and record shops were being pestered for it. As a result, when it was finally released shops ordered enormous quantities, enough to have the record enter the charts at number 5. Radio couldn't ignore it. And with the resultant airplay, it got all the way to the top, in the meantime alerting the UK public at large to the joys of reggae.

While living in London, Dekker was recording vocals locally on to backing tapes sent over by Kong, and it was after the producer's death in 1971 that the string of hits began to dry up. Indeed, although he had minor success with such self-produced efforts as 'Sing A Little Song' and 'Hippopotamus', his biggest post-Kong hit was a re-release of 'The Israelites' in 1975.

In spite of remaining one of the most important figures in Reggae As An International Concern, Desmond Dekker was also yet another victim of the music's somewhat relaxed approach to bookkeeping: in 1984 he was declared bankrupt, citing management mishandling of earnings as probable cause. He still performs on a regular basis, accepting that, musically, his past is perhaps more interesting than his present.

The Best Of Desmond Dekker; Music Club International MCCD115

Kong-period Dekker, that doesn't waste its tracklisting on what went on after that. 'You Can Get It If You Really Want', 'Problems', 'The Israelites', 'Pickney Gal', 'It Mek' ... It's enough to make you go out and buy a tonik suit and pork-pie hat.

SEE ALSO:

Tougher Than Tough – The Story Of Jamaican Music; Mango IBXCD1
The Roots Of Reggae; Music Club MCBX003
Reggae Attack; Attack CDAT113
20 Reggae Classics Volume One; Trojan CDTRL222
20 Reggae Classics Volume Two; Trojan CDTRL224
Celebration – The Best Of Reggae – 25 Years Of Trojan Records; Quality QTVCD010

Clement 'Coxsone' Dodd

➦ It's safe to say that post-rock steady, at the very end of the 1960s and the beginning of the 1970s, Coxsone's previously pro-lific output slowed to a comparative trickle. Producers like LESLIE KONG, LEE PERRY, Lloyd Charmers, NINEY and JOE GIBBS – more than one of whom had learned their trade under Dodd – were carrying the swing as reggae began to shape itself beyond the pop style it initially became. Not that Coxsone was finished or anything like that. It's just that he wasn't as innova-tive as he had been back in the previous decade when he, PRINCE BUSTER and DUKE REID were virtually inventing Jamaican music as we'd come to know it. Dodd's influence around this time was indirect, but no less important.

The reggae that was coming out of Brentford Road at that time was far more subtle and restrained than that enjoying such a high profile in the UK. Not only were technical advances allowing music to be finished to a much more delicate level, but under the smoove tutelage of Jackie Mittoo, musical arranger for so much of what was being cut, the music was perhaps far closer to rock steady than elsewhere. It incorporated a lot of US sweet soul and southern soul influences, to offer an unsurpassed approach to melody and harmony which absorbed the reggae beat almost organically in a way that further enhanced the legendary Studio One warmth. Mittoo had by now switched wholeheartedly to the organ and his oozing, bubbling tones would be way out front of the mix to keep things even cooler. Subject matters were predominantly affairs of the heart, so what was happening here was really the founding father of what would later be called lovers' rock.

The starting point was THE HEPTONES' 'Pretty Looks Isn't All'. That trombone is melting all over a rock steady beat, and Sibbles and the guys are giving it up out front. From there Coxsone/Mittoo translated the hornlines to the softer sounds of the organ, pumped up the beat a bit to get that chopping synchronicity and, basically, didn't do much more than that. Suddenly, with not much more than a flick of your musical wrist, you've arrived at 'Melody Life' by MARCIA GRIFFITHS. Or 'Love Me Forever' by Carlton and His Shoes. Or 'What Kind Of World' by The Cables. This was the stuff that deejays played at about three in the morning at a ram-packed Dalston blues when people wanted just to feel nice and finally grab the gal they'd been eyeing up since midnight. Coxsone's old sound man instincts kept him precisely in tune with what *his* crowd wanted and he served it up with a series of serious reggae cuts from such artists as Cornell Campbell, DENNIS BROWN, DELROY WILSON, JOHN HOLT, DENNIS ALCAPONE, SLIM SMITH, JOHNNY OSBOURNE, Freddie Mackay, FREDDIE MCGREGOR, KEN BOOTHE, Ken Parker and HORACE ANDY.

It kept Studio One's stylistic integrity intact too. They had effectively brought the next wave of Jamaican music to them, rather than having to go out and meet it. It continued the Brentford Road commitment to a melody, even on the dub sides, which was what took Dodd forward even further. The new generation of deejays who were starting to make records wanted radio to pick them up, and so they needed tracks that were strong enough for them to climb all over or reduce to a bass 'n' drum riddim, yet still finish up with something that had a melody – they took to Studio One tunes like fish to a pond. As well as the deejays who were actually signed to the label, Dennis Alcapone was the groundbreaker, there were legions who just appropriated Studio One records – either vocal cuts or the numerous Soul Vendor instrumentals – and recorded over them. Jamaica had no copyright laws at the time, so more than a few Coxsone originals from the rock steady and early reggae eras have been versioned literally hundreds of times. And while Dodd or the original artists and writers wouldn't get a penny for this, it meant that old Studio One cuts were being presented to a new generation in a way that was entirely modern. It allowed what Dodd did to be almost organically updated and, with literally no effort whatsoever, stand ready for what was coming next. ••

For Studio One compilations covering this era, check the Coxsone entry in the previous section. The compilations cross time barriers – a handy overview of how it all fits together – but have been put in the earlier chapter as that's where it all began. Also, as was suggested on page 31, the best thing to do is to check the credits on albums by the artists mentioned above and see what was cut at Brentford Road. If you like some of it, then chances are you'll go for the rest as well.

Eric Donaldson

(Born 1947; Kingston, Jamaica; singer)
If you're going to be a One Hit Wonder, then that big record might as well be 'Cherry Oh Baby'. Produced by BYRON LEE in 1971, that year's Jamaica Festival Song Competition winner and an enormous hit on the island, it was one of those rare records that would lighten up a blues dance – everybody would join in the chorus – but at the same time its slow, sinewy bassline made it an unparalleled piece of rub-off-the-wallpaper deep lovers' rock rhythm. 'Cherry Oh Baby' stayed a sound system favourite in its original form for years, taking on an extended life through the ridiculous number of versions – deejay, singer and instrumental – and crossing over to make an impression on a respectable amount of mainstream buyers. Years later the song

regained its high profile by being covered by both UB40 and The Rolling Stones (Mick Jagger's fascination with reggae is legendary).

And this meant that the song stayed in the public eye much longer than Eric Donaldson himself. Just as he'd been recording all over town before he fetched up at Lee's Dynamic, so success on that scale eluded him once again. True, his 'Miserable Woman' enjoyed a lot of sound system play the next year – largely because us guys thought it was particularly sharp to sing it to our girlfriends – but other than that and numbers called 'Blue Boot' and 'What A Festival', the singer's biggest moments were confined to the Festival Song Competition which he won a further four times. Today he owns and runs the Cherry Oh Baby Bar outside Kingston, occasionally getting up on stage more as a hobby than a career move. Presumably some of the money from sales of his one monster song found its way back to him.

*Love of the Common People; Jamaican Gold JMC200115

The most important thing is that this has got 'Cherry Oh Baby' on it, but more than that it'll give you 'Blue Boots' and 'What A Festival'. There's also a rather bizarre reggae cover of 'Sylvia's Mother', but Eric Donaldson's falsetto isn't really enough to stay interesting across a whole album – that's why his success was so sporadic, as it was always much more about the songs.

There are a couple of hard-to-find Eric Donaldson Best Ofs on CD, featuring different permutations of his better known tracks – 'Miserable Woman' included – so there's probably little to choose between them and the above.

Meanwhile, 'Cherry Oh Baby' can be found on:
Trojan Explosion; Trojan CDTRL246
Tougher Than Tough – The Story Of Jamaican Music; Mango IBXCD1
20 Reggae Classics Volume One; Trojan CDTRL222
From Bam Bam To Cherry Oh Baby; Jamaican Gold JMC200 101
Monkey Business (20 Skinhead Hits); Trojan CDTRD407

Errol Dunkley

(Born 1951; Kingston, Jamaica; singer)

It's unfortunate that one of the enduring memories of Errol Dunkley is of him performing his UK Top 10 hit, a cartoon version of John Holt's 'OK Fred', on BBC Children's TV with all the integrity of Lenny Henry's Algernon Razzmatazz. There was always much more to him than this – after all, this was the man who wrote 'Little Way Different', which became a roots/lovers' classic, and was a founding partner in GREGORY ISAACS' African Museum record label. It was during this early reggae period that Dunkley established himself as a singer of note. He'd been cutting late-model ska and rock steady tunes for the likes of PRINCE BUSTER, JOE GIBBS and COXSONE since he was barely out of short trousers, but it was at the end of the 1960s that he settled down into a reggae groove as the new style proved perfect for his light, lilting alto voice. Among his early successes were 'Get Up Now' for Studio One, a reggae-style re-recording of earlier rock steady numbers entitled 'Three In One', the rather marvellous 'Black Cinderella' and a tune that was one of the London sound systems' rub-up regulars, 'Darling Ooh'. However, it was in the 1970s that he made the most impact. He wrote and had a hit with the first, somewhat lighter, version of 'Little Way Different', he changed DELROY WILSON's 'I Don't Know Why' into 'Movie Star' and broke big again, while other successes included 'Where Must I Go', 'Down Below' and 'Baby I Love You'.

Although Errol Dunkley's voice was never disagreeable, it tended to lack the character to make anything special out of average material. When the roots revolution happened he did well, provided what (and who) he had to work with was good – he did well in the studio with NINEY and, of course, the DENNIS BOVELL reworking of 'Little Way Different' – but he contributed little to this new development. Then came 'OK Fred'!

Darling Ooh; Attack CDAT117

Originally entitled *Presenting Errol Dunkley*, this was cut with SONIA POTTINGER in 1972. It's particularly effective as Pottinger's light touch brings out the best in Dunkley's plaintive voice, making sure the melodies lift him up rather than drag him down and swamp him. As well as 'Little Way Different', we have 'Movie Star', 'Created By The Father', 'You'll Never

Know', 'Baby I Love You' and 'It Was Nice While It Lasted'. While this set may not have the gustiness of the later material – which says more about the producers than the star – it's probably the finest presentation of what Dunkley does best, which is sing gentle love songs.

SEE ALSO:

*Errol Dunkley and Sly and Robbie: *OK Fred*; Rhino RNCD2017

20 Reggae Classics Volume Three; Trojan CDTRL256

Remarkably, there is no Errol Dunkley whatsoever on *Tougher Than Tough – The Story Of Jamaican Music* (Mango IBXCD1). Why not? What's wrong with 'Little Way Different'?

Clancy Eccles

(Born 1941; Kingston, Jamaica; singer/producer)
Although there are no dedicated Clancy Eccles CDs on the market at the moment, the man had his own Trojan imprint, Clandisc, and an enormous following among black and white kids for about five years starting around 1968. Also, as his work crops up so frequently on Trojan compilations – but, amazingly, not on *Tougher Than Tough – The Story Of Jamaican Music* – I figured he was worth the inclusion.

After recording a number of ska and rock steady sides for COXSONE and SONIA POTTINGER – the most successful were 'River Jordan', 'Freedom' and 'Sammy No Dead' – Eccles branched out by himself in 1967. It has been said he deeply resented what he saw as exploitation on the part of the big producers, and it's common knowledge he played a major role in talking LEE 'SCRATCH' PERRY into leaving Coxsone in 1968 – Eccles was musical arranger on Scratch's anti-Dodd hit 'People Funny Boy'. But Eccles didn't really hit his stride until the next year when he scored huge with the early toasting records 'Fire Corner', Herbman', 'Herbsman Shuffle', 'Vigorton 2', 'Dance Beat' and 'The Ugly One' by King Stitt, a none-too-pretty deejay who was equally well known by the latter song's title! It's no coincidence that Stitt was one of Coxsone's top sound system deejays either. But what Eccles managed to do, which relatively few others did at that time, was capture the excitement of the dancehall on record with a brilliant balance between Stitt's whooping and the backing track's rhythm. And he put it together in such a way that it sold by the truckload in the UK – maybe because his productions on Stitt were always aware the deejay was *part* of the record, not just something grafted on top.

Eccles was the man behind the work of misty-eyed genius that is LORD CREATOR's 'Kingston Town'. He cut Cynthia Richards' 'Foolish Fool'. And he did well for himself too: his bawdy anthem 'Fattie Fattie' has long been a dancehall classic, while 'Freedom' and 'Africa' displayed his fierce political leanings. A bent so strong that in 1972 he took up a post within Michael Manley's government, as consultant on all things music business – by now, it was officially acknowledged how important reggae was for the economy. That was more or less the end of Clancy Eccles's career, and although he continued recording through the 1980s he now concentrates his efforts and expertise managing his singing son.

Examples of Clancy Eccles at the controls can be found on:
The Trojan Story Part One; Trojan CDTAL 100
20 Reggae Classics Volume One; Trojan CDTRL 222
20 Reggae Classics Volume Two; Trojan CDTRL 224
20 Reggae Classics Volume Four; Trojan CDTRL 284

Joe Gibbs

(Born Joel Gibson, 1945; Montego Bay, Jamaica; producer)
Although Joe Gibbs's direct contribution will not be felt until the mid-1970s and the unstoppable rise of roots reggae, and in spite of there being no dedicated CDs of Gibbs's rock steady and early reggae productions, his presence was such that he has more than earned his place in this section.

Originally an electrical equipment repairman, when he expanded his business into a shop in the early 1960s, he used some of the extra space to sell records. Which, pricking his love of music into positive action, led him to start producing them and to set up his own label, Jogib, in 1966. Immediately grasping the new rock steady style, Gibbs had early success with such genre classics as the highly influential 'Hold Them' by Roy Shirley, STRANGER COLE's 'Just Like A River' and Lyn Taitt's 'El Casino Royale'. However, it was as the music shifted to the reggae beat that he began to come into his own. By the end of the decade he had fallen back on his skill with the soldering iron and had built what was a fairly sophisticated two-track studio in the shop. And, maybe because of this relative hi-techness, it was very much the place to be. A veritable nursery slopes for the original reggae stars: The Slickers, ERROL DUNKLEY, Jimmy London, The Reggae Boys and JUNIOR BYLES all started off with Gibbs; Nicky Thomas recorded the big UK hit 'Love Of The Common People' there; THE PIONEERS' Long Shot Period took place under Gibbs's wing and THE HEPTONES turned up there after leaving Studio One to record a series of classics including 'Freedom For The People', 'God Bless The Children' and a re-recording of 'Hypocrite'. Although it could be said that by that time Gibbs's role was more to do with overseeing what the producers he employed were doing, his influence is undeniable. And don't forget, these producers included such class acts as LEE PERRY (who did quite a long spell there after leaving Coxsone), NINEY and Errol T. All names who provided the groundwork for what was to be Gibbs's most memorable work. But that wasn't going to happen until well into reggae's next development.

*Various Artists: *The Heptones And Friends Volumes One and Two*; Trojan CDTRL357

The Heptones, Save The Last Dance For Me, Hypocrite; **Julie Anne**, The Gardener; **The Heptones**, Our Day Will Come; **Nicky Thomas**, Have A Little Faith; **The Heptones**, Freedom For The People, Every Day And Every Night; **Peter Tosh**, Maga Dog; **The Heptones**, God Bless The Children, Love Has Many Faces; **Nicky Thomas**, Mama's Song; **Ken Parker**, The Dynamic Ken Parker (a medley of 'Prisoner Of Love', 'True True True', 'My Whole World Is Falling Down' and 'The Chokin' Kind'); **Peter Tosh**, Them A Fe Get A Beatin'; **The Heptones**, The Magnificent Heptones ('Baby', 'Why Must I?', 'Why Did You Leave'); **Jackie Brown**, People Of Today; **The Ethiopians**, The

Ring; **Uriel Aldrel**, Let True Love Begin; **Dennis Brown**, Money In My Pocket; **Alton Ellis**, Knock On Wood; **The Heptones**, I've Got A Feeling; **The Versatiles**, Wareika Hill; **Delroy Wilson**, Baby I Need Your Loving; **Big Youth**, A So We Stay.

This CD is both volumes of the original, by-now-impossible-to-find vinyl albums that wonderfully sum up Joe Gibbs in his pre-roots phase. They even go some way to explain his graduation into the next development by going as far as BIG YOUTH, PETER TOSH, THE ETHIOPIANS and The Versatiles. Naturally, the sets concentrate on The Heptones, as they were Gibbs's biggest act back then, and although their tracklisting contains a worrying amount of MOR-ish cover versions, this shouldn't serve to put anybody off. The trio's sheer soul power is unstoppable; in fact the undeniable catchiness of numbers like 'Save The Last Dance For Me' and 'Love Has Many Faces' only seems to spur them on. Thus we end up with some of the classi-est pop reggae there was. Not just from Leroy Sibbles and the boys either, but also Nicky Thomas, Dennis Brown and Ken Parker. Plus it's good to see that the likes of Julie Anne and Jackie Brown won't be forgotten.

*Joe Gibbs and Friends: *The Reggae Train 1968–1971*; Trojan CDTRL261

Lee Perry, The Upsetter; **The Versatiles**, Trust The Book; **Lee Perry**, Kimble; **Sir Gibbs**, People Grudgeful; **The Reggae Boys**, Me No Born Yah; **The Young Souls**, Man A Wail; **The Immortals**, Bongo Jah; **The Slickers**, Man Beware; **The Tommy McCook Band**, Soulful Mood; **The Joe Gibbs Allstars**, Hijacked; **Ken Parker**, It's Alright; **The Soul Mates**, Jump It Up; **The Reggae Boys**, The Wicked Must Survive; **The Slickers**, Mother Matty; **The Versatiles**, Push It In; **The Reggae Boys**, The Reggae Train; **Ken Parker**, Only Yesterday; **Peter Tosh**, Arise Blackman.

Not the most obvious Joe Gibbs selection, but by far the better for it. Put together by Steve Barrow and probably worth the asking price for that scorching instrumental 'Hijacked' alone.

Greyhound

(It's proved impossible to track down details of the group members, and the most popular theory is that they were anonymous session singers hired in for the occasion.)
One of the very few British-based reggae groups making music aimed solely at the UK market. This group were really the culmination of the Trojan philosophy of taking the poppiest, most melodic reggae, sweetening it up even further, then going for the pop hit riding off the back of the older Jamaicans who tended to approve of this sort of thing – music with a distinct back home feel, but which adapted itself so as to fit in with the host market.

'Black And White' was as dumb a piece of pop optimism as ought to be allowed, but it was kind of fun. Like the group themselves. While they have earned their place in this book by epitomizing exactly how far reggae could go pop and still stay, technically, reggae, they were too insubstantial to make it last. Over the course of about a year they hit the UK charts three times – as well as 'Black And White', there was 'Moon River' (January 1972) and 'I Am What I Am' (March 1972) – and just missed out on a couple of other occasions. Then, after riding out the fag end of the pop reggae boom playing live up and down the British Isles, they called it a day in the middle of the decade when that sort of music really didn't count for anything any more.

*Black And White; See For Miles C5CD539

As well as the title track, there's a generous helping of Greyhound schmaltz in the shape of 'Dream Lover', 'Unchained Melody' and 'Only Love Can Win'. Why the other two hits aren't there is completely beyond me.

Derrick Harriot

►► By the time reggae broke, the man they called The Chariot was in full flight. Capitalizing on the smoove rock steady reputation he'd built up, Derrick Harriot eased into reggae in a move that, he claimed at the time, suited him down to the ground, simply because it allowed him greater scope. It gave him more room to make the most of covering the new style of US soul – Harriot's Afro was always one of pre-roots reggae's better moments; the space to expand the way of doing things to bring back the instrumental as an end in itself; the means to introduce to the music the kind of broad-based black nationalism that was being established in America, as opposed to purely local politics; and the chance to produce the kind of pop-songs-with-attitude-reggae that Harriot understood so completely. There is a story, verified by more than one person, that right after ERIC DON-ALDSON won the Festival Song Contest with 'Cherry Oh Baby', he 'tore the theatre up' looking for Derrick Harriot to ask him to produce it on record. Apparently, it's only after the singer could-n't find Harriot (he'd opted to stay with his girlfriend instead of going to the show) that he did a deal with BYRON LEE.

By this time Harriot had achieved financial independence and was running his Crystal and Move 'N' Groove labels in a way that allowed creative freedom without the serious overhead of a recording studio: he'd rehearse and experiment with his musi-cians at great length in the large room at the back of the record shop he owned, and only when they'd achieved exactly what he wanted would he hire a studio. And then, in true Jamaican style, once the tape started rolling there'd be the regulation amount of improvization. This resulted in some of the most exciting early reggae, which, in spite of its accessibility, never made much of an impact in the UK outside of the specialist markets.

Harriot worked on material for his own honeyed tones – a sensational cut of 'Riding For A Fall', a reggaefied version of KEN BOOTHE's rock steady great 'Home Home Home', a cover of The Temptations' 'Message From A Black Man', and all points in between these. He produced all manner of other artists – DENNIS BROWN, Nicky Thomas, Eric Donaldson, The King-stonians ('Singer Man' is a Harriot production), Scotty (some of the first deejay recordings in 1970 and 1971) and Glen Brown, to name but a few. But, most importantly, Harriot worked with his regular backing group The Crystalites (Lloyd Charmers, Boris Gardiner, 'Deadly' Headley Bennett, Vin Gordon, Lyn Taitt, Bongo Herman and so on) to put out a succession of instrumen-tal tunes based on the spaghetti westerns that were so popular in West Kingston cinemas. Although this wasn't an original move – what Harriot was doing was following the lead taken by LEE PERRY's Upsetters and their highly popular Django series – he took it beyond the cowboy theme to produce a thoroughly rounded collection of some of the best instrumentals that weren't cut at Studio One. Understandably, given the UK success enjoyed by The Upsetters, Dave and Ansil Collins and HARRY J, it was these spikey instrumentals that found favour among a dance-happy skinhead audience, and by 1970 Trojan had turned their Song Bird subsidiary label exclusively over to Derrick Harriot productions.

From these inventive instrumentals it was never going to take a man like Derrick Harriot too long to arrive at dub reggae. Or much longer to find his way down to KING TUBBY's studios in Waterhouse. Harriot had experimented with his own mild dub mixes, more as complicated arrangements from as far back as 1970, but the first brass neck dub cuts came with the *Scrub A Dub* album four years later. It was one of the very first dub albums, and featured different, spectacular Tubby mixes of a few hand-picked Crystalites tunes. It was received so well by both sound systems and consumers alike that the next year produced *More Scrubbing The Dub*, and the same approach achieved more or less equal acclaim. Both of these albums shifted large amounts of expensive import copies in the UK, and totally reclaimed Harriot from his skinhead fanbase, not least thanks to the cartoon dancehall scenes on the covers and the, at the time, outrageous titles. It was as if the LPs brought more than just the music of Kingston to the chilly streets of north London. These are among the greatest dub albums ever made, and twenty years later each mix still sounds as fresh as it did when King Tubby cut them, while just a glance at the sleeves invokes ever more misty-eyed memories.

Derrick Harriot dipped a toe in roots reggae around this time as well. Always a proud black nationalist, even from when he was recording schmaltzy cover versions of American hits he welcomed Rasta's growing prominence. During the second half of the 1970s he produced some very credible roots music with artists like AUGUSTUS PABLO, I-ROY, Bongo Herman and Ray-I. But he never went too far down that road. Maybe it simply wasn't for him and he didn't feel entirely confident up against the rising young stars of the next generation. Remember, by now he'd been in the music business for over two decades.

Derrick Harriot continued recording throughout the 1980s, mostly reverting to his natural environment of soulful reggae versions of US hits, and today runs his profitable record labels, licensing and retail business from his base in Constance Springs, Kingston. Anyone who has been to the shop will testify as to how he is obviously enjoying his role as one of reggae's elder statesmen and most intact survivors. However, it is said it doesn't take a great deal of coaxing to get him up on a stage.

14 Chartbuster Hits; Crystal CRCD01

The first half-dozen or so on this set are what Harriot does brilliantly – R&B-ish (almost doo-wop) crooning. While they may not be strictly reggae, or even remotely reggae for that matter, they show where Harriot's gentle lovers' rock reggae came from. But once they're out of the way, The Musical Chariot gets into stride with some superb reggae. At this point his approach to a beat was always up, with the bass and drum taking the perky, bubbling option, further buoyed up by bright piano or guitar lead lines and an always prominent melody. 'Standing In', 'Born To Love You', 'Walk The Streets' and a reggae-ed up cover of The Chi-Lites' 'Have You Seen Her' display Harriot the singer in the best possible light. 'Psychedelic Train' is about as odd as the title might suggest, and shows how Harriot was thinking 'dub' way before the term became official. 'Lollipop Girl' and 'Sugar Dandy' are The Jiving Juniors' finest moments revisited. But the real gem on this set is 'Solomon', the original cut of the tune on which so many of Harriot's wild west instrumentals were based.

Derrick Harriot And The Crystalites: *For A Fistful Of Dollars*; Jamaican Gold JMC200211

'Undertaker, make me three coffins' . . . 'My mistake, make that four!' Dialogue outrageously filched from The Man With No Name opens this totally serious instrumental album. They're the opening words from 'The Undertaker', which is built on the 'Solomon' rhythm and serves as a marvellous statement of intent for a set that runs to such thematic titles as 'True Grit', 'A

Fistful Of Dollars', 'The Overtaker', 'The Undertaker's Burial' and, rather ominously for those who remember the film from which the album takes its name, 'Ramon's Last Remark'. It's not all shoot-em-up, though: Harriot's crisp, sometimes startling method of instrumental arrangement relies on a strong rhythm with all manner of gimmicks and solo breaks ushered in to whip the tune into a tightly synchronized top gear. Then he applies this notion to an almost unrecognizable version of The Beatles' 'Lady Madonna' and such mellower numbers as 'Biafra', 'Musical Madness' and 'Tonight'. The first twelve tracks are the original vinyl album, with the final five as bonus recordings. With this new, digitally enhanced clarity these are timeless reminders of how musically powerful instrumental reggae could be in the hands of somebody as good as Derrick Harriot.

*_Songs For Midnight Lovers_; Trojan CDTRL198

Much of this crosses over with the reggae tracks on *14 Chartbuster Hits*, but this album comes into its own by going into The Chariot's later career and including such gems as 'No Man Is An Island', 'Message From A Black Man', 'Eighteen With a Bullet' and 'Groovy Situation'.

***Various Artists**: _From The Chariots's Vaults Volume Two – Sixteen Reggae Hits_; Jamaican Gold JMC200215

Nicky Thomas, Gypsy; **Keith and Tex**, Down The Street; **Junior Soul**, The Hustler; **Tinga and Ernie**, She's Gone; **The Prunes**, Come A Little Closer; **Glenmore Brown**, Love I; **Noel Brown**, The Phoenix; **Rudy Mills**, Lemi-Lemi-Li; **Bongo Les and The Chrystalites**, Home Sweet Home; **Tinga Stewart**, Hear That Train; **The Kingstonians**, Right From Wrong; **Denzil Laing**, Medicine Stick; **Bongo Herman and Bingy Bunny**, Freedom Fighters; **I-Roy**, Melinda; **Augustus Pablo**, The Bells Of Death; **Augustus, Derrick and Fay**, Bedroom Mazurka.

Backed by The Crystalites and given Harriot's bright treatment, this shows how if an approach is strong enough it can stretch across a number of different executions with neither side suffering. The majority is smoove lovers' rock – The Kingstonians,

Noel Brown and Tinga and Ernie stand out – but it moves up to the embryonic roots styles of Augustus Pablo and Bongo Herman and Bingy Bunny. The final track even proves that a respectable family man like Derrick Harriot was entirely capable of getting rude! A kicking cross-section of the man's reggae days.

SEE ALSO:

The Sensational Derrick Harriot Sings Jamaican Rock Steady – Reggae; Jamaican Gold JMC200 213 (discussed in detail in the previous section)
20 Reggae Classics Volume Three; Trojan CDTRL 256
The Magnificent Fourteen – 14 Shots Of Western Inspired Reggae; CDTRL283
Yesterday – 16 Fab Beatle Reggae Classics; Trojan CDTRL 294

Harry J

(Born Harry Johnson, 1945; Kingston, Jamaica; producer)
This man will always be remembered as the guy who nicked The Staples Singers' 'I'll Take You There' bassline and parlayed it into an enormous reggae hit both in Jamaica and the UK. But his story didn't start and finish with The Harry J Allstars' one-off hit. In fact that wasn't even the first time he'd appropriated that bassline! A musician-turned-insurance-salesman, Johnson opted for production in 1968 and straightaway found something he was good enough at to give up selling pension plans. Among his first recordings was The Beltones' enormous JA hit 'No More Heartaches' and he was up and running. He followed it up with 'Cuss Cuss' (Lloyd Robinson), 'Shine Eye Gal' (Vince Foster) and, the first time he used that Staples Singers' riff, 'What Am I To Do?' (Tony Scott), each one smoove and steady. And they weren't only JA hits – they made a reasonable impression on the British market too. And it was there that he was about to hit huge. By taking the vocal off 'What Am I To Do?' and replacing it with a bubbling lead line from organist Winston Wright, he upped the tempo and took the song to number 9 in the UK charts in November 1969 – quite literally a foot-stomping skinhead classic as the more-on-the-case boot-boys would stamp in time

to the four popping beats that finished off the chorus' riffs. Early the next year, he continued to prove he had the measure of the international market when his equally bouncy 'Young Gifted And Black' took BOB AND MARCIA to number 5.

Then as the 1970s rolled around, Harry J seemed to drop out of sight, preferring to concentrate on building a state-of-the-art studio that became the preferred environment for such roots stars as BURNING SPEAR, AUGUSTUS PABLO, BOB MARLEY and CULTURE, but his role was strictly administration. Although he popped up occasionally with pop reggae classics like 'Breakfast In Bed', 'Skank In Bed' and 'The Bed's Too Big Without You', THE HEPTONES' rather wonderful *Party Time* album – although much of the credit for that must go to Leroy Sibbles' arrangements – plus a host of locally successful deejay records and sound system one-offs, for the last twenty years he has concentrated on running his studio and keeping it at the cutting edge of available technology.

*Harry J and Friends: *The Return Of The Liquidator*; Trojan CDTRD412

The original *Liquidator* album – which, essentially, is the hit and a bunch of other organ led instrumentals that, other than 'Reach For The Sky' and 'Jack The Ripper', are pretty dull. But then the second CD in this set is the best of Harry J's early productions: a couple from The Beltones', 'What Am I To Do?', 'Young Gifted And Black'; and a few surprises in the shape of two saxophone scorchers from Val Bennett, 'Festive Spirit' (Dave Barker and Glen Brown) and Glen Adams' 'Rich In Love'. Although the album's got enough Harry J Allstars instrumentals to keep The Liquidator's fan club happy, it's also all the proof you'll need that there was more to the man.

The Heptones

•• In 1971 The Heptones left Studio One. It was not a happy parting. Leroy Sibbles maintains it was for both artistic and financial reasons, inasmuch as they were, by then, among the biggest stars on the label but were still being treated as jobbing singers and were being held back as reggae began to blossom into a much wider form. All this was particularly galling for him as he'd been responsible for so much of the label's vocal output, both as an arranger and talent scout. But while the likes of us can only speculate as to what might have been had the group stayed and the relationship remained cheerful, the change of scenery seemed to do The Heptones no harm at all. Such was their reputation after the Studio One hits, they virtually had a queue of producers looking to sign them up. JOE GIBBS was the one they went to first, which became something of a dream ticket, as the producer's shrewd ear for commercialism gelled perfectly with the trio's sweet rootsy harmonies to produce a musical feast lasting the best part of two years. And after they left Gibbs, they seemed to go from strength to strength, cutting new tunes or updated versions of their old ones with just about every producer in town – PABLO, Harry Mudie, RUPIE EDWARDS to name but three. The best was yet to come, though.

It was around 1974 when the group hooked up with LEE PERRY and it was as if they'd come home. Scratch's sensibilities were perfect for The Heptones at precisely that time – he understood roots reggae so well he could adapt it to anything he wanted; he was in the forefront of the escalating technological revolution in Jamaica's studios; his productions were so warm they virtually glowed; and he never forgot that every great record has to start with a good tune. The Heptones cut an album called *Party Time* for Perry, which versioned a lot of their Studio One successes to reinvent the works as some of the best cool roots music ever made. The album remains a reggae classic. But it was more or less the group's swansong. They went on to cut some crisp singles for HARRY J during the first half of the 1970s, including the magnificent 'Country Boy', 'Book Of Rules' and 'Mama Say', but these tended to get overly overdubbed with strings on UK release so are not, perhaps, appreciated for the cool roots wonders they were.

However, in terms of sheer consistency and sly innovation, nothing really came close to the Lee Perry sessions. When Sibbles left in 1977, he was replaced by Naggo Morris and The Heptones' eleven-year stint at the top was effectively over. All original members remain active today, and, happily, the current revival trend has meant they get together with increasing frequency.

*Various Artists: *The Heptones* And Friends Volumes One and Two; Trojan CDTRL357

Covered in detail in the earlier Joe Gibbs entry, this is the best possible record of the group's time with him. And the most interesting easily available example of The Heptones from this period.

*Night Food; Island RRCD19

Post-Perry and just before the-break up, this 1976 album is, simultaneously, exhilarating and a frustration. It's largely a collection of re-recordings of the trio's finest moments – 'I've Got The Handle', 'Fattie Fattie', 'Book Of Rules' among them – which can never be ignored. And the chance to pick them up in glorious digital clarity shouldn't be missed. But it's produced by Danny Holloway, and while there's nothing actually wrong with it, compared with the almost frightening three-dimensionality Lee Perry gave to his work it sounds flat. However, I'm probably being overly picky, and if you've never heard the Perry stuff you'll quite rightly love this.

For some reason the *Party Time* album is no longer available in its original form on CD. The only other Heptones CD dealing with reggae rather than rock steady is *Good Vibes* (Prestige, CDSGP 048), and as Leroy Sibbles is not part of the line-up at this point it doesn't really count.

SEE ALSO:

Lee Perry: *Reggae Greats*; Mango RRCD10
Tougher Than Tough – The Story Of Jamaican Music; Mango IBXCD1
Out Of Many, One – Jamaican Music Part Two; Trojan CDTRS2
Rupie Edwards And Friends: *Let There Be Version*; Trojan CDTRL280

John Holt

(Born 1948; Kingston, Jamaica; singer)
For somebody who grew up with John Holt Mk 1, it's always

been hard to come to terms with what he became. By the end of the 1970s he'd grown his beard and his dreadlocks and was recording some righteous roots reggae. But the time we're concerned with in this chapter involved pure pop and such delights as *The John Holt Reggae Christmas Album* and covers of lounge music specials like 'The Girl From Ipenema' and 'Alfie'. Not that this was nearly as schmaltzy as it might have been. John Holt's rich tenor could give anything an injection of soul, while the crisp productions behind him always kept it on the tougher side of that street marked Easy Listening.

Holt was another child star of the Vere Johns Talent Shows, winning on a regular basis since the age of eleven and capitalizing on his ready-made audience five years later when he began recording for LESLIE KONG in 1963. Then, at age eighteen, he joined THE PARAGONS to become lead singer during the group's most successful period – 'Happy Go lucky Girl', 'War You To The Ball', 'The Tide Is High' and so on – which lasted up to the end of the decade. In fact it was largely down to Holt's charisma and vocal presence at the front of the group that kept DUKE REID up with what THE HEPTONES were doing over at Studio One.

But, in terms of sales and profile, this was just the beginning for Holt. He quit the group at the end of 1970, to join up with BUNNY LEE – a man who understood the true nature of easy-action love-song-style reggae – and, straight out of the gate, cut 'Stick By Me'. An instant classic, Jamaica's biggest selling record of the year, a sound system smash in the UK. From there John Holt became the undisputed Don when it came to cool lovers' rock reggae. The trick was to get pre-release copies brought in from Jamaica as, by the time much of his stuff got British release, additional strings and keyboards had sweetened tunes so far it made your teeth hurt just to think about them. (Mind you, it worked. During the early 1970s John Holt had a string of UK mainstream chart hits, culminating with 'Help Me Make It Through The Night', which spent five weeks in the Top 20.)

Not that it made any difference to how John Holt was perceived by his core audience. His Harry Mudie-produced *Time Is The Master* album (1974) is a byword in Jamaican balladeering, while the *Volts Of Holt* series cut for Bunny Lee further defines the island's obsession with covering US hits. As the decade progressed, Holt edged towards a rootsier approach, which came as a surprise only to his pop fans. For although he never rammed it down anybody's throat, Holt had never shied away from nationalistic numbers – few made it to the UK as anything other than import singles, but one of his early solo albums was called *Still In Chains*, with the title song stating that slavery had been abolished in name only. So when he cut the deep roots rhythm 'Up Park Camp', it seemed like a natural progression, as did the drawing of a locksed up John Holt on the cover of *The Further You Look* (although it was a collection of silky-tonsilled love songs!). But what did cause a few raised eyebrows was Holt's latter-day signature tune, 1987's 'Police In Helicopter'. The rhyme went 'Police in helicopter/They come fe look fe marijuana', and it proved a little too much for the mums and dads who'd always seen the singer as a bastion of respectability.

Still working, Holt has flirted with just about every style from disco to rap to ragga, but remains best known for some of the most brilliant balladeering to come out of Jamaica. If you hear the original cut of 'Stick By Me' at a dance today, you're pretty much guaranteed a result.

Time Is The Master; Rhino RNCD2002

This is the classic, vintage, undisputed champion John Holt. The luxuriant, strong tenor pipes, the totally three-dimensional Harry Mudie productions and a collection of smoove, street-smart songs that combine to present the absolute best in Jamaican popular music – in the dictionary definition of the term. Just wallow through a tracklisting that boasts 'Stick By Me', 'Looking Back', 'Riding For A Fall' and 'Everybody Knows' as well as the title cut itself. Each one was a London sound system regular, both in original form and the countless versions that tunes this strong can take. A genuine Jamaican gem.

1000 Volts Of Holt; Trojan CDTRL75

This 1973 album is the first in a series of LPs recorded by Bunny Lee – there was also a *2,000* and *3,000 Volts Of* – and the only one still available. It's also the best of the trilogy, and as it's the one that features a reggaefied reading of 'The Girl From Ipenema' then you know it must be pretty good! Its focus is covers of US hits: '(You've Got Me Going) Stoned Out Of My Mind', 'Killing Me Softly With Her Song' and 'Help Me Make It Through The Night' are stand-out tracks, with the last of these providing a good example of what made this apparent gloop-fest work – it would be shifted up several gears with Lee's buoyant arrangements and taut rhythms, turning a potential dirge into a lively skank. It's an approach applied to the whole album.

ALSO RECOMMENDED:

*Reggae Christmas Hits Album; Trojan CDTRL230

Guaranteed to break the ice at parties, this fully festive occasion features John Holt in both a crooning ('When A Child Is Born' and 'Lonely This Christmas') and kicking rub-a-dub style ('Santa Claus Is Coming To Town', 'White Christmas' and 'My Oh My'). Not nearly as bad as some might imagine!

*20 Golden Love Songs; Trojan CDTRL192

The sort of record you'd have bought your mum for Christmas twenty-odd years ago, but is much better than you think. Holt at his most lurrrvesome, with tracks collected from the *Volts Of* series, including 'Rainy Night In Georgia', 'Touch Me In The Morning', 'When I Fall In Love', 'Too Good To Be Forgotten' and 'You'll Never Find Another Love Like Mine'.

SEE ALSO:

20 Reggae Blockbusters; Trojan CDTRL176
20 Reggae Classics Volume Two; Trojan CDTRL224
The Trojan Story; Trojan CDTRD402
Tougher Than Tough – The Story Of Jamaican Music; Mango IBXCD1
Yesterday – 16 Fab Beatle Reggae Classics; Trojan CDTRL294 (John Holt's contribution is a version of 'Hey Jude')

Unfortunately, *The John Holt Reggae Christmas Album* has yet to be released on CD. In original vinyl form it features such festive cheer as 'I Believe In Father Christmas', 'Santa Claus Is Coming To Town', 'Auld Lang Syne' and 'Lonely This Christmas'. On the other hand, maybe its lack of digital availability isn't such a bad thing after all.

Leslie Kong

•• As mentioned in the previous section, Leslie Kong was one of the few producers *not* to own a sound system, and so, without the need to keep a hyped-up crowd on their toes all night, he was far freer to experiment in the studio. Also, he was a record retailer, so was well aware of what people actually wanted to take home. He knew it wasn't necessarily the tuffest rhythms that would find favour on the family radiogram, but the ones that would stand playing over and over again, and the ones that wouldn't be removed too far from whatever was on the radio – which was still very American-influenced. He took to the emerging sounds of reggae as a golden opportunity to feed in outside influences in a way that would broaden the music and give it a bit of a lift abroad to continue the international success he'd had with early DESMOND DEKKER stuff. This has often been given short shrift for softening or commercializing the music, which is grossly unfair. Kong broadened it and its appeal. Pure and simple. Whether he softened or lightened it is irrelevant. And as for the wails of 'commerciality', point me out any producer making records, anywhere in the music business at any time, who didn't want to sell as many copies as possible.

Kong made the transition into reggae with enormous ease, opening his account with Desmond Dekker's 'The Israelites' – the first reggae record to become a UK pop chart number 1 – while tunes by DERRICK MORGAN, KEN BOOTHE, JIMMY CLIFF, THE MAYTALS and THE PIONEERS turned out to be, from an export perspective, among the most accessible Jamaican music so far. His Beverley's productions – released in the UK mostly on Pyramid or Trojan – weren't nearly as rigid as other producers' work, meaning he and his arrangers used the possibilities offered up by reggae's inherent spaciousness to stir in deftly other poppier influences and secondary rhythm patterns. His bassline rhythms were always enormously strong – it was easily Kong as much as anybody else who advanced the cause of the bass guitar within Jamaican music – allowing the extra emphasis on melody not to damage the original vibes. This, and his insistence on the best musicians, welcoming their creative input, gave Kong's work enormous home crowd credibility while it refused to throw up the barriers to anybody else.

Maybe this was down to Kong's not being black. Or perhaps he was just far shrewder than he's ever been given credit for. Big Kong records were The Pioneers' 'Long Shot', Ken Boothe's 'Freedom Street', Jimmy Cliff's 'Wonderful World, Beautiful People' and 'Many Rivers To Cross', THE WAILERS' *Best Of The Wailers* album and, of course, THE MELODIANS' 'Sweet Sensation' and 'Rivers Of Babylon', an arrangement which was used, virtually unchanged, for the massive Boney M pop hit.

Sadly, Leslie Kong died of a heart attack in 1971. His death occurred not long after his accountant told him he was reggae's first millionaire. It would have been so good to see how he and his open-minded approach would have succeeded through reggae's changing future.

*The Best Of Beverley's Records; Trojan CDTRL199

Bob Marley and the Wailers, Soul Shakedown Party; **The Gaylads**, There's A Fire; **The Maytals**, She's A Scorcher; **Peter Tosh**, Soon Come; **Ken Boothe**, It's Gonna Take A Miracle; **Bruce Ruffin**, I'm The One; **The Melodians**, It Took A Miracle; **Bruce Ruffin**, Dry Up Your Tears; **Bob Marley and The Wailers**, Caution; **Ken Boothe**, Now I Know; **Peter Tosh**, Stop That Train; **The Melodians**, Rock It With Me; **The Pioneers**, Battle Of The Giants; **Bob Marley and the Wailers**, Cheer Up.
A marvellous opportunity to see how what Kong did worked so well in a number of different contexts.

Other than that, for Kong on CD check out The Wailers' *In The Beginning* (Trojan CDTRL221), discs by the other artists mentioned above, just about any Trojan compilation, especially *Celebration: The Best Of Reggae – 25 Years Of Trojan Records* (Trojan CDTRD413), and, as you'd probably expect by now, *Tougher Than Tough – The Story Of Jamaican Music* (Mango IBXCD1).

Bunny 'Striker' Lee

•• Using the pick of the new generation of studio musicians – guys like the Barrett Brothers, Gladstone Anderson and Lloyd Charmers, who were reshaping Jamaican music – Bunny Lee behaved as if reggae had been invented just for him. Kicking off in the style, more or less, with SLIM SMITH's 'My Conversation' in 1968, he grabbed the accelerating beat and constructed a rhythm track so solid it's still being versioned nearly thirty years later. The way Striker went from here was clearly marked UP. During the next five years he became the man to beat. While he didn't exactly invent any brand new way of doing things, he refined what was already there to a high degree. He took possession from COXSONE or DUKE REID to arrive at a situation whereby his style and sound was so distinctive, practically anybody who went in the studio with him was guaranteed a hit. It was that rare combination of artistically credible and commercially viable, which came about because Lee was so much a man of the people he knew what they wanted before they did. He never took what was being done too far from its origins, but tweaked it, buffed it up and softened reggae's naturally angular feel, paying incredible attention to detail – there'd be an enormous amount going on in a Bunny Lee mix, but it was so cleverly balanced it appeared completely straightforward. So clever, it would come over as simple. And he had an enormous natural warmth that spilled all over every song he produced, which was something reggae lent itself to with particular aplomb.

Between 1968 and 1974 Bunny Lee cut over a hundred hits, including several particularly empathetic covers of post-1960s sweet US soul (it was a natural vehicle for the 'Bunny Lee Warmth') and more than a few of the most memorable records to grace (quite literally) deejay turntables on either side of the Atlantic: 'Long Time Me No See You Girl' (The Sensations); 'How Long Will It Take' and 'If It Don't Work Out' (PAT KELLY); 'Too Proud To Beg' (Slim Smith and The Uniques); 'Everybody Needs Love' (Slim Smith); 'Warming Up The Scene', 'Dance Hall Arena' and 'Musical Train' (Roy Shirley); the toasters' favourite 'Hey There Lonely Girl' (Glen Adams); 'Last Flight To Reggae City' (Lester Stirling); 'Hold You Jack' (DERRICK MORGAN); 'This Old Heart Of Mine' (DELROY WILSON); 'Deejay's Choice' and 'The People's Choice' (Winston Williams) 'A Change Is Gonna Come' (Ken Parker); and 'Hook Up' and 'Warfare' (The Bunny Lee All Stars).

But of course a list of Bunny Lee's pop reggae achievements wouldn't be complete without special mention of four tunes.

The first was one of the biggest selling reggae records up to that point, and still claims its place in the memories of anybody who so much as dropped a foot to the music at the time – the recut of 'Hold You Jack', MAX ROMEO's 'Wet Dream'. In spite of assurances that the lyrics told of a man trying to fix a leaky roof – 'Lie down so I can reach over and push this piece of slate up into the hole above the bed?' *Sure!* – it was banned by the BBC in the UK. This didn't seem to do it a great deal of harm, though, as it went Top 10 in 1969 and sold over a quarter of a million copies. The others are three of the biggest, most nice-up-a-dance lovers' rock regulars: JOHN HOLT's absolutely wonderful 'Stick By Me', Delroy Wilson's timeless 'Cool Operator' and ERIC DONALD-SON's double-mega 'Cherry Oh Baby', each song launching a thousand versions, dub plates and deejay styles.

Within such a reputation for pop choices, though, Bunny Lee was developing a healthy political bent. Another Striker masterpiece was Delroy Wilson's brooding, sufferah anthem 'Better Must Come', which was taken up as a theme song by Michael Manley's People's National Party in the run-up to the 1972 election, in one of the first open attempts to attract the ghetto vote. As was indicated by such an early excursion into serious subject matter, when the beat began to change again, Lee had roots music covered. Both in lyrics and in rhythm. ⇥

There aren't, at present, any compilations specializing in Bunny Lee productions from this period. No, I can't imagine why either. Probably one (more) of those instances when the business is getting in the way of the music. Sets by the above-named artists are the best starting points for Lee's work. 'Stick By Me', 'Better Must Come', 'Cherry Oh Baby', 'Wet Dream' and 'My Conversation' all feature on *Tougher Than Tough – The Story Of Jamaican Music* (Mango IBXCD1), while permutations of these plus a few more of the better known examples can be found on the Trojan Various Artist compilations.

Dandy Livingstone

(Born Robert Livingstone Thompson, 1944; Kingston, Jamaica; singer)
Dandy Livingstone's family emigrated to the UK in 1960, where

he grew up to become not only one of the first home-grown heroes of reggae, but also one of the principal movers and shakers behind the scenes in those early days. The music-mad teenager's first job in Britain was for a record shop, which occupied the ground floor of the building that also housed the Island and Planitone record companies. It was, literally as well as figuratively, a short step to making, instead of selling, records, and he was soon cutting ska sides first as part of The Keynotes, then as half of the duo Sugar and Dandy. His success with the latter and then as a solo singer was enough to convince the owners of the Ska Beat label (for whom he recorded) to create Giant, specifically for Livingstone and his productions – remember, he'd not long turned twenty.

In 1968, after doing OK, but not marvellously, he received an offer from Lee Goptal, an old friend from the record shop days, who was now a partner in the newly-independent-from-Island Trojan Records. The wheeze was: have your own label, Down Town, as part of the company that was releasing almost 75 per cent of the reggae in Britain. The label's first release was 'Move Your Mule', written, produced and recorded by Dandy, and as fine a piece of early reggae as could have been made in Jamaica. He followed it up too: 'I'm Your Puppet', 'Raining In My Heart' and 'Reggae In Your Jeggae' were his own releases and not far short of a pop chart placing, while his Down Town productions included 'Version Girl' by Boy Friday, 'The Burial Of Long Shot' (a reply to THE PIONEERS' 'Long Shot Kick The Bucket') by The Prince Of Darkness (aka Dandy Livingstone), The Music Doctors' 'Bush Doctor' and 'Johnny Dollar', and Desmond Riley's 'Tear Them'. But the one that lives on is his production of Tony Tribe's 'Red Red Wine'. This cover of the Neil Diamond song was an enormous reggae hit – just getting into the mainstream Top 50 – and provided the blueprint for UB40's smash several years later.

Dandy Livingstone played a huge part in establishing UK-made reggae as a viable proposition – both artistically and financially. For alongside running a successful label, his residence in England meant he'd absorbed what was going on around him to help shape the pop-influenced sound that did so well here. He earned a reputation as a dynamic performer too, cutting a thoroughly modern figure in his wide-lapelled, flared suits, glasses and mutton chop sidewhiskers, and acquired a huge British following of reggae-obsessed skinheads. This eventually paid off in 1972 when his 'Suzanne Beware Of The Devil' went Top 20, with 'Big City' following it a few months later.

But that was about it. It's believed he returned to Jamaica in 1974, and apart from his resurfacing briefly a couple of years later with an unsuccessful US album, nothing else has been heard from him.

There used to be a couple of compilation albums of Dandy Livingstone productions available on vinyl, but they've long since disappeared. Now all that remains is samples of his own releases, and Tony Tribe's 'Red Red Wine' on the following:

20 Reggae Blockbusters; Trojan CDTRL176
Tighten Up Volumes One And Two; Trojan CDTRL 306
Tighten Up Volumes Three And Four; Trojan CDTRL 307
Trojan Explosion; Trojan CDTRL 246
20 Reggae Classics Volume One; Trojan CDTRL 222
20 Reggae Classics Volume Two; Trojan CDTRL 224

Dandy Livingstone productions *won't* be found on *Tougher Than Tough – The Story Of Jamaican Music* (Mango IBXCD1) because, strictly speaking, it isn't Jamaican music.

The Maytals

•• That McCarthy and Gordon waited for Hibbert to finish his 'porridge' isn't altogether surprising. Quite apart from the fact they were best friends, the peculiar balance of The Maytals' raw, signifyin'-type gloriousness couldn't have been repeated with any other permutation of performers. It owed more to the soul raised with Toots out front and each pushing the other two higher than to any technical expertise, and so it was never going to be a matter of just auditioning a replacement or, even, continuing as a duo. Also waiting at the gate in 1968 was LESLIE KONG, who took the group to Beverley's for three of the most productive years reggae would ever witness. The tunes flowed like a river and it was, quite literally, every one a winner.

The first recording proved that a year and a half in a particularly grim prison had in no way broken Hibbert's spirit: in spite of the fact that (or maybe because) it was essentially a trumped up charge – the police would routinely harass prominent Rasta believers by arresting them for the collie weed they'd usually have about their persons. The group's first Kong cut was '54-46 That's My Number', a reference to Hibbert's prison number, with lyrics about doing time under dubious legal circumstances. It became an immediate and enormous Jamaican hit – so many sufferahs related to it personally! – and went on to cross the ocean. Big style. It remains one of the best loved reggae songs anywhere, the opening riff one of the music's most instantly recognizable sequences of notes. Thanks to a combination of serious song writing – Hibbert had developed into a writer of remarkable inspiration – a wicked sense of humour (this is the group that gave us 'Monkey Man'), singing that never went off the boil and Kong's deceptively tricky productions, the group kicked hits until 1971. A chartbusting run that made as big an impression in the UK as it did at home, elevating The Maytals to the top international reggae act. (They were always far more consistent than the sometimes stellar competition.) It's a widely held belief – but one never actually verified – that Island Records boss Chris Blackwell only signed THE WAILERS because he couldn't get The Maytals.

Then, in 1971, Leslie Kong died. The Maytals were by now established on a worldwide basis, but with Kong gone they simply couldn't keep it up. They went to BYRON LEE, then to Blackwell. The latter, in keeping with his rock-orientated ideas of groups having to have focal points, renamed them Toots and The Maytals, but it didn't seem to do them a lot of good. As the 1970s progressed it became increasingly obvious that the trio's best days were now behind them. Although the album *Reggae Got Soul* (1976) sold well enough to climb into the UK charts, it didn't add anything to their body of work that hadn't been done (better) before. McCarthy and Gordon left in the 1980s, leaving Toots to continue with two new Maytals. He's still a regular on the international live circuit, but it's not the same any more.

Do The Reggae 1966-1970; Attack CDAT103

More or less The Maytals' Greatest Hits. Although it gets things started as far back as 'Bam Bam', the real deal is the Leslie Kong reggae productions: 'Do The Reggay', cut in 1968 and generally accepted to be the first song to use the word in a title; 'Sweet And Dandy', that classic from *The Harder They Come*; 'Johnny Cool Man', a piece of rude boy nonsense and a masterpiece that has for so long been underrated; the previously hard to find 'Water Melon'; and, of course, '54-46'. Enough Maytals joyousness to uplift even the most miserable.

Reggae Greats; Island IMCD38

The perfect companion piece to the above, as this is the disc with 'Monkey Man', 'Pressure Drop' and 'Funky Kingston'. Also, by way of a bonus, there's 'Reggae Got Soul' and 'Time Tough'. The two sets cross over on '54-46' and 'Bam Bam', which, I suppose, are good enough tunes to make it acceptable.

Funky Kingston; Mango RRCD21

The title track was a big hit, and elsewhere 'Poomps And Pride' and the threesome's riotous reading of 'Louie Louie' do the business, but there's not much else here.

ALSO RECOMMENDED:

In The Dark; Trojan CDTRL 202

Much later stuff, from when Toots Hibbert was experimenting with other styles of music. Not too many of which were successful – witness 'Got To Be There', 'Havin' A Party' and 'Take Me Home Country Roads'. Even the inevitable inclusion of '54-46' can't refloat this sinking ship.

Most Trojan collections will include at least one of the Leslie Kong-produced Maytals numbers, while *Tougher Than Tough – The Story Of Jamaican Music* (Mango IBXCD1) features '54-46'.

Lee 'Scratch' Perry

➻ 'A musical injection-tion-tion. . . . Sounds from the Upsetting Station-tion-tion . . . Now move your feet to this musical version-sion-sion!' When the deejay got to shrieking either that or something very close to it over the mic at an early 1970s blues dance you'd tense up. Ready. Poised for the needle to drop on some kind of scorching, quirky instrumental, courtesy of Lee 'Scratch' Perry. In fact maybe this section entry should be renamed The Upsetter, because that was how Perry was best known both in Jamaica and in the UK. The nickname came from a tune of that name which he cut for JOE GIBBS in 1968 – yet another pot-shot at COXSONE. He also later named his studio band The Upsetters and formed a record label with the same handle in Jamaica, while Trojan launched its similarly titled counterpart in 1969 exclusively for Perry productions.

But it was the band that really made Perry's name at this point. A band that was the incubator for the next wave of Jamaican musicians, with SLY DUNBAR, GLEN ADAMS, The Barrett Brothers, Boris Gardiner, Steelie Brown and Mickey Richards all serving time in the unit.

After working for Joe Gibbs and CLANCY ECCLES, Perry set up on his own and proved himself to be one of the most pro-active producers in the music so far. Rather than leave his musicians to get on with it and sort out their own arrangements, he had very definite musical ideas and relished his freedom to experiment. Virtually his first effort was destined for immortality – 'Tighten Up' by The Untouchables, a crisp piece of dance floor syncopation that took reggae's rhythm to an absurd conclusion and became a huge hit. The song also lent its name to that most excellent of early reggae compilation series. From there, show Lee Perry a rhythm pattern and he'd mess with it – slow it down, speed it up, compress it, echo it, stretch it out or turn it backwards. Sometimes there'd be a singer out front, but more often the lead would be taken up by Val Bennett's saxophone or Glen Adams' organ. Witness 'The Return Of Django', over a month in the UK Top 10, or 'Live Injection', or 'The Vampire', or the lunacy that occurred on 'Shocks Of Mighty' or 'Ram You Hard', one of the many vocal cuts of the seriously good 'Dry Acid' instrumental.

This was one of the major turning points in Jamaican music. Guys like Dodd and REID had taken it as far as they were going to; now Perry, somewhat younger, was far more in tune with the emerging technology and the idea that Jamaicans were far more artistically adventurous than they'd ever been given credit for. As well as creating the lively pop cuts that did so well on both sides of the Atlantic, as the 1970s progressed Perry began expressing himself in a far more spiritual manner. He slowed the beat down and started utilizing dub technique to astonishing effect, translating Rastafari into something much more than mere music, but presentations that were never less than musical. He would work to catch a vibe by whatever sonic means necessary, then graft it on to a fragmented rhythm. Yes, there probably was a mountain of ganja in there somewhere!

By the time Trojan closed down their Upsetter imprint in 1974, Lee Perry no longer seemed interested in knocking out catchy little pop tunes. The work he appeared to be taking most seriously was the deeper stuff he was doing with DENNIS ALCAPONE ('Alpha and Omega'), JUNIOR BYLES ('Beat Down Babylon'), U-ROY ('Earth's Rightful Ruler) and THE WAILERS (three albums, containing early versions of what became some of the most famous numbers in their later repertoire). That same year he opened his own studios, Black Ark, at the back of his Kingston home, and moved into Phase Three of his career. It was to be the most exciting yet. Even by existing Perry standards. ➥

The Upsetter Collection; Trojan CDTRL195

This is the one for any fan of those vibed up, irresistibly syncopated, sometimes just plain weird tunes that came out on the Upsetter label in the UK starting in 1969. Naturally things get underway with 'The Return Of Django', but we venture further down that road with the spaghetti western-inspired lunacy of 'Django Shoots First' and 'Kill Them All'. Then this set scores extra points for including the oft-forgotten 'French Connection' – remember, 'This is musical injection called French Connection!' – as well as the ever-popular 'Vampire' and its harder than hard B-side 'Check Him Out' by The Bleechers. And if you like your 'quirkiness' in almost transcendental proportions, this set runs as far as two versions of 'Cow Thief Skank'.

Lee Perry and Friends: *Give Me Power*; Trojan CDTRL254

Neville Grant, Sick And Tired; **Junior Byles**, Rasta No Pickpocket; **Little Roy**, Don't Cross The Nation; **The Stingers**, Give Me Power; **King Iwah**, Give Me Power Version Two; **Leo Graham and The Upsetters**, News Flash/Flashing Echo; **Lee Perry and The Upsetters**, Justice To the People; **Max Romeo/Niney/Lee Perry**, Babylon's Burning; **The Upsetters**, Ring Of Fire, The Thanks We Get, Dig Your Grave; **Max Romeo**, Public Enemy Number One; **Dillinger and The Upsetters**, Mid-East Rock; **The Stingers**, Forward Up; **Prince Django**, Hot Tip; **Shenley Duffus**, To Be A Lover.

All tracks cut between 1970 and 1973. As well as being an excellent cross-section of the more interesting artists Perry produced, this selection also shows how, even back then, he was moving away from pop reggae to something with a greater message and a deeper beat. While the set opens with a vocal version of 'The Return Of Django', and contains more western-style silliness in 'Dig Your Grave', that side of things is soon left behind with the righteousness of tunes like 'News Flash', 'Ring Of Fire' and 'Babylon's Burning' – two versions of 'Beat Down Babylon' – and such straight up political denunciation as 'Public Enemy Number One'. Although it might come as a bit of a shock for the Django/Vampire/Clint Eastwood fans – i.e. reggae's skinhead aficionados of the day – it's Perry at his best before he completely rewrote the rules.

*The Upsetters and Friends: *Upsetting the Nation*; Trojan CDTRL 330

The Upsetters, Eight For Eight/Outer Space; **Buster Brown**, To Love Somebody; **The Upsetters**, Soulful-I; **Lee Perry and The Upsetters**, The Man From MI5; **The Termites**, I'll Be Waiting; **Lee Perry and The Upsetters**, Ten To Twelve; **The Muskyteers**, Kiddy-O; **The Upsetters**, Medical Operation/Night Doctor; **Buster Brown**, Crying About You.

This is an excellent example of what Lee Perry really meant around the time of 'The Return Of Django'. It's quirky, but not yet barking mad. And to have the dub cuts of such instrumentals as 'Eight For Eight' and 'Medical Operation' is a bonus. But really this album is Premier League stuff quite simply because it includes a personal favourite of mine, 'The Man From MI5'.

ALSO RECOMMENDED:

*Various Artists; *People Funny Boy (Early Upsetter)*; Trojan CDTRL339

Burt Walters, Honey Love, Evol Yenoh; **Val Bennett**, Popeye (Stranger) On The Shore; **The Mellotones**, Nonesuch Busted Bet; **The Upsetters**, Handy Cap; **Lee Perry**, People Funny Boy; **Burt Walters**, Blowing In The Wind; **Val Bennett**, Spanish Harlem; **The Mellotones**, Uncle Charlie; **The Inspirations**, Tighten Up; **David Isaacs**, Place In The Sun.

Probably a bit on the tame side for anybody who arrived at Lee Perry much later, but it's still a valuable lesson in where it all began. And it's good to see that the title track – a typically antagonistic Perry-style musical attack on former colleague Joe Gibbs – hasn't been lost.

**The Upsetter Box Set*; Trojan CDPRY1

Later, slightly more spiritual and less immediate Upsetter material. While nothing Lee Perry has done is anything less than interesting, this one tends to fall between the two stools of outright pop and woozy, righteous dub rock and is not recommended for Upsetter novices.

*Lee Perry and Friends: *Shocks Of Mighty 1969-1974*; Attack CDAT104

Although this one's spread across a slightly longer period of time, it doesn't manage to communicate as accessibly as the above. So while it's still rich in the spirit of the man – anything featuring 'Shocks Of Mighty', 'French Connection 2', 'Pound get a Blow' and 'Black Man's Time' will have so much spirit it can't keep it quiet – it doesn't seem to illustrate as interestingly how both he and, subsequently, the music changed.

SEE ALSO:

Tighten Up Volumes One and Two; Trojan CDTRL 306
Tighten Up Volumes Three and Four; Trojan CDTRL 307

The Magnificent Fourteen – 14 Shots Of Western Inspired Reggae;
Trojan CDTRL283
The Trojan Story; Trojan CDTRD 402
20 Reggae Blockbusters; Trojan CDTRL176
Tougher Than Tough – The Story Of Jamaican Music; Mango
IBXCD1

The Pioneers

(Sydney Crooks, Jackie Robinson and George Dekker; all born
1940s; Kingston, Jamaica; vocal group)
This was the line-up that scored the UK Top 20 hit with the race-
track story of 'Long Shot Kick De Bucket', and as that raw,
jump-reggae jolly-up was as big fun as it was a hit, they've
earned their place in this book. Originally the group was
Sydney Crooks, his brother Derrick and keyboard player/
vocalist Glen Adams, but they achieved little success. The
second incarnation under the name was Sydney and Jackie
Robinson. As this duo they had the huge hit 'Dem A Laugh And
A Ki Ki', except they chose to call themselves (or rather producer JOE GIBBS chose to call them) The Soulmates. It was
around this time that the first chapters of the racehorse saga
were recorded – 'Long Shot', 'Dip And Fall Back', 'No Dope Mi
Pony' and 'Jackpot' – all of which made a considerable impression on London dancehalls at the end of the 1960s. Their other
biggies from around then were 'Give Me Little Lovin'', 'Catch
The Beat' and 'Mama Look Deh'.

It was after George Dekker joined that they went back to
KONG (the original Pioneers had started there, unsuccessfully,
in 1965) and recorded a string of Jamaican hits, of which 'Long
Shot Kick De Bucket' was just one of them. Although a move to
the UK in 1969 brought them chart hits – 'Let Your Yeah be
Yeah' was a monster, and there were a few minor efforts – it did-
n't do much for their music. After spending a couple of years
touring, the group split in 1973.

It's a pity there's no CD record of their time with Joe Gibbs,
other than 'Dem A Laugh And A Ki Ki', as their work is a good
example of what the Jamaican vocal group became after rock
steady. When they got lively. Otherwise, it's possible to find

'Long Shot Kick De Bucket' on a large selection of Trojan Various Artist compilations.

Duke Reid

➻ The Duke may have been The King when it came to rock steady, but the arrival of reggae left him rather at sixes and sevens. His late-1960s output – wicked tunes like 'Love Up Kiss Up' (THE TERMITES), 'Moonlight Lover' and 'Kansas City' (Joya Landis), 'Love Is All I Had' (Phyllis Dillon) and the much-versioned 'You Don't Care' (THE TECHNIQUES) owed far more to rock steady. It seems Reid couldn't get to grips with the new beat in a way that would allow him to leave his mark on it.

Then, in 1970, he hit upon an idea that altered the face of reggae to such a degree that today's dancehall style might not exist had he not had such a rush of blood to the head. He started putting out deejay records as entities in their own right rather than quickly knocked out optional extras sometimes found on B-sides, or dub plates exclusive to certain sound systems. And the really clever thing was, he did it over his classic old rock steady rhythms.

Like every other sound system operator, Duke Reid employed deejays to toast at his dances, and he was aware of their power over an audience, but it was only after a chance intervention by KING TUBBY that he took them seriously as a saleable commodity. Tubby had recorded U-ROY – one of his sound system deejays – over a unique dub version of The Techniques' 'You Don't Care' and took it down to Duke Reid's place for cutting. Reid was so impressed he took U-Roy into the studio there and then to record a spontaneous toast over the instrumental track of ALTON ELLIS's 'Girl I've Got A Date'. It came out as 'Wake The Town', and Jamaica woke up to a musical phenomenon. It went right to the top of the charts, where it was followed by a string of other U-Roy/Duke Reid recuts of old Treasure Isle favourites – at one point, for a period of several weeks, the combination held four out of the top five spots with the other instant classics 'Wear You To the Ball', 'Everybody Bawling' and 'Rule The Nation'.

It was a typical example of Jamaican ingenuity and a way of

life that recycles just about everything. Although, initially in the UK, it was a bit hard for people who weren't sound system regulars to come to terms with the idea of, what was, after all, somebody shouting over somebody else's record, it soon caught on largely thanks to U-Roy's personality and bubbling tones, plus Duke Reid's light productions and the musical pedigree of the backing. By that time, Reid was cutting tunes with DENNIS ALCAPONE, and dominating the style that was now being copied all over town.

Once Duke Reid got back on the top spot, he held it for about three years and then his status began to fade. By this time there was already a second generation of deejay artists in place, and they were being treated like singers in the studio as well as the shops. They were recording over specially prepared rhythm tracks and making the most of the swing towards deep roots and Rastafari. Something which The Duke could never get a grip on. Maybe it was a by-product of his law enforcement background, but Duke Reid actively resisted recording Rasta reggae, and that, ultimately, was his downfall as he simply got left behind by changing tastes.

Still, starting two musical styles in the one lifetime is considerably more than most people get round to doing. Duke Reid died in 1974, leaving behind a musical legacy that will outlast everybody who contributed to it.

Duke Reid compilation albums have been detailed in his entry in the previous section (pages 72-78). Other than those, check U-Roy and Dennis Alcapone albums for his production credit, plus the deejay compilation sets *Keep On Coming Through The Door* (Trojan CDTRL255) and *With A Flick Of My Musical Wrist* (Trojan CDTRL268) and, for 'Wake The Town', check *Tougher Than Tough – The Story Of Jamaican Music* (Mango IBXCD1).

UB40

(Robin Campbell, born 1954, guitar/vocals; Ali Campbell, born 1954, vocals; Earl Falconer, born 1957, bass; Jimmy Brown, born 1957, drums; Brian Travers, born 1957, saxophone; Astro, born Terry Wilson, 1957, trumpet/vocals/toasting; Norman Hassan, born 1958, percussion/trombone; Mickey Virtue, born 1957, keyboards. All born Birmingham, UK)

When UB40 first started playing in 1979, they got lumped in with the ska revivalist 2-Tone bands of the time – largely because they played reggae (albeit rather different to ska, but, hey, it's all Jamaican!); they came from the Midlands (2-Tone was based in Coventry, not quite Birmingham but, hey, it's close enough!); and they were a 'multi-racial' band and therefore must've been making the same 2-Tone statement (they were actually eight guys who used to hang out together and all liked reggae, but, hey! . . .). It was a label that took far longer than the demise of 2-Tone to shake off. For a few years music critics tended to write that UB40 were a 2-Tone band who didn't have what it took to move on. Then they labelled them a plastic reggae act. Rather curiously, the same people who saw Madness or The Selecter as ska acts off the same top shelf as PRINCE BUSTER or THE SKATALITES were affronted that UB40 should be attempting such numbers as 'Red Red Wine', 'Cherry Oh Baby', 'Wear You To The Ball' or 'Kingston Town'. But this has never seemed to bother UB40 particularly. They've only had one line-up change in sixteen years (which was before they ever made a record and because their original percussion player got deported to Nigeria), and neither have they deviated remotely from their chosen path of gentle, post-rock steady reggae. And their fans don't appear to have any problems either – it's not unusual for a UB40 album to sell several million worldwide, while on tour 10,000-seater arenas are the order of the day.

UB40's history is, like so much else about the band, refreshingly straightforward. They grew up in the less salubrious part of Birmingham and, during their teenage years, Caribbean neighbours had introduced them to the delights of reggae and late-night blues parties. Hence the fixation with a certain period, i.e. late-1960s reggae. As much as any of them actually founded the band, it was the Campbell brothers who understood a bit about the Midlands music business, as their parents were renowned local folkies Lorna and Ian Campbell. In 1979 the group played their first gigs in 1979 in local pubs, signed to a local management company and recorded their first single for a label that was operated by a local record shop. At that point Chrissie Hynde spots them and takes them out of the area as support act on The Pretenders' tour; the first single sells over half a million; and the first album, *Signing Off* (it kept up the train of thought that named them after the unemployment benefit card the UB40) stays on the charts for a year and a half.

And with very few hiccups, it all got better from then on, with the band demonstrating a capacity for loyalty seldom seen in the music business – they've never moved away from Birmingham (in fact, they leave it as little as possible, holding all album launches and business meetings locally), and when their bass player was imprisoned for a road accident that caused the death of his brother (the band's engineer) he rejoined the group as soon as he was out.

But the question that is still being asked is: Are they real reggae? Of course they are. Over a dozen albums testify to this. And even if they somehow weren't 'real', they've done as much as anybody to promote reggae around the world. As with BYRON LEE, if UB40 records act as the catalyst to bring non-believers to the music then they're twice as important.

The Best Of UB40 Volume One; Dep International CDUBTV1
The Best Of UB40 Volume Two; Dep International CDUBTV2

The two of these between them are the best way to approach UB40, as like any other reggae band they express themselves through singles rather than across whole albums. These CDs are also a no-hiding-place record of the group's improvement over the years, from that first single, 'Food For Thought' (which was originally the B-side of the also-included 'King', but was the tune radio deejays preferred), up to the mega-hit of 1993 '(I Can't Help) Falling In Love With You'. Whereas the former gets by on little more than enthusiasm, the latter is a truly sophisticated example of modern techniques and sounds applied to an old-fashioned way of doing things.

Indeed it's expertise and a detailed understanding of how reggae works – and how it works with recent studio developments – that characterizes *Volume Two*. The first set contains, among its eighteen tracks, '1 In 10', 'Red Red Wine', 'Rat In Mi Kitchen', 'Don't Let It Pass You By', 'I Got You Babe' and 'The Earth Dies Screaming'. The second is a far more varied package, in terms of arrangements within the style, and covers 'Where Did I Go

Wrong', '(I Can't Help) Falling In Love With You', 'Homely Girl' and 'Wear You To The Ball'.

Labour Of Love; Dep International DEPCD5
Labour Of Love Volume Two; Dep International DEPCD14

Two volumes of cover versions of classic reggae tracks. These are the tunes the band grew up with – hence the title – and it's these albums that really have the purists spluttering. What they are though, are two sets of songs of the calibre of 'Red Red Wine', 'Wear You To The Ball', 'Singer Man', 'Sweet Sensation', 'Cherry Oh Baby', 'Version Girl', 'Stick By Me' and so on, carefully selected and delivered in a style that never claimed to be 'authentically' Jamaican but shows enormous respect for the material. Interestingly, the group claim that although the first *Labour Of Love* set came about because they had to deliver an album but hadn't written any songs, they found that having to discipline themselves to other reggae, instead of writing to their own strengths, greatly improved their musicianship.

ALSO RECOMMENDED:

UB40 Live; Dep International DEPCD4

Recorded on tour in 1982, it's proof that enthusiasm and onstage invention can more than make up for lack of technical expertise, and thus provides a vital record of the band's vibrant approach to live performance.

Promises And Lies; Dep International DEPCD14

The most recent, mega-selling set that demonstrates the breadth of reggae knowledge the band now possesses as they stir in dancehall, ragga and roots influences without detracting from the UB40 vibe. This is the album with '(I Can't Help) Falling In Love With You'.

U-Roy

(Born Ewart Beckford, 1942; Kingston, Jamaica; deejay)
'I originate, so you must appreciate, while others have to imitate!' So

went one of the vibrant, whooping intros to a U-Roy record. But unlike so many other deejays who used lyrics along these lines, with U-Roy it wasn't just empty boasting. This was the man they called The Teacher. The original Big Daddy of studio deejay music. U-Roy had a buoyant, altogether musical style that set the trend for years to come, and he was the first real Jamaican toaster so many of us in England ever heard. And thanks to his working over rock steady rhythms and a pre-dread approach to life – although this may be down to Duke Reid more than anything – along with DENNIS ALCAPONE he was the only deejay accepted by the white reggae fans of the time, the original skinheads.

Beckford got into music professionally as a teenager. Inspired by the likes of King Stitt and, particularly, Count Machuki, he started deejaying local sound systems and quickly progressed to the respectably-sized outfit Sir George The Atomic. His stage name had already been decided by his infant nephew whose diction wasn't quite up to pronouncing 'Ewart'. Towards the end of the 1960s, he joined KING TUBBY's HiFi, one of the main contenders for the Reid/DODD crown, thanks to Tubby's innovative way with his control tower and the dub selections he was making specifically for his sound. It was here U-Roy really began to shine, as the slates Tubby would create were tailored to allow breaks for toasting. It was while cutting these plates, featuring U-Roy's toasting, that the idea of deejay records came to the attention of Duke Reid (Tubby cut discs at Treasure Isle) who saw the value of exploiting them commercially. Though there is some argument as to whether U-Roy's first recordings were produced by LEE PERRY ('Earth's Rightful Ruler') or KEITH HUDSON ('Dynamic Fashion Way'), if this was the case it was definitely the Duke who successfully marketed the deejay first. His initial releases, 'Wake The Town', 'Rule The Nation' and 'Wear You To The Ball', stayed in the top three positions in the Jamaican charts for three months, an occupancy only interrupted by his fourth single, 'Everybody Bawling'.

But best of all was U-Roy's 1971 Trojan album *Version Galore*. The blue cover was exactly the sort of thing you wanted to be seen carrying around, and the music was like U-Roy's Greatest Hits, each one a Treasure Isle classic. The swooping, soaring, sheer joyousness of The Teacher's voice as he scatted across them was about the most exciting reggae there was in 1971.

Like the song says, 'keep coming on through the door': U-Roy opened the gates for a rush of deejays to start recording. They were already there, working the sound systems, and it was simply a matter of getting them into the studio. Most prominent in this first wave were Dennis Alcapone, King Stitt, Sir Lord Comic, Lizzy, Winston Scotland and Sporty. At one point, such was the demand for deejay music in Jamaica that the radio stations banned toasting records in order to give singers a chance! This was the beginning of something that would not only profoundly affect reggae but would also have an enormous bearing on US soul – it's unlikely rap would ever have happened had it not been for toasting. And U-Roy was at the start of it.

He stuck with Duke Reid until 1973. By then the beat was changing and the subject matter becoming more considered. U-Roy moved with the times. ↝

*U-Roy And Friends: *Your Ace From Space*; Trojan CDTRL359

Don't let the title mislead you into thinking this is some kind of Various Artists album. The Friends in question are the artists who made the original records over which U-Roy toasts – THE PARAGONS, THE MELODIANS, ALTON ELLIS, Hopeton Lewis, THE TECHNIQUES and so on. Yes, this is a collection of U-Roy's Treasure Isle sides, and Trojan's spirit of generosity goes further than just the credits as the thirty tracks include nearly everything the deejay made for Duke Reid: that is both Treasure Isle albums, plus a few more sides that didn't appear on either. In every way it's an early Greatest Hits set, with 'Version Galore', 'Wake The Town', 'Wear You To The Ball', 'Tom Drunk', 'Rule The Nation', 'On The Beach', 'Words Of Wisdom', 'Flashing My Whip' and 'Ain't That Loving You'. In the absence of an old blue cover copy of the original *Version Galore* LP (and that is really only for sentimental reasons), this is all the first period U-Roy anybody could ever want.

ALSO RECOMMENDED:

*Version Of Wisdom; Frontline CDFL1903

Very much a distillation of *Your Ace From Space*, and although all of the absolutely crucial tracks are there, there's still only seventeen of them. So while there's really nothing *wrong* with this set, it could actually be a lot righter.

*U-Roy and Friends: *With A Flick Of My Musical Wrist – Jamaican Deejay Music 1970-1973*; Trojan CDTRL 268

U-Roy and Delroy, You Keep On Running; **King Sporty**, For Our Desire; **Charley Ace**, Ontarious Version; **U-Roy**, Love I Tender; **Ramon and The Chrystalites**, Golden Chickens; **Cat Campbell and Nicky Thomas**, Hammering; **U-Roy**, Festival Wise; **U-Roy and Ken Boothe**, Medley Train; **I-Roy**, Space Flight; **U-Roy**, Top Of The Peak; **Big Youth**, Opportunity Rock; **King Tony**, Speak No Evil; **U-Roy**, Hard feeling; **I-Roy**, Musical Drum Sound; **Prince Jazzbo**, Freedom From Chains.

Led by U-Roy, this is a stunning cross-section of the first crop of Jamaican deejays and, such is the power and grace of what they're doing, it doesn't sound nearly as naïve as it ought to when put up against later models.

SEE ALSO:

Keep On Coming Through The Door – Jamaican Deejay Music 1969-1973; Trojan CDTRL 255 (only two U-Roy tracks, but as one of them is 'Wet Vision', a hard to find, Bunny Lee-produced toast to MAX ROMEO's 'Wet Dream', we can't really complain)
Tougher Than Tough – The Story Of Jamaican Music; Mango IBXCD1
The Trojan Story Part Two; Trojan CDTAL200

Delroy Wilson

➡ In 1971 Wilson was back with BUNNY LEE and cut a record that ultimately held far greater significance than the simple fact it would raise the temperature at a dance when everybody joined in with the chorus. 'Better Must Come' was originally an apolitical slice of sufferah rock, about waiting for salvation from the crippling ghetto environment. But then it got taken up by the opposition People's National Party as their rallying song for the 1972 election. Party leader Michael Manley had shrewdly figured that the ghetto vote could hold the key to government and openly courted it through music. He was right too: the PNP swept to victory, no small thanks to Delroy Wilson.

From then on, Wilson established himself as a spokesman for the people as well as a love man supreme. His catalogue was peppered with cuts like 'Mash Up Illiteracy' and 'Have Some Mercy', even though it was songs such as 'I'm Still Waiting', 'Pretty Girl' and 'Love' and his cover of 'It's A Shame', a massive, wallpaper-endangering hit, that were his true stock in trade. But the really big tune was 'Cool Operator'. Another slinky Bunny Lee rhythm, topped off with Delroy's oozing vocals, this was guaranteed to rock any party from Kingston to Kensal Rise. It still does today – because every guy fancies himself as a cool operator and every girl wants to meet one. Back in 1972 it was something of a theme song, played in your head or sung out loud to any of your spars who'd just made prats of themselves. It was this one record, more than anything else, that established Delroy Wilson as the island's premier vocalist.

It was a position he held throughout the first half of the decade, consolidating it with the excellent *Sarge* album in 1976. But during the 1980s he began to fade. In spite of a couple of big dancehall reggae hits – 'Don't Blame It On Me' and 'Ease Up' – he was never to achieve any form of consistency again. Many who knew him blamed his drinking, which caused the cirrhosis of the liver that was to kill him in March 1995. In spite of leaving behind half a dozen brilliant records, it's still very easy to think that, somehow, Delroy Wilson never did fulfill his potential.

There's very little of Delroy Wilson's later work available on CD in this country at present. The greatest hits collections were discussed in the previous section (pages 90-91) and they spill, partially, over into this area. 'Better Must Come' features on *Tougher Than Tough – The Story Of Jamaican Music* (Mango IBXCD1), while 'Cool Operator' crops up on several Trojan compilations. Without wishing to appear ghoulish, maybe we can expect a comprehensive Delroy Wilson compilation now that he's passed on.

VARIOUS ARTISTS

The albums listed below may start to read like a Trojan catalogue, but I'm not on any sort of bung, I promise. Quite simply, during the first half of the 1970s, roughly three-quarters of all reggae released in this country came out on a Trojan-affiliated label, and the company still retains the UK rights to much of it.

20 Reggae Classics; Trojan CDTRL222

Tony Tribe, Red Red Wine; **The Melodians**, Sweet Sensation; **Nicky Thomas**, Love Of The Common People; **The Slickers**, Johnny Too Bad; **The Maytals**, Pressure Drop; **Harry J All Stars**, The Liquidator; **Symarip**, Skinhead Moonstomp; **The Pioneers**, Long Shot Kick De Bucket; **Winston Groovy**, Please Don't Make Me Cry; **Jimmy Cliff**, Many Rivers To Cross; **Desmond Dekker and The Aces**, 007 (Shanty Town); **Dandy Livingstone**, A Message To You Rudy; **Boy Friday**, Version Girl; **Eric Donaldson**, Cherry Oh Baby; **Clancy Eccles**, Fattie Fattie; **The Melodians**, Rivers Of Babylon; **The Ethiopians**, Last Train To Skaville.

20 Reggae Classics Volume Two; Trojan CDTRL224

The Maytals, 54-46 Was My Number; **Roland Alphonso**, Phoenix City; **John Holt**, Love I Can Feel; **Augustus Pablo**, Java; **Dandy Livingstone**, Reggae In Your Jeggae; **Andy Capp**, Pop A Top; **Dave and Ansel Collins**, Double Barrel; **U-Roy and John Holt**, Wear You To The Ball; **King Stitt and The Dynamites**, Herbsman Shuffle; **Bob Marley and The Wailers**, Small Axe; **The Upsetters**, Battle Axe; **Desmond Dekker and The Aces**, The Israelites; **Andy Capp**, The Law; **Derrick Morgan**, Fat Man; **Winston Groovy**, So Easy; **The Ethiopians**, The Whip; **The Maytals**, Pomps And Pride; **John Holt**, The Further You Look; **The Upsetters**, The Return Of Django; **Bob Marley and The Wailers**, Soul Shakedown Party; **King Stitt**, Fire Corner; **The Dynamites**, The Next Corner.

20 Reggae Classics Volume Three; Trojan CDTRL256

Al Brown and Skin Flesh and Bones, Here I Am; **Derrick Harriot**, Some Guys Have All The Luck; **Errol Dunkley**, A Little Way Different; **Louisa Mark**, Keep It Like It Is; **The Diamonds**, Just Can't Figure Out; **Ken Boothe**, Everything I Own; **Bob And Marcia**, The Pied Piper; **Horace Faith**, Black Pearl; **Derrick Harriot**, Groovy Situation; **Hopeton Lewis**, Boom Shacka Lacka; **The Upsetters**, Live Injection; **Nora Dean**, Barbwire; **Lloyd Parks**, Baby Hang Up The Phone; **Big Youth**, Hit The Road Jack; **Nicky Thomas**, Rainy Night In Georgia; **Bob Marley and The Wailers**, Mr Brown; **Derrick Harriot**, 18 With A Bullet; **Peter Tosh**, Them Fe A Get A Beating; **The Paragons**, The Tide Is High; **Delroy Wilson**, Better Must Come.

20 Reggae Classics Volume Four; Trojan CDTRL284

Lord Tanamo, I'm In the Mood For Ska; **The Kingstonians**, Singer Man; **Lord Creator**, Kingston Town; **Eric Donaldson**, The Way You Do The Things You Do; **Hopeton Lewis**, Groovin' Out On Life; **John Holt**, Stick By Me; **Dave Barker**, On Broadway; **Jackie Robinson**, Homely Girl; **Scotty**, Draw Your Brakes; **Ken Parker**, Help Me Make It Through The Night; **Rupie Edwards**, Irie Feelings; **Boris Gardiner**, My Commanding Wife; **Slim Smith**, Everybody Needs Love; **Susan Cadogan**, Fever; **Johnny Clarke**, Tears On My Pillow; **Marcia Griffiths**, When Will I See You Again; **Pat Kelly**, He Ain't Heavy He's My Brother; **Max Romeo**, Wet Dream; **Ken Boothe**, Who Gets Your Love; **The Cimarons**, Rock Your Baby.

The *Reggae Classics* series was always far more considered than the *Tighten Up*s, and therefore probably makes up for in variety what it lacks in character. Or perhaps not. But then I grew up with *Tighten Up*, so I'm biased.

Adults Only, Volume One; Trojan CDTRL 305

Lee Perry and The Soulettes, Rub And Squeeze; **Phyliss Dillon**, Don't Touch Me Tomato; **Dermot Lynch**, Adults Only; **The Termites**, Rub Up, Push Up; **The Versatiles**, Push It In; **The Tennors**, Kahki; **The Soul Sisters**, Wreck A Buddy; **Kid Gungo**,

Hold The Pussy; **Lloydie and The Lowbites**, Birth Control; **The Inspirations,** Wet Dream; **Nora Dean**, Barbwire; **Clancy Eccles**, Open Up; **Dave Barker and The Gaylads**, She Want It; **Lloydie and The Lowbites**, Fat Fat Girl; **The Observers**, International Pum Pum; **Charley Ace and Fay**, Punanny; **Max Romeo**, Sexy Sadie; **Lloydie and The Lowbites**, Pussy Cat.

Adults Only, Volume Two; Trojan CDTRL 308

Justin Hines, Rub Up Push Up; **Owen and Leon**, Want Me Cock; **Stranger Cole**, Pussy Cat; **Lee Perry**, Doctor Dick; **The Termites**, Push It Up; **Calypso Joe**, Adults Only; **Lloyd Charmers**, Mr Rhya; **The Ethiopians**, Satan Girl; **The Soul Mates**, Pussy Catch A Fire; **U-Roy**, Big Boy And Teacher; **U-Roy**, Rough Rider; **Max Romeo**, Play With Your Pussy; **Lloyd and Patsy**, Papa Do It Sweet; **Flowers and Alvin**, Inna De Pum Pum; **Charlie Ace And Fay**, Mr Whittaker; **Max Romeo**, Hole Under Crutches; **Lloydie and The Lowbites**, Yum Yum Pussy.

Rude reggae was a big deal in the late 1960s/early 1970s, widely assumed to be a continuation of the calypso and mento tradition for bawdy ballads and a precursor to the 'slackness' of the 1980s and 1990s. At this point, though, it's not nearly that offensive and still good fun. Sort of.

I Shall Sing!; Trojan CDTRL289

Judy Mowatt and The Gaytones, I Shall Sing!; **Phyliss Dillon**, Picture On The Wall; **Cynthia Schloss**, Words (Are Impossible); **Lorna Bennett**, Run Johnny; **Judy Mowatt**, The Gardener; **Bobbi Huston**, Make It With You; **Elizabeth Archer and The Equations**, Feel Like Making Love; **Marie Pierre**, Somebody Else's Man; **Judy Mowatt**, Emergency Call; **Jenny Taylor**, Come Lay Some Loving On Me; **Judy Mowatt**, Way Over Yonder; **Janet Kay**, Loving You; **Phyliss Dillon**, I Can't Forget About It; **Louisa Marks**, Keep It Like It Is; **Marcia Griffiths and Lloyd Charmers**, No Me Without You; **Marie Pierre**, Can't Go Through With Life.

I Shall Sing! Volume Two; Trojan CDTRL316

June Powell, The Best Thing For Me; **Marcia Griffiths**, I See You My Love; **Sharon Forrester**, Silly Wasn't I; **Phyllis Dillon**, The Love That A Woman Should Give A Man; **Judy Mowatt**, She Kept On Talking; **June Powell**, Please Mr Please; **Roslyn Sweet**, Mother Nature; **Audrey Hall**, Heart Made Of Stone (Vocal); **The Hit Squad**, Heart Made Of Stone (Version); **June Powell**, You Can Wake Up With Me; **Phyllis Dillon**, Love The One You're With; **Cynthia Richard**, Promises; **Naomi**, You're Not My Kind; **Barbara Jones**, I Can't Help It Darling; **Sharron Forrester**, Put A Little Love Away; **Sidonie Jordon**, Something About You; **June Powell**, I'll Be Everything To You (Vocal); **The Hit Squad**, I'll Be Everything To You (Version).

These two collections of the finest in Jamaican female vocalists are probably the best proof there is that reggae wasn't 'all the same'. Although these women mostly handle lovers-ish ballads, there's so much range and scope in production, writing, arrangement and approach that these two CDs never ever get boring.

Keep On Coming Through The Door – Jamaican Deejay Music 1969-1973; Trojan CDTRL 255

King Stitt and Clancy Eccles, Dance Beat; **Sir Lord Comic**, Jack Of My Trade; **Samuel The First**, Sounds Of Babylon; **King Stitt**, Fire Corner; **I-Roy**, Heart Don't Leap; **Herman**, To The Fields; **Dennis Alcapone**, Mosquito One; **Prince Jazzbo**, Mr Harry Skank; **Dennis Alcapone**, Alpha and Omega; **U-Roy**, Wet Vision; **Dillinger**, Headquarters; **Dennis Alcapone**, Back Biter; **Lloyd Young**, High Explosion; **U-Roy**, The Higher The Mountain; **Prince Far-I**, Deck Of Cards; **I-Roy**, Rose Of Sheron; **Prince Heron**, Ten Commandments; **Scotty**, Salvation.

The best example available of across-the-board early deejay work. The grass roots of today's dancehall styles, and the reason for Snoop Doggy Dogg and the like. A vital record for anybody remotely interested in Jamaican musical history.

*The Magnificent Fourteen – 14 Shots Of Western Inspired Reggae; Trojan CDTRL283

Sir Lord Comic and The Upsetters, Django Shoots First; **Derrick Harriot and The Chrystalites,** Fistful Of Dollars; **The Upsetters,** Paint Your Wagon; **Dice The Boss,** Gun The Man Down; **Richard Ace,** Hang 'Em High; **The Upsetters,** Dollar In The Teeth; **Rupie Edwards Allstars,** The Magnificent Seven; **The Upsetters,** The Return Of Django; **Bongo Les Herman and The Chrystalites,** True Grit; **Gladstone Adams,** Dollars and Cents; **The Upsetters,** Eastwood Rides Again; **Clancy Eccles and The Dynamites,** Van Cleef; **Winston Wright and GG Allstars,** Bonanza; **The Upsetters,** The Good The Bad and The Upsetter.

In the ghettos of Kingston, aside from the dancehall, the next best place to be was the cinema. Before the US blaxploitation films of the 1970s reached Jamaica, westerns were the preferred viewing – it wasn't unusual for rude boys in the audience to get so caught up with the action they'd start shooting at the screen! This set of tunes represents what was something of a national obsession, and as most of the tracks owe a debt to Lee Perry, it's never short of surprises.

*Out Of Many, One – Jamaican Music 1962-1975; Trojan CDTRS1

Don Drummond and Tommy McCook, Music Is My Occupation; **The Ethiopians,** Owe Me No Pay Me; **Sir Lord Comic,** Jack Of My Trade; **Carl Bryan,** Run For Your Life; **Neville Grant,** Sick And Tired; **Busty Brown,** Don't Look Back; **Ken Parker,** Only Yesterday; **Junior Byles,** A Place Called Africa; **The Tennors,** Hopeful Village; **Delroy Wilson,** Better Must Come; **The Crystalites,** Stop That Man; **I-Roy,** Space Flight; **Bob Marley and The Wailers,** The Sun Is Shining; **Niney The Observer,** Ital Correction; **Junior Byles,** Fever; **Keith Hudson,** Satan Side; **Scotty,** Skank In Bed; **Cornell Campbell and The Eternals,** Let's Start Again.

Out Of Many, One – Jamaican Music Part Two; Trojan ZCDTRS2

Big Youth, Mammy Hot Daddy Cool; **Ken Boothe,** Who Gets Your Love; **Johnnie Clarke,** Everyday Wondering; **Dennis Alcapone,** It Must Come; **King Tubby,** A Serious Version; **Michael Rose,** Clap The Barber; **Lloyd Parks,** Everybody Needs Love; **The Techniques,** Drink More Wine; **Bunny and Ricky,** Freedom Fighter; **Roy Shirley,** Hold Them; **Monty Morris,** Strongman Samson; **The Duke Reid Group,** The Rude Boy; **Bennett and Dennis,** Puppy Love; **Pat Kelly,** Little Boy Blue; **The Heptones,** Give Me The Right; **Carlton Jackson,** History; **Junior Ainsworth,** Thanks And Praise; **Cornell Campbell,** I Will Never Change.

Not the obvious Trojan compilations, thus the *Out Of Many, One* CDs make a good companion pair to what else is available.

Reggae Attack; Attack CDAT113

Harry J All Stars, The Liquidator; **Bob Marley,** Soul Shakedown Party; **Nicky Thomas,** Love Of The Common People; **Ken Boothe,** Crying Over You; **Tony Tribe,** Red Red Wine; **Symarip,** Skinhead Moonstomp; **The Upsetters,** Dollar In The Teeth; **Desmond Dekker,** 007 (Shanty Town); **Dave and Ansil Collins,** Double Barrel; **The Ethiopians,** Last Train To Skaville; **The Pioneers,** Long Shot Kick De Bucket; **Dandy Livingstone,** Suzanne Beware Of The Devil; **Desmond Dekker,** The Israelites; **The Maytals,** Monkey Man; **Jimmy Cliff,** Many Rivers To Cross; **Lord Tanamo,** I'm In The Mood For Ska.

The Roots Of Reggae; Music Collection International MCBX003

DISC ONE: **Bob Marley,** Soul Shakedown Party; **Ken Boothe,** Everything I Own; **Desmond Dekker,** You Can Get It If You Really Want; **Greyhound,** Black And White; **Susan Cadogan;** Hurt So Good; **Don Drummond,** Man In The Street; **Mikey Dread,** Barber Saloon; **Dennis Brown,** Let Me Down Easy; **Lee Perry,** I Am A Madman; **Desmond Dekker and The Aces,** The Israelites; **John Holt,** Help Me Make It Through The Night;

Toots And The Maytals, 54-46 Was My Number; **Bob Marley**, Kaya; **The Pioneers**, Let Your Yeah Be Yeah; **Bob And Marcia**, Young Gifted And Black; **Linval Thompson**, Rock Me In Dub; **Augustus Pablo**, Java; **Prince Far I**, What You Gonna Do On Judgement Day.

DISC TWO: **Dandy Livingstone**, A Message To You Rudy; **The Ethiopians**, Last Train To Skaville; **Desmond Dekker**, 007 (Shanty Town); **Phyllis Dillon**, Perfida; **Harry J All Stars**, The Liquidator; **The Pioneers**, Long Shot Kick De Bucket; **Roland Alphonso**, Phoenix City; **The Upsetters**, Return Of Django; **The Skatalites**, Confucius; **Dave And Ansil Collins**, Double Barrel; **Bob Marley**, Trenchtown Rock; **The Maytals**, Pressure Drop; **Augustus Pablo**, East Of The River Nile; **Symarip**, Skinhead Moonstomp; **Gregory Isaacs**, All I Have Is Love; **Inner Circle**, I Shot The Sheriff; **Big Youth**, Hit The Road Jack; **The Heptones**, Book Of Rules; **Barrington Levy**, Shine Eye Gal; **Niney The Observer**, Blood And Fire.

DISC THREE: **Bob Marley and The Wailers**, Caution; **Jimmy Cliff**, Miss Jamaica; **The Maytals**, Monkey Man; **Lee Perry**, People Funny Boy; **Desmond Dekker**, It Mek; **Bob And Marcia**, The Pied Piper; **Dandy Livingstone**, Suzanne Beware Of The Devil; **Evan and Jerry With The Carib Beats**, Rock Steady Train; **Peter Tosh With Bob Marley and The Wailers**, Stop That Train; **Scotty**, Skank In Bed; **Bob Marley and The Wailers**, Keep Moving; **Laurel Aitken**, Bartender; **The Ethiopians**, The Whip; **The Melodians**, Sweet Sensation; **Honey Boy Martin**, Dreader Than Dread; **Lord Tanamo**, I'm In The Mood For Ska; **Freddie Notes and The Rudies**, Montego Bay; **The Techniques**, Oh Ba-a-by (Sick and Tired); **Augustus Pablo**, African Queen; **Alton Ellis**, Rock Steady.

Tighten Up Volumes One and Two; Trojan CDTRL 306

Lee Perry, Tighten Up; **Joya Landis**, Kansas City; **Val Bennet**, Spanish Harlem; **David Isaacs**, Place In The Sun; **George A Penny**, Win Your Love; **Brother Dan All Stars**, The Donkey Returns; **Joyce Bond**, Ob-La-Di Ob-La-Da; **Joya Landis**, Angel In The Morning; **Derrick Morgan**, Fat Man; **Byron Lee**, Soul Limbo; **The Kingstonians**, Mix It Up; **The Uniques**, Watch This

Squad; **The Pioneers**, Long Shot Kick De Bucket; **Rudy Mills**, John Hones; **Clancy Eccles**, Fire Corner; **The Soul Sisters**, Wreck A Buddy; **Dandy Livingstone**, Reggae In Your Jeggae; **Clancy Eccles**, Fattie Fattie; **The Upsetters**, The Return Of Django; **The Kingstonians**, Sufferer; **Joya Landis**, Moonlight Lover; **The Bleechers**, Come Into My Parlour; **The Soulmates**, Them A Laugh And A Ki Ki; **The Upsetters**, Live Injection.

Tighten Up Volumes Three and Four; Trojan CDTRL 307

The Maytals, Monkey Man; **The Upsetters**, Shocks Of Mighty; **Ken Boothe**, Freedom Street; **Dandy**, Raining In My Heart; **The G.G. All Stars**, Man From Carolina; **Jo Jo Bennett**, Leaving Rome; **The Kingstonians**, Singerman; **Jimmy Cliff**, Suffering; **King Stitt**, Herbsman; **Nora Dean**, Barbwire; **Delano Stewart**, Stay A Little Bit Longer; **Lloyd and Claudette**, Queen Of The World; **Niney**, Blood And Fire; **The Slickers**, Johnny Too Bad; **The Ethiopians**, The Selah; **The Maytals**, One Eye Enos; **Merlene Weber**, Hard Life; **The Gaytones**, I Shall Sing; **Hopeton Lewis**, Grooving Out On Life; **The Pioneers**, Starvation; **The Music Doctors**, Bush Doctor; **The Ethiopians**, Good Ambition; **The Lowbites**, I Got It; **Merlene Weber**, Stand By Your Man.

Tighten Up Volumes Five and Six; Trojan CDTRL 320

Delroy Wilson, Better Must Come; **Jackie Edwards and Julie Anne**, In Paradise; **The Dynamites**, Hello Mother; **Clancy Eccles**, Rod Of Correction; **Dennis Alcapone**, Ripe Cherry; **Errol Dunkley**, Three In One; **Julien and The Chosen Few**, Joy To The World; **Bongo Herman**, Know For I; **The Maytals**, It's You; **Jimmy London**, Bridge Over Troubled Water; **The Chosen Few**, Shaft; **Bob Marley and The Wailers**, Duppy Conqueror; **Ernie Smith**, Pitta Patta; **The Chosen Few**, Do Your Thing; **Mikey Chung**, Breezing; **The Maytones**, As Long As You Love Me; **Harry J All Stars**, Down Side Up; **Dandy Livingstone**, Suzanne Beware Of The Devil; **The Cimarons**, Struggling Man; **The Maytals**, Redemption Song; **I-Roy and The Jumpers**, Hot Bomb; **Shortie**, President Mash Up The Resident; **Jackie Edwards**, Who Told You So; **Clancy Eccles**, Unite Tonight.

The *Tighten Up*s used to be the heart and soul of reggae in this country. Retailing at under a quid, they were the only way Saturday job money could stretch to buying the hottest tunes. Together with their never better than tacky artwork, they remain a marvellous document of Trojan Records and how reggae developed in the UK. No, they're part of your heritage.

*Tougher Than Tough – The Story Of Jamaican Music; Mango IBXCD1

↔ DISC TWO: *Reggae Hit The Town 1968-1974*
Desmond Dekker, The Israelites; **The Maytals**, 54-46 (That's My Number); **The Ethiopians**, Reggae Hit The Town; **Max Romeo**, Wet Dream; **The Uniques**, My Conversation; **Stranger Cole and Lester Sterling**, Bangarang; **The Upsetters**, The Return Of Django; **Harry J Allstars**, The Liquidator; **The Melodians**, Rivers Of Babylon; **Jimmy Cliff**, The Harder They Come; **Bob and Marcia**, Young Gifted And Black; **U-Roy**, Wake The Town; **Pat Kelly**, How Long; **Dave and Ansil Collins**, Double Barrel; **Niney**, Blood and Fire; **Eric Donaldson**, Cherry Oh Baby; **Delroy Wilson**, Better Must Come; **Dennis Brown**, Money In My Pocket; **John Holt**, Stick By Me; **Dennis Alcapone**, Teach the Children; **Big Youth**, S.90 Skank; **Ken Boothe**, Everything I Own; **Dennis Brown**, Westbound Train; **Johnny Clarke**, Move Out Of Babylon; **Junior Byles**, Curly Locks.

And so *Tougher Than Tough – The Story Of Jamaican Music* continues into the second phase, with no relaxation of standards whatsoever. This combines the commercial, the oblique and the sound system hits with stunning accuracy, to present a truly rounded picture of the music as it progressed through to the roots period. (Discussed in the previous section, page 99.)

*The Trojan Story Volume Two; Trojan CDTAL200

I-Roy, Musical Pleasure; **The Ethiopians**, The Selah; **Delroy Wilson**, Better Must Come; **Little Roy**, Hard Fighter; **Niney**, Blood and Fire; **The Eternals**, Push Me Into A Corner; **U-Roy**, Earthquake; **El Paso**, Mosquito; **Dennis Brown**, What About The Half; **Shortie The President**, President Mash Up The

Resident; **Dizzy and The Soul Syndicate**, Riot; **Winston Scotland**, My Little Filly; **Trevor Lambert**, Bald Headed Teacher; **The Heptones**, Our Day Will Come; **Alton Ellis**, Big Bad Boy; **Scotty**, Skank In Bed; **Freddie McKay**, Our Rendezvous; **The Upsetters**, Jungle Lion; **I-Roy**, Hijacking; **Delroy Wilson**, Living In the Footsteps; **Dennis Alcapone**, DJ's Choice; **Alton Ellis**, Truly; **Pablo and Fay,** Bedroom Mazurka; **Jah Berry**, Whole Lotta Sugar Down There; **Gregory Isaacs**, Bad Dah; **Johnny Clarke**, Hold I Up; **Big Youth**, Hit The Road Jack; **Ken Boothe**, That's The Way Nature Planned It; **The Heptones**, Cool Rasta; **John Holt**, Ghetto Girl; **Lizzard**, Milk And Honey; **Ras Michael**, Unity; **Michael Rose**, Born Free; **Sugar Minott**, Strange Things; **Linval Thompson**, I Love Marijuana; **Thompson Allstars**, Rock Me In Dub; **Ashanti**, Babylon Wrong; **Mikey Dread**, Barber Saloon; **Ranking Joe**, Choice Of Colour; **Barrington Levy**, Rob and Gone; **Bim Sherman,** Lightning And Thunder; **The Viceroys**, Mission Impossible; **Prince Jammy**, Throne Of Blood; **Prince Far-I**, Every Time I Hear The Word; **Ken Boothe**, You're No Good; **Barry Brown**, Mr CID

The second part of the massive, full-length *Trojan Story* set, taking us up to the end of the company's dominance and showing how they began to adapt to the changing times, but just didn't seem to go the distance. It was as if their heart wasn't in the roots movement. All the same, this early dread beat is first class, and the set is the ideal complement to the Mango box *Tougher Than Tough*.

The Trojan Story; Trojan CDTRS402

DISC ONE: **The Skatalites**, Guns Of Navarone; **Roland Alphonso**, Phoenix City; **The Techniques**, Oh Ba-a-by; **Alton Ellis**, Get Ready Rock Steady; **The Maytals**, Do The Reggae; **Marlene Webber**, Stand By Your Man; **Tony Tribe**, Red Red Wine; **Jimmy Cliff**, Miss Jamaica; **U-Roy**, Version Galore; **Screaming Target**, Big Youth; **Dennis Alcapone**, Cassius Clay; **I-Roy**, Black Man Time; **Dennis Brown**, Silhouette; **Ken Parker**, Jimmy Brown; **The Diamonds**, Just Can't Figure Out; **Johnny Clark**, Enter Into His Gates With Praise.

DISC TWO: **Desmond Dekker**, Pretty African; **The Heptones**, Save The Last Dance For Me; **Zap Pow**, Nice Nice Time; **Toots and The Maytals**, Take Me Home Country Roads; **Tito Simon**, Time Is The Master; **The Pioneers**, Mama Look Deh; **Judge Dread**, Big Eight; **Peter Tosh**, Them Fe Get A Beating; **Freddie Notes and The Rudies**, Montego Bay; **Byron Lee and The Dragonaires**, Elizabethan Reggae; **Desmond Dekker**, 007 (Shanty Town); **Ken Boothe**, Crying Over You; **The Upsetters**, The Return Of Django; **John Holt**, Mr Bojangles; **Dandy Livingstone**, Reggae In Your Jeggae; **The Pioneers**, Long Shot Kick De Bucket.

A condensed version of the set that makes up *The Trojan Story Parts One and Two* (Trojan CDTAL100 and 200), going right from the start up to the 1970s. An excellent cross-section of Jamaican music, and although the tracklisting will struggle to impress the specialist, it's ideal for the nervous beginner.

*Yesterday – 16 Fab Beatle Reggae Classics; Trojan CDTRL294

Dandy, Yesterday; **John Holt**, Hey Jude; **The Israelites**, Come Together; **Phyliss Dillon**, Something; **Nicky Thomas**, Let It Be; **Anonymously Yours**, Get Back; **Joe's Allstars**, Hey Jude; **Keith Lynn With Byron Lee and The Dragonaires**, My Sweet Lord; **Del Davis**, World Without Love; **The Maytals**, Give Peace A Chance; **The Chrystalites**, Lady Madonna; **Nicky Thomas**, Isn't It A Pity; **Harry J Allstars**, Don't Let Me Down; **Roslyn Sweet and The Paragons**, Blackbird; **B.B. Seaton**, Eleanor Rigby; **The Johnny Arthey Orchestra**, World Without Love.

*The Black Album – Yesterday Part Two; Trojan CDTRL338

Jackie Edwards, Yesterday; **Ken Boothe**, My Love; **John Holt**, Happy Christmas (War Is Over); **The Johnny Arthey Orchestra**, Something; **The Rudies**, My Sweet Lord; **Marshall Williams**, Norwegian Wood; **Joyce Bond**, Ob-La-Di-Ob-La-Da; **The Dynamites**, Hey Jude; **John Holt**, I Will; **Marcia Griffiths**, Don't Let Me Down; **Jackie Robinson**, In My Life/Version.

The Sounds Of The 1970s – Reggae Style; Trojan CDTRL321

Lloyd Charmers, I Can't Get Next To You; **The Chosen Few**, You're A Big Girl Now; **Nicky Thomas**, Rainy Night In Georgia; **Keeling Beckford**, Groove Me; **Dave Barker**, Just My Imagination; **John Holt**, Sister Big Stuff; **Lloyd Charmers**, Shaft; **Ken Parker**, Help Me Make It Through The Night; **Margaret Elaina**, Ben; **B.B. Seaton**, Lean On Me; **Derrick Harriot**, Have You Seen Her; **Marcia Griffiths**, The First Time Ever I Saw Your Face; **Dennis Brown**, Let Me Down Easy; **Leroy Sibbles**, Break Up To Make Up; **Susan Cadogan**, It Hurts So Good; **Alton Ellis**, It's Too Late To Turn Back; **Barrington Spence**, Living A Little Laughing A Little; **Cynthia Richards**, (If You're Ready) Come Go With Me; **Boris Gardiner**, You Make Me Feel Brand New; **The Inner Circle**, When Will I See You Again.

Three examples of the obsession with pop cover versions that reggae had at this time, an obsession rooted in the Jamaican music industry by so many musicians having to play Jamaican-ized versions of popular hits for tourists in the hotels. It carried over to recording, as there were no copyright laws in Jamaica until much later. Also, the radio had no problems playing stuff like this. Although so much of it is cheesy (there are four volumes of reggae covers of 1970s soul ballads on the market, *Just My Imagination – Soulful Reggae For Lovers*, which space and good taste prevents me from going into here), some of it wasn't too bad. The three detailed above are included as much for their kitsch value as for illustrating a widespread early reggae trait.

3

NATTY ROOTS, NATTY CULTURE

J amaica gained its independence from Great Britain in 1962, and for a while the country surfed on a wave of optimism and the short-term financial gains that accompanied an upturn in tourism and bauxite mining. But long before it became apparent to the country in general that Jamaica's go-it-alone status was all but unworkable, the harsh realities of the post-colonial economic climate were being felt in the ghettoes of West Kingston. An apparently endless stream of fortune-seekers had arrived in town, assuming that an independent Jamaica meant increased opportunities, then the thousands displaced by newly opened bauxite mines ended up alongside them in the city's growing shanty towns. Overcrowding made an enormous contribution to the rude boy riots of the second half of the 1960s. Things didn't get any better, either. For a vast majority of Jamaicans, a decade on from Independence, money was too tight to even think about, let alone mention. And an alternative culture was flourishing.

Rastafari had been present on the fringes of Jamaican society since the 1930s, when a combination of Marcus Garvey's Back To Africa teachings, Emperor Haile Selassie's coronation and the rise of the African Methodist Episcopal church in Jamaica combined to create the circumstances for the establishment of the faith. By the 1950s it had grown to become the religion of choice among Kingston's dispossessed young men. But to hold such beliefs was seen as an act of insurrection by the authorities, so in order to avoid persecution the many ghetto musicians who followed Rastafari were not open about it.

By the 1970s though, the notions of American black power

and the riots in major US cities had a profound effect on Jamaica. The number of poor was rapidly rising, Rasta converts were increasing out of all proportion, and nobody was prepared to keep quiet about it any more.

Black expression was by now an international affair, and in Jamaica this manifested itself as Rastafari. It seemed like every singer on the island was 'locksing' up as the notion of black roots and culture took over the music business to an almost total degree. During the first couple of years of the 1970s, reggae turned righteous. In a manner from which it has yet to recover.

The beat slowed down, as the whole purpose of the music seemed an act of deliberate intimidation. Of dread. The balance of instruments changed as the bass and drums became more dominant. Horns took on an Eastern feel, evoking visions of Ethiopia. Lyrics concerned themselves with all matters Old Testament, statements of black pride, or rallying cries against the system. And very little else. Acts were now called things like Black Uhuru, Culture, Burning Spear, Prince Far-I, The Observer, Israel Vibration and Ras Michael. It was an intensely spiritual time for the music, and in turn it produced some of the most moving tunes ever to come out the island, as reggae confirmed its folk music status by becoming an absolute expression of the lives of the people who were performing it.

The sound system was now of the utmost importance, as once again national radio ignored the music of the people. Although the ultra-conservative programmers had come to accept the vibrant, poppy reggae of the past few years as fit to be broadcast, this new style was a completely different matter. It was more than just subversive, it was downright anti-social. Not only did these people sing in ghetto slang, but they didn't comb their hair either! So suddenly the sound system deejay was king. The ghetto communicator who was best placed to advance these new ideas that were sweeping the area. Whereas deejay recordings had been in existence for several years, they were only just establishing themselves as an art form in their own right, with guys like U-Roy and Dennis Alcapone looking for maximum entertainment value. Roots reggae changed that. Instantly. New style toasters like Prince Jazzbo and Tappa Zukie had an agenda to chant down Babylon, and would urge crowds on to do the same as Rasta scattergun logic, word play, Old Testament teachings and black nationalism tumbled out together to present some wildly inventive lyrics. At the same time the singers added a real poignancy to either solo outings or the classic JA three-part harmony approach, by voicing songs of spirituality or sufferation.

Advancing studio technology played its part in the dread revolution too, as the generation of producers now coming to the fore were looking to re-invent the music as blatantly as possible. This new breed were constantly seeking fresh angles, therefore investigating the potential of the rapidly improving studio equipment with much greater gusto than their predecessors. And so the mixing desk itself became something of an electronic playground to the likes of Lee Perry, Joe Gibbs and Errol Thompson, Augustus Pablo, Bunny Lee and the legendary King Tubby. Their adventures in sound created dub as an end in itself rather than simply a by-product of the versioning process. And the more startling the better. What began merely with skilful use of the cross-fader, rapidly evolved into the complete reinvention of tunes as remixing involved echoes, delays, reverb, distortion, shifts in time signatures, additional instrumentation and a battery of SFX from telephones ringing and explosions to animal noises and TV dialogue.

All of this, in spite of sounding deliberately unnatural, successfully boosted the cause of Jah Rastafari, as the ferocious, rumbling or just plain overwhelming results invoked a very Old Testament idea of dread. Fire and brimstone would be a walk in the park compared with a King Tubby mix of an Augustus Pablo instrumental.

Natty culture spread around the world too, thanks to the arrival of one Robert Nesta Marley, reggae's first international superstar. Naturally enough, it took a firm hold in the UK. Dreadlocks had been a common sight on British streets long before the 1976 Notting Hill Carnival ended with pitched battles between police and black kids. By then dissatisfaction with police attitudes and the racially imbalanced unemployment figures were spilling over into frustration. Rasta ideology, with its sense of black pride, Caribbean roots and spectacular soundtrack seemed to suit so many of the UK's sufferahs far better than the American approach. Roots sound systems appeared in every city that had a large black community, while artists such as Aswad, Steel Pulse, Misty and Dennis Bovell brought a uniquely British slant to the creation of deep roots music.

It wasn't all dread inna England either. As reggae mush-roomed in popularity among British black kids, so it broadened its appeal to a more pop-orientated audience with the develop-ment of lovers' rock. Which was exactly what the term implies – much lighter, smoove-flowing reggae that concerned itself more or less solely with affairs of the heart. It was a natural progres-sion from the pop reggae of the previous era that did so well in the UK, but took on board the techniques and sound balances of the roots material, in order to make sure it stayed black, just far more melodic. The lovers' rock sound systems and record labels knew their audience – mainly young girls who had grown out of The Jackson Five – and tailored their approach to fit. During the second half of the 1970s, the UK produced a stream of teenage girl artists and groups – Janet Kay, Susan Cadogan, Louisa Mark, Brown Sugar and 15, 16, 17 (a trio so named because of its members' ages) – in response to the enormous market for some-thing both culturally correct and easily enjoyable. Plus there was the added bonus that this stuff was far more likely to cross over into the mainstream, the best example of which was Janet Kay's 'Silly Games', a number 2 pop chart hit in 1979.

Indeed reggae seemed unstoppable as we went into the 1980s. Not only was it succeeding, but it was doing so on a worldwide basis, and on what appeared to be its own terms as the big-time roots acts refused to compromise.

Then in 1981 Bob Marley died and the music was thrown into a tailspin. Without such a charismatic, internationally recog-nized figurehead, the roots movement lost direction, and all musical development seemed to go on hold as producers and record labels looked for 'the new Bob Marley'. It took two or three years for people to realize they weren't going to find one, by which time reggae-as-we-knew-it had all but disappeared as a global force.

It wasn't to be away for too long, though, and when it did return it was vastly altered . . .

The Abyssinians

(Donald Manning; Linford Manning; Bernard Collins; all born 1940s; Kingston, Jamaica; vocal group)

How did you know, reggae-wise, the 1970s were going to be something really rather special? That what had, over the last ten years, evolved into a true Sound Of The People was about become a genuinely spiritual folk music? The answer came in 1971 in five words: The Abyssinians' 'Satta Massa Gana'. Cut at Studio One over two years earlier, it based itself on the Carlton and His Shoes hit 'Happy Land' and was a deep and moving hymn to Jah Rastafari, delivered in part in Amharic, the first language of Amhara, an ancient country that became the north-western section of Ethiopia. The stirring blend of low, rootsy harmonizing and trance-like rhythms set off with cascading percussion conjured up a smoky crossroads of soul power where Addis Ababa collided with downtown Kingston, the Wareika Hills and little pockets of London, Birmingham and Bristol. This was the way forward for the music in a manner that would satisfy the heart, the head and the feet. Testament to the importance of 'Satta Massa Gana' is found in the fact it's been versioned more times than anybody cares to count.

The group was founded in 1968 as a duo, Donald Manning and Bernard Collins, when Manning left Carlton and His Shoes, the group he was in with his two brothers Linford and Carlton. Hence the 'Happy Land' musical connection. Then when Linford joined a few months later, it precipitated the break up of Carlton's group. The first thing they wrote and recorded was 'Satta', but COXSONE DODD refused to release the record, consigning the tape to his vaults where it was promptly forgotten about. This actually isn't so remarkable – not only was Dodd from another musical era, but socially he always had one eye on uptown and was very slow to appreciate the value (both commercial and otherwise) of roots reggae. The group never forgot it though, and after over a year of saving were able to buy the tape from Studio One, who might not have wanted to put it out but weren't about to give it away either! It shows a shrewd judgement on the part of The Abyssinians that they opted to hold out for the wonderfully atmospheric Studio One production rather than go elsewhere and cut the tune again. It was such

177

an instant and enormous hit when they put it out themselves that Dodd immediately re-recorded it and cashed in with numerous quick versions, all of which were, ironically, vastly inferior.

Not only was this song a definite starting point for roots vocalizing, but it marked the beginning of The Abyssinians as the foremost singing group of the 1970s. Although they never hit those astonishing heights again, 'Declaration Of Rights', 'Prophecy' (two more much-covered roots classics), 'Poor Jason White', 'This Land Is For Everyone', 'Reason Time' and 'Maabrak' (their own version of 'Satta Massa Gana', supplementing the lyrics with readings from the Old Testament) kept them up near the top for the next ten years. By the end of the decade Collins had left, to be replaced by Carlton Manning – thus creating a kind of dread version of Carlton and His Shoes – but the group split in 1980, with Donald continuing the same spiritual path under the name Donald Abyssinian.

Very recently, as the roots revival gathers pace, they have reformed and, by performing some of the very best concerts, are a living embodiment of the power of genuine roots reggae.

Satta Massa Gana; Heartbeat HBCD190

The nearest you're going to get to an Abyssinians Greatest Hits on CD at the moment, and the fact that this has the title track on it is worth the cost of admission alone. That it's got 'Declaration Of Rights', 'Maabrak', 'Poor Jason White' and 'Love Comes And Goes' too is really just a bonus. To let this set play all the way through is like immersing yourself in a bath of roots reggae, a dread-beat primer. It offers all the explanation ever needed as to why The Abyssinians are so important. The urgency of the rhythm tracks communicates the notion of time running out, while there's a deep earthy softness to every production that prevents any edginess – they didn't lose a thing when, post-'Satta', they started producing themselves. And as for the harmonizing, if a heartbeat had a voice this would be it. It's immeasurably close, rich and luxuriant, but still the sound of sufferation and as militant as hell. If they didn't actually change the world, for nearly an entire decade The Abyssinians made it a much more bearable place to be.

Arise; Frontline CDFL9010.

Recorded in 1978, relatively late in the trio's first life, this is their second album. While all the technical expertise is still very much in place, there seems to be a certain weariness of spirit about the group and so the album didn't ever hit the heights of its predecessor, the currently (and criminally) unavailable *Forward To Zion*. Although any disc which can boast 'This Land Is For Everyone', 'Meditation' and 'Oh Lord' on its tracklisting has got to represent a good deal, maybe by this time they'd simply been doing it too long. They would split up not long after.

SEE ALSO:

Reggae Refreshers Volume Two; Mango RRCDS102/524 030-2
Jammin'; Mango CIDM1010
Nice An' Ruff – A Crucial Brew Of Roots, Dub and Rockers; Music Club International MCCD092
Roots and Culture Serious Selection Volume One; Rewind Selecta CDREG3
Roots 'N' Culture; Music Club International MCCD128

The Aggrovators

(Studio session group)
This was BUNNY 'STRIKER' LEE's studio band, a name that disguised the shifting pool of players who worked for the producer over the years, in the same way THE SKATALITES worked for COXSONE DODD. But the particular significance about this band is that they were the first formalized unit of the new roots strain of reggae (or as near as it was possible to be in the Jamaican music business of the 1970s).

Lee had begun the various incarnations of The Aggrovators at the end of the rock steady period in the late 1960s, but they came into their own as the first regular riddim kings a couple of years into the next decade, as versions became desirable in their own right. Striker was one of the pioneers of this vocal-less approach and, thanks to his early patronage of master mixer KING TUBBY, The Aggrovators' instrumental sides from this time were never less than interesting.

Johnny In The Echo Chamber; Attack ATCD106

Although there's a few Aggrovators albums available on vinyl, this is the only UK-released CD. However, for what you miss in quantity it makes up for in quality. The album comprises the dub tracks to JOHNNY CLARKE's *Don't Trouble Trouble* album (a collection of Lee-produced scorchers), and on these cuts you have one of the very best in roots backing bands. Not just as working for Bunny Lee, but anywhere. Among the players are Chinna Smith (guitar); ROBBIE SHAKESPEARE and Family Man (bass); Carlton 'Santa' Davis (drums); and Bobby Kalphat (keyboards). Mixed down Tubby-style, the title doesn't lie: it offers up a dubwise selection covering all points in between the rootsy 'Too Much War' ('Not Enough Dub'), the reggaefied R&B 'Tears On My Pillow' ('Dub On My Pillow') and the swinging lovers' rock of 'Do You Love Me' ('Do You Dub'). It's a stunning example of the individual and collective talents of all involved.

Dr Alimantado

(Born Winston Thompson, 1952; Kingston, Jamaica; deejay)
Back in the summer of 1976, then Sex Pistol and punk icon Johnny Rotten was playing his personal all-time Top 10 on a London radio station. In at number 3 was 'Born For A Purpose (Reason For Living)' by Dr Alimantado. Within days, the good Doctor's name was spray-painted on what seemed like every wall in Ladbroke Grove, and Greensleeves, its tiny UK label, was frantically repressing the track and the album it came from. It seemed every punk in Britain had to have it, with the single eventually selling over 50,000 copies. Dr Alimantado had achieved instant cult status.

The Doctor's deejaying career began on LEE PERRY-operated sound systems at the beginning of the 1970s and so it was natural that Scratch should be the first to record him. Nothing came of it though, and Alimantado set up by himself to produce tracks that had absorbed the whole spectrum of Perry-istic quirks and left-field attitude but with a slightly harder undercurrent. It worked too. 'Best Dressed Chicken', 'Born For A Purpose', 'Son Of Thunder', 'Unitone Skank', 'Gimme Mi Gun' and 'Sons Of Thunder' were instant hits in a market far removed from punk, and presented a teetering, towering sound with some of the busiest, most fragmented mixes outside of Black Ark, topped off by the Doctor's persuasively melodic toasting.

The Johnny-Rotten inspired burst of fame wasn't the best thing that could have happened to him, though. In order to make the most of it he moved to London – with his trademark red, gold and green college-style scarf, sunglasses, dreadlocks and a big smile, he became a familiar figure around the Westbourne Grove frontline. But the music he recorded here lacked the inspired lunacy of his Jamaican efforts, and although he continued cutting albums all through the 1980s, they just don't compare with the first two.

Sons Of Thunder; Greensleeves GRELCD22

This is the album first released as *Born For A Purpose*, and is probably the best example of Dr Alimantado's bizarre, irrepressible style. It's obvious the man is from the Lee Perry School Of Sound, but whereas his mentor's output often seems to exist for no other reason than Scratch's personal pleasure, Alimantado never forgets he has an audience. And that they want to rock. No matter what's on top, or where the echo's spinning to, or just how mad the fading and phasing is, at the heart of everything is a tune. Here, as well as the entirely melodic 'Born', which had become an easy skanking classic long before that radio programme, there's two other cuts of it – 'Reason For Living' and 'Still Alive', each offering a more studiedly dread approach – there's a cover of 'Sitting In The Park' and the strictly lovers' 'Marriage License'. Of course, he gets rootsy too with the overwhelming rhythms and screwball mixes of 'Sons Of Thunder' and 'Call On Jah'.

ALSO RECOMMENDED:

The Best Dressed Chicken In Town; Greensleeves KMCD1

The killer cut on this is the title track, a wild toast and a wilder mix structured around the melody lines of Bill Withers's classic 'Ain't No Sunshine'. Elsewhere there's 'Ride On' and 'Unitone

Skank', but it was really not until *Born For A Purpose/ Sons Of Thunder*, which was recorded a year later, that it all started to come together.

SEE ALSO:

Natty Rebel Roots; Frontline CDFL9013
If Deejay Was Your Trade – The Dreads At King Tubby's 1974-1977;
Blood And Fire BAFCD001

Horace Andy

(Born Horace Hinds, 1951; Kingston, Jamaica; singer)
His friends called him 'Sleepy', which was as much in tribute to his easy-going nature as to his laid back way with a tune – either in his singing or his writing. Horace Andy's swooping and soaring falsetto was a regular sound around Studio One from the end of the 1960s, arriving after a couple of unproductive years with Phil Pratt. Once at Brentford Road, though, he kicked off on a series of hits that was to establish him as one of the island's premier vocalists: 'Got To Be Sure', 'The Love Of A Woman', 'Just Say Who', 'Elementary' and 'Skylarking', the biggest song of the early-1970s. All absolutely wonderful early reggae, but none of it in the rootsman style his voice seemed to be perfect for. *That* didn't come until he left COXSONE in 1972.

First, with BUNNY LEE he cut such gems as 'Pure Ranking', 'Serious Thing' and 'Better Collie', but it was with Everton DaSilva in New York that he came into his own. Writing and co-producing/arranging, Sleepy could tailor material to fit his voice precisely and give it that haunting, sufferah quality that adds a spectacular lift to the work around this time. 'Do You Love My Music' was the opening cut off *In The Light*, the album he made with DaSilva in 1977, and the answer was a resounding 'Yes please' as the hits flowed until 1979 when the producer was shot dead. 'Problems', 'Youths Of today', 'Government Land' and 'Fever' are just a few of them.

After that the singer freelanced around, recording with, among others, Bullwackie in New York, JAMMY, BOBBY DIGITAL and Morwell, his biggest hit from this period being 'Natty Dread A Weh She Want' with Tappa Zukie. Most recently, Horace Andy has guested with the Bristol-based Massive Attack and is big in Japan. No kidding.

In The Light/In The Light Dub; Blood And Fire BAFCD006

A brilliant value double-CD, featuring that one DaSilva album and the accompanying dub tracks to provide almost eighty minutes of classic roots in a single easy-to-use package. The first ten tracks are the vocal cuts, a series of carefully woven complex big band instrumentals featuring players of the calibre of Horsemouth Wallace, AUGUSTUS PABLO, Bobby Kalphat and TOMMY MCCOOK. Horace Andy's voice manages to float just above the music, while at the same time becoming part of it and reacting to every nuance – choice cuts like 'Do You Like My Music', 'Problems' 'In The Light' and 'Collie Herb' are examples of a master at work. The corresponding dub cuts, however, take this to undreamt of heights. For a long time only available as a pricey Jamaican import LP, this is mixed by Prince Jammy at TUBBY's just as the sorcerer's apprentice was about to strike out on his own. It is a truly startling sonic sculpture, exploding with depth-charge drum beats, murderous basslines, skipping staccato percussion and faders that'll mess with your head long after you've turned the stereo off and gone to bed. To hear it in digitally restored splendour is not much short of an honour.

ALSO RECOMMENDED:

Seek And You Will Find; Blackamix BLKMCD015

Modern-day Horace Andy, made in the UK, but the eerie vocals are still very present and entirely correct.

SEE ALSO:

'Skylarking' can be found on *Respect To Studio One*; Heartbeat CDHB 181/182
'Elementary' can be found on *Reggae Dance Party*; Ras RASCD3018
Nice An' Ruff – A Crucial Brew Of Roots, Dub And Rockers; Music Club International MCCD 092
Lovers' Rock: Serious Selection Volume One; Rewind Selecta CDREG1

Keith Hudson And Friends; Studio Kinda Cloudy; Trojan
CDTRL258

Aswad

(Brinsley Dan, born Brinsley Forde, 1952, Guyana, vocalist/ guitar; Drummie Zeb, born Angus Gaye, 1959, London, UK, vocal-
ist/drums; Tony Gad, born Tony Robinson, 1958, London, UK,
bass/keyboards)
When you hear a tune like Aswad's 'Warrior Charge', it's as if a
light has been turned on over the style that is roots reggae. It was
the main theme from *Babylon*, a movie set in the volatile world
of London sound systems (a film that starred Brinsley Dan who,
in a previous life, was a BBC TV child actor), and the record
played its part in the script as the killer tune that would allow
the hero's sound to sweep all before it. Which is exactly what it
did in real life. All its sounds and sound balances were classic
roots reggae – the bass, the drums and the horns – while the
arrangements and tempos set traditional rhythms on their heads
to create one of the most powerful pieces of instrumental reggae
ever put down on tape. In fact, it's quite a puzzle as to why
something this hot didn't set fire to the recording equipment.
Though the likes of KING TUBBY, LEE PERRY, PRINCE
JAMMY and SCIENTIST were geniuses in their own right, and
recreated what already existed, they were still operating within
reggae's very traditional confines. With 'Warrior Charge',
Aswad shook themselves free of such claustrophobia yet
remained undeniably reggae. Perhaps the track couldn't have
been done anywhere else except Great Britain, and it remains
one of the most singularly inspired pieces of music ever written.
By anybody. Anywhere. In any style.

And it's unique – even Aswad never did anything remotely
like it again. In many ways this isn't too surprising. They are
indisputably talented, staggeringly innovative, technically correct and have the hearts of lions, they are the UK's longest
serving resident roots reggae act, plus they have put out some of
the most sound system credible reggae *and* enjoyed a number 1
pop hit, but you still can't help thinking Aswad could've done
much better for themselves. Essentially, their story reads like a

catalogue of unfulfilled potential and missed opportunities. Most of them not their fault either.

They started off, in the mid-1970s, with a bigger line-up and a style that greater reflected the musical melting pot that used to be London. Although, as their name would suggest – Aswad is Amharic for 'black' – Rasta ideology was a motivational force, their approach involved such other black London influences of the time as soul, fusion and jazz/funk over a reggae beat that would've done any Jamaican proud. They bounced dub sides down with different ears too: 'Back To Africa' had a dub plate that succeeded more on its use of space and a theoretically ludicrous rewriting of the time signature than on echo or artful crossfade, and quite literally tore up the London sound systems all through that long hot summer of 1976. It's not at all surprising that the cream of visiting reggae talent, from BURNING SPEAR to DENNIS BROWN to BLACK UHURU to BOB MARLEY, would use Aswad as a pick-up band.

But by now rock critics were arriving at reggae through punk, and the popular opinion was that Aswad weren't 'real', weren't heavy enough – curiously, what this amounted to was a bunch of white people deciding the group somehow wasn't black enough. Never mind, their peer group loved them. But on the second album, after the departure of the more jazz-minded George Oban, the direction became far more conventionally reggae, as they topped bills at Rock Against Racism concerts, above acts like The Police and Elvis Costello. The new sound wasn't rubbish or anything – they were still crisp and could come up with some serious dub – but after the spectacular debut it just seemed like marking time.

Record company wranglings followed and they found themselves on a major label. Which in theory was A Good Thing. Except, by the time they came to release a record, everybody who had been involved in bringing them to the label had left and nobody seemed to know (or care) what to do with a London roots band who had a reputation for being surly with the press. And by then (1982) wasn't reggae a bit old hat anyway? *New Chapter* was their best work for years, but such was the lack of specialist marketing skills not many people got to hear it – ironically, the dub plate from this set, *New Chapter Of Dub*, was released by a much smaller label and sold a great deal more.

After this the group lost momentum for several years, perhaps understandably, and turned back to their own world of West London blues dances, cutting a series of quite superb singles on their own Simba label – 'Bubblin', 'Kool Noh' and 'Hooked On You' standing out and marking their shift into the then embryonic digital reggae.

Then they went pop. Brilliant songwriters as they were, with their own compositions they found it all but impossible to step outside their chosen field, so they opted for cover versions. Almost immediately, as they reverted to their original formula of soul and funk built on a reggae foundation, they had a number 1 pop chart hit with 'Don't Turn Around'. Their natural on-stage exuberance and explosive performance skills once again endearing them to a broader audience. But the pop world is a fickle one and it went for the song rather than the band. Further attempts to crossover didn't fare nearly so well and had it not been for the shrewdly balanced *Rise And Shine* album in 1994 – a subtle blend of traditional and dancehall reggae, with extraneous sensibilities stirred into the mix – they might have lost their home crowd too.

Aswad's story is, unfortunately, all too typical of British reggae artists, who fall prey to the whims of a mainstream that is never more than flirting with the style, and would much rather a white group provided it. The problem is, though, that anything perceived as too pandering to the rock market means increasing distrust from original fans who want to keep the band as 'theirs'. Handily, Aswad have had the intelligence – musical and otherwise – to survive this and are still a practising, happening unit. So many others from the mid-1970s wave of British roots bands weren't so fortunate.

Showcase; Mango IMCD57

Aswad's greatest hits, going right back to 'Back To Africa', taking in the wickedly entertaining 'Three Babylon' – 'Three Babylon come to make I and I run/They come to have fun with their long truncheon' – the live show favourite 'Drum And Bassline', 'African Children', 'Natural Progression' and of course the superb 'Warrior Charge'. It's probably the best of Aswad. At their best.

Aswad; Mango IMCD58

The first album, cut in 1976, when the group was deliberately writing with other influences. Although it doesn't display some of the mesmerizing skills of their later work, through tracks like 'Back To Africa', 'Ethiopian Rhapsody', 'Concrete Slaveship' and 'Can't Stand The Pressure' it proves how it was possible to broaden reggae's base without losing touch with the root. In many ways (along with the later 'Warrior Charge'), it sums up what UK reggae could've been – maybe should've been – and how Aswad had everything they needed to define the parameters.

New Chapter; Mango CID9711
New Chapter Of Dub; Mango IMCD55

New Chapter is the one that got away, the album recorded for a major label then allowed to languish on the shelves of all the wrong shops as nobody at the company knew quite what to do with it. It remains, however, one of the best reggae albums ever made. By now (1982) they were highly skilled musicians and studio technicians, their songwriting had matured to great effect and they had money to spend on making this. Furthermore, encouraged by their new, far more rock-orientated surroundings, they approached it as an album rather than as a collection of singles and it carries through on a centric thread of brilliantly put together music. Needless to say, the dub tracks are so startling in their stripping down of these tunes they ought to carry a government health warning for those of a nervous disposition.

To The Top; Mango IMCD59

This is mostly the stuff they put out on Simba during the so-called wilderness years of the mid-1980s. Listening to it now, it becomes obvious how happy the group must have been to have the pressure of life on a big-time label removed. The tracks are superbly relaxed early dancehall, showing how easily players of this calibre can adapt, featuring the sound system hits 'Bubblin'', 'Kool Noh' and 'Hooked On You', and revealing Drummie Zeb to have the best voice in the band.

ALSO RECOMMENDED:

Live And Direct; Mango IMCD54

While this is an able demonstration of Aswad's stage show expertise, it's ultimately a bit frustrating as you can't actually be there.

Renaissance; Stylus SMD886

A later model greatest hits. It may feature 'Warrior Charge', 'Kool Noh' and 'African Children', and may be the only way you can get 'Roots Rockin'' on compact disc – but it doesn't do itself any favours with a remix of 'Smoky Blues'.

Rise And Shine; Bubblers BUBBCD1

Aswad get modern, with dancehall rhythms and hi-speed toasting kept on the right side of righteous with their olde worlde sensibilities adding a comforting warmth. The bonus is a surprisingly successful dancehall update of 'Warrior Charge' ('Warrior Charging'), proving you can't keep a good tune down.

SEE ALSO:

Reggae Refreshers Volume Two; Mango RRCDS102/524 030-2
Roots and Culture: Serious Selection Volume One; Rewind Selecta CDREG3
Jammin'; Mango CIDM1010
On A Reggae Tip; Island CIDTV5
Crucial Reggae; Mango RRCD37
Reggae Hits Volume One; Jetstar JETCD1001
Pure Reggae; Island CIDTV8

Cuts by Motion, the band George Oban formed after Aswad, can be found on *Lovers' Rock: Serious Selection Volume One* (Rewind Selecta CDREG1) and *Reggae Classics: Serious Selection Volume One* (Rewind Selecta CDREG2).

Big Youth

(Born Marley Buchanan, 1950; Kingston, Jamaica; deejay)

After U-ROY and DENNIS ALCAPONE established the art of the deejay as a recording proposition, somebody was going to have to move the art form on to the next level. What was less obvious was that that particular somebody would have red, green and gold inserts in his teeth, an enormous grin and would announce himself from off the back of a motorbike.

For the first couple of years of the 1970s, Big Youth, who was hotel porter by day, had been deejaying the Tippertone sound system – one of the era's top steppers outfits. By never forgetting that crowds had come to dance as well as reaffirm Jah Rastafari, he'd developed a style that was as exuberant as it was righteous. This was a man who understood the delicate balance of those streets, the relationship between having fun and the harsh realities, because it was *his* territory. He was the first genuine ghetto youth to find success as a recording deejay and so knew exactly how to write lyrics and deliver the rhymes in a way that was just right.

His first hit was a shining example of his knowing what time of day it was. 'S.90 Skank' was about the then current Kingston craze for Honda S.90 motorbikes, as a status symbol as much as a means of transport, and the record opened with a revving S.90 that had been smuggled into the studio by producer KEITH HUDSON (someone else who understood the new sufferah culture). Success came about after several attempts with other producers, who didn't allow the Youth the head of steam he needed to whip up a dancehall-type storm in the confines of the recording studio – his best known effort before S.90 was the sound system hit 'The Phil Pratt Thing'.

But once he'd hooked up with Hudson there seemed no stopping him. Whether he was just toasting a nonsense lyric ('Hit The Road Jack'), taunting other deejays ('Natty Dread She Want'), praising Jah ('House Of Dreadlocks' or 'Dread Inna Babylon'), discussing social issues ('Train To Rhodesia') or covering smooth soul tunes ('Papa Was A Rolling Stone'), Big Youth's exuberance touched everybody that heard him. Of course by now the coloured inserts in his front teeth made the smile that much more spectacular! Big Youth formed his own label in the second half of the 1970s, and his output seemed to slow down about the same time. Nowadays, he still performs on a fairly regular basis and hasn't lost any of his spark. A spark that ignited the deejay phenomenon to such a degree that without Youth's lyrical and vocal wildness, the later generations of less conventional fast-talking performers might never have happened.

Reggae Phenomenon; Trojan CDTRD411

Although back in 1974, when this first came out, it was a straight-up studio album, hindsight makes it look like something of a Best Of Big Youth – 'Hit The Road Jack', 'Natty Dread No Jester', 'Wolf Inna Sheep's Clothing', 'Dread Inna Babylon' and 'The Phil Pratt Thing'. . . This was cut a couple of years into his recording career so he had by then perfected his style and was well established in both the eyes of the industry and the ears of the public, all of which add up to what is perhaps his most adventurous series of recordings. Indeed, the only thing that's keeping this from being a total compilation is that you're missing 'S.90 Skank', 'Screaming Target' and 'Lightning Flash (And The Weak Heart Drop)', which, although genius tunes, aren't omission enough to seriously mar this magnificent collection by one of the top three roots toasters.

Screaming Target; Trojan CDTRL61

When this came out in 1973, it was the one to own. Everything about it was spot on. Heavyweight duotone cardboard sleeve, a picture of the artist with his locks out and music that was so exciting it could rock the house in a mortuary. In fact, in original vinyl, this became one of the most collectable (i.e. expensive) reggae records not to have a Studio One label – thank you Trojan for putting it out on CD. Across a selection of different moods, Big Youth's resonant baritone toast rings across such works of wisdom as two versions of the title track, 'Solomon Grundy', 'I'm Alright' and 'Tippertone Rock', a tribute to his old sound system.

ALSO RECOMMENDED:

Dreadlocks Dread; Frontline CDFL9006

This is the album with 'Lightning Flash' and 'House Of Dreadlocks'.

SEE ALSO:

Tougher Than Tough – The Story Of Jamaican Music; Mango IBXCD1
Dubble Attack; Greensleeves GRELCD601
Roots 'N' Culture; Music Club International MCCD128
Beyond The Frontline; Frontline CDFRONT1

Black Uhuru

(Duckie Simpson, born Derrick Simpson, 1952, Kingston, Jamaica; Michael Rose, born 1955, Kingston Jamaica; Puma Jones, born Sandra Jones, 1953, Columbia, South Carolina; vocal trio)
If ever there was a link between the roots era of the 1970s and the dancehall sounds of the next decade, it is Black Uhuru. Militant as you'd want them to be – Uhuru is Swahili for 'freedom' – yet with a sound that dragged reggae into the 1980s, with all the new studio technology that involved. Once they hooked up with The Riddim Twins SLY DUNBAR (drums) and ROBBIE SHAKESPEARE (bass), and took full advantage of the pair's experimentation with digital drum kits, a computerized space bass and new methods in the studio to have their haunting vocalizing become part of something that was equally unforgiving. The Black Uhuru sound, as displayed on albums like *Red*, *Chill Out*, *Anthem* and *Sensimilla*, was a chilling, uncompromising warning to the world that it was going badly astray. Post BOB MARLEY, they were three of the few rebels left in town.
   A few years earlier, it must have seemed to Simpson that the group was never going to get going. They were on their third line-up in five years when he recruited Michael Rose in 1977, and cut an album for PRINCE JAMMY. At the time it was received as just another Rasta vocal group LP, although it was later re-released as *Black Sounds Of Freedom* and did quite well. Soon after, the third member left. It was roughly a year later that Rose and Simpson literally happened across Jones, who was singing to herself in her apartment – the devout Rasta was in Jamaica working with RAS MICHAEL AND THE SONS OF NEGUS. This was the third leg they needed to support their

stool: the perfect ethereal offset for Rose's militant tones, which Simpson's haunting harmonizing had never quite been able to supply. As a result the in-yer-face revolutionary songwriting and posturing of Michael Rose was now softened into something people could listen to without flinching (too much). This was so important in getting the group's message over; as Rose admitted at the time, he could only sing and write 'militant', and his lyrics were often put together in the studio where they tumbled out as a kind of stream-of-consciousness rant against every one of society's evils, from lack of gun control to police persecution of Rastas, to racism, imperialist foreign powers and corrupt domestic governments.

Sly and Robbie's studio sorcery was perfect to back this up. Modern and forward-looking, it was still undeniably reggae but was constructed out of a series of groundbreaking sounds and timings, thus could revitalize the whole notion of Rasta protest, which by now (the very end of the 1970s) was starting to sound a little tired. It had a power and a glory that took Black Uhuru all over the world – not least as the opening act on the Rolling Stones' 1982 World Tour – and won them the first ever Grammy Award for Reggae for the *Anthem* album in 1984. And as their stage performance matched their music, they endeared themselves to audiences who expected more from a live performance than that offered by the average reggae artist.

But their problem was that just as they moved things on, so they got stuck in their own rut. The dynamic, taut electronic sound they built up with Sly and Robbie failed to evolve over the years, and although it never got soft there were only so many albums of it you wanted to own at any one time. It's felt by many that The Riddim Twins had taken their eye off the reggae ball, because their success with Uhuru had meant they had become internationally in-demand producer/players, across all types of music.

Michael Rose left in 1985, to be replaced by Junior Reid, but this failed to breathe new life into the group. Puma was replaced soon after, and died of cancer in 1990 after a long battle against the illness. Although, in retrospect, Black Uhuru may have stayed a bit too long, they left behind some of the most exciting reggae of the era.

Liberation – The Island Anthology; Mango CRNCD1

Two CDs, twenty-eight tracks, and if you think of your favourite Black Uhuru songs they'll be there. It takes the best of the best albums, a sampling of dub cuts and a couple of singles, B-sides and previously unreleased tracks and gives them enough time to show off in their full glory. It's worth mentioning that one thing that made Uhuru special was they weren't afraid to take tracks beyond the apparently regulation three minutes – most are five or six minutes, while 'Spongi Reggae' lets rip with a little over ten! It's a mark of the producers' skills that it doesn't really make sense at much less. Complete with an informative and entertaining booklet by New York reggae expert Tom Terrell, it's the ideal Uhuru.

Red; Mango RRCD18

Cut in 1981, this is considered by most – by me anyway! – as Black Uhuru at their peak. They were still fresh, yet, together with Sly and Robbie, had more or less come to terms with what they could do. The two best tracks on it, 'Spongi Reggae' and the chilling 'Youth Of Eglington', are on *Liberation*, but this one has a couple of gems that aren't: 'Carbine' and 'Rockstone'. It's also about the only Black Uhuru album that has a centric thread running through it, and taken as a whole is greater than the sum of its parts.

ALSO RECOMMENDED:

When looking back like this, it becomes apparent that quality control wasn't high on Sly and Robbie's agenda. Or maybe five albums, numerous dub sets and a live LP in just four years, plus touring, meant they didn't spend as much time as they should have done in the studio. But either way, outside of the popular tracks – which all show up on *Liberation* – there seems to be an extraordinary amount of filler on these records. And without the vocal takes in front, the dub albums (*Dub Extravaganza, Brutal Dub* and *The Dub Factor*) don't really hang together.

*Anthem; Mango RRCD41

This is the album with 'What Is Life', 'Botanical Roots' and 'Somebody's Watching You'.

*Sensimillia; Mango RRCD12

The title track.

*Chill Out; Mango RRCD43

'Darkness', 'Chill Out' and 'Mondays'.

*Reggae Greats; Mango IMCD3

A less comprehensive version of *Liberation*.

SEE ALSO:

Tougher Than Tough – The Story Of Jamaican Music; Mango IBXCD1
Reggae Refreshers Volume Two; Mango RRCDS102/524 030-2
Jammin'; Mango CIDM1010
Nice An' Ruff – A Crucial Brew Of Roots, Dub and Rockers; Music Club International MCCD092
Reggae Dance Party; Ras RASCD3018
Crucial Reggae; Mango RRCD37
Planet Reggae; Charly CDINS5056
Pure Reggae; Island CIDTV8

Dennis Bovell

(Born 1953; St Peter, Barbados; multi-instrumentalist/producer/band leader)
One Christmas Eve, about fifteen years ago, Matumbi, Dennis Bovell's London reggae band, played the prestigious festive slot at The Venue, which was then one of the capital's hippest concert halls. They performed for about two hours, running through selections of their vast back catalogue, providing their own dub versions, displaying a few nifty dance routines, cracking jokes and generally enjoying themselves as much as the crowd – many of whom will still tell you it was the best reggae

show they'd ever seen. Matumbi, under Bovell's guidance, had more than one mainstream chart hit too. They put out a series of killer singles and albums under a variety of names from 4th Street Orchestra to Blackbeard – more than a few of these would feature Bovell on every instrument except the brass section. As well as this, he provided the backing for LINTON KWESI JOHNSON's dub poetry and produced pop acts such as The Slits, The Pop Group and Bananarama. He virtually invented UK LOVERS' ROCK with his productions of syrupy love songs for teenage black British singers – a state of affairs culminating in the Bovell-produced 'Silly Games' by Janet Kay, which spent several weeks at number 2 in the pop charts. It was his crisp, innovative production that shaped Errol Dunkley's 'Little Way Different' into the huge UK sound system hit it was. And as he was always open to whatever could be learned from what was going on around him, he adapted rock, pop and soul affectations into his wildly experimental mixing techniques to advance the cause of British dub considerably. Although, as with ASWAD, self-styled taste-shapers were queuing up to pronounce Dennis Bovell's efforts as not the genuine article, to a generation of 'born here' black kids, during the 1970s and early 1980s, this man was Britain's Mr Reggae. He was an ex-sound system operator who knew exactly what the indigenous audience wanted – how far the envelope could be pushed with them – and had the skills and passion to serve it up. Much as COXSONE DODD had done in Jamaica over a decade previously.

So why aren't there great big statues of Dennis Bovell up in reggae-friendly locations around London? Or why isn't everything he's done fanatically collected and about to be reissued on CD? I mean, why isn't he lionized in the way someone of his influence ought to be – during the 1970s, it wasn't unusual for him to have had something to do with over half of the records in the British Reggae Top 20. Why is Dennis Bovell's profile so low it's virtually horizontal? I'll be damned if I know.

*Dennis Bovell and The Dub Band: *Audio Active*; Meteor MTLP008CD

The Dub Band were one of the later incarnations of the floating-but-pretty-regular pool of London-based reggae players that made up Matumbi and Bovell's other musical identities. Cut in 1986, this comes as the digital revolution was starting to take hold, and Bovell takes no prisoners in an edgy, explosive dubfest that turns the computerized revolution on its head by using the thoroughly modern sounds merely as counterpoints to a traditional bass, drum 'n' horn workout. Moving from a heavy dread stance to smoove lovers' rock and back again, the producer's instinctive feel for reggae allows him to fool around with the stylistic boundaries, and his clever use of the fader and sequencer proves that computers needn't sound faceless, that dancehall reggae had more than one option open to it. A point which, some ten years later, the new wave of producers finally seem to have accepted.

Blackbeard: *Strictly Dubwize*; Moving Target MTD017

This was a set that came out towards the end of the 1970s, and you quite literally had to be in the right place at the right time to get a copy. Much like Bovell's *Yuh Learn* LP. To find it on CD was a rare treat, as through such dub depth-charges as 'Cut After Cut', 'Ites Of Dub' and 'Strictly Dub' it's Bovell's mixing desk alchemy at its unrestrained peak.

Linton Kwesi Johnson: *LKJ In Dub*; Mango RRCD34

A set of totally intriguing dub mixes – they're not quite as brain pounding as some of Bovell's other work – from LINTON KWESI JOHNSON's *Forces Of Victory* and *Bass Culture* albums. Unlike so many after-the-event dub albums, these actually make sense away from their originating sets.

SEE ALSO:

Matumbi's 'After Tonight' can be found on *Lovers' Rock: Serious Selection Volume One* (Rewind Selecta CDREG1). Their 'Man In Me' is on *Reggae Classics: Serious Selection Volume One* (Rewind Selecta CDREG2).
Janet Kay's 'Silly Games' is on *Jammin'* (Mango CIDM1010) and numerous other compilations.

Dennis Brown

(Born 1957; Kingston, Jamaica; singer)

I had a birthday party a little while ago, for an embarrassingly old age, and at about three in the morning one guy was getting ready to leave. He was saying he didn't want to go yet but he had a bunch of stuff to do that day and had been up from early. We said goodbye, he left and we shut the door behind him. A couple of minutes later I looked up from the record decks and saw him back in the living room dancing very close with a young lady.

'How did you get back in? I thought you were knackered,' I ventured, not unreasonably.

'You didn't tell me you were going to play Dennis Brown,' was all the explanation he felt he had to give.

And all anybody needed.

DB has that effect on people. BOB MARLEY may have been reggae's biggest star on a worldwide basis, but Dennis Brown was always ours. Even though he has scored a few hits in the outer regions of the mainstream charts, what Dennis Brown did best was be big in his own back yard – both in the UK and Jamaica. Big enough to survive changes in style, potentially self-destructive personal problems and the fact that, in his twenty-five years as a recording artist, he's made over two hundred albums and not even come near to getting boring.

In spite of the size of his presence in the reggae world, Dennis Brown's story isn't nearly as complicated as it might have been. Not because his tale is particularly unimpressive, but because he does one thing very well and that's pretty much all he's been doing since he started off cutting sides for COXSONE as a 12 year-old. In fact, since his days as a Studio One child rock steady star, Dennis Brown's CV is pretty one-track. His voice got richer in tone as he got older, but never lost the choirboy-type sweetness that had made it so special when he was a youth. He worked with nearly every producer in Jamaica, particularly successful with NINEY, JOE GIBBS, Errol T. and GUSSIE CLARKE. He spent some time living in London in the 1980s, where he contributed enormously to the indigenous lovers' rock scene. He's survived the transition from roots to dancehall, unlike so many of his peers. And that's more or less the extent of it. If he's playing a show tomorrow – which he probably is – he'll sing in his rich melodious tenor, injecting life and soul into even the flattest of material. He'll ease from strictly roots to silky lovers' with utter conviction. Women will come over all wobbly and guys won't go home when they really know they ought to.

Dennis Brown is a reggae phenomenon. It's probably best to let his singing do the talking.

What follows is a highly selective, er, selection of Dennis Brown albums. As I said earlier, the man is counted as prolific in an industry where it's not unusual for an artist to make two LPs in the same afternoon, and over half of his back catalogue is available on CD. Which'll put what's on offer well into the three-figure bracket. It's safe to say that just about anything with Dennis Brown's name on it will be worth further investigation, and if it's before 1986 it's more than likely worth buying. Those detailed below are probably the most easily available of the albums that show off the best cross-section of his classic tracks. The cursory descriptions are due to space restrictions rather than any lack of respect. Besides, there's really very little to discuss. It's all good.

Wolves and Leopards; Blue Moon CDBM046

The second of two albums cut for Niney in the late 1970s records that (particularly this one) cemented DB's standing as one of the all-time great roots artists. The producer, probably at his peak here too, interplays horns, organ and guitar to create the kind of fractured melodies that were always perfect for sound system consciousness, then Dennis Brown oozes all over them to put the tune back together. As steppers lovers' rock, this album has yet to be beaten. If for no other reason than the title track and 'Here I Come' – you know, the one that starts off 'Love and hate can never be friends . . .'

Unchallenged; Greensleeves GRELCD138

Gussie Clarke's at the controls for this 1990 recording, and at that time the Music Works environment was exactly right for Dennis Brown. The set has all the modern dancehall sounds it needed to get the singer across to a new generation of reggae fans, but Clarke always had an understanding of melody and was wise enough to know DB couldn't leave the old style behind completely. This is the sort of album that people who don't like dancehall end up taking home with them.

The Prime Of Dennis Brown; Music Club International MCCD118

Probably the best of the dozen or so Best Of Dennis Browns on the market at the time of writing. Eighteen tracks, seven of which are 'Money In My Pocket', 'Ain't That Lovin' You', 'Wolves And Leopards', 'Here I Come', 'Cassandra', 'Malcolm X' and 'Boasting'.

Live At Montreux; Blue Moon CDBM016

Recorded in the late-1980s, the voice is seasoned to a smokey croon and the set list is a veritable catalogue of hits, including 'Don't Feel No Way'.

Super Reggae And Soul Hits; Trojan CDTRL57

Cut in his mid-teens for DERRICK HARRIOT, and, as you'd expect from the man they call The Musical Chariot, this involves a lot of soul song cover versions and is 100 per cent smoove. None of which did young Dennis any harm at all.

Visions; Blue Moon CDBM021
Joseph's Coat Of Many Colours; Blue Moon CDBM010

After leaving Niney, DB fetched up at Joe Gibbs's, where, under the guidance of Gibbs and Errol Thompson, he cut these two. Smoother than the previous releases, while they wrap up the voice far more carefully, the relentless rhythms and subtle fades makes sure they lose nothing in terms of roots credibility. The former features 'Malcolm X', 'Concrete Castle King' and 'Love Me Always'; the latter boasts 'Well Without Water', 'Slave Driver' and 'Three Meals A Day'.

Money In My Pocket; Trojan CDTRL197

Something of an alternative greatest hits, and although it crosses over enormously with *The Prime Of Dennis Brown*, this CD includes 'Yagga Yagga' and 'Ah So We Stay'.

Dennis Brown and Gregory Isaacs: *Two Bad Superstars*; Trojan CDTRL335

One of many double-headers DB was involved in, several of which were with his frequent touring partner ISAACS. The best thing about this set is that the tracks – including 'Funny Feeling' and 'Let Love In' – are all full length so feature some serious dub versions.

Dennis Brown and Gregory Isaacs: *Judge Not*; Greensleeves GRELCD72

More Dennis and Gregory, this time the later model with dance-hall influences starting to creep in.

SEE ALSO:

There are so many Dennis Brown tunes floating about that it would be easier to list the roots reggae compilations he *hasn't* got a track on. Best to check the listings when you're in the shop.

Glen Brown

(Born 1951; Kingston, Jamaica; producer)
Back in the mid-1970s at a club in Wembley, while playing a tune called 'Mr Harry Skank' by Prince Jazzbo, the deejay would lift the needle off the record and shout 'Spider Time!' into the mic. At this, whatever shape you were throwing while you were skanking you had to hold until he dropped the needle again. An irie version of musical statues, I guess. But it was a good laugh, as the crowd would attempt to outdo each other with increasingly precariously balanced poses, and from the opening notes, even before Jazzbo's croak came in, 'Mr Harry Skank' triggered

an outbreak of wildly exaggerated dancing. The man responsible for 'Mr Harry' – and therefore responsible for normally sensible blokes making fools of themselves on Friday nights – was one of roots reggae's most underrated producers, Glen Brown.

A rock steady singer from the sixties, Brown turned to production in 1970 with his own Pantomine (sic) label and immediately showed an understanding of the new style that astonished the more established operatives. Working on the theory that once you got your foundation right the rest will be no trouble at all, he'd build up on bone-crunching bass 'n' drum rhythms. Such was the strength of these rhythms, they could support sweet harmonizing (his own experiences as a solo crooner and in duos with Dave Barker and HOPETON LEWIS), deejay toasting or any amount of dubwise remixing – and Glen Brown was a man who made full use of KING TUBBY's mixing desk. Such was the respect Glen Brown commanded, he brought a veritable who's who of the JA music business to Pantomine: toasters like U-ROY, Jazzbo and BIG YOUTH; and singers such as GREGORY ISAACS, JOHNNY CLARKE and Tinga Stewart; and the very best session players. And while he may not have been the first to cut them, he always seemed to get that little bit extra out of them – U-Roy's 'No 1 In The World', Gregory's 'One One Cocoa' and, of course, Jazzbo's 'Mr Harry Skank' are close to the best things those artists ever did. He kept this up for most of the 1970s, never afraid to prolong a tune's active life by versioning it himself, but come the new decade Glen Brown kind of faded away.

These three albums are the ultimate Glen Brown cross-section. They take each of the three aspects of the Pantomine back catalogue, vocal, deejay and instrumental, at a time when the label was flying, and present the best surviving recordings of it.

Boat To Progress – The Original Pantomine Vocal Collection 1972-1974; Greensleeves GRELCD602.

Ritchie McDonald and Glen Brown, Realize; **Roman Stewart**, Never Too Young To Learn; **Little Roy**, Father's Call; **Ritchie McDonald**, Do Your Thing; **Glen Brown**, Take A Step; **Glen Brown**, Tell It Like It Is; **Keith Poppin**, Get Together; **Gregory Isaacs**, One One Cocoa; **Glen Brown**, Boat To Progress; **Johnny**

Clarke, Really Gotta Hold On Me; **Tinga Stewart**, Brand New Me; **Glen Brown and Lloyd Parks**, I'm Your Puppet; **Glen Brown**, Away With The Bad; **Glen Brown and Glenroy Richards**, Save Our Nation.

*Dubble Attack – The Original Pantomine Dee-Jay Collection 1972-1974; Greensleeves GRELCD601.

U-Roy, No 1 In The World; **Big Youth**, Opportunity Rock; **Prince Jazzbo**, Meaning Of One; **I-Roy**, Rasta On A Sunday; **Dean Beckford**, Father's Call; **Godsons**, This A Year Fe Rebels; **Big Youth**, Spider To The Fly; **I-Roy**, Brother Toby Is A Movie From London; **Prince Jazzbo**, Mr Harry Skank; **Big Youth**, Dubble Attack; **Berry Simpson (Prince Hammer)**, Whole Lot Of Sugar; **I-Roy**, Festive Season; **Prince Jazzbo**, Mr Want All; **Lloyd Young**, Butter Bread.

*Check The Winner – The Original Pantomine Instrumental Collection 1970-1974; Greensleeves GRELCD603.

Tommy McCook and Richard Hall, Dirty Harry; **Glen Brown**, The Winner, Pantomine Rock, Glen Brown At The Crossroads, No More Slavery, Crisp As A Ball, Sunshine Showdown, Sgt Crackers, School Call, 2 Wedden Skank, Mitchville Rock, High Holborn St Song; **Glen Brown and Joe White**, Merry Up; **Ron Wilson and Lennox Brown**, Scatter Lite Rock; **Ron Wilson**, Get Up; **Bobby Ellis, Don Drummond and Glen Brown**, Determination Skank; **Tommy McCook and Ron Wilson**, More Music; **Bobby Aitken**, Mr Baldhead Aitken.

Burning Spear

(Born Winston Rodney, 1945; St Ann's, Jamaica; singer)
If there is a godfather, a wise elder of roots reggae, it's Burning Spear. Now grey of beard and lock, and a good deal smaller than you'd expect, the man looks every one of his fifty years, but a more commanding figure you are unlikely to meet.

When Burning Spear played the Finsbury Park Astoria about twenty years ago, the band chugged out the opening lines of 'Slavery Days' for what seemed like an age, then Spear took the stage and, staff in hand, strode towards the mic. 'Do-o-o-o you remember the days of slavery?' he intoned. The respondent 'Yes!' nearly raised the roof. It was a spine-tingling, genuinely magic moment. It's probably no coincidence that Spear, BOB MARLEY and Marcus Garvey all share the same birthplace of St Ann's in Jamaica, as it's through this trinity that most youth outside of the island first got to hear about Rastafari and the Back To Africa Movement. In his twenty-five years in the music business Burning Spear has not wavered from the path of righteousness he set himself, and his music still smoulders with the same intense spiritual passions as it did back then.

Not that it's always been easy for him. In the very beginning, when Marley took him for an audition at Studio One in 1969, he was immediately signed up but for the next five years released records to no or very little commercial success. It's not hard to see why: back then, COXSONE wasn't as fully empathic with dread performers as he later became (but saying that, Spear's voice has a hypnotic power that anybody with ears wouldn't turn away). Also this was a time when the Jamaican radio was deliberately ignoring Rasta music, sound systems had a duty to entertain their crowds and Spear's direction was so deeply religious many of his sides sounded more like chants or prayers than actual tunes.

But this all changed when Spear hooked up with Ocho Rios sound system owner and classy (woefully unheralded) dub producer Jack Ruby. Ruby understood what Spear was about, put him with two backing vocalists to add a ghostly harmony to the haunting lead vocals and set to work on an album of unashamedly Rasta material that, in its use of horns and dread beat bass 'n' drums, *was* commercially acceptable. It helped that times had changed, too, and there was now that much more Rasta reggae being made.

That album finished up as *Marcus Garvey*, required listening for anybody who hung out at sound systems or clubs – even the funk clubs – back in 1976. It was also the start of a run of recording that many believed ought to have put Burning Spear in the Bob Marley bracket of international superstardom. Those who knew, however, realized this wouldn't happen as the man was too uncompromisingly black. But the records were still genius pieces of roots reggae.

Man In The Hills was the only other record Spear recorded for Jack Ruby, before he dropped the backing singers and started producing himself. And the upward curve continued, with *Dry And Heavy*, *Social Living* (featuring members of ASWAD in the backing band), *Hail H.I.M.*, and *Farover*.

Since his peak at the end of the 1970s/beginning of the 1980s, bar a few experiments involving rock musicians and a more conventionally musical approach, Spear hasn't changed all that much – witness *Live In Paris*, recorded at the end of the 1980s and very much in the same classic Spear vein. Likewise the recent studio albums, or his performance in London in 1994. But this isn't a bad thing, as Spear has always been so far out on his own limb there's room for him to be exactly what he feels comfortable with in every new trend – he'll never fit in, so he'll always provide a welcome relief. The last thing anybody would want is a jungle version of 'Social Living'.

When looking at the best of Burning Spear, approach the albums as one whole body of work rather than individually, because the style is so pronounced and utterly unique the basis doesn't change from album to album. Every one possesses that inimitable Spear Quality, as his voice comes at you out of the hazy middle distance, conjuring up misty visions of Africa, slavery, poverty and, most importantly, hope for a brighter tomorrow. Then the music, whether it's Ruby or himself at the controls, is the same smokey, ghostly arrangement as the horns fade in and out, leaving a lasting impression of Ethiopia, while the beat and guitar flourishes create some of the deepest steppers' rhythms known to man.

The only things that make the CDs I've detailed below stand out from the others are personal preference for some subtle touches and the number of truly classic Spear songs on the tracklisting.

Social Living; Blood And Fire BAFCD004

By this time (1978) Spear had left Jack Ruby and was at his most adventurous. This set stirs in all sorts of ethereal elements into a mix that suspends time and motion, as Spear weaves his magic to present a notion of Africa that is strictly spiritual. While the deep, slow rhythm track bolts it all down, the horns leave enough for percussion, SFX and subdued echo (the entire approach is like a dub mix with words) to be dropped in with a fluidity and perfectly placed spontaneity most jazzmen would kill for. So solid is the backing that the vocalist clearly knows he has nothing to worry about and stretches himself with scats and chants way beyond the call of the lyrics. This is the album on which Aswad lined up next to the Jamaican likes of SLY, ROB-BIE, Familyman, RICO, Bobby Ellis and Horsemouth. It's also everything Burning Spear was ever about. Musically and spiritually.

Living Dub Volume One; Heartbeat HBCD131

Sylvian Morris-mixed dub cuts to *Social Living*. Some people who have heard this record have never been quite the same again.

Marcus Garvey/Garvey's Ghost; Mango RRCD20

That first LP from Jack Ruby, doubled up with the dub set of the whole album, is a bargain you really ought not to refuse. All those early Spear classics – the ones that made the initial impression in London twenty years ago – are there: 'Marcus Garvey', 'Slavery Days', 'Jordan River' and 'Resting Place' among them.

Dry and Heavy; Mango RRCD40

With titles like this, Burning Spear will never get caught under the Trades Descriptions Act. The first time he produced himself, it takes the opportunity to redress the Studio One situation by redoing a few of the tunes from that period in the way they should have been done in the first place. 'Creation Rebel' benefits particularly.

Reggae Greats; Mango IMCD5

The Best of Burning Spear, containing a dozen of the better known tracks, and while it's an absolutely first-rate introduction it only really tells half the story.

Live In Paris; Greensleeves GRELCD120

Spear really comes into his own in concert. This one captures him and The Burning Band (reggae's only all-female horn section) in full flight, and while that might not mean recreating every little musical flourish from the album, they more than make up for this with atmosphere. Spread over two CDs, it brings you the whole 100-minute experience that is Spear In Concert. There are few more vibeful live albums.

ALSO RECOMMENDED:

People Of The World; Greensleeves GRELCD100

More about The Burning Band than Burning Spear, but enjoyable nonetheless.

Mek We Dweet; Mango CIDM1145

Late model roots (1990) that is as heavy as it should be, but lags behind a bit on inspiration.

Man In The Hills; Mango RRCD15

The second Jack Ruby set, and in spite of 'Door Peep' and 'Lion', the songs aren't quite as strong as those on its predecessor.

(Burning Spear's Studio One 1969-1974 recordings are only available on two hard-to-find import vinyl albums, *Studio One Presents Burning Spear* and *Rocking Time*. *Hail H.I.M.* is on an equally obscure import CD and *Farover* seems to have been lost in the mists of time.)

SEE ALSO:

Tougher Than Tough – The Story Of Jamaican Music; Mango IBXCD1
Reggae Refreshers Volume Two; Mango RRCD102/524 030-2
Roots And Culture: Serious Selection Volume One; Rewind Selecta CDREG3
Planet Reggae; Charly CDINS5056

Junior Byles

(Born Keith Byles, 1948; Kingston, Jamaica; singer)
Recording as Junior Soul, Chubby and even, for some reason, under his God-given name of Keith, Junior Byles never really made it as a rock steady or early reggae singer. And would probably have passed from view completely had it not been for one particular tune that has ensured his immortality: 'Curly Locks'. Produced by LEE PERRY, in 1975, in typical Scratch style – an almost organic balance between the individual instruments and the voice, plus the softest-edged dub effects imaginable – it summed up the reaction in London (and Jamaica, for that matter) to the by now very visible dreadlocks culture. If you had locks, or at the very least wore a woolly hat, respectable people wouldn't let you near their daughters. It was an enormous sound system hit, so huge it actually nudged the mainstream charts with no airplay at all. It'll still raise a loud cheer if you drop it at a party full of 40 year-olds.

Junior Byles actually had a few more big hits – 'A Place Called Africa', 'Beat Down Babylon' and 'Fade Away' – but huge as they were, they've not got the instant recognition factor of the much-versioned 'Curly Locks'. After a lengthy spell in a mental hospital at the end of the 1970s, he went back to recording but so far has had little success.

Junior Byles features on:
Reggae Classics: Serious Selection Volume One; Rewind Selecta CDREG2

'Curly Locks' can be found on the following:
Tougher Than Tough – The Story Of Jamaican Music; Mango IBXCD1
Out Of Many, One – Jamaican Music 1962-1975; Trojan CDTRS1
Reggae Hits Volume Two; Jetstar JECD1002

Al Campbell

(Born 1954; Kingston, Jamaica; singer)
If ever a singer had seemed misplaced in the roots market it was

Al Campbell. Still in his teens, the former Studio One backing singer cut all sorts of low-key roots tunes, before discovering the way to go was all the way. All the way smoove, that is. Under the watchful eye of producer Phil Pratt, he reinvented himself as a lovers' rock singer to give the world a series of rub-up-the-wallpaper classics through the first half of the 1980s – he was the man who voiced those smokey, four-in-the-morning, packed-house-party perennials 'Ain't That Loving You' and 'Late Night Blues'. But the most remarkable thing about Al Campbell is that when he returned to rootsier music after his lurrrve man excursion he brought with him a far greater soulfulness than he'd shown before, and was thus able to straddle the two camps with comparative ease.

*Rasta Time; Lagoon LG21056

Unfortunately, the rather wonderful *Mr Lovers' Rock* album has yet to make it on CD, but this really is the next best thing. Recorded relatively late (in the 1980s), it illustrates perfectly Campbell's silky way with a tune; how the laid back emotional quality of his singing powers lovers' selections to the point at which a crowd will be completely swept away, and at the same time delivers the roots material with the restrained urgency it needs to make an audience take notice. Produced by Phil Pratt, this set features 'Ain't That Loving You', 'You Must Get A Beating', 'If You Don't Love Jah' and the glorious 'Hit Me With Music'.

Johnny Clarke

(Born 1955; Bull Bay, Jamaica; singer)
There are few more uplifting examples of two people meeting at the right time and in the right place in culture than when Johnny Clarke and BUNNY 'STRIKER' LEE hooked up in the mid-1970s in a roots reggae situation. Up until then, Clarke had been wasting his soulful falsetto on throwaway pop-style tunes and Lee had yet to create a singer of this calibre in the new style. Together, with the aid of the happening session band THE AGGROVATORS and KING TUBBY's mixing desk, they turned

out a string of dread beat classics – 'Move Out Of Babylon', 'Cry Tough', 'Cold I Up', 'Enter His Gates With Praise', 'None Shall Escape The Judgement' and so on. And they didn't neglect the loveman side of things either, thus Clarke/Lee rub-ups were a big deal at all the better educated dances. It was a marriage made in heaven.

Clarke had come to recording relatively late – he didn't figure he'd have a chance of making it as a singer in the big city until he'd won a home town talent contest at the age of eighteen. Once in town, he started recording for RUPIE EDWARDS, and had more success in Britain than at home with tunes like 'Julie' and 'Everyday Wandering'.

But by 1974, he was at work with Striker. And 'work' was probably the right word for it, as the Lee and Clarke partnership, responding to the sound systems' demand for new roots product, turned out several sides a day. But this was never merely a matter of quantity over quality. During the course of the next few years, Johnny Clarke established himself as one of the era's top vocalists voicing a string of sound system and commercial hits, equally as at home with as with a rockers rhythm, a sweet love song or a reworked ska beat favourite. Albums from that period – *Rockers Time Now*, *Enter His Gates With Praise* and *Authorised Version* – remain hugely influential as the easy-going finish washed over even the hardest roots sentiments and made them accessible to just about every strain of reggae fan.

After the leaving the exclusive company of Bunny Lee at the end of the 1970s, Clarke freelanced around, and spent the main part of the 1980s out of the music business. His recent return has yet to enjoy success on anything like the scale he had with Striker.

**Authorised Rockers*; Frontline CDFL9014

Johnny Clarke and Bunny Lee's greatest hits. A wonderful record of the spell the twosome could weave over a tune – they could pick up a beat and keep it taut but all soft at the edges so it kind of flowed over you rather than hit you in the guts. Then Clarke's superbly relaxed style would ease you along into whatever it was he was singing about until, without quite realizing it, you were gently rocking. On the tracklist are the twosome's

best-known triumphs: 'Crazy Baldheads' (a killer reworking of
the MARLEY song), 'Declaration Of Rights', 'Cry Tough', 'Natty
Roots Natty Congo', 'Rockers Time Now' . . . Do I need to go on?

**Don't Trouble Trouble*; Attack ATCD107

Steve Barrow-compiled, so although many of the songs aren't
that obvious, you know it's not going to let you down. Which
means it presents an excellent companion to *Authorised Rockers*,
and so it should do, as I strongly believe nobody can have
enough Johnny Clarke records. There's perhaps a greater
emphasis on the lovers' material here, so along with 'Stop The
Tribal War' and 'Don't Trouble Trouble', you get 'Bring It On
Home To Me', 'You Keep On Running', 'Don't Call Me Daddy'
and 'Tears On My Pillow', many of which are on album for the
first time.

The companion dub set to *Don't Trouble Trouble* is available as
Johnny In The Echo Chamber (Trojan ATCD106) and is looked at
in greater detail in The Aggrovators' entry.

SEE ALSO:

Natty Rebel Roots; Frontline CDFL9013
Tougher Than Tough – The Story Of Jamaican Music; Mango
IBXCD1
Roots 'N' Culture; Music Club International MCCD128
Irie Feelings – Chapter And Version; Trojan CDTRL281
Beyond The Frontline; Frontline CDFRONT1

The Congos

(Cedric Myton, born 1947; St Catherine, Jamaica; Roy Johnston,
born 1948; Hanover, Jamaica; Watty Burnett, born 1951;
Kingston, Jamaica; vocal group)
There are times when a piece of work can go on to vastly over-
shadow whoever made it. The Congos' *Heart Of The Congos*
album is exactly such a work. It all started as the fulfilment of
one of LEE PERRY 's dreams to record a traditional Jamaican
Impressions-based vocal trio, handling roots material, in his
own personal toybox that was The Black Ark Studios. (The

Congos were actually a duo, but Perry was so impressed with
their devoutly dread approach to life and music that he took
them on and added Burnett to cover the bottom end.) Then,
because of Perry's own complicated business set-up – like every
other genius he was a law unto himself – he withdrew the album
from Island Records after a row with the company over one of
his own vocal albums, thus *The Heart Of The Congos* didn't get
the worldwide release his other projects had done. And apart
from the odd battered vinyl copy floating around, and a limited
market US CD release, it soon ceased to exist. The album became
something of a Holy Grail to collectors – while proper people
wondered if it could possibly live up to the hype – and the group
were all but forgotten. Well, nothing else they did could have
possibly lived up to these expectations. The album had a low
profile UK release fifteen years ago, as part of the reggae revival
that accompanied 2-Tone, but that was so limited it served only
to heighten interest.

The group split with Scratch soon afterwards, on bad terms
because, quite correctly, they objected to being used as pawns in
his business dealings, believing their chances of selling a lot of
records had been vastly diminished. So *Heart Of The Congos* was
a situation never likely to be repeated.

Now the revival label Blood And Fire have seen fit to put it out
on a sparklingly remastered CD. Complete with the dub of it
that few people outside the inner sanctum of the roots reggae
industry even knew existed, and, as a further bonus, a handful
of previously unreleased tunes. But is it any *good*?

Heart Of The Congos; Blood And Fire BAFCD009

The answer isn't merely 'yes', it's more like 'YES!' It's difficult to
imagine what Island Records had done to upset Lee Perry to the
degree he would withhold this totally inspired piece of music
from them. It's probably the best album he made – remember,
this includes *Super Ape* and *The Battle Of Armageddon* – because,
quite simply, it makes perfect sense. The Congos' vocals are
every bit as soft and embracing as Perry's production, but what
he did (which is why he wanted a traditional trio) is to leave
them alone and let them play it straight. Or as straight as their
finely textured, spiritual harmonizing can play it. Then behind

them, over his insistent beats, he unleashes the whole battery of Scratch effects – babies crying, cattle mooing, discreet echoes, subtle cross-fades and more than one bomb is dropped. It's one of the most marvellously three-dimensional reggae records ever made, quite simply because the textures involved are so tricky they give it an astonishing depth. Sure, the dub tracks are an enormous plus point, massively satisfying to own, but what's going on in the regular album is so off-handedly interesting it more than stands up by itself. It's little wonder so few people paid any attention to what the group did apart from this.

Culture

(Joseph Hill, born 1952; St Andrews, Jamaica; Albert Walker, born 1949; St Andrews, Jamaica; Kenneth Paley, born 1950; St Andrews, Jamaica; vocal group)

The prophesy of St John The Divine in the Book Of Revelations is deep at the heart of Rasta doctrine, and the 'sevens' were always taken as heralding the arrival of the Apocalypse. On 7 July 1977, record levels of absenteeism from work and schools was recorded in Jamaica, as people were terrified to leave their homes, and the army was on stand by to deal with any natural disaster.

It was against such an onset of dread that a Rasta vocal trio called The African Disciples allowed JOE GIBBS to change their name to Culture and put out a record called 'Two Sevens Clash', detailing the sort of devastation that could be expected on that fateful date. The record flashed their name all over the world as it seized the moment in Jamaica, the UK and America, and the trio's rough hewn-harmonies, fronted by the charismatic, fiercely devout Joseph Hill, stood on the verge of international stardom.

They got there too. By this time the Rasta approach to reggae was as accepted as it was ever going to be – i.e. while it may not have had mainstream appeal, it had replaced pop reggae or rude boy bragging as the dominant way of doing things. Now people wanted a new hero. Culture, with an uncompromisingly militant approach, and production that played up the Africanness of Rasta percussion incorporated into a lively reggae beat, were perfectly placed to nudge market leaders aside momentarily.

For Joe Gibbs, and later SONIA POTTINGER, they recorded some vital Rasta albums and secured a worldwide deal with Virgin. It should have come to something big, but just as they'd arrived late so the scene began to wane by the time they really hit their stride.

They never changed either. Almost twenty years since the two sevens clashed – or didn't, as the case may be – the real legacy of that wonderful music continues to pay off as Joseph Hill is still touring as Culture. To appreciative locks-wearing, herb-fuelled audiences.

Two Sevens Clash; Shanchie SHANCD44001

Those first Joe Gibbs recordings that have been described, rather accurately, as 'sounding like they're singing through a thick fog'. The whole approach is far more relaxed than, say, anything BURNING SPEAR was doing at the time, but far more specialist than later MARLEY, as if Hill and Gibbs had conspired to introduce Rasta culture to the masses by stealth – it can't be that militant if it's got a tune you could whistle at a bus stop. Sweeping hornlines and percussion on overload give it that genuinely heavy sense of dread, while the balance of Hill and his harmonizers conjures up something from about 400 years ago. As well as the title track we get 'See Them A Come', 'Black Star Liner' and 'Natty Dread Taking Over'.

Cumbolo; Shanchie SHANCD44005

A Sonia Pottinger production from 1979 that in no way lets up the sense of dread injected by Gibbs on that first album. If anything, because the production is more restrained and eases up on the bassline a little, Hill, Walker and Paley work just that little bit harder and manage to keep the dread quota up while singing just that little bit sweeter. The title track is an excellent example of this, as is 'Natty Dread Nuh Run' and 'They Never Love In This Time'.

Strictly Culture – The Best Of Culture 1977-1979; Music Club International MCCD158

Pretty much everything you should have if you just want to dip a toe into the cultural delights that are Culture. Mixing Gibbs and Pottinger to great effect: 'Two Sevens', 'Behold', 'Calling Rasta For I', 'Jah Love', 'Cumbolo', 'International Herb', 'Holy Mount Zion' and 'Lion's Gate' among them.

Peace And Love; Charley CPCD8024

Although it's not the first division, with 'Capture Rasta', 'Soon Come', 'Five To One' and 'Praise Him' this isn't exactly Culture The B-Sides either.

SEE ALSO:

Tougher Than Tough – The Story Of Jamaican Music; Mango IBXCD1
Nice An' Ruff – A Crucial Brew Of Roots, Dub And Rockers; Music Club International MCCD092
Roots 'N' Culture; Music Club International MCCD128
Beyond The Frontline; Frontline CDFRONT1

Dillinger

(Born Lester Bullocks, 1953; Kingston, Jamaica; deejay)
Just as BIG YOUTH rode in on an S.90, so Dillinger made his entrance on the favoured bike of 1975, the CB200. Although the man had served his apprenticeship on some of Kingston's larger systems, and had enjoyed dancehall hits with 'Brace A Boy', 'Freshly' and 'Killer Man Jaro', his style was never anything to get excited about. It was always more about the songs he was toasting over than what he was doing to them, as shown with the series of rock steady-based sides he cut for Studio One, among which was the one that broke him in the shops as well, 'Ready Natty Dreadie'. Which is why it came as an enormous surprise when the *CB200* album became regulation for half the student population of the UK in 1976. It was OK, but it wasn't another *Screaming Target* or *Version Galore*.

That Dillinger didn't really have that much more to offer became obvious with his follow-ups, which seemed to cash in on the single 'Cocaine' and represented something of an affront to any righteous Rasta man.

*CB200; Mango RRCD30

The title track remains a crisp little rocker, and the words come across like agreeable nonsense, but it's still impossible to work out what all the fuss was about.

SEE ALSO:

Classic Reggae Volume One; Profile PCD 1434
Planet Reggae; Charly CDINS5056

Coxsone Dodd

➤➤ By now, the golden period for Coxsone Dodd was pretty much in the past. Although Studio One was far from finished, many of the artists he'd started off had left and such innovative producers as LEE PERRY, Jackie Mittoo and NINEY THE OBSERVER had gone. It was felt that Coxsone was far too much a part of the old school, when tunes were tunes and singers combed their hair and dressed smartly. In other words, although he didn't actually lose his touch for making brilliant music, he never really came to terms with dread culture. This is underlined by the fact that acts like BURNING SPEAR, THE VICEROYS, DILLINGER, HORACE ANDY and SUGAR MINOTT all did excellent stuff there – 'Door Peep', 'Skylarking', 'Ready Natty Dreadie' and 'Vanity' were cut at Studio One – but the bulk of their most inspired music was recorded after they'd moved away.

For much of the late 1970s and early 1980s, things went quiet, but it wasn't all over yet. Dodd spent much of this period organizing and re-releasing his enormous back catalogue, which had a knock-on effect once the music shifted gear again. By the second half of the 1980s, the dancehall deejays carried the swing and they were plundering old Studio One rhythms from which to construct their ever-so-modern reggae. Because the tracks were so strong they'd support just about anything – it was much like the gangsta rappers recycling the heavy duty P-Funk of twenty years ago. Thus revitalised, Dodd got back into production, dealing with such young Turks as MICHIGAN AND SMILEY, The Lone Ranger and JOHNNY OSBOURNE. He cut some credible stuff too, but his heart didn't seem to be in it. Before the end of the decade he'd closed the studios and moved to New York, where he has as little as possible to do with the music business. But try as he might, he can't get away from it – as long as there's a Studio One record out there he'll still be part of reggae. In fact, if it hadn't been for him and a couple of others, there might not be *any* reggae.

Tracklistings for a selection of Studio One compilations, several of which include the artists mentioned above, can be found in the previous section (pages 117-119).

Mikey Dread

(Born Michael Campbell, 1958; Port Antonio, Jamaica; deejay/producer)

If anybody had been marked to take over LEE PERRY's mantle of mixing desk lunatic, it was Mikey Dread. His productions and mixes were outrageous even by Scratch's standards, as they built up on some of the hardest rhythms, then put everything in and around it – real instrumentation, snatches of TV dialogue, radio jingles, explosions, bells, animal noises, gun shots, whistles, what sounded like household appliances. . . Then he'd half sing, half toast, half shriek on top. And, unbelievably, he'd make it work, as in the mix would be some bizarre musical quality that carried it through. But perhaps the most amazing thing about the man was that it was the inherent conservatism of Jamaican establishment radio that was the breeding ground for his technique and which had sent him into the recording studio in the first place.

Mikey Dread, a former sound system deejay and electronics student, had the only reggae show on the nationally owned JBC. While figuring it was politically sound to pander to the sufferahs in this way, the management's relentless snobbery put him on in the graveyard shift of Saturday night/Sunday morning when, quite literally, it was figured he would offend as few 'decent' people as possible. He called his four-hour session 'The Dread At The Controls', taking the viewpoint that he had hijacked the airwaves, and grasped his opportunity with both hands. He would cut his own dubs for the show, mix live on air, ladle on the SFX and record some of the most outrageous jingles ever heard in radioland. And, naturally enough, he started releasing his recordings to his ever growing public. Indeed it was the size of this public that eventually threw him out of JBC. In the space of a couple of years, at the back end of the 1970s, he had grown from cult figure to commanding one of the station's biggest audiences, and other presenters (they didn't like to call themselves 'deejays') weren't happy. Apart from a basic jealousy, they were terrified for their jobs as they feared his popularity might lead to a generally reggaefied policy. They got together, had a word with the management and The Dread At The Controls was fired.

But JBC's loss was our gain. As well as making records and building up a roster on his DATC label during the mid-1980s, he moved to the UK where he had his own local radio show in Bristol. Today Mikey Dread broadcasts on radio and television, does occasional record production and mixing and deejays dances.

When discussing Mikey Dread's body of work, it's worth bearing in mind that one of his early albums carried the sleeve note 'Dread At The Controls records are not for night clubs displaying signs saying "No Hats – No Tams" . . . By Order, Mikey Dread.' This is an entirely appropriate warning.

African Anthem; Ras RASCD3035

Engineered by Errol T, Ernest Hoo-Kim, Errol Brown and The Dread himself, and featuring the absolute cream of Jamaica's roots players, including a four-pronged keyboard assault of AUGUSTUS PABLO, Frankie Waul, Gladstone Anderson and Ansel Collins (such was the exposure value of DATC, he had no trouble recruiting the best), this album is sub-titled *The Mikey Dread Show* and could almost have been recorded straight off the airwaves. Dub plates like 'Saturday Night Style', 'Pre-Dawn Dub', 'Mikey Dread In Action' and 'Technical Selection', with jingles thrown in between the tracks, exactly capture the spontaneous, adrenaline-charged atmosphere of his late-night sessions. It leaves you wondering not why they sacked him, but how he ever got the job in the first place.

*S.W.A.L.K.; Heartbeat CDHB11568

A late-model Mikey Dread album that's far more conventional than the earlier straight-from-radio epics. And finds the Dread rather in the mood for romance as songs like the title track, 'Problems' and 'Rocky Road' swing with a definite lovers' rock approach. Not that this affects the overall feel in any way. It's still some of the most inventive mixing of its time (1982), as it makes use of the recording studio's creeping computerization, while getting its point across through musical texture rather than gimmicks.

SEE ALSO:

Roots Rockers; Attack CDAT112

There are at least three other Mikey Dread albums from this golden, start-of-the-1980s period. Any chance of getting them on CD, so I can replace my scratchy old vinyl?

Rupie Edwards

(Born 1945; St Anns, Jamaica; producer/vocalist)
Remember 'Irie Feelings (Skenga)', that deeply irritating novelty single that assaulted us back around Christmas 1974? Well there was always much more to both that and its creator, Rupie Edwards.

The former schoolboy musician came up through the Kingston talent shows in the early 1960s, and cut records for minor league sound systems until, in 1968, he released one for sale and the figures were enough to convince him to give up his job as a garage mechanic. From there, he realized the money was to be made in producing rather than singing, and although he'd still step up to the mic himself, he quickly built a reputation through his recording of THE ETHIOPIANS, I-ROY, JOHNNY CLARKE and BOB ANDY in the early 1970s. Which is, in a roundabout way, where that 'skenga skenga' business comes in.

Edwards was always a far more innovative producer than he's ever been given credit for, and was always looking for methods to advance the cause of dub. In 1974 BUNNY LEE gave him an old rock steady tune, 'My Conversation' by SLIM

SMITH, which Edwards was determined not only to revamp for a new-style reggae audience, but also to use to demonstrate exactly how much life could be breathed into a second-hand rhythm. He cut it in at least fifteen different ways – toasts, instrumental, singing, dubbing, with any amount of lyrics from the fiercely political to Christmas carols – put 12 of them on an album titled *Yamaha Skank*, and it virtually flew out of the shops to start a trend for one-rhythm LPs. A trend he was quick to get in on himself, when he recorded Johnny Clarke singing 'Everyday Wondering' and recut it some two dozen times. Two of which were 'Irie Feelings (Skenga)' and its almost chart-friendly follow-up 'Leggo Skenga'. It only goes to prove it's all too easy to have too much of a good thing.

Tracklisted below are *Yamaha Skank* (retitled *Let There Be Version* and with three extra tracks – each one another reading of 'My Conversation') and *Irie Feelings – Chapter And Version* which was sixteen different approaches to 'Everyday Wondering', including Johnny Clarke's original and the title track. Thankfully we've been spared 'Leggo Skenga'. While to the uninitiated so many versions of the same tune must seem about as interesting as rinsing a vest, it's actually a musical manifestation of Jamaica's capacity to recycle just about anything, and a fascinating exercise in how something that is inherently the same can be so different. So many times.

Let There Be Version; Trojan CDTRL280

Slim Smith and The Uniques, My Conversation; **The Success All-Stars**, 100,000 Dollars; **U-Roy Junior**, Doctor Come Quick; **Shorty The President**, Half Way Tree Pressure; **El Cisco Degado**, Mi Nah Matta; **Tyrone Downie**, Tribute To Slim Smith; **The Success All-Stars**, Doctor Satan Echo Chamber; **Shorty The President**, Yamaha Skank; **Earl 'Chinna' Smith**, Riding With Mr Lee; **Shorty The President**, President Mash Up The Resident; **Joe White**, President Rock; **Bongo Herman and Les**; Dew Of Herman; **The Heptones**, Give Me The Right; **Shorty The President**, Underworld Way; **Rupie Edwards**, Christmas Rush.

Irie Feelings – Chapter And Version; Trojan CDTRL281

Rupie Edwards, Irie Feelings, Feeling High; **Johnny Clarke**, Everyday Wondering; **Rupie Edwards All-Stars**, Buckshot; **Jah Woosh**, The Wanderer; **Tyrone Downie**, Dub Master Special; **Rupie Edwards All-Stars**, Dub Master; **Rupie Edwards**, Spangy; **The Heaven Singers**, Rasta Dreadlocks; **Rupie Edwards All-Stars**, Rasta Dreadlocks Dub; **Rupie Edwards**, Free The Weed; **Milton Henry**, What Can I Do?; **Rupie Edwards All-Stars**, Wandering Dub; **Joy White**, Feeling Time; **Rupie Edwards All-Stars**, Feeling Horn; **Mr Bojangles**, The Dread Commandment.

Prince Far-I

(Born Michael Williams, 1945; Spanish Town, Jamaica; deejay)
On record, Prince Far-I was the embodiment of living dread. His rhythms never displayed anything less than city-flattening potential. They rolled out of speaker boxes riding on a bass 'n' drum oppressiveness that went beyond merely 'heavy', and the Addis-style horns offered a strength of purpose and a celebratory, triumphant appeal that would rock any kind of dance. And the only thing that could possibly hope to live up to this threatening rumble was Prince Far-I's deep, gravelly toasting style. It sounded like it was coming from the back of a cave in the Wareika Hills, was waking up from 400 years of sufferation and was mad as hell. This wasn't 'Young, Gifted And Black'. There'd been a definite shift in emphasis over the intervening years. This was 'Black Man Time'. Not reggae for the faint hearted.

In fact, one of the few things more physically intimidating than Far-I's music was Far-I himself. Actually a very pleasant, obliging chap, he presented an enormous, muscular figure, with the scars on his face bearing evidence that he hadn't always followed the ways of Jah Rastafari – indeed, before he turned to music full-time he was the security force at COXSONE's Brentford Road studio; not a job for a delicate flower. Far-I's apprenticeship in music had come via toasting at various sound systems and cutting a couple of tunes for BUNNY LEE in the 1960s. Calling himself King Cry Cry, he even very occasionally stepped up to the mic at Studio One, but it wasn't until he changed his name to Prince Far-I that he began to make a difference. His *Under Heavy Manners* album, cut for JOE GIBBS, with some appropriately serious rhythms, was an enormous hit in 1977. ('Heavy manners' was a phrase beloved by Jamaican politicians of the day, which referred to how law breakers would be severely punished. Far-I turned it round to claim it for Jah and Rastafari as an expression of how Babylon would be brought down.) The album set him up for some staggering work – *Message From the King*, *Livety* and the *Cry Tuff Dub Encounter* series remain cornerstones of black reggae music, whatever era you approach them in.

Of virtually all Jamaica's roots deejays, Prince Far-I was about the only one who remained totally true to the cause throughout his working life. Not for him slackness, gun lyrics or even love songs, he was strictly righteous, believing his one purpose in the recording studio or on stage was to spread the word of Jah. Although to more than a few this made him something of a one trick pony, maybe if there had been more like Prince Far-I still actively involved in Jamaican music during the period of the late 1980s/early 1990s it wouldn't all have gone off the rails so badly.

Tragically, Prince Far-I was shot dead in an apparently random act of violence in 1984. This happened shortly after he'd returned to the island, following a long spell in the UK, and was just starting to re-establish himself with his home crowd.

Black Man Land; Frontline CDFL9005

That vital Joe Gibbs-produced album, *Under Heavy Manners*, is unavailable on CD, but this is an entirely worthy substitute. It's made up of a combination of tracks from the next two, equally awe-inspiring, bodies of work, *Black Man Time* and *Livety*. Self-produced, both sets had everything you want from a Far-I record: thundering, threatening, claustrophobic rhythms; horns perking it up and steering it east; and toasting of the fullest fire and brimstone fashion. On the tracklisting here are 'Message From The King', 'Black Man Land', 'Badda Card', 'Ghetto Living' and 'River Of Jordan'.

Dubwise; Frontline CDFL9019

Made up of *Cry Tuff Dub Encounter Volume Two*, cut in 1979, and eight previously unreleased tracks. The *Cry Tuff* stuff is an excellent example of Far-I taking his notion of musical intimidation to the mixing desk and back. It structures some towering, brain-damaging, dreader-than-thou dub, sparse and dark, yet surprisingly textured as upper register percussion and fragmented melodies rip through the basslines. Likewise, the four other tracks and their dub versions – 'Throw Away Your Gun' and 'Jah Do That' are two of them – prove that, if anything, Far-I's dub technique was so overwhelming the tunes actually increase in menace when the vocals are taken out. Beat down Babylon? You wouldn't really need to – just point a Prince Far-I dub plate in the right direction.

ALSO RECOMMENDED:

*Cry Tuff Dub Encounter; Danceteria DANCD075

The first of the series, which isn't quite as texturally interesting as *Volume Two*, and although good righteous music, it suffers from not having the bonus tracks.

*Voice Of Thunder; Trojan CDTRL204

Late-model toasting that offers little progression from the earlier classics.

SEE ALSO:

Roots 'N' Culture; Music Club International MCCD128
Natty Rebel Roots; Frontline CDFL9013
Beyond The Frontline; Frontline FRONT1

Dean Fraser

(Born 1957; Kingston, Jamaica; saxophonist)
Given the disproportionately high number of superb brass players Jamaica has produced, and a tradition among them for indigenously made jazz, it's difficult to see why so few of them have careers outside of backing other people. Luckily, Dean Fraser is an exception to that rule. And while backing just about everybody who counted during the last twenty years, since JOE

GIBBS first recorded him in 1978 he's also had a career as a front-man. Also, as dancehall rhythms became increasingly machine-generated, Fraser found himself in enormous demand from producers who wanted an instant injection of humanity into their work. Such has been Dean Fraser's contribution to Jamaica's music industry that in 1993 he was awarded the civic honour of The Musgrave Medal. A bit like an OBE.

Rather than attempt to list the records Fraser has played on, it'll save a lot of time and space if you just check the credits. The chances are that if said album was made after 1975 – when he did his first recording session as part of Lloyd Parks's We The People band – Fraser will be on it. Probably with his regular musical partners Ronald Robinson (trombone) and Junior Chinn (sax), which means you're in for a bit of a treat.

Sings And Blows; Greensleeves GRELCD113

Cut in the late 1980s for dancehall producer Dennis Star, this shows how Fraser could bring a roots earthiness to the reggae of the day, while revisiting the idea of the sax man as singer as well – he had recorded some reasonably successful vocal sides for DONOVAN GERMAIN a few years earlier. It works too, as his soulful tenor isn't that far removed from his sax.

Raw Sax; Greensleeves GRELCD129

Just playing this time, as Fraser brings out all the warm, sweet jazziness, laced with flashes of fire, with which he made his rep-utation.

Pablo Gad

(Born early 1960s, Kingston, Jamaica; vocalist/keyboards)
Although resident in the UK and still recording for various inde-pendent London labels, roots singer Pablo Gad is a shadowy figure. What makes this low profile even more remarkable is that Gad cut one of the very best late-roots records of the early 1980s. 'Hard Times Style', with its crashing clavinet, machine-gun steppers rhythm and Gad's impassioned singing, stated the

case for British reggae with an eloquence few others got near. It rocked parties every time it was dropped. Still does today. So it's brilliant that somebody's seen fit to put it out on CD (with as little information as possible on the sleeve, of course). Your roots reggae collection can now be complete.

**The Best Of Pablo Gad*; Roots ROTCD001

Not only is this built around 'Hard Times Style' and its blistering dub, but it also features those two equally rocking follow-ups 'Guns Fever' and 'Beggarman Child'. Complete with dub mixes. So don't let the no-frills packaging put you off, it's the tunes that count. All together now: 'When I was a yout' I used to burn collie weed in a Rizla/Now I am a man I jus' a burn collie weed in a chalwah . . .'

Joe Gibbs

➻ Into the 1970s, by which time Gibbs was embracing roots reggae with gusto. He'd already hinted at what he was capable of after he opened his own two-track studio in 1969, took on NINEY THE OBSERVER (after the latter had one too many rows with LEE PERRY) and, under such spartan conditions, cut 'Jack Of My Trade' with Sir Lord Comic, an instant early roots classic. In fact it was from there, after Niney had left, that the combination of Joe Gibbs and master engineer Errol 'Errol T' Thompson recorded DENNIS BROWN's original cut of 'Money In My Pocket', BIG YOUTH's version of 'Ah So We Stay' and some of PETER TOSH's best work including 'Them Fe Get A Beating' and 'Maga Dog'. But it was after he moved to a more luxurious set up in 1975, that he really came into his own.

Gibbs/Thompson productions had a much harder quality to them than anything else that was going on; the bass and drum balance slapped rather than bounced and the horns and guitars did nothing to soften the effect. While so much Rasta-influenced music had a woozy spirituality about it, this was up-on-its-hind-legs militancy – in a style which had its place as black nationalism openly swept Jamaica, and which, from a strictly artistic point of view, was perfect for raw-edged deejays such as Trinity

(*Three Piece Suit*), Prince Hammer and Dillinger (it was with Joe Gibbs and Errol T that PRINCE FAR-I recorded the seminal *Under Heavy Manners* album). At the same time singers like JUNIOR BYLES, Earl Sixteen and GREGORY ISAACS all benefited from the tough sound they'd be guaranteed from a Joe Gibbs production. He got CULTURE started with the fearsome 'Two Sevens Clash' and continued on the international trail with Dennis Brown – a swinging recut of 'Money In My Pocket' – and the enormous UK pop success 'Uptown Top Ranking' by one-hit wonders Althea and Donna. But where Joe Gibbs left his own name indelibly stamped on the Book Of Reggae was with the *African Dub* album series. Half a dozen 'Chapters' of escalatingly experimental dub selections that split opinion as to whether they went 'too far', and which, due to their confrontational qualities, eventually found great favour with British punks. Perhaps that was a big factor in turning the reggae crowd off them.

Gibbs and Thompson continued in the next decade too, linking the roots era with what was coming next as they put together fast-moving, mildly digital Jamaican hits for EEK-A-MOUSE and Nigger Kojak. But, in spite of the envelope-pushing *African Dub* albums, Gibbs was too much of a traditionalist to fully come to terms with the new sounds. Creative alienation and legal battles over ownership of songs have put him into semi-retirement in Miami, with his only music business involvement being back catalogue exploitation.

*African Dub Chapters One and Two; Rocky One Records RGCD020
*African Dub Chapters Three and Four; Rocky One Records RGCD024
*African Dub Chapters Five and Six; Rocky One Records RGCD028

That this series is now available on CD must be much to the chagrin of second-hand record dealers everywhere, who were charging increasingly silly prices for vinyl copies. And to get two albums on the one disc is more than just VFM, it's probably the nearest most of us will get to committing robbery.

The series allows us to see how Gibbs and Thompson

progressed on this epic journey to the outer limits of dub. And how they came back again. In each case, they begin with a series of well-known tunes, reduce them to their absolute essence – more often than not, this would mean paring the tune down to the foundation rhythm (the bass 'n' drums tracks) and dissecting even that to leave just a snatch of the bass line being repeated, with bits of the drum pattern being dropped in at rhythmically appropriate points. Then, among the weird and wonderful sound effects, certain key notes and chords would be sequenced in to provide some startlingly off-beat rhythmic emphasis. And of course, just about everything added would be distorted, echoed or just musically messed about with.

What made Gibbs and Thompson dubs so accessible, though, was, ultimately they kept tunes as tunes by making sure each out-of-left-field rhythm had a thick coating of melody. But – and this is what made their work really clever – it was precisely their use of this melody that made the series so challenging. While so many other producers shaped their dubs out of pure rhythm, this dynamic duo fooled around with lead instruments with equal enthusiasm: not-very-obvious samples of the original lead lines would be treated to the Gibbs box of tricks, then thrown back into the mix; melody excerpts would be rerecorded on different instruments; individual bits of records would be remixed separately then reapplied with a radically altered sound, which in turn would more or less rewrite the tune in a couple of bars. But what they always did was swing. And all this was done twenty years ago, by instinct, exuberance and speed of hand on sixteen-track analogue equipment.

Chapter Three was where the series peaked. Always more than merely a version excursion, it took such reggae classics as 'I Love You So', 'Love You Always' and 'Hypocrites' and reworked them with a vengeance. These tunes would be cut up, redressed, rebalanced, and in a couple of cases rewritten, then re-presented to us with such guile and subtlety the original – something we knew and loved – would occur as merely a subliminal idea. The high point of this work of genius, 'Tribesman Rockers' demonstrates the Gibbs approach perfectly. It takes the bits of the tune that lead up to an instantly recognizable chorus, and by repeating them holds you on the edge for about as long as humanly possible. By the time the phrase that usually defines the tune looms up out of the SFX background – once, and on a totally unexpected instrument – your head is somewhere else completely. This and the other frequent, but thickly veiled, references to the original work leave you knowing what it once was, thus able to get into it immediately. The problem is you won't realize what happened until two or three records later, when it sinks in that the wild, cutting-edge dread, techno-dub monster you'd just spent a perfect three minutes rocking to was in fact 'Kingston Town'.

To use an old rock steady rhythm as the basis for their experiments wasn't all that unusual. Such records were selected for the strength of the drum and bass foundations laid down by producers such as Duke Reid or Bunny Lee, and that the cool rock steady tempo was entirely suitable for the heavy-lidded atmosphere of dread they succeeded in creating. It was probably such acts of sacrilege that set so many self-appointed guardians of reggae against the *African Dub* series, claiming it was nothing more than gimmickry – Lee Perry was actually far more open to such a charge, but because the majority of his ground-breaking dubs were original compositions, he seemed to get away with it. *Chapter Three* was especially reviled – by people who had never rocked to its contents in a packed, heaving house party – and whether in reaction to this or simply because they were running out of puff, from *Chapter Four* onwards the series seemed to get straighter and straighter. Not that this is in any way a criticism. Most producers could make 600 dub albums and not come up with anything remotely as enticing as *African Dub Chapter Three*. Or *One* or *Two* or *Four* or. . . .

The Gladiators

(Albert Griffiths, Clinton Fearon, Dallimore Sutherland; all born early 1950s; Kingston, Jamaica; vocal trio)
Another prime example of how the changes occurring in reggae had led to COXSONE's grip being loosened – The Gladiators were one more roots act that did better away from Studio One than they did when they were there. This isn't to say their time with Dodd was in any way wasted: their schooling at Brentford Road as a classic Jamaican vocal trio, from their outset in the

mid-1960s, doubtlessly shaped their harmonizing into the powerful, well-oiled machine it was; and they did have a string of roots successes in the early 1970s.

However, it was after they left and began producing themselves that the full emotion of their Rasta philosophies and clever writing and arrangements were given a free rein. Signed to the UK label Virgin, who jumped into the reggae market with both feet in BOB MARLEY's slipstream (and reportedly sent reps to Jamaica to wave money at anybody with dreadlocks and a demo tape), they recorded a string of classic albums – *Trenchtown Mix Up, Proverbial Reggae, Naturality* and *So Sweet Till* – featuring some fine updating of tunes recorded for Dodd ten years previously.

Dreadlocks The Time Is Now; Frontline CDFL9001

None of The Gladiators's excellent Virgin albums are currently available in original form on CD, but this is surely the next best thing. Going across the entire catalogue at the label, it shows exactly what made the trio so special as they manage to mix up the light and the heavy in the same songs. Everything complies with what Virgin were looking for in their ultimate quest for a Marley-esque roots crossover act: it's entirely melodic, there's a great airiness to the mix and a conventional-rock instrumentation is well to the fore with a lead guitar and keyboards – but at the same time the rhythm track is tough enough to stop anything floating away. And the harmonizing, built round Griffiths's falsetto, is pure Trenchtown sufferation. While remaining culturally correct, it's among the most accessible roots reggae ever made.

SEE ALSO:

Natty Rebel Roots; Frontline CDFL9013
Roots 'N' Culture; Music Club International MCCD128
Beyond the Frontline; Frontline FRONT1

Joe Higgs

(Born 1940; Kingston, Jamaica; singer/cultural and musical mentor)

It would be impossible to tell the story of modern reggae, especially the roots rock chapter of it, without mention of Joe Higgs – in spite of the fact that his most successful musical effort belonged in a previous era. Teamed up with Roy Wilson as Higgs and Wilson in 1959, he was one of the earliest Jamaican recording artists, and the duo's single 'Manny Oh' was the first huge local hit by indigenous artists. A vivid example of the Jamaican Boogie style that formed the link between US R&B and home-grown ska on the island, it was produced by Edward Seaga who later became leader of the Jamaican Labour Party and eventually the country's prime minister.

Where Joe Higgs left his mark, though, was as a singing and music teacher and moral adviser to Trenchtown's youth. A devout Rasta from the time it was spoken of in hushed tones (Higgs had been subject to great police persecution for his beliefs) he was determined to steer the local teenagers away from the rude boy life. His yard, on Third Street in the heart of the ghetto, was open house to any youngsters who wanted to drop in and 'reason' – that is, talk about just about anything but with constant spiritual undertones. He'd espouse Rasta doctrine and encourage attendees to follow the path of righteousness, but to get them there in the first place he'd provide singing and guitar lessons. As music represented one of the very few roads out of poverty, these afternoon sessions were always packed. He was a hard taskmaster too, insisting the kids learned scales, mastered correct breathing methods and practised properly and regularly. Most of the stars to come out of Trenchtown in the 1960s and 1970s had passed through Joe Higgs's yard at least once, his most famous graduates being THE WAILERS. Indeed, on many an occasion Bob Marley publicly credited Joe Higgs for teaching the original group to sing and harmonize, for introducing him to the teachings of Jah Rastafari and for giving him his first taste of the herb.

Although Joe Higgs possesses one of the sweetest voices in Jamaica and made a string of well-received roots singles and a few innovative albums during the 1970s, he never really got the acclaim he might have as a singer. He still lives in Jamaica – though no longer in Trenchtown – as one of reggae's elder statesmen.

*Life Of Contradiction; Grounation GRCD508

Recorded in 1975, this self-produced set is, at the time of writing, the only Joe Higgs album available on UK CD release. Therefore it will be hard to track down, but ultimately worth it. Higgs's first musical love was jazz – while he was growing up it would have been mostly jazz that was played on Jamaican radio and by local bands – and this album expresses that perfectly within the roots reggae idiom. On top of a gently swinging dread beat, the instrumentation is treated to a jazz-type arrangement with soul-of-the-day influences stirred in (the line-up features US jazz/funk guitarist Eric Gale). But topped with Higgs's sweet roots voice and sufferation lyrics, it was never going to be any-thing other than Rasta reggae. It's a pity this didn't get wider exposure at the time, as it was an excellent pointer to how Jamaican music could've broadened its base without going off course. As it is, it remains a tribute to the musical knowledge and cultural intelligence of Joe Higgs.

Keith Hudson

(Born 1946; Kingston, Jamaica; producer/vocalist)

Perhaps 'innovator' would be a more accurate title for Keith Hudson. One of the first significant producers to enter reggae outside the Treasure Isle/Studio One axis of ex-rock steady men, he always had a style very much his own – he'd concen-trate on what could be done with what he had (the players and their instruments) rather than bring in such outside elements as sound effects or studio gimmicks. 'S.90 Skank' notwithstanding. As a result, the Jamaican session-playing fraternity of the time deeply respected Hudson and would usually pull something special out of their bags for him.

It's probably Hudson more than anybody else who is the father of deejay recording: when he cut U-ROY on a track he called 'Dynamic Fashion Way' in 1970 – a version of the first Hudson hit, KEN BOOTHE's 'Old Fashioned Way' – it was such a success it converted toasting from a sound system art form into a commercial prospect. The early, and many say best, DENNIS ALCAPONE tracks are Hudson's, and it was 'S.90 Skank' that took BIG YOUTH from the Tippertone sound system and into the recording studio.

Hudson voiced a few mid-1970s scorchers himself too. Albums such as *Flesh Of My Skin*, *Torch Of Freedom* and *Entering The Dragon* proved him to have a unique half-singing half-toasting style and a view of life that was as militant as it was optimistic. And, as well as producing some classics by HORACE ANDY, AUGUSTUS PABLO and DELROY WILSON, with the 1975 release *Pick A Dub* Hudson produced the first deliberately thematic dub album – tracks mixed down with the full intention of appearing next to each other on an LP, rather than a fairly random collection of versions.

Hudson was an all-round nice guy too. Anybody who knew or worked with him will testify to that – I say 'knew' because, sadly, Keith Hudson passed away from lung cancer in 1984. He was one of the few producers at the time who actually went out of their way to see that (a) their artists got paid, and (b) that they looked after the money – Dennis Alcapone still recounts the story of how, after they put out their first record together, Hudson took him to a bank to open an account.

Perhaps the truly remarkable thing about Keith Hudson, though, is that he used to be a dentist. It was from his successful ghetto practice that he financed his first recordings and eventually the building of his own studio.

Pick A Dub; Blood And Fire; BAFCD003

This is that marvellous release of twenty years ago, and it's an enormous relief that Blood And Fire have had the nous to depict the original sleeve as part of the reissue's design. That unsophisticated drawing of a dread under a palm tree was like a badge of cool, as whoever owned this album carried it round with them to show how hip they were. Featuring players who were a virtual who's who of roots sessioneering at the time (Pablo, the Barrett brothers, Chinna Smith and so on), this set reintroduces some of Hudson's finest moments – 'S.90 Skank', 'Declaration Of Rights' and 'Satta Massa Gana' among them. It's a virtual shop window of his brilliance, as the tunes are stripped back to the bone and rebuilt, in part, to blistering effect. The results hinge entirely on what the producer does with what he had to start off with. The only additions are scant, scat vocals from himself and Horace Andy, meaning this set is dub in its purest form.

*Keith Hudson and Friends: *Studio Kinda Cloudy*; Trojan CDTRL258

A brilliantly titled, completely brilliant collection of Hudson productions for other people, including many of the tracks that made his (and their) reputations. Most Wanted on this is U-Roy's excellent 'Keith Hudson Affair', which for over twenty years in this country hasn't existed outside a very limited white label import. But I'll shut up, and let the tracklisting do the work:

Ken Boothe, Old Fashioned Way; **Dennis Alcapone**, Spanish Amigo; **U-Roy**, Dynamic Fashion Way; **Dennis Alcapone,** Shades Of Hudson, Revelation Version; **Phillip Samuel**, Hot Stick Version; **Keith Hudson**, Satan Side; **The Soul Syndicate**, Riot; **U-Roy**, The Hudson Affair; **Horace Andy**, Don't Think About Me; **Jah Woosh**, I'm Alright; **Dino Perkins**, Skin Him Alive.

SEE ALSO:

Beyond The Frontline; Frontline FRONT1

I-Jahman

(Born Trevor Sutherland, 1946; Kingston, Jamaica; singer)
Although the man also known as I-Jahman Levi had began his musical life as a graduate of the JOE HIGGS academy of singing, then moved on to become one of DUKE REID's adolescent ska hopefuls, his arrival in the UK in 1963 changed everything. Almost immediately he formed a soul band, enjoying mild acclaim on the London live circuit, then a few years later discovered Jah Rastafari. From that point on he became something of a father figure to the UK roots scene, collaborating with that other relocated Rasta man RICO and blending his soul influences into his reggae to produce some unique black British music.

Still prolifically recording, he may never have had the enormous success his lively local following felt he deserved, but in his day I-Jahman recorded some excellent singles. Not least 'Jah Heavy Load' and 'I Am A Levi'.

Hail I Hymn; Mango RRCD35
We Are A Warrior; Mango RRCD25

This is vintage I-Jahman. On the former you'll find 'Jah Heavy Load', 'Jah Is No Secret' and 'I Am A Levi', while the latter will give you 'Miss Beverly', 'Two Sides Of Love' and the title track. They're all songs that perhaps best display the man's combination of deep roots sensibilities over a deceptively light arrangement, and the ability to apply the same degree of soulfulness to his righteous material as he did to his love songs. Yes, the rhythms were dread, but his sweet voice and way with a melody was uplifting in every respect.

ALSO RECOMMENDED:

King Far-I; Jahmani CDJMI 1400
Love Smiles; Jahmani CDJMI 1200

More of before, but this time more modern and although excellent value, somehow not quite as powerful.

I-Roy

(Born Roy Reid, 1950; Spanishtown, Jamaica; deejay)
It would be wrong to dismiss I-Roy as nothing more than a U-ROY impersonator as so often happened twenty years ago. The most articulate and apparently intellectual of the early recording deejays, while a few of his touches were recognizable AL-CAPONE-isms and his name immediately put you in mind of U-ROY, this one-time civil servant had a remarkable style of his own. He talked proper English. Or near as dammit. Although his subject matter and vocabulary were straight outta Trenchtown, the syntax was pre-Independence mother tongue, as still taught in Jamaica's better schools. His subject matter was pretty unique too, inasmuch as I-Roy was equally at home with Rasta

233

philosophies, political diatribe or bawdy sex rhymes. And he was the main instigator in deejay battles, whereby toasters issued 'answers' to each other's records, often over the same backing track. I-Roy was involved in memorable lyrical conflicts with JAZZBO, U-Roy and BIG YOUTH. The battle with the former produced some ludicrously wordy insults – for example 'Jazzbo if you were a jukebox I wouldn't put a dime in you' – and when I-Roy released his classic slackness saga 'Welding' ('ah wah de young gal want'), Big Youth came straight back at him with the righteous 'Natty Dread (A Wah De Young Gal Want)'. It shouldn't be forgotten either that I-Roy cut some excellent tunes too: with GUSSIE CLARKE, GLEN BROWN, BUNNY LEE and Tony Robinson. 'Black Man Time', recorded with Clarke, remains one of the all-time best deejay singles.

For some reason, the I-Roy/Clarke collaboration album, *Presenting I-Roy*, is only available on vinyl. This is a great shame, as it's practically a catalogue of the finest moments they had together, and therefore represents a great deal of the deejay's best work.

Crisis Time; Frontline CDFL9015

One of the later albums, recorded for Virgin under the guidance of Tony Robinson. It lacks some of the spark of the Clarke releases, but even if there were other I-Roy albums available on CD it would still be worth it. Features 'Heart Of A Lion', 'Roots Man Time' ('Black Man Time' revisited), 'African Herbsman' and 'Don't Touch I Man Locks'.

SEE ALSO:

Dubble Attack – The Original Pantomime Dee-Jay Collection 1972-74; Greensleeves GRELCD601.
Tougher Than Tough – The Story Of Jamaican Music; Mango IBXCD1

Inner Circle

(Ian Lewis, bass; Roger Lewis, guitar; both born late 1940s; Jacob Miller, vocals; born mid-1950s; all born Kingston, Jamaica; band)

How many times do you see an actual band coming out of Jamaica, a self-contained unit of musicians as well as singers? Not that often. And it's probably because Inner Circle were such an outfit, and the fact they used to earn a good living out of the North Coast hotel lounges, that they have been written off as nothing more than ersatz reggae. This has never been strictly true, though, and even if it was that's no reason to run them down.

When the group were first formed in 1968, they included several players who would go on to become Third World, and immediately assumed lightweight pop group status. However, once Cooper, Coore and Daley had departed a few years later, the Lewis brothers added Miller to a line-up supplemented by session players. The singer who had enjoyed solo success with such mild roots moments as 'Tenement Yard' and 'Forward Jah Jah Children', now brought a definite focus to the group. They began growing dreadlocks, and growing in bulk – at one point the threesome had a combined weight of well over 50 stone. Their repertoire consisted of cover versions of roots hits plus their own equally two-tiered writings (pop style, deep sentiments), and it won such enormous international acclaim that they were big in the USA long before BOB MARLEY. Indeed, it was probably this that saw off their reggae following, as they edged so close to the US *Saturday Night Fever*-style club scene, they actually fell in with a couple of highly KC and The Sunshine Band-ish disco albums. When Miller was tragically killed in a car accident in 1980, Inner Circle split up, with the Lewis brothers opening a studio in Miami.

The thing about Inner Circle was they knew what they did best, and if it involved presenting an acceptable face of natty to the tourists, so what? Not everybody can be PRINCE JAZZBO. And with no light relief, the others wouldn't sound so heavy. The way we looked at the group back in the day was that it was better to have them in the Top 20 than The Bay City Rollers, or whoever. Also, like Byron Lee before them, if what they did turned even one visiting tourist on to the deeper stuff then they'd done their job. In fact when the Lewises found vocalist Carlton Coffey (just as well-nourished and long-locked) and came back two years ago with 'Sweat (A La La La La Long)' it was like welcoming home a couple of old friends.

The Best Of Inner Circle; Trojan CDTRL318

A good cross-section of what they did before they went solely soul – covers of, among others, 'Duppy Gunman', 'Curly Locks', 'I Shot The Sheriff', 'Book Of Rules' and 'Forward Jah Jah Children', plus reggaefied versions of 'T.S.O.P.', 'When Will I See You Again' and 'Rock The Boat'. It's all one hundred per cent pleasant, and a reminder of how much of an understanding they had of reggae in order to be able to sweeten it up like this. Also, it goes a long way to showing off how technically good they were.

SEE ALSO:

Crucial Reggae; Mango RRCD37

Gregory Isaacs

(Born 1950; Kingston, Jamaica; singer)
There's been a great deal written and even more said about Gregory Isaacs's legendary unpleasantness. Apparently the bloke could strop for his country. Then there's the drugs. Not the weed of wisdom or the healing herb – we're talking major contributions to Bolivia's balance of payments. It isn't the sort of thing that'll improve anybody's disposition. He's frequently found himself at odds with the local constabulary and has even done serious time in one of Kingston's fearsome gaols. And, as he'll put it, he's done what he's had to do to survive for thirty years in an industry in which acts of violence are everyday currency.

Of course, in theory, the world would be a much better place if Gregory Isaacs didn't carry on like this, but if he didn't he wouldn't be Gregory Isaacs. And when you consider the prospect of no Gregory at all, any reported behavioural problems are merely a technicality.

The man they call The Cool Ruler is exactly that. To reggae people over the age of thirty, and quite a few under it, Isaacs rules the dance, with a style so laid back it's practically bent double. So astonishingly three-dimensional is his voice that every time a deejay e-e-e-eased a tune such as 'Night Nurse' on to the deck we'd all be able to see the man in front of us: a big crown hat on his locks, a trademark three piece suit and his eyes barely open. Then he'd start to sing in what could accurately be described as a groan. Women would go weak and the guys would hold them up that little bit tighter. For the full three minutes. Then, when it was over, we'd shout 'More Gregory' until the deejay licked it back more than one time.

There was a soulful quality to Isaacs's voice that few others ever got near. It totally transcended anything that may have been going on away from the studio. In his love songs he'd play the underdog, either pleading for the woman in question to give him a break or telling how he'd been wronged. He'd give up a little-boy-lost air of 'please mother me, or, at the very least, feel sorry for me'. With complete conviction. Even though you knew the man was so dangerous you wouldn't trust him in a room by himself, let alone with a woman. When it came to the righteous stuff, too, such a vulnerability was perfect for expressing the hurt and suffering of Jah People. In spite of his obviously having strayed off the path every now and again. And again. And the lazy, hazy delivery of some distracted soul, not quite sure of himself, only served to heighten these effects.

This was all there from his beginnings in the early 1970s, when, like so many other Trenchtown youth, he'd do the rounds of Kingston talent shows looking for a break. Once he got in the recording studio, he didn't wait too long for a hit. 'Love Is Overdue' came courtesy of Alvin Ranglin and it established a style that has changed very little since. Hits flowed: 'Loving Pauper', 'Lonely Lover', 'All I Have Is Love', 'Promised Land' . . . Even his own African Museum label going belly up wasn't enough to stop him growing into reggae's Original Mr Loverman. Indeed the only real hiccup came at the beginning of the next decade with Isaacs's incarceration for firearms offences. And that was eventually turned to his advantage – after he came out, in order to restore his fortunes, he put himself on the open market for any producer who would have him. Which turned out to be most of them, and in the second half of the 1980s the market was flooded with Gregory Isaacs material on a level that made even DENNIS BROWN look slothful.

Isaacs rode out the change in styles by doing very little other than what he'd always done – dancehall producers were so keen to make use of his inherent soulfulness they'd adapt their rhythms to suit. Problem was, the sheer volume of material and the strains of the Isaacs's personal life were conspiring to edge quality control somewhere near the window, if not actually out of it. This got worse as the 1990s rolled around, and the toll began showing in the one place it couldn't afford to – the Gregory Isaacs pipes. What was previously 'seasoned' began to sound more like 'shot'. Nowadays it's necessary to ask to hear a Gregory Isaacs record before you buy it. Hopefully he'll sort out whatever it is that ails him before he becomes one more reggae museum piece. Then the rest of us can get back to taking him on trust.

What follows is merely a selection of the best Gregory Isaacs on offer at the moment. There are over 300 albums on different catalogues, and a vast amount of it appears on CD. Suffice to say, anything made before 1990 is worth further investigation and anything involving either GUSSIE CLARKE, NINEY, GLEN BROWN or Alvin Raglin or The Roots Radics band shouldn't be ignored.

Night Nurse; Mango RRCD9

This is absolutely classic mid-period Gregory. Cut in 1982 – before the substances had really taken hold – self-produced, backed by The Roots Radics and achieving that springy, semi-stepping feel that provides exactly the right support mechanism for the man's ultra-relaxed croon. Like the very best soul singers, on more than one occasion he'll lapse into lurrrve-type noises as the apparent overwhelming rush of emotion renders the lyrics somewhat redundant. As well as the title track, there's its virtual clone 'Stranger In Town', the sublime 'Cool Down The Pace' and the righteous rock of 'Material Man'.

The Cool Ruler Rides Again; Music Club International MCCD144

The sub-title is '22 Classics From 1978-1981' and it's not lying either. 'Slave Market', 'Mr Brown', 'Permanent Lover', 'The Fugitive', 'Poor And Clean'... I could go on, but I really shouldn't need to.

The Early Years; Trojan CDTRL196

The original hitsound. Young Gregory sounding sweeter than he ever did after this and wrapping you up in such wonders as 'Loving Pauper', 'Lonely Lover', 'Financial Endorsement', 'Promised Land', 'Rock Away', 'All I Have Is Love' and, of course, 'Love Is Overdue'. Let this play and it won't take long to understand why the man became The Cool Ruler.

Love Is Overdue; Munich Records NETCD24

The Soul Syndicate backing him up on this one, as a bunch of the old tunes are revisited in 1990. The real star of the show is 'Love Is Overdue', done over again in an original style, but with a toast from U-ROY to round it off. Then as a bonus there's a 'discomix' (again with U-Roy) of 'Financial Endorsement', and an extended 'How Long'.

Private Beach Party; Greensleeves GRELCD85

Fast forward to 1985 and Gussie Clarke. By now the computer-ized rhythms are more than just creeping in and Clarke puts it together expertly to create some real digitized excitement going on behind the groaning. The killer tracks are 'Private Beach Party', 'Let Off Supm' and 'Wish You Were Mine', but really this is one of the last consistently good albums.

Live At The Academy; Kingdom CDKVL 9027

A vivid example of the power of an in-form Gregory live on stage. The set list reads like a Cool Ruler's Greatest Hits, the band is tighter than they've got any right to be, the crowd – at the Brixton Academy in 1984 – is so wildly on his side that the vibes reach out of the speakers and drag you back there.

Set Me Free; Vine Yard VYDCD2

Cut in 1991 with BOBBY DIGITAL, this is Gregory going head-to-head with the dancehall dons of the day and coming out on top. The rhythms may be high-speed and computerized, but the singing is pure Gregory, so although, in theory, the two should be pulling in opposite directions, the Isaacs croon dominates to such a degree it stays soulful.

Memories; Riddim 112082

Most recent Gregory, in which the voice sounds, er, delicate. In fact, gone to hell would be a better description. But, surprisingly, this doesn't make a lot of difference to the soulful quota involved – if anything it helps as there's a pleading edge to it that hadn't been present for a few years. What this set also shows, though, is how the modern, techno reggae producers are turning their equipment to producing a more traditional song structure and musical arrangement in their backing material. What we have here could almost be called – with apologies to BLACK UHURU – digital roots.

Number One; Charly CPCD8026

To have 'My Number One', 'Loving Pauper', 'Border' and 'If You're Feeling Hot I Will Cool You' all on the same CD has got to be worth considering.

SEE ALSO:

Like Dennins Brown, with whom he frequently duetted, Isaacs was so prolific an artist that there's few halfway decent compilations that don't feature one of his tunes.

Israel Vibration

(Skeleton, born Cecil Spence; Apple, born Albert Craig; Whiss, born Lascelle Bulgrin; all born late 1950s; Kingston, Jamaica; vocal group)
This remarkable trio were all polio-myelitis victims as babies (an epidemic hit Jamaica at the end of the 1950s), and came together and began singing as they grew up in a rehabilitation centre – until they discovered Rastafari in the early 1970s and began to 'locks up'. They were all thrown out and lived rough for five years – if it wasn't for busking and financial as well as spiritual

aid from Rasta organization The Twelve Tribes, they would have starved. Indeed it was The Twelve Tribes who met the studio costs for their first recording sessions in 1976. Even this was surprising, as many Rastas refused to have anything to do with the trio, believing that their disability was a punishment from Jah. The first album was an immediate hit and they went on to sustain considerable success in both Jamaica and the USA, where they have been based for several years.

The Same Song; Pressure Sounds CDPS003

The group's first and greatest album, recorded in 1978, with extended versions of the title track and 'Crisis' (the latter featuring an AUGUSTUS PABLO-led dub). Their three-part harmonies are classic Jamaican, the voices are plaintive without being pitiful, the lyrics are strictly dread and the rhythms are suitably lazy with a great deal of top end offsetting the loping basslines. This is, quite simply, brilliant melodic roots. Apparently, in live performance, as they grooved to the beats on crutches and walking sticks, the crowds were never less than totally overwhelmed.

Linton Kwesi Johnson

(Born 1952; Clarendon, Jamaica; dub poet)
Dub poetry was a big deal in Britain in the late 1970s. Its potential audience was enormous too, for while it wasn't *quite* toasting, it wasn't nearly as dry as the popular notion of a poetry reading either. It was that era's take on the Jamaican oral tradition: more concerned with telling a story than with catchphrases or rocking a dance. The dub poets who got noticed at the time concerned themselves with social injustice and racial politics by articulating the resentment they saw festering on the street corners – it's no coincidence that this style came to the fore as so many inner cities across the country were rocked by riots. It appeared far more intellectual than what was going on at the sound systems, but still retained enormous roots credibility. Johnson was the highest profile exponent among such others as Mutabaruka and Benjamin Zephaniah.

Johnson had arrived in the UK aged ten, and graduated in sociology before becoming a journalist and a founder member of the Race Today Collective. Reacting against the commonplace police brutality and widespread institutional racism in London in the 1970s, his poetry developed to get his messages across in a way the youth could understand but, at the same time, would be taken seriously. What made it so instantly popular, though, was that his love of reggae music led him to DENNIS BOVELL whose Dub Band provided a series of totally rocking backing tracks that turned LKJ albums and shows into something special.

LKJ was never really that comfortable in the spotlight, though, and just when dub poetry was at its biggest he seemed to lose interest. He returned to journalism – both print and broadcast – and today runs LKJ Records, performing only rarely. Shame.

Bass Culture; Mango RRCD26

This 1980 album was dub poetry at its peak. Witty, articulate, angry, passionate and spread across a wider range of subject matter than was previously associated with the style. That is, alongside the polemics was a love ode and couple of pieces about nothing more controversial than raving. The album is packed with references to the politicians of the day, has a track about the police's Special Patrol Group ('Reggae Fi Peach', in memory of school teacher Blair Peach, who was killed during SPG action at a demonstration) and the poem 'Di Black Petty Booshwah', which addressed white-collar black folks and their growing depoliticization – a black middle class in Britain was a relatively new concept in 1980. The set provides a vivid picture of black life fifteen years ago. With some serious music from Dennis Bovell.

The Poet and Roots: *Dread Beat An' Blood*; Frontline CDFL9009
Forces Of Victory; Mango RRCD32

Although the former was recorded under a different name, it is LKJ and Dennis Bovell on their first excursion into the recording studio. Both of these albums are far more uncompromising than

242

Bass Culture – Dread Beat being the harder of the two – as if once LKJ relaxed into what he was doing he could start to move around more in terms of subject matter.

ALSO RECOMMENDED:

*Reggae Greats – Linton Kwesi Johnson; Mango ICM2033

A selection from *Bass Culture* and *Forces Of Victory*.

*LKJ In Dub; Mango RRCD34

A selection from *Bass Culture* and *Forces Of Victory* given the Dennis Bovell dub treatment.

Other dub poetry worth investigating:
Mutabaruka: Any Which Way ... Freedom; Greensleeves GRELCD131
Mutabaruka: The Mystery Unfolds; Shanachie SNANCD430370
Benjamin Zephaniah: Us An Dem; Mango CIDM1043

Bunny 'Striker' Lee

➻ When the roots revolution happened in reggae music, it was Bunny Lee who was at the back of it. The big two – REID and DODD – had come into the business before there was even ska, and therefore had taken the R&B-based music they understood to its logical conclusion. The idea of reggae, and roots reggae at that, wasn't in their way of thinking: the balance of instruments was completely different, the vibe of the music was in entirely another direction and the sentiments of so much of the lyrical content were diametrically opposed to ska's jolly-ups or rock steady's rude boy-isms. But Lee came to the style much later, and so his starting point was at a stage of much greater development. And, perhaps most importantly, as he had no past to pay attention to there was nothing to get in the way of his looking forward.

Striker took to roots reggae as if this was what he'd been waiting for, and by bringing what were essentially tunesmith credentials to the style produced some classic melodic Rasta reggae. His productions with JOHNNY CLARKE and Owen Grey became the yardstick against which other roots singing was measured; while in the case of Cornell Campbell he took one of the island's most popular LOVERS' ROCK singers and, with the single 'Gorgon', transformed him into a righteously dread artist, giving rise to a rash of 'Gorgon rock' in the process (the Gorgon's head of snakes were likened to dreadlocks). Most crucially, though, Bunny Lee was one of the first to make use of the talents of mix master KING TUBBY and his Waterhouse laboratory that turned out some of the finest, most enduring dubs the world has ever witnessed.

Lee was fascinated with the technological advances being made in the recording studio during the 1970s and was determined to see it play its part in what he was doing. Working closely with Tubby, Lee was one of the first to 'play' the studio and its equipment like another instrument, sitting alongside the bass, drums, horns and so on, rather than as a box of tricks to be sprinkled on after the event. This is why the duo's dub mixes have survived within reggae, rather than sitting just outside it. Dub mixes were in Lee's natural order of things rather than an optional extra. He'd record tracks with the specific intention of taking them to Tubby for a refit: all the required musical elements would be in place and strong enough to take the pounding they'd get from the reverb, echoes, SFX and adventures in space and time. Lee encouraged the mixer to experiment, and became one of the earliest exponents of the one-rhythm album in a successful attempt to prove how much great music could be wrung out of the same set of tapes.

It was a musical revolution. Because Lee/Tubby music was exactly that – music. For all the gimmicks and spaced-out notions that went into it, it was never forgotten that these were tunes first and foremost, which allowed the mixes to cross to a much wider audience than would normally be attracted. Whereas dub this deep had previously been the sole preserve of the dreadlock, now it was played among the lighter reggae and lovers' rock with no noticeable loss of enjoyment. In other words, Striker had made dub respectable, turned it into an art form in its own right. This was no mean feat. So while it's taken as read that King Tubby is a genius as his fingers were actually on the controls, it should never be forgotten that during so many of those magic moments Bunny Lee was standing just behind him.

There are no UK-released compilations of this material under the name Bunny Lee. But if you check the King Tubby entry (page 000), you'll find so much of this stuff is out there it's simply been credited to Tubby.

Otherwise, Striker was as at home producing deejays as he was singers and his productions can be found on albums by, among others from this period, Johnny Clarke, ALTON ELLIS, Cornell Campbell, U-ROY, DENNIS ALCAPONE, Leroy Smart, Trinity, DR ALIMANTADO, Owen Grey, PRINCE JAZZBO, Tappa Zukie, HORACE ANDY and Linval Thompson.

Lovers' Rock

Although lovers' rock is in many ways diametrically opposed to roots reggae, in London during the 1970s and early 1980s the two were inseparable. Lovers' sprang up as kind of B-side of roots reggae. Made in the UK, it was where the reggae of the previous section went after it had been exposed to pop soul, Motown and bubblegum pop music. It was sweet, lively, uncomplicated reggae music sung – largely – by teenage girls or beardless youths and provided entertainment for the legions of reggae fans who either viewed Rastafari with suspicion, or couldn't be bothered with everything that went along with being dread or just fancied something a bit more conventionally sophisticated. It was developed by British-based producers such as DENNIS BOVELL and THE MAD PROFESSOR (Neil Frazier), and performed by the likes of Janet Kay, 15-16-17, Louisa Mark and Carol Thompson. And, despite being reviled by the self-appointed guardians of reggae in Britain at the time – middle-class white journalists – it thrived within the black areas. Dedicated lovers' rock record labels and sound systems advertising themselves as 'Pure Lovers' would pull a young, sharply dressed crowd with as many women as men.

Curiously, although there have always been balladeers in Jamaica, lovers' rock as a genre never really had an equivalent over there – maybe well-brought-up Jamaican girls weren't allowed near the music business!

As the roots revival takes hold in the UK in the mid-1990s, so lovers' rock is being rediscovered too. There are probably more lovers' compilations available now than at any other time since the 1970s. Names to look for, apart from the above, are SUGAR MINOTT, Deborahe Glasgow, Sandra Cross, Kofi, Jean Adebambo and The Investigators.

Lovers Rock – Serious Selection Volume One; Rewind Selecta CDREG1

Rudy Thomas, Key To The World; **Fil Callender featuring Jah Stitch**, Baby My Love; **Matumbi**, After Tonight; **Horace Andy and Tappa Zukie**, Natty Dread A Weh She Want; **Barry Biggs**, Wide Awake In A Dream; **Portia Morgan**, Let Me Be Your Angel; **Louisa Marks**, Caught You In A Lie; **Motion**, Walk On By; **Bunny Maloney**, Lady Of Magic; **Jean Adebambo**, Paradise; **Errol Dunkley**, Betcha By Golly Wow; **The Tamlins**, Ting A Ling.

Ariwa 12th Anniversary Album; Ariwa Sounds ARICD067

Susan Cadogan, Together We Are Beautiful; **Sandra Cross**, Country Living; **John McLean**, I Gave My Heart To You; **Macka B**, Proud Of Mandela; **Jocelyn Brown and Robotiks**, Daydreaming; **U-Roy and Sister Audrey**, True Born African; **Carroll Thompson**, Show Some Love; **John McLean and Dego Ranks**, Runaround Girl; **Macka B**, Don't Drink Too Much; **Aisha**, Creator; **Davina Stone and Ranking Ann**, Love On A Mountain Top; **Aquizm**, True True Loving; **Delena**, Stylers; **Mother Nature**, Ganja Smuggling; **Mad Professor and Mafia and Fluxy**, Six Million Dub.

These are two of the very best compilations, from the 1970s and 1980s respectively. Other albums worth investigating are:
Deborahe Glasgow: *Deborahe Glasgow*; Greensleeves GRELCD135
Sandra Cross: *This Is Sandra Cross*; Ariwa ARICD066
Sandra Cross: *100% Lovers Rock*; Ariwa ARICD096
Susan Cadogan: *It Hurts So Good*; Trojan CDTRL122
Janet Kay: *The Ultimate Collection*; Arawak ARKCD106
Pure Lovers series; Charm CCD 101-107

Lovers For Lovers series; Business WBRCD 901-909
Out The Lights Volumes One-Eight Disco Tex DTCD 11-18
Sugar Minott: *20 Super Hits*; Sonic Sounds SON0009

The Mad Professor

(Born Neil Frazier, 1959; Guyana; producer/mixer/record com-
pany mogul)
At the time of writing, The Mad Professor's *Dub Me Crazy* series
is up to Volume Twelve, and has featured sub-titles such as
*Schizophrenic Dub, Beyond The Realms Of Dub, Science and The
Witchdoctor* and *Dub Maniacs On The Rampage*. All made in south
London, where Frazier has lived since childhood, these are dub
adventures on a scale so grand they go much further than
merely remixing an existing tune. Like the further reaches of
LEE PERRY or JOE GIBBS, this is dub for dub's sake – i.e. it's
both the beginning and the end product, as a studio band will
create tracks with the intention of having them mixed directly
into a space-age dub creation. Then the Professor weaves his
magic at the desk, blending in all manner of outboard effects,
samples, digitally created and digitized sounds, with the one
intent: to surprise as many people as possible. You're never
quite sure what's going to happen next in a Mad Professor mix,
other than that, with consummate craftsmanship, it'll always
remain rooted in a rich reggae rhythm.

Of course this isn't everybody's cup of tea – like Gibbs, Perry
and even KING TUBBY, such a distinctive sound tends to polar-
ize the punters – but it's unlikely The Mad Professor is too worried about the sneering press he's attracted in the past. Because
he's also attracted names like Lee Perry, JAH SHAKA, BOB
ANDY and JOHNNY CLARKE from Jamaica to his London studio to work under his guidance. And this studio, Ariwa Sounds,
established in 1979 in his spare room, is now the biggest, most
sophisticated black-owned recording operation in the UK, while
the record label is this country's longest-surviving black-owned
reggae outfit.

Then there's his contribution to LOVERS' ROCK. Frazier is
probably solely responsible for the style surviving into the 1980s
and beyond, as his increasingly sophisticated approach to its

production technique helped it survive in the face of dancehall's growing nihilism.

As well as the *Dub Me Crazy* series (all twelve volumes of which are available on Ariwa CDs) and the lovers' rock albums mentioned in the entry of the same name, Frazier productions worth checking out are:

The Lost Scrolls Of Moses; Ariwa ARICD87

Lee Perry Meets The Mad Professor (Chapter One); Lagoon LGCD21068

Lee Perry Meets The Mad Professor (Chapter Two); Lagoon LGCD21069

A Feast Of Yellow Dub; Ras RASCD3069

U-Roy: *True Born African*; Ariwa ARICD071

SEE ALSO:

Time Warp Dub Clash (Old School vs New School); Mango CDIM1105

Bob Marley and The Wailers

➥ During the summer of 1969, when Bob Marley came back from working in the USA, he immediately fell back in with Peter and Bunny. But the threesome weren't so much rebels without a cause as rebels without a clue. They themselves were by now focused enough on what they wanted to get across, but this was the post-rock steady/pre-roots period and – in commercial terms – something of a spiritual vacuum. The rude boy protests hadn't been taken anywhere to speak of, indeed they were now being frowned upon as studio bosses distanced themselves as much as possible from that era, and the most visible reggae was the bouncy, uptempo stuff that was being lapped up in the UK.

Then The Wailers happened across LEE PERRY.

Scratch was as disgruntled as the trio with the state of the nation as much as with the studio system. Both the group and the producer were beginning to come to terms with Rastafari as making particular sense for black Jamaicans. Both wanted to make music that expressed all their dissatisfactions. And neither were particularly bothered about the accepted way of doing things – from either an artistic or a business point of view. Perry put them together with The Upsetters, took them to Randy's studio in Kingston and as 1969 rolled into 1970 cut a series of tunes – including reworkings of a few of their old Studio One sides – that would establish the group as true soul rebels and do much to set the pace for the sufferah style that would come to dominate reggae music. The songs from this period are the best the group, or Bob by himself, ever wrote, as proved by the fact so many of them were re-recorded later in his career.

Perry all but dismantled The Wailers' traditional-type harmonizing, preferring to have Bob make more effort on lead, while Peter and Bunny functioned as background singers, accentuating the songs' lyrical focus. He eschewed horns too, concentrating on sparse, tightly syncopated abrasive reggae rhythms. It was aggressive in the extreme, thus well suited to such songs as 'Small Axe' (an attack on the 'big t'ree' producers of the time, KONG, DODD and BYRON LEE); 'Duppy Conqueror'; 'Soul Rebel'; '400 Years'; and 'African Herbsman.' These sessions turned the trio into a proper band too, as Perry encouraged the cornerstones of The Upsetters – Aston ('Family Man') and Carlton Barrett, on bass and drums respectively, and organ player Glen Adams – to become fully fledged Wailers. (This was just after The Upsetters had completed a lucrative tour of Great Britain, and Scratch, rather shrewdly, saw The Wailers would need to be a self-contained group if they wanted to court international success. He knew playing was a vital part of establishing yourself abroad, and also knew that pick-up bands couldn't be relied on if your sound was in any way distinctive.)

The results were released in the UK either on Trojan Records or on Perry's personal imprint, the Upsetter label, and established Bob Marley and The Wailers (as Perry had them called on record sleeves) on Britain's black reggae scene. Which brought them to the attention of Island Records boss Chris Blackwell, a white Jamaican who understood the UK rock scene.

Blackwell desperately wanted to promote reggae on a worldwide level, and believed that any black Jamaican reggae act with enough talent could become as big as the big rock acts provided it had the right marketing campaign and understood the needs of the rock audience. It is said that his first choice for this bold experiment was JIMMY CLIFF, but he'd already left the label. Then, apparently, Blackwell went for THE MAYTALS but they opted to sign with Leslie Kong. At exactly that time, the start of 1972, The Wailers were on a disastrous visit to Europe and had become stranded in London unable to perform because their work permits had been held up and the management team that had brought them over had gone to America on more pressing business. They were miserably cold and had no money for tickets back to Jamaica, so Brent Clarke, a friend connected with Island Records in the UK, approached Blackwell in London to negotiate a deal. Blackwell signed the group, and offered up an advance to allow them home, on the understanding that Bob returned before the year was out with the tapes for an album. Marley kept the group's side of the deal and came back to London at the end of the year with the masters of *Catch A Fire*.

In order to make the album 'acceptable' to a rock audience, Blackwell himself remixed the rhythms slightly, rebalancing the bass 'n' drum, and further lightened the tunes by having various white rock session men overdub guitars and keyboards. But what really stood this album apart was the packaging: a sleeve constructed like a Zippo lighter, with a fully flipping top, the actual album peeping out from behind a cut-out flaming wick. It was as spectacular as it was impractical – the rivet hinge soon wore out the cardboard around it so the thing fell apart, and the wick took a severe battering every time the record was put back. But all of this trickery worked inasmuch as it got The Wailers noticed by the mainstream media, which, together with a tour of Europe and US to support the April 1973 release, meant it sold well enough to ensure they got the chance to make a second album for the company. However, the sales weren't anywhere near high enough to warrant this sort of high-profile, big budget treatment for the next one. The follow-up, *Burning*, came out just before Christmas in that same year and was pretty much as The Wailers intended it – i.e. it sounded like a conventional reggae record, with all the right instruments in all the right places. It was also a very mature, subtly inventive reggae record, marking The Wailers as prodigious writing, playing and producing talents. And, perhaps unsurprisingly, it was this LP that broke the band big, proving once again that nobody understood how this music worked better than people who originated it.

During 1974 the band exploded on to the international scene. At exactly the same time, Tosh and Livingston chose to quit.

There are two favoured reasons for the split – it was probably a bit of both – a) they didn't like touring; and b) they deeply resented Chris Blackwell renaming the group Bob Marley and The Wailers (the record company boss felt the act needed a focus).

That it was now Bob Marley and a backing group (albeit some of the best players in Jamaica, with harmonies provided by his wife ,Rita, along with Marcia Griffiths and Judy Mowatt) did it no harm at all, though – 1975 was Marley's biggest year yet. The release of the *Natty Dread* album consolidated the position taken by *Burning*, and a triumphant tour climaxed in the now legendary concerts at London's Lyceum Theatre.

It was this album's title track, and Bob Marley's now full head of dreadlocks, that more than anything else announced the arrival of Rastafari to the world. As well as becoming a byword for reggae music around the globe, Marley was soon an equally international figurehead for the Third World as a social situation, bringing the slums of West Kingston into living rooms everywhere. But, importantly, it was his uniquely humanitarian viewpoint that cut across class, race, nationality and political persuasion to represent those less fortunate, whatever their situation. And he remained true to his roots throughout. No matter what properties the now millionaire international superstar owned, Bob was never based anywhere other than Kingston. Indeed, he'd recreate the Trenchtown vibe in the Hope Road mansion he bought from Chris Blackwell. In the same street as the Prime Minister's palatial dwelling, livestock grazed in Bob's grounds and dreads from downtown would drop by for front-verandah reasoning sessions.

Because of such closeness to the Jamaican people, Bob's influence was strongest at home. Politicians vied for his endorsement, but he was always careful to avoid being seen as allied to one side or the other. Until 1976, when in the midst of the political violence that tore through Kingston's ghettoes, gunmen burst into the Hope Road house and shot Marley and his manager Don Taylor. Local wisdom has it that the assassination attempt was because Marley had agreed to do a huge concert in Jamaica 'for the people', at the specific request of Prime Minister Michael Manley, and the opposition wanted to make sure this didn't happen. He left Jamaica for eighteen months after that, returning in 1978 to perform the One Love Peace Concert, at which the two rival political leaders, Manley and Edward Seaga, and their respective chief gunmen, Bucky Marshall and Claudie Massop, shook hands on stage. Nobody other than Bob Marley could have organized such an event.

In fact, during the second half of the 1970s, until his tragic death from cancer in 1981, Bob Marley meant much more as an international statesman for the dispossessed than he did as a musician. Essentially, once his reggae settled down into the arena-friendly, internationally accessible rock-tinged hybrid it became after *Natty Dread*, it stopped developing. Lyrically, he continued to prove himself a ghetto poet on a par with Curtis Mayfield, Marvin Gaye or James Brown – with love songs as well as the political stuff – but even his brilliant singles were becoming increasingly isolated.

But by this time what Bob Marley meant to reggae went way beyond mere music. And it's as such that his talent will never be replaced. ↔ (PETER TOSH and BUNNY WAILER)

Songs Of Freedom; Tuff Gong/Island TGCBX1

This beautifully packaged, 77-song four-CD box set goes from the first recordings with Leslie Kong, through the Studio One days and back to Kong, it takes in the Lee Perry sessions and the Blackwell-overseen releases, and goes up to the very end with the 1980 self-productions. It's got a number of alternative takes, live recordings and studio cuts that have never seen the light of day before, plus a lavishly illustrated booklet, and could well be all the Bob Marley many people need. It's also a fitting souvenir for anybody who's already got all the albums.

African Herbsman; Trojan CDTRL62
Rasta Revolution; Trojan CDTRL89
Soul Revolution One And Two; Trojan CDTRD406

More or less the Lee Perry sessions in full, and probably the group at their very best. Perry's experimentation stays within the conventional reggae boundaries, just stretching them a bit with an in-yer-face high-stepping rhythm and arrangements that pull you into the mix, while his attention to vocals makes the most of The Wailers' Studio One harmonizing days. These tunes are raw, as all concerned seem to be revelling in their newly defined rebel status, particularly *Rasta Revolution* (which originally came out in 1970 as *Soul Rebels*, with a host of different sleeves). Elsewhere, they contain a lot of prototypes or songs that became much more famous a few years later. *African Herbsman*, for instance, features '400 Years', 'Small Axe' and 'Duppy Conqueror', while *Soul Revolution One* boasts 'Put It On', 'Kaya' and another cut of 'Duppy Conqueror'. The best thing about these CD reissues, though, is *Soul Revolution Two*, the previously much sought after dub mixes of *Soul Revolution One*.

Catch A Fire; Island TGLCD1

The one with all the extra twiddly bits – which, it must be said, has improved enormously over the years. At the time it irritated many people who had already bought the Lee Perry stuff because it seemed to be saying 'we know what reggae needs to make people like it'. But since then so many different routes have been tried it now appears to be just one more attempt at broadening the horizon.

Burning; Island TGLCD2

It was songs like 'Burnin' And Lootin'', 'I Shot The Sheriff' and 'Get Up Stand Up', done in a true Trenchtown style, which actually broke Bob Marley. Quite deservedly so. Incidentally, this album went a long way to recapturing the UK sound system ground lost by *Catch A Fire*.

Natty Dread; Island TGLCD3

This album more than any other – by anybody – defines commercial reggae as it should be. While the sentiments of 'Rebel Music (3 O'Clock Roadblock)', 'Talkin' Blues', 'Natty Dread' and 'No Woman No Cry' are exactly what his original audience wanted, they presented a clear window into another world for the outsiders. Also, at this point, the music still had some character and was clever enough to be incredibly varied within the context of tuff bass 'n' drum reggae. The album any newcomer should start at, and everybody in the world ought to own.

Live At The Lyceum; Island TGLCD4

That historic concert from 1975, that two decades later at least half a million people will claim there were at. Curious really, as the theatre only ever held a couple of thousand. But at least now everybody can enjoy it as these recordings genuinely capture the excitement of something very special.

ALSO RECOMMENDED:

The following are best judged on individual tracks rather than as overall albums.

Exodus; Island TGLCD6

The title track, 'Jamming', 'Natural Mystic' and 'Waiting In Vain'.

Uprising; Island TGLCD9

'Redemption Song'.

Confrontation; Island TGLCD10

'Buffalo Soldier' and 'Blackman Redemption'.

Freddie McGregor

(Born 1955; Clarendon, Jamaica; singer)
It's remarkable that Freddie McGregor is only forty years old – it seems like he's been around for ever. But then he did start his professional career a as member of THE CLARENDONIANS at the tender age of seven. It's just as remarkable that Freddie McGregor isn't a much bigger star, as he seems to have always been standing on the verge of it. He's got the looks, the voice, the engaging disposition, and he's had major label backing on more than one occasion, yet he's never quite got there. It can't be lack

of experience either – the man started off in rock steady, progressed into reggae and roots reggae, then managed to segue into dancehall and out the other side into what they're calling 'new roots' (righteous singing, on top of tunes played on modern computerized instruments). He's had hits in every style, yet never seems to stamp his personality on the public long enough to cash in on anything. Maybe that's the problem: Freddie McGregor may be a brilliant singer and an all-round nice bloke, but he just doesn't have a forceful enough personality to get himself across beyond the songs he's singing. However, when the songs are of the calibre of Freddie McGregor's hits, perhaps this doesn't matter so much.

Bobby Bobylon; Heartbeat CD3502

This 1980 Studio One solo album was always something of an anachronism – recorded at a time when the rest of Jamaica was following SLY AND ROBBIE into computerization, these rhythms could have been cut at any time in the late 1960s – yet it's become a roots reggae classic. Maybe because it's so relaxingly old-fashioned. But what it does show, on tunes like the title track, 'The Wine Of Violence', 'Bandulo' and 'Rastaman Camp', is COXSONE's perfect understanding of what worked with Freddie McGregor's easy falsetto. The album is also all the proof anybody needs of Coxsone's refusal to move with the times, even when he was acknowledging Rasta reggae.

Big Ship; Greensleeves GRELCD

The title track was probably Freddie McGregor's theme song in my part of the world a dozen or so years ago. It's the classic easy-action roots reggae that has you rocking – with or without a gal – before you realize it. As this set also features 'Roots Man Skanking' and 'Holy Mount Zion', it's probably, along with *Bobby Bobylon*, the McGregor peak.

Carry Go Bring Come; Greensleeves GRELCD197

Produced by GUSSIE CLARKE, this 1990s style teams Freddie up with some thoroughly modern artists – Snagga Puss, JC

Lodge etc – and is by far the best of his later stuff. The title track was his biggest hit for years.

Freddie McGregor; Polydor 833-567 2

It's got 'Just Don't Want To Be Lonely', 'That Girl (Groovy Situation)' and 'Slow Down', which is probably all you need to know.

The Meditations

(Ansel Cridland, born Westmoreland, Jamaica; Winston Watson; Danny Clarke; both born Kingston, Jamaica; all born mid-1950s; vocal trio)
The accepted idea was that classic Rasta vocal harmonizing was little more than the traditional Jamaican vocal trio with different subject matter. The Meditations, however, make mockery of this regimented one lead and two backing singers arrangement. They were three lead singers who would each take turns to step out to the front, often within the same song. This gave a particular depth to their work – no matter how superficially lightweight it seemed, as each voice pulled the listener in a different direction.

The group came together in the mid-1970s as righteous dreads and immediately courted controversy with the massive hit 'A Woman Is Like A Shadow', the lyric to which advanced a very Old Testament notion of feminism. Not that it appeared to do them any harm, as they went from strength to strength into the next decade as their lilting, peaceful arrangements lived up to their name. At the roots sound systems, Meditations cuts such as 'Wake Up', 'Warmongers', 'Lucifer' and 'Woman Piabba' provided the same light relief as LOVERS' ROCK. Only with a lot more credibility.

The Meditations' early period recordings survive as a fine example of sensitive roots music and of the versatility of the three-part harmony within a reggae structure, and the group still make a living from touring. This is mostly in the USA, and their rare visits to the UK are more than worth the price of admission.

Unfortunately, none of The Meditations' wonderful early albums – *Message From The Meditations*, *Wake Up* and *Guidance* – are available on CD. Although what does exist is superb, the overall warmth of their initial, less sophisticated recordings seems somehow closer to the essence of the group.

*No More Friend; Greensleeves GRELCD52

Produced by Linval Thompson, and backed up by The Roots Radics, this was The Meditations' first set to be aimed as squarely at the dancehall as it was at the place of worship. And it succeeds quite brilliantly. Cut in 1983, computerization is creeping in, with the taut, springy sounds providing an ideal setting for the trio's gentle vocalizing as it shows up their intricate lead swapping and easy-action crooning in sharp relief. With stand-out cuts being the title track, 'Carpenter Rebuild', 'Fuss And Fight' and the discreetly dubwise 'Jack On Top', this remains one of the best available examples of how roots can come to the dancehall and everybody go home happy.

ALSO RECOMMENDED:

*For The Good Of Man; Heartbeat HBCD42

From 1988, and proof that they still weren't overwhelmed by advancing studio technology.

SEE ALSO:

Nice An' Ruff – A Crucial Brew Of Roots, Dub and Rockers; Music Club International MCCD092

Ras Michael

(Born Michael Henry, 1945; Kingston, Jamaica; master drummer)

At the point at which true Rastafarianism meets roots reggae you'll find Ras Michael And The Sons Of Negus. His drumming arrangements are so complex, so three-dimensional and, as a result, downright musical, that with the addition of the voices they stand up as an entirely valid reggae expression. Indeed, on the recordings which involve guitar, bass and organ, the drums are leading the way rather than merely marking time.

One of Jamaica's original Rastafarian community, having been born into it over fifty years ago, Michael was the natural inheritor for the mantle passed down by COUNT OSSIE. As a child he learned the intricacies of traditional drumming, along with his grounding in the faith, and formed his troupe of drummers while still in his teens. The group would hire themselves out for recording sessions – they provided percussion for Studio One sessions throughout the second half of the 1960s – as a means to raise finance for Michael's radio show in which he would spread the word of Jah.

In the 1970s the troupe expanded to include vocalists and dancers, when they began to perform at home and abroad – BLACK UHURU's Puma Jones first came to Jamaica to be one of Ras Michael's dancers. Recording was a natural extension, but it had to be on the right terms – i.e. it had to be a Rasta drum troupe with a supplement of conventional instrumentation arranged to fit in with it, *not* the other way round. There were, of course, as with Ossie, strong jazz overtones. The result was reggae approached from an entirely different angle. Which doesn't usually work, but in this case, as Michael's soul is so completely at one with the sufferahs that 'invented' reggae as we know it, it was unlikely he was going to go far wrong. Up until the mid-1980s Ras Michael turned out some deeply spiritual yet very listenable roots sounds.

Rastafari; Greensleeves GRELCD153

This is the one that really introduced Ras Michael as bona fide reggae artist rather than just some odd outsider. His use of regular instruments is so subtle and skilful that it carries the listener along more on the *idea* of reggae than on anything solid enough to get in the way of what he really does, which always turns out to be far more intricate.

Love Thy Neighbour; Greensleeves LLCD001

Cut in 1983 and Ras Michael's last really innovative album. It had an enormous advantage over the rest, inasmuch as it was produced by LEE PERRY. Not over-produced either, as Scratch really had no need to prove what a total rhythm master he was: the brilliance is more in the arrangements as he sensibly leaves the drummers to get on with it.

Kibir Am Lak; Greensleeves GRELCD158

Produced by Tommy Cowan, this is subtle, uncompromising late 1970s roots, and features as one of the additional musicians TOMMY MCCOOK on flute – the sax man was closely involved with Rasta culture, as since the early 1960s he had taught music as Count Ossie's Community And Cultural Centre.

The Mighty Diamonds

(Donald Shaw; Fitzroy Simpson; Lloyd Ferguson; all born early 1950s, Kingston, Jamaica; vocal trio)
To this day, Rasta vocalizing as part of mainstream reggae can be pretty much summed up in three tunes: 'The Right Time', 'Country Living' and 'Pass The Koutchie'. All by The Mighty Diamonds. Each one taking a different aspect of Rasta philosophy – Marcus Garvey's teachings, the natural, ital, lifestyle and good quality ganja. Yet in spite of the tuff, sound system-friendly rhythm, they were all so sweetly melodic they appeared innocuous enough for your mother to sing around the house without realizing they were natty dread anthems. The tunes remain classics, but in 1976 the first two were such enormous hits ('Country Living' didn't come out until 1978 when it was massive too), they established the group as international superstars. A position they still hold today, as touring the US and Europe continues to earn them a good living.

Although their super-tight, high-pitched harmonizing deserved such recognition, fortunate timing played its part. The group had formed in 1969, had recorded without success for RUPIE EDWARDS and had one minor hit for producer Pat Francis in 1974 before they fetched up at Jo-Jo Hookim's Channel One the following year. There, the trio's very traditional Jamaican close harmonizing proved the perfect counterbalance to the crisp 'rockers' reggae sound being developed under Hookim's guidance by drummer SLY DUNBAR. Very much a drummer's style, the upfront, uptempo beats presented a more militant-edged alternative to the 'flying cymbal', taking melody lines from old Studio One tunes and presenting them in this most modern style. Which, when coupled with the infectiousness of The Mighty Diamonds' singing and songwriting, made it impossible to ignore. The 'rockers' approach went on to dominate reggae for the rest of the decade, with The Diamonds playing no small part.

Right Time; Shanachie SHANCD43014

That brilliant 1975 album, which goes a long way to explaining what all the fuss was about. The textural balance between the singing and the rockers rhythms seems to sum up the two sides of reggae and how, when they work as well as this with each other, they can't fail to make everlasting music. The guys' singing was probably never better either, as they plead sweetly through the title track, 'I Need A Roof', 'Them Never Love Poor Marcus', 'Why Me Black Brother Why' and 'Africa'. All that's missing is 'Country Living', which – as a studio version – doesn't seem to be on CD anywhere, but it'll take more than that to detract from the sheer, unadulterated joy of rediscovering 'The Right Time'. All together now: 'Natty dread ain't gonna run away/No, no, no/Natty dread ain't gonna run away/When the right time comes.'

Live In Europe; Greensleeves GRELCD124

This is the album that really gives testimony as to how technically correct The Mighty Diamonds are as singers. As well 'The Right Time', 'I Need A Roof' and 'Country Living', they ease through an entirely appropriate cover of THE HEPTONES' 'Party Time' – appropriate because Sibbles' crew is the group the Diamonds were closest to in style. You even end up taking their version of 'Putting On The Ritz' far more seriously than you might imagine.

Go Seek You Rights; Frontline CDFL 9002

The *Right Time* album – which originally came out on Front Line in this country, with some extra tracks added. The bonus here is you get such numbers as 'Sweet Lady' and 'Let The Answer Be Yes', which display the other side of The Mighty Diamonds, as honey-dripping balladeers.

SEE ALSO:

Jammin'; Mango CIDM1010 (this contains 'Pass The Koutchie')
Roots 'N' Culture; Music Club MCCD128
Beyond The Frontline; Frontline FRONT1
Tougher Than Tough – The Story Of Jamaican Music; Mango IBXCD1

Sugar Minott

(Born Lincoln Minott, 1956; Kingston, Jamaica; singer)
It's rare that a roots reggae record squarely impresses the general public and manages to retain any specialist market cred-ibility. Sugar Minott's 'Good Thing Going' did exactly that in 1981. A cover of a Michael Jackson Motown song, he took it to the pop Top 10 in April of that year, yet it was guaranteed to rock the dancehall both before and after that event. For a *long time* afterwards. It couldn't have happened to a nicer chap either. His ridiculously gap-toothed grin (one of his front teeth was missing) and sunny disposition were the trademarks of a man who was willing to help others, often at his own expense. He devoted so much time and energy both to his Youth Promo-tion/Black Roots organization (dedicated to giving Kingston's underprivileged youth a break into music through recording) and to his sound system that he never seemed to capitalize on his own talent. However, he's been an integral part of the reggae business in Kingston and London for twenty years now, com-bining roots spirituality and LOVERS' ROCK smoove with his perpetual good humour to enjoy underground hits more or less at will. And the best part is, he's recently teamed up with JAMMY, and seems to be getting near the potential he's shown in the past.

*Good Thing Going; Heartbeat HBCD13

Still as totally kicking as it was fifteen years ago, the title track is a jaunty, lovers-style hymn to optimism that pretty much sums up Sugar Minott and his approach to life – 'It's all good!' It's a vibe that continues through an album that gives an enormous variety of tone and tempo to the notion of the modern(ish) reggae love song.

Black Roots; Mango RRCD39

The other side of the Minott coin is just as enjoyable, if perhaps not quite so relentlessly cheerful. His roots music always presented itself with dignified spirituality, while at the same time offering hope – by tone of voice as much as anything else. Maybe this set shows off his wonderfully expressive singing more than the love songs for which he is best known.

A Touch Of Class; Jammy's JMCD001

A collaboration with King Jammy from the early 1990s, which, with good material, empathetic production and subtle use of computers, appears to push the singer to heights he hasn't reached for years.

SEE ALSO:

Nice An' Ruff – A Crucial Brew Of Roots, Dub and Rockers; Music Club International MCCD092

Pablo Moses

(Born Pablo Henry, 1955; Kingston, Jamaica; singer)
Although he didn't start recording until the almost pensionable age of twenty, Pablo Moses' initial records made up for lost time. Immediately. He announced himself in 1975 with an album called *Revolutionary Dream* and a single titled 'I Man A Grasshopper'. The latter wasn't nearly as daft as it seems, as it was a reference to the TV series *Kung Fu* in which the central character, a Shao Lin monk nicknamed Grasshopper, roamed the land, slightly detached from but always 'at one' with his environment. Which is exactly how Moses' devastating delivery came over: he was slightly removed from the music, more float-

ing above it than part of it, but always giving the impression of a man completely in control of what was going on around him. He had this kind of quiet intensity that made his hymns to Jah that much more potent.

Moses followed up *Revolutionary Dream* with two more albums that lacked nothing except their predecessor's initial impact, then decided to produce himself through the 1980s and very little more was heard from him. Until very recently, when he resurfaced, based in New York, with an album recorded at SLY AND ROBBIE's studio, self-produced and engineered by Geoffrey Chung, the man who produced those previous works of art. And this must have made all the difference because this one isn't bad at all.

Revolutionary Dream; Musidisc 198832

Beautiful, esoteric roots reggae. Pablo Moses at his absolute best, sounding like he's singing for himself rather than an audience or even a studio mic. Chung's production keeps the music working but well away from him, as if the vocals were recorded first, then the players did their bit on top. Features 'I Man A Grasshopper', 'Revolutionary Dream' and 'Come Mek We Run'.

A Song; Island CID9541

One of the two that came after *Revolutionary Dream*, and that air of guileless, slightly distracted innocence is still very much intact.

ALSO RECOMMENDED:

Mission; Riddim 111962

The most recent (1995) Pablo Moses album, and although the sounds are modern, that enchanting vibe seems to be back in place.

Junior Murvin

(Born 1950; Port Antonio, Jamaica; singer)
If you're going to be a One Hit Wonder, then nobody's going to

complain if that one hit is 'Police And Thieves'. As well as being the biggest selling record in Jamaica during 1976 – it perfectly summed up the breakdown of law and order on the island at the time, in a manner that cleverly took the side of the hapless sufferah caught in the middle – it became a London sound system anthem and something of a theme for that year's Notting Hill Carnival, which erupted into anti-police rioting. And it also had the power of LEE PERRY's productions when applied to a workmanlike song. Scratch took the composition by the singer, who had recorded it before to no great success, and reinvented it in his Black Ark Studio. He transformed a simple folk song into a strikingly plaintive, but undeniably forceful, work. He played up the key elements in the lyric – essentially the lines 'Police and thieves in the street/fighting the nation with their guns and ammunition/all across Jamaica hear what's happening . . .' – into a musical mantra, reworked the instrumentation until it had exactly the right pleading, nagging high-pitch and then dropped a bass that would wipe you out. Lee Perry Magic. This was much more a producer's record, with the artist simply along for the ride.

Murvin and Perry did a whole album together, but this was the only track anybody played. And anybody who was halfway shrewd had bought the twelve-inch instead, because that way you got three different mixes. They even recorded a few more singles in the ensuing couple of years, but nobody I've asked can remember what they were called, let alone what they sounded like. Still, when you've got your name on a tune like 'Police And Thieves', nobody will ever forget you.

Police And Thieves; Mango CID9499

This has just been taken off catalogue, and although it's still relatively easy to find, this situation won't last. The point to remember is don't be fooled into thinking everything on it is as blindingly brilliant as the title track. If this is the only way you can get hold of a copy of the single 'Police And Thieves' then take it, but otherwise you won't be losing anything by seeking it out on a compilation set.

SEE ALSO:

'Police And Thieves' is featured on:
Tougher Than Tough – The Story Of Jamaican Music; Mango
IBXCD1
Pure Reggae; Island CIDTB8; 1994
Jammin'; Mango CIDM1010
On A Reggae Tip; Island CIDTV5
Reggae Greats; Mango 162-539 792-2

Niney The Observer

(Born Winston Holness, 1952; Montego Bay, Jamaica; producer)
So many of the developments in roots reggae during the 1970s
have Niney The Observer's fingerprints on them, yet he remains
best known for his one hit record, 1970's 'Blood And Fire'. But
what a hit. The sparse, apocalyptic rhythm chugged relentlessly,
the sentiment referred to Babylon and the chorus line went 'Let
it burn/let it burn/let it burn, burn, burn'. It was that year's
Record Of The Year in Jamaica as the sound systems couldn't
stop playing it and it sold into the tens of thousands.

The story is that Niney was setting off to get the first copies of
the record pressed, when he and one of his studio musicians got
into a fight about whether the rhythm was original or ripped off
from something else. When he finally presented the disc to the
pressing plant it is said 'Blood And Fire' was actually covered in
blood.

This isn't that easy to believe, as everybody who's ever met
Niney maintains he's one of the most mild-mannered, good-
humoured people in the music business. He also has a fair sense
of the ridiculous, as his nickname derives from the fact he lost a
thumb in an industrial accident during his first job as an engineer. Maybe that was what convinced him to try his luck in the
music business.

Once he started work as BUNNY LEE's assistant in the mid-
1960s and progressed to working with LEE PERRY at JOE
GIBBS' at the end of the decade, there was no holding him back.
By 1970 he'd set up his own operation and used the income
generated from his hit to sponsor his own productions. Calling

himself The Observer, his sound was characterized by its uncompromising toughness, as the stripped-down, spaced-out rhythm tracks provided ideal backing for the new generation of studio deejays. U-ROY, DENNIS ALCAPONE, BIG YOUTH, I-ROY and DILLINGER all felt the benefit of Niney productions, while his dub albums such as *Dubbing With The Observer* and *Sledgehammer Dub* remain sought-after vinyls.

Then there was the other side to him – the side that produced some of the best Jamaican balladeering of the decade, largely from DENNIS BROWN, but as importantly – if less prolifically – from GREGORY ISAACS, JUNIOR BYLES, HORACE ANDY, DELROY WILSON, Junior Delgado and Leroy Smart. It was here that he virtually redefined the love song by bringing his roots music elements to ballads, thus toughening them up to the degree that even the fiercest of rebel sound systems would spin them. His work with Dennis Brown in this area was a big factor in DB's success.

After a very quiet 1980s, Niney has recently surfaced to repackage and repromote his extensive back catalogue of Observer productions.

At present there are no dedicated Observer compilations or dub albums on release on CD in this country – although Trojan have the comprehensive Niney and Friends set *Bring The Couchie 1974-1976* on vinyl. For Observer productions, it's best to check the artists mentioned above and their albums' production credits. Notably Dennis Brown.

Johnny Osbourne

(Born 1950; Kingston, Jamaica; singer)
The album *Truth And Rights*, produced by COXSONE DODD and sung by Johnny Osbourne, still stands out, some fifteen years after it was recorded, as the absolute zenith of Studio One's roots music. Cut in 1980, just after Johnny Osbourne returned from ten years spent living and working in reggae bands in Canada, it makes you wonder what he could have achieved if he'd been in Jamaica during the 1970s, when some of the most inventive, yet musically based, producers had been crying out for a rich, seasoned voice like his. He made a few

more singles for Dodd after that, but they were something of an anti-climax. Indeed, the only time he's come close to those heights during the last ten years is on a few isolated singles: 'Folly Lover', 'Water Pumping' and 'Rougher Than Them', for instance. His recent recordings actually seem to suggest his voice is improving as it gets older, so any problems have to be down to bad material.

Truth And Rights; Heartbeat HB3513

As its basis, this set utilizes the old rock steady rhythms that Coxsone made his own almost twenty years earlier, merely sparking them up a bit by slightly raising the tempo and adding dashes of the sharpest of horns to point it all Eastward. But the real cleverness is that this album gives the impression of being a righteous roots set – really it's an old rock steady album given a new lick of paint. Which, when coupled with Osbourne's thoroughly relaxing voice, is a bit like putting on an old pair of slippers. Along with the title track, look out for 'Nah Skin Up', 'The Children Are Crying', 'Love Jah So' and the completely brilliant 'Sing Jay Style'.

Count Ossie

(Born Oswald Williams, 1930; Kingston, Jamaica; master drummer/Rasta figurehead)
What became known as Rasta drumming always owed a huge debt to the Burru people of The Dungle area of Kingston. The Burrus were descendants of slaves who previously lived in Clarendon, and their drumming techniques, which originated in Ghana, were one of the few African cultural expressions to have survived in Jamaica through to the twentieth century. Rastas would make regular visits to the Burru camps for reasoning sessions (rambling, apparently open-ended, philosophical discussions) and it was on these cultural exchange visits that Ossie, a lifelong Rasta, learned Burru drumming which he incorporated into his own style. What emerged was a highly innovative, infectious style that was obviously darkly African in its roots, but was intricate and sophisticated enough to entertain in its own right.

And it might have remained hidden in Ossie's camp – he had no interest in Babylon's recording industry – had PRINCE BUSTER not convinced him and his drummers to play on his 'Oh Carolina' sessions in 1959. What Buster was looking for was an indigenous Jamaican sound to blend into the US-derivative recording scene, to promote black Jamaican culture and to get the drop on his rivals. He and Ossie ended up rerouting Jamaican music and the new drum patterns altered the balance of R&B and Boogie, putting it on the road to ska.

The Count Ossie Group continued to play sessions during the 1960s, even recording under their own name from time to time, but it seemed they'd made their big contribution to Jamaican music. Until 1973. At that point they emerged from a quiet spell with the triple album *Grounation*. Under the name Count Ossie and The Mystic Revelation Of Rastafari, it brought together The Ossie Group with Cedric 'Im' Brooks's more conventional band – a double bass, a brass section, and a snare drum – and dread vocalist Sam Clayton whose speciality was spiritual monologues. Always intended more as a statement of Rastafari than as a commercial proposition, the album sold astonishingly well as it became a cultural touchstone for Jamaicans and Rastas around the world. And its improvisational nature also gave it a strong appeal to jazz fans. Sadly Ossie died three years later, just months after the ensemble issued the equally attractive *Tales Of Mozambique*.

Grounation; Ashanti CD301

This won't, of course, be everybody's cup of tea. A far more esoteric statement than anything by RAS MICHAEL, it lines up Ethiopian chants, African spirituals, free-form poetry, jazz improvisation, Rasta music and reggae in a way that both intrigues and sustains interest. Jazz is about the best yardstick here – there's even a cover of The Crusaders' 'Way Back Home' in there – as the music has a Miles Davis-ish overtone in the way the instruments are seemingly at odds with each other and you have to observe the work as a whole rather than just bits of it. It won't be the easiest thing you've ever listened to, and it's pretty hard to find the CD – nobody's quite sure what rack to put it in! – but perseverance on both counts will pay off.

SEE ALSO:

Prince Buster's 'Oh Carolina', featuring Count Ossie's drumming, can be found on *Tougher Than Tough – The Story Of Jamaican Music*; Mango IBXCD1

Augustus Pablo

(Born Horace Swaby, 1953; St Andrews, Jamaica; melodica and keyboard player/producer)

When Augustus Pablo's album *King Tubby Meets The Rockers Uptown* hit in north London in the mid-1970s, it was as if a light had been turned on. Of course, we all knew who Pablo was and had been hip to dub versions for years – his earlier album *Ital Dub* had been required listening and thus took care of both counts. But this was different. Right from a title that was about the coolest thing we'd ever heard. As TUBBY's sheer dub madness meshed with the 'Somewhere East Of Java' sound Pablo had been perfecting over the previous few years, you were offered the sort of spiritual experience that usually involves controlled substances. It was one of the few dub sessions that would work at a dance with a non-roots crowd – and work on a level that, back then, would leave the people momentarily lost for words. The tunes came at you with a power you couldn't ignore, but that was standard for Tubby's adventures in sound. What was happening here was something that touched us on a level that took us back to Africa. Before the slave ships landed. Contained within that forty minutes or so were all the reasons for reggae. The logical conclusion to what PRINCE BUSTER had been doing fifteen years previously when he got COUNT OSSIE involved in 'Oh Carolina'. And to think Augustus Pablo made his mark playing a melodica, an instrument with less credibility than a stylophone. Or perhaps that's why he had to try a bit harder.

Pablo hit his mark almost immediately. Which, when you look at his history, is hardly surprising. He'd taught himself piano at age thirteen and mastered the melodica and organ while still at school. As a sixteen year-old, he and his older brother operated their Rockers sound system and had a reputation for pushing their crowds to the limits as their tone control experimentation yielded astonishing results. When Pablo cut his first records in 1969 and 1970 he combined this keyboard wizardry and a taste of adventure to create the wistful 'East Of The River Nile' sound. His woozy melodica floated on top of a high-stepping drum 'n' bass that sparked itself off with skipping, ricochetting percussions, flying cymbal and powerful horn stabs. It had a swing all of its own right from the start, and, in recognition of the Swabys' sound system, became known as 'rockers style'. *This Is Augustus Pablo* was recorded in 1970 (although it wasn't released in the UK until 1974) and is regarded as one of the classic instrumental reggae albums of all time.

But Pablo soon became unhappy with his treatment (or payment) from other labels and in 1972 set up his own Rockers International label and record shop, so he was then free to do pretty much what he wanted. Which involved hooking up with King Tubby – the one event that, as much as anything else, turned Augustus Pablo into the roots reggae icon he is. Tubby's mixes brought another dimension to arrangements and productions that were already taking notions of time and space, as well as tone and tempo, into areas unknown to reggae. By the middle of the decade their collaborations were being applied to his productions on a string of artists – Jacob Miller, Hugh Mundell, Tetrack to name but three – resulting in some superb and superbly varied roots music.

Although it got really sublime when they were deconstructing an Augustus Pablo instrumental. In spite of the tone of this work being dread from the roots, it was never less than obvious how much Pablo and King Tubby were plain enjoying what they were doing. Which brings us neatly back to 'King Tubby Meets The Rockers From Uptown', the single. A tune of such unrestrained joy, playfulness and celebration, it couldn't be anything other than righteous. And if everything was as explanatorily titled then buying records would be a whole lot easier.

Pablo actually came to terms with digital technology and the mid-1980s shift in reggae music far better than many might imagine – his productions on Rockers International have remained a regular fixture in the Jamaican charts, and include that brilliant Junior Delgado album *Ragamuffin Year* (1990).

In spite of that, though, the late 1980s and early 1990s weren't particularly kind to him. Ill-health as much as changing fashion meant he was nowhere near as active as he was during the 1970s. However, the roots revival of the mid-1990s has – entirely understandably – put Pablo back in favour. His back catalogue is widely available on CD; he's touring as much as he's physically able to – Pablo shows in London are always instantly sold out, in spite of no publicity at all, and give up instrumental roots reggae music like dancehall never happened; and he's recording both himself and other artists in an original Rockers style. It's such a pity Tubby isn't there to kick off with him any more.

There are currently about fifty Augustus Pablo CDs on offer, both UK-released and easily available import. What follows is a selection of the most vital, which is as good a starting place as any. Reviews are brief, quite simply because there is a Pablo and Pablo/King Tubby vibe – the Rockers International sound – that is totally unique and drips off every recording with his name on. As was discussed above. Although in no way do they 'all sound the same': if you like one, the chances are you'll like the rest. And probably vice versa.

King Tubby Meets The Rockers From Uptown; Sanachie MESSCD1007

If, for some strange reason, you only see the need to own one Augustus Pablo CD then it has to be this one. It's worth far more than the twelve quid or whatever it costs, just for the privilege of being able to play the title track whenever you want to. Of course there's so much more to it than that. The opening cut, f'rinstance – 'Keep On Dubbing' is a cascade of different keyboards, layered on top of each other and a drum 'n' bass track that doesn't quit. They are then passed on to King Tubby to weave it into a Rockers tapestry that sounds all the more startling twenty years later. Or what about 'Stop Them Jah', which pulls in the full horn section to take the lead. Then there's eight other Rockers International gems – all approaching their task with an enormous array of keyboard instruments driving the rhythm instead of the traditional guitar. Most of the tunes are either the most spectacular remixes of his previous hits or recuts of old Studio One rhythms, as Pablo always liked the natural swing found in so much rock steady. But in all of them you can literally hear how much fun these two musical giants were having as they manipulated the control board. I could go on about them, forever, but while you're reading you're wasting time when you could be on your way to the record shop.

East Of The River Nile; Sanachie MESSCD1003

'East Of The River Nile' is what Pablo's woozy, deeply spiritual melodica sound became known as. This is the album on which it all came together after several years of refinement. On the whole a little slower and more meditative than the usual Rockers International output. Which shouldn't put anybody off, as this is so much of what Pablo and his music is about away from the King Tubby mixes and in-yer-face dub tracks. The *East Of The River Nile* experience is very close to what Pablo is like on stage – subtle, thoughtful and more drawn into himself than you'd expect.

AUGUSTUS PABLO PRESENTS: **Tetrack** *Let's Get Started* and Augustus Pablo *Eastman Dub*; Greensleeves GRELCD505

A double header that is an absolutely indispensable accessory for anybody who is captivated by *East Of The River Nile* as they ought to be: the two albums on this CD are, respectively, the vocal tracks and the dub mixes to *East Of The River Nile*. The former is performed by classic roots-style trio Tetrack, with lyrics written by their leader Carlton Hines that combine Rasta hymns, social commentary and lover songs, while the latter is masterfully mixed by Pablo himself.

This Is Augustus Pablo; Heartbeat HBCD34

His first album, and, as it was cut in 1970, before he'd set up his own company, it's produced by Clive Chin. This set shows where it all came from, as much of the tracklisting is early versions of the tunes with which Pablo later made his name. Although it's by no means as inventive as what was to come, in its quality of restraint it goes a long way to allowing us to see

272

what a truly classy keyboard player Augustus Pablo is.

Blowing With The Wind; Sanachie SHANCD43076

Cut in 1990, there is no other proof needed that Pablo didn't, in any way, 'lose it' when the digital revolution took hold. Although production methods and many of the sounds are as modern as you like, the soul of the album is pure Pablo. Pure Rockers. Pure roots reggae. The stand-out tracks are 'Ancient Harmonies', 'Drums To The King' and 'Zion UFO'.

Augustus Pablo and Various Artists: *Classic Rockers*; Mango RRCD52

Jacob Miller, Baby I Love You So; **Augustus Pablo,** King Tubby Meets The Rockers From Uptown; **Tetrack**, The Time Is Right; **Augustus Pablo**, Jah In The Hills; **The Immortals**, You Can't Keep A Good Man Down; **Paul Blackman**, Earth Wind And Fire; **Leroy Sibbles**, Love Won't Come Easy; **Earl Sixteen**, Changing World; **Junior Delgado**, Blackman's Heart; **Hugh Mundell,** Jah Says The Time Has Now Come; **Delroy Williams**, You Never Know; **Rockers All-Stars**, You Never Know Dub; **Delroy Wilson**, Stop The Fighting; **Rockers All-Stars**, Stop The Fighting Dub; **Augustus Pablo,** Suki Yaki; Eastern Promise.

One hundred per cent produced by Pablo and in most cases mixed by King Tubby, all these tracks date from between 1975 and 1985. They represent the best imaginable cross-section of Rockers International, showing how Pablo managed to pull another level of performance out of artists you thought you knew back to front.

Bewilderingly, that early example of Pablo's dub strengths *Ital Dub*, an enormous favourite back in the day – not least for its herb stalk cover – remains available only on vinyl.

SEE ALSO:

Blow Mr Hornsman – Instrumental Reggae 1968-1975; Trojan CDTRL257
Nice An' Ruff – A Crucial Brew Of Roots, Dub And Rockers; Music Club; MCCD 092

Lee 'Scratch' Perry

➤➤ Around the beginning of the 1970s, Lee Perry more or less decided he'd had enough. Had enough of playing by the rules, that is. By that point he'd established his Upsetter sound (as in 'recorded sound' not 'system') as being somewhat to the left of reggae's rather conservative centre – whether it was knocking out quirky pop-style tunes with The Upsetters or adding breadth to the early deejay recordings. He was allowing his commitment to Rastafari and black nationalism increasing amount of space in his artistic game plan – witness his work with THE WAILERS between 1969 and 1971 – yet he didn't want to settle for anything as straightforward as the roots hymns that were being made back then. (It's worth noting that it was Perry who put The Wailers together as a self-contained group when he took the Barrett brothers out of The Upsetters to join Bob, Peter and Bunny.) He was also fascinated by what could be done in the modern recording environment. And as he was in possession of one of the most fertile imaginations known to man, this all came together in an explosion of sound, structure and texture.

As you'd expect, Lee Perry was among the first in the queue at KING TUBBY's Waterhouse studios, looking for that extra edge. In fact it was he, along with BUNNY LEE, who talked Tubby into setting up his own studio. Between them Lee Perry and King Tubby produced a series of killer releases, culminating in 1973 with the gloriously deep roots dub album *Black Board Jungle Dub* – alternative mixes of The Upsetters' *Black Board Jungle* album – so heavy you practically needed a forklift truck to get it on to the turntable.

But in spite of having this and the previous year's *Rhythm Shower* LP and singles like 'Jungle Lion' and The Gatherers' 'Word Of My Mouth' on their joint CV, in 1974 when Perry set up his own studio he seemed to move up to yet another level, leaving Tubby behind. This was for two reasons. The first was that the Waterhouse mix master's dub innovation was peaking around 1975 – although his rhythms remained championship contenders until the end of the decade, much of what he was doing in the second half of the 1970s was merely a further refinement of previous technique. The second reason was quite simply that Perry's sound didn't suit King Tubby as well it might – initially, Perry had used Tubby to create exclusive mixes of his tunes for sound system use only, as a method of publicizing the records. True, the work they did was excellent, but sets like *Blackboard Jungle Dub* said far more about Tubby than they did about Scratch. King Tubby was all about space, and the contrast created against it, while Perry's method filled in the gaps with all manner of sounds and tones, creating an apparently random *mélange* of music, only to pull it all together in the mix to perfect sense. And the vibe Perry looked for was much warmer, seeking to unsettle by stealth rather than push it all up in your face.

In his own Black Ark Studio, set up behind his house in Kingston, he embarked on a journey that would redefine roots reggae to such a degree that British rock bands would often turn up there looking for the Lee Perry Magic. Here, free from the constraints of having to pay for studio time, he'd spend hours experimenting with sounds and sound effects – some of the earliest examples of sampling happened in Black Ark as he recorded toy noises, animal sounds, babies crying, TV and radio dialogue; anything he thought was vaguely interesting. Although only a four-track, he utilized every available technological device to record his music, filtering, phasing (Perry introduced the phaser to the Jamaican recording studio) and distorting instruments to create the required tone and feel, softening any sharp edges, then he'd compress the layers of different sounds into what became the trademark Lee Perry multi-texture. A deep, comforting affair that might have been chanting down Babylon, but was doing it from inside a big fluffy pillow while still managing to stay tough.

But Perry really came into his own behind the mixing desk. Always a natural showman, he'd play the board like an instrument. Spliff in hand, eyes shut, shirt hanging open and with nothing on his feet, he'd be caught up in a fluid, skanking dance of his own invention, shifting the sliding controls as he moved to the rhythm, whipping his arm out and down as he hit switches and bounced echoes. It was as if he'd become part of the mix, a situation rewarded by the overwhelmingly attractive human quality he bought to everything he did. It didn't seem to matter what he was using as a lead instrument – or how it finished up sounding – it always played a tune and Perry couldn't fail to be melodic. Whether it was a deep dub cut, one of his own snatches of musical mayhem, THE HEPTONES or THE CONGOS singing sweet harmony, PRINCE JAZZBO's gruff toasting, Susan Cadogan's LOVERS' ROCK or such lilting songs of sufferation as 'Curly Locks' or 'Police And Thieves', everything had this accessible, intricate, soothing Perry vibe. This was peaceful roots, an astonishing expression of Jah Rastafari.

Perry's personal life was never that peaceful, though. Hints that the man was touched by more than just genius had been there for some time – from his fiery, resentful split with DODD back in the 1960s. The fact that The Wailers had gone on to worldwide success, after they'd done what's widely acknowledged as their best work with him, didn't help his disposition either. Following his success with JUNIOR MURVIN's 'Police And Thieves', UK punk band The Clash hired Perry to produce a reggae album for them in an attempt at serious street credibility. Though one of the producer's longstanding complaints being his lack of worldwide exposure, he gave the band such a hard time they left Jamaica with only one track recorded. By the end of the 1970s he'd fallen out with Island Records, who'd successfully handled his UK releases – MAX ROMEO, The Heptones, George Faith, etc – and refused them *The Heart Of The Congos*, one of the greatest reggae albums ever made. And he'd also decorated the gate that opened on to the street from Black Ark's yard with a selection of old electric toasters – because, he claimed, he was a toaster. He'd hollowed out part of the studio floor to make a duck pond, and situated the drum riser on a kind of bridge across it. Then, in 1980, he trashed the equipment and set fire to the building.

By then, Lee Perry's music was increasingly difficult to understand, and becoming further and further removed from the notion of reggae. During the last fifteen years he's spent much of his time living and working in Europe – most recently in Switzerland, apparently married to one of the local aristocracy. His music has, for the most part, been all but unlistenable, and sold accordingly, but every once in a while he comes up with an album that would let you know, in no uncertain terms, that the 1970s pretty much belonged to Lee 'Scratch' Perry.

The following four albums are a mixture of Perry's productions on other people, Upsetter instrumentals, his own vocalizing and some serious dub cuts. Everything that makes up the four titles has the Lee Perry Magic sprinkled all over it, and really needs no further explanation than that given in the main text. The only real difference between them is that *Reggae Greats*, with only ten tracks, several hits and no dub mixes, is by far the most commercially orientated and easily accessible of the sets. All in all, though, they're the best way for a novice to approach Lee Perry, as it's not quite as intense an experience as it might be. Also, such songs as 'Party Time', 'War Inna Babylon', 'Neckodeemus' and 'Talk About It' show exactly how Perry both fitted into and totally subverted what was happening in reggae at the time.

For the more seasoned listener, the albums represent a brilliant chance to reassess the man's talent and, in the case of the first three discussed, to get hold of some very rare twelve-inch singles in a handy digital format.

It should also be noted that what follows is merely a selection of Lee Perry albums. As a rule of thumb for further investigation, pretty much anything with a 1970s date on it will be worthwhile, but anything after that should be checked out carefully before you actually part with money, as by then the errant genius was much more errant than genius.

*Lee 'Scratch' Perry and Friends: *Open The Gate*; Trojan CDPRY2

Anthony 'Sangie' Davis and Lee Perry, Words; **Devon Irons and Dr Alimantado**, Vampire; **The Heptones**, Babylon Falling; **The Upsetters**, Version; **The Heptones**, Mistry Babylon; **The Upsetters**, Version; **Leroy Sibbles**, Garden Of Life; **Carlton Jackson**, History; **Junior Delgado**, Sons Of Slaves; **Watty Burnett**, Open The Gate; **The Diamonds**, Talk About It; **The Upsetters**, Yam A-Ky; **Eric Donaldson**, Cherry Oh Baby; **Watty Burnett**, Rainy Night In Portland; **Horace Smart**, Ruffer Ruff; **The Upsetters**, Ruffer Dub; **The Congos**, Neckodeemus; **The Twin Roots**, Know Love; **Lee Perry**, City Too Hot; **Lee Perry**, Bionic Rats; **Junior Murvin**, Bad Weed.

*The Upsetters With Lee Perry and Friends: *Build The Ark*; Trojan CDPRY3

Leo Graham, My Little Sandra; **The Upsetters**, Dubbing Sandra; **Sharon Isaacs**, Feelings; **The Upsetters**, Version; **Winston Haywood**, Long Time; **The Upsetters**, Long Time Dub; **Junior Dread**, Ah Wah Dat; **The Upsetters**, Dub Dat; **Lee Perry**, White Belly Rat; **The Upsetters**, Judas De White Belly Rat; **Eric Donaldson**, Freedom Street; **The Upsetters**, Freedom Dub; **Shaumark and Robinson**, Peace And Love; **The Upsetters**, Peace A Dub; **The Sons Of Light**, Land Of Love; **The Upsetters**, Land Of Dub; **The Meditations**, Think So; **The Upsetters**, Dub So; **Junior Murvin**, Cross Over; **The Upsetters**, Cross Over Dub; **The Congos**, At The Feast; **Debra Keese and The Black Five**, Travelling; **The Upsetters**, Nyambie Dub; **Peter and Paul Lewis**, Ethiopian Land; **The Upsetters**, Landmark Dub; **Lord Sassafrass**, Green Bay Incident; **The Upsetters**, Green Bay Dub; **The Shadows**, Brother Noah; **The Upsetters**, Noah Dub; **Junior Ainsworth**, Give Thanks And Praise; **The Upsetters**, Dub And Praise; **Danny Hensworth**, Mr Money Man; **The Upsetters**, Money Dub.

*Lee Perry and Friends: *Public Jestering 1974-1976*; Attack CDAT108

Judge Winchester, Public Jestering; **The Upsetters**, I'm A Dreadlocks; **The Upsetters**, Dreadlocks Version; **Lee Perry**, Stay Dread; **The Upsetters**, Kingdom Of Dub; **Truth, Fact and Correct**, Babylon Deh Pon Fire; **Truth, Fact and Correct**, Jungle Fever; **Jimmy and Glen**, Hypocrites; **Jimmy and Glen**, Nine Fingers Jerry Lewis; **Leo Graham**, Black Candle; **The Upsetters**, Bad Lamp; **Leo Graham**, Big Tongue Buster; **The Upsetters**, Bus-A-Dub; **Leo Graham**, Doctor Demand; **The Upsetters**, Black Bat; **Horse Mouth**, Herb Vendor; **Prince Jazzbo**, Penny Reel.

***Reggae Greats*; Mango 162-539 792-2

The Heptones, Party Time; **Junior Murvin**, Police And Thieves; **Keith Rowe**, Groovy Situation; **Lee Perry**, Soul Fire; **Max**

Romeo, War Inna Babylon; **Jah Lion**, Wisdom; **George Faith**, To Be A Lover; **Lee Perry**, Roast Fish And Cornbread; **Prince Jazzbo**, Croaking Lizard; **Lee Perry**, Dreadlocks In Moonlight.

Jah Lion: Colombia Colly; Mango RRCD47

Jah Lion was a Perry alias, thus this 1976 set features a lot of his vocals. It's the best CD example of pure roots Perry, taking several of his cuts from the time and doing them over inna rub-a-dub style with some wildly scatological toasting on top. A vital album, summing up where Perry wanted to take the Rasta music he kicked off with The Wailers some seven years previously.

Battle Of Armagideon (Millionaire Liquidator); Trojan CDTRL227
Time Boom X De Devil Dead; Syncopate CDP 748 442 2

A brace of mid-1980s albums that remain remarkably consistent throughout, both retaining the Perry warmth and subtlety as the rhythms flow with a quiet strength, enough to drive the melodies and support any amount of oddness spread on top. The mixes are as intriguing as you'd want them to be, leading you by the hand into a dense forest of musical expressions in which you just *have* to hear what'll be sprung on you next. And whatever it is, it never disappoints. As to Scratch's mental state, the former features a track entitled 'I Am A Madman', while the latter contains those immortal lines 'I slew the Bank Of England/I slew the Barclays Bank'. Barking. In the best possible way.

Original Black Board Jungle Dub; Orchid ORCHCD1

The absolute apex of the union between two of reggae's biggest talents, this album is everything you'd want it to be. The Upsetters' *Black Board Jungle* album was always an event in itself, performed by the group's best line up – the Barrett brothers, Gladstone Anderson, Skully Simms, Winston Wright and Glen Adams – featuring tunes that are almost entirely gimmick-free (this is relatively early in Perry's career as a maniac) and so laid back they're already way past horizontal. Tubby doesn't so much alter the structure of anything as just stre-e-e-etch it out a bit, extending rhythm breaks, repeating horn lines, looping lead lines and fading sounds so that they hover on the very edge of what you can consciously hear. It pulls you into a third dimension of the music that wasn't so accessible in the LP's original form.

The overall effect is of time standing still, as these tunes don't seem to go anywhere other than round and round your frontal lobes. Which means that while it remains superficially quite light as all the melodies survive – somehow – a couple of seconds after each track has finished, you're left struggling with the weight of it. *Black Board Jungle Dub* remains the most effective tribute to what two geniuses can do with merely the most basic recording equipment and enormous imaginations.

Lee Perry And King Tubby; Creole REG108
Lee Perry And King Tubby Volume Two; Creole REG108

The next best things to the above are these two selections of Scratch productions given the Tubby treatment. And in spite of the two not perhaps being as mutually compatible as they might have been or as cohesively fluid as BBJD – they weren't recorded as albums, but made up of selected recordings – there are some magnificent moments contained here. Maybe they're made all the more enjoyable because so much of it isn't as self-consciously dense.

Anybody remotely interested with Lee Perry's Black Ark period will notice one glaring omission at this point. *Superape*. This collection of Perry-produced/mixed Upsetter tracks (revisits to stuff we already know) is, quite simply, his most brilliant album. Yet it's only available *on cassette*! The nearest we're going to get to this work of magic inna digital format is one track from it, the Prince Jazzbo toast 'Croaking Lizard', which can be found on *Reggae Greats* (Mango 162-539 792-2) and is enough of an example to let you know what you're missing.

SEE ALSO:

Lee Perry-produced albums from this period include:
The Congos: *The Heart Of The Congos*; Blood and Fire BAFCD009

Max Romeo: *War Inna Babylon*; Mango RRCD23
The Wailers: *African Herbsman*; Trojan CDTRL62
The Wailers: *Soul Revolution One And Two*; Trojan CDTRD406
The Wailers: *Rasta Revolution*; Trojan CDTRL89
Prince Jazzbo's *Natty Passing Through* is available on US import
CD under the title *Ital Corner*.

Maxi Priest

(Born Maxwell Elliot, 1960; London, England; Singer)
It's really difficult to figure out why Maxi Priest isn't a star of
global proportions. In the years immediately after the death of
BOB MARLEY, practically every record company in the UK who
had previously so much as sniffed a reggae record began looking
for 'the new Bob Marley'. Preferably a British version, given that
we were now making plenty of reggae in this country, as it would
save all that bother of having to go to Jamaica and deal with
artists who didn't understand the British way of doing things.
Although this was a particularly dumb undertaking, it had the
advantage of meaning reggae was taken seriously for a while,
and Maxi Priest was the perfect candidate for such mainstream
largesse. He had roots credibility as he'd come up through the
London sound system scene, first as a builder of bespoke speaker
boxes, then as a deejay/singer with the top-ranking Saxon
sound. Having been brought up in England, he understood both
the local reggae and mainstream markets. He was good-looking,
personable and intelligent. He exuded star quality with his taste
for sharp Italian suits, his flashing smile and his waist-length
dreadlocks. And he could sing like an angel. Here was a man
who was so absolutely right to bridge the pop and reggae divide
and not short change either side. Yet in spite of major record label
push and a long-term contract, he never lived up to the enormous potential he displayed when he'd steal the show on his *Top
Of The Pops* appearances in the late 1980s.

To the utter confusion of many – both inside and outside reggae circles – despite all he had going for him and several mainstream chart successes, which allowed him to introduce himself
to the public as something of a media star too, Maxi Priest
seemed to turn his back on stardom as the 1990s rolled around

and opt for life in the specialist market. Our gain, I guess, but the really curious thing is how on earth can the London under-ground reggae scene manage to contain a talent as big as this? The last I saw of him was a few years ago, when he came on stage at the Brixton Academy as SHABBA RANKS' special guest (they duetted on one of the many versions of 'Mr Loverman'). He comprehensively stole the show then, as well.

Maxi; 10 DIXCD64

Cut in Jamaica with SLY AND ROBBIE and a host of top session men, this is a stunning example of late roots reggae and the best available advertisement for Maxi Priest's talent. Although it was cut a couple of years after the digital watershed, and features an array of computerized studio trickery, it's got an enormous heart and never forgets that the front man is a singer. And a singer of yearning, pleading emotions at that. Slapping, crisply uptempo rockers like 'Wild World' and 'Some Guys Have All The Luck' (extended version) combine with the smoove lovers' rock of 'Reasons' and 'How Can We Ease The Pain' to provide the ideal bridge between two styles of reggae.

You're Safe; 10 DIXCD11

Cut in the UK, two years before *Maxi*, this is his first big-time album and as such is far more conventionally reggaefied. In fact it's a swinging, celebratory statement of where he came from: a largely lovers' rock sound system. This album rocks with such favourites as 'Should I', 'Hey Little Girl' and 'Dancin' Mood', only falling over when he moves away from the easy action stuff and into a rapid fire dancehall mode – it just doesn't suit him. Quite aside from being a deft example of the state of UK reggae just prior to 'Sleng Teng', *You're Safe* also ought to be enough to prove to Priest's detractors that he's quite capable of writing some killer songs. And if they are a bit overly reminiscent of GREGORY ISAACS, then that's probably not a bad thing.

The Best Of Me; 10 DIX111

The greatest hits collection, featuring all the well-known stuff –

'Some Guys', 'Strollin' On', 'Should I', 'How Can We Ease The Pain?', 'Close To You' and so on – plus a few surprises.

SEE ALSO:

On A Reggae Tip; Island CIDTV5

Rico

(Born Emanuel Rodriguez, 1934; Kingston, Jamaica; Trombonist)

Even on an island as rich in brass talent as Jamaica, Rico stands out. This premier horn player is, as near as anybody will ever prove, the man responsible for the 'Addis Ababa' horn sounds that typified Rasta reggae during the 1970s. Formally educated in music at the Alpha Boys Catholic School, Rico's prodigious talent had him sitting in with the island's best big bands and jazz combos while still in his teens. At the same time he discovered Rasta and took to spending time at COUNT OSSIE's camp in the Wareika Hills just outside Kingston, where he began to adapt his trombone sounds to express the same vibe as the voices of the brethren's drum-powered chants. Which became the sound he was to introduce to the recording industry years later. It was up in that camp that Rico felt the crack of the police batons as the organised harassment of Rastas became commonplace. Indeed such was the state of things that, in 1961, Rico became one of the first musicians to quit Jamaica to live in the UK, leaving behind a promising recording career as an in-demand sessioneer for every producer on the island. It's Rico's trombone that's on the ground-breaking 'Easy Snappin''.

Although numerous artists followed and a lively recording industry was set up in Britain during the 1960s, Rico earned as much from painting and decorating as he did from blowing his trombone. This all changed in the 1970s, though. With Rasta very much the place to be as far as reggae was concerned, Rico was signed to Island and returned to Jamaica to record *Man From Wareika*, which remains a milestone in Rasta music. Deeply spiritual in the way the bass and percussion set up psalm-like rhythm tracks – varying tempos but each one solemn as the last – the brass takes over to elevate it up into the sky somewhere.

All of Rico's jazz and classical experience comes to bear as he
recreates the chanting vibe but with an intricacy and spirited-
ness that keeps it worlds removed from the conventional idea of
a prayer. The lead instruments (mostly his 'bone, a guitar or keyboard) interact with each other as they ease out of the pack and
somewhere, way in the back, are some voices. The only album
that comes near it in terms of sheer class is its dub album *Wareika
Dub*.

Although he cut more than a few interesting singles over the
next few years, he never repeated this feat and remains resident
in London, gigging frequently inna jazz-tinged rootsman style.

Roots To The Bone; Mango RRCD54

A worthy 1995 replacement for *Man From Wareika*. It features
nearly all of the 1976 set and show's the man's versatility by supplementing the tracks with some of the singles mentioned above
– including Rico's fascinating version of Dave Brubeck's 'Take
Five', the Java-jazz of 'Midnight In Ethiopia', the dubwise 'No
Politician' and the easy-action 'Far East'.

Max Romeo

(Born Maxwell Smith, 1947; Kingston, Jamaica; singer)
There were two spectacular examples of what wonders the LEE
PERRY Magic could do for a little more than average singer.
Check back to the JUNIOR MURVIN entry for one, while Max
Romeo has to be the other. Prior to 1976 his one claim to fame
had been the bawdy early reggae classic 'Wet Dream' in 1960.
You remember, getting it played at a school disco then watching
teachers' faces as all that 'Lie down girl let me push it up, push
it up' boomed out of the speakers. The tune actually went Top 10
in the UK despite a BBC radio ban, which an enterprising record
company tried to get round by having Max explain to whatever
media would take any notice that the record wasn't rude at all –
it was about was a leaky roof. (his dreams were wet because the
rain was coming in, and he wanted his wife to lie down so he
could reach over her to plug the gap with a piece of wood). They
got nothing for effort, and the ban remained.

Fast forward to the mid-1970s, by which time he's had a few novelty hits in Jamaica, discovered Rastafari and hooked up with Lee Perry. In 1976, after a string of serious roots singles and the Revelation Time album, he recorded 'War Inna Babylon'. An instant classic. One of the defining records of that long hot summer in London, remaining as brilliant a piece of music today as it was when I first heard it at a blues dance in Tottenham nineteen years ago. But it was always a Lee Perry record, with Max Romeo just one more instrument in the master's orchestra. Everything Scratch ever dreamt about at the mixing desk comes together in that four minutes of sheer roots reggae bliss. The balance of rhythm and melody is so careful it must have been arrived at in a laboratory. The odd sounds and effects bubble just below the surface to pull you into its depth. Very little happens quite when you expect it to, thus you have to pay attention. It's as dread as anything. Yet it oozes out of the speakers, with such silkiness it's taken over the room before you realize it. Deejay, lick it back.

Romeo and Perry messily fell out after this – Perry's tune 'White Belly Rat' (see **The Upsetters With Lee Perry and Friends**: *Build The Ark*; Trojan CDPRY3) was, apparently, written and recorded with Max Romeo in mind. And nothing Max Romeo has done since then has really amounted to anything.

War Inna Babylon; Mango RRCD23

That it's got the title track on it is all the recommendation anybody needs, but there's an enormous bonus here – the album opens with one more reason to thank Lee Perry: 'One Step Forward'. This may effectively have been Max Romeo's swansong, but what a way to go.

SEE ALSO:

You can find 'War Inna Babylon' on:
Reggae Greats; Mango 162-539 792-2
Tougher Than Tough – The Story Of Jamaican Music; Mango IBXCD1

One Step Forward is on:
Reggae Refreshers Volume Two; Island/Mango RRCDS102

Scientist

(Born Overton Brown, 1962; Kingston, Jamaica; mixing desk wizard)

As the 1980s rolled around, dub was fading fast. It seemed as if the likes of LEE PERRY, JOE GIBBS and KING TUBBY had taken it about as far as it would go while still being reggae.

Then came Scientist, a young upstart who'd apprenticed as an engineer at Studio One, then been taken under King Tubby's wing. Youthful, forward-looking and entirely technology literate, Scientist was so sure of himself he came forward with a string of preposterously titled albums – *Scientist Wins The World Cup*, *Scientist Beats The Space Invaders*, *Scientist Rids The World Of The Curse Of Evil Vampires* and so on. Each with an appropriately daft cartoon of himself carrying out said deed, more than likely still seated at his mixing desk.

What Scientist did with his wildly inventive, effects-littered, cheeky dub mixes was to bring a sense of humour to reggae. But although his work perked things up for a couple of years, the writing was on the wall for reggae-as-we-knew-it. Although Scientist was young and vital, at the heart of his work were some pretty traditional arrangements, thus he cut less and less ice as dancehall rhythms began to establish themselves. He now lives and works as an independent producer in New York.

Scientist Meets The Space Invaders; Greensleeves GRELCD19
Heavyweight Dub Champion; Greensleeves GRELCD13
The Big Showdown – Scientist vs Prince Jammy; Greensleeves GRELCD9

During his few years in the sun, Scientist put out an astonishing number of albums, a dozen of which are currently available on CD. It is, however, pretty much an acquired taste as the dubbing is far more self-conscious than his predecessors – you tend to end up listening to the mixes rather than the tune, thus they can quickly start to sound gimmicky. However, they've all got such a vitality that they're never less than enjoyable and form a fitting bookend to dub's golden age. The three detailed above are probably the easiest to get into, and have also remained fresh the longest, but the last is perhaps the most spectacular, as he battles it out with JAMMY, each producer taking it in turns to mix BAR-RINGTON LEVY tracks.

Jah Shaka

(Born 1950s, Jamaica; sound system operator/producer/deejay) The name comes from the Zulu King Shaka, a conquering warrior leader whose armies for years held up the advance of colonization in Africa. Likewise Shaka's sound was all-conquering in London and has been so synonymous with London dread there was a time when Shaka's dances were akin to spiritual experiences. At the Notting Hill Carnival, before they closed off the sections under the flyover, Shaka's sound had the tightest packed, most militant crowd. Dub mixes on his label have been the most crushing, unremitting bass 'n' drum cuts. His philosophies have been by far the blackest, taking the teachings of Jah Rastafari and blending them with the black power politics of America of the 1960s and early 1970s.

Coming to the UK as a child in the 1960s, Shaka – he will admit to no other name – played in a band before realizing he could get his message across much quicker with a towering sound system. And his system took on all-comers with sheer physical power and depth of dub experience.

As public interest in roots reggae declined during the eighties, Shaka continued to do just what he'd always done – play heavy, deeply righteous Rasta reggae. For a while there were few takers and it's now that his recordings began in earnest. But, maybe as a reaction to dancehall or as testimony to the man's innate skills and the true power of Rasta reggae, during the 1990s the crowds started coming back. Jah Shaka now plays dances as big as anything he deejayed twenty years ago.

Dub Symphony; Mango CIDM 1044

Nowhere near as crushingly dread as a Shaka live set; the deejay is in no doubt that so much of the rumbling, thunderous bass 'n' treble polarity of the dancehall would be pointless in the average living room. The album more or less lives up to its title, with an impressive range and tunefulness within the spectacular dub style.

Shaka productions of MAX ROMEO and HORACE ANDY, with appropriately heavy vibes, are currently available on CD as, respectively, *Fari Dub Ship* (Shaka SHAKACD989) and *Jah Shaka Meets Horace Andy* (Shaka SHAKACD947).

SEE ALSO:

Various Artists: *Time Warp Dub Clash (Old School vs New School)*; Mango CDIM1105

Sly and Robbie

(Born Lowell Dunbar, 1952, drummer; Robbie Shakespeare, born 1953, bass guitarist; both born Kingston, Jamaica; producers/mixers)
Sly and Robbie are known as The Riddim Twins, and their playing has been the backbone for, quite literally, hundreds of reggae artists during the last twenty-five years. But to look on them as mere session musicians, or even as musician/producers (they've mixed some of the biggest reggae hits), would be doing them down. Sly and Robbie are *innovators*. They've been at the heart of two major upheavals in reggae's development, and, second only to BOB MARLEY, they've taken Jamaican music to the rest of the world.

The two had known each other for years on the Kingston music scene – Sly working mostly with LEE PERRY and in the club/studio band Skin, Flesh and Bone, and Robbie as a regular member of BUNNY LEE's AGGROVATORS. They had even worked on the same sessions on frequent occasions. But they didn't team up until the mid-1970s, when they came together in The Revolutionaries, Jo-Jo Hookim's Channel One Studio's house band. It was here that the uptempo 'rockers' sound that led the way, rhythm-wise, for the rest of the decade was developed, but although it had been attempted, it wasn't until Shakespeare actually joined the band that it was achieved. Sly had been pushing the rhythm upwards by playing double time within a pretty conventional beat, but it took Shakespeare's nimble fingers on the bass to drive it to the levels it needed to reach. Channel One succeeded in taking over as reggae's hottest studio, and, largely thanks to Sly and Robbie's crisp playing, held on to that crown for years with artists like THE MIGHTY DIAMONDS, DILLINGER, HORACE ANDY, JUNIOR BYLES, Trinity and instrumental and dub albums by The Revolutionaries. Sly and Robbie, however, soon wanted to move things on.

By the end of the 1970s, they'd set up their own label and were embracing the advancements made in studio technology with all four arms. Their new Mixing Labs studio was home to all sorts of digital gadgetry – not least one of the first electronic drum kits and computerized bass guitars seen on the island – and their own Taxi record label gave them the opportunity to work on their own terms. Immediately, their taut, muscular productions propelled BLACK UHURU to international stardom. Which did wonders for The Riddim Twins' standing too – as they toured the world with Uhuru as the foundation for their backing band, offers of work flooded in from such characters as Bob Dylan, The Rolling Stones and Grace Jones. They weren't neglecting the home front, either. The fact that they've never relocated from Kingston and remain in close contact with the local scene has played a big part in Sly and Robbie's ability to stay on top for so long. In Jamaica their new digital sound was scoring hits for, notably, Junior Delgado, The Tamlins, SUGAR MINOTT, THE VICEROYS, Jimmy Riley, GREGORY ISAACS, DENNIS BROWN and, of course, Black Uhuru.

It was the success of this distinctive, obviously computerized style that set the reggae business on the road to the entirely digital sounds of dancehall. In which, of course, Sly and Robbie were a force to be reckoned with. ↵

There are no Revolutionaries instrumental albums currently available on CD, so to find that original rockers sound, check out albums by the artists mentioned that were recorded in the second half of the 1970s. If they were Hookim-produced, with Sly and Robbie among the credits, then they're what you're looking for. For that classic early 1980s Taxi sound, once again you're best off looking for the artists concerned from that timespan, or enquiring about the several Taxi compilations from the period on easily available import CDs.

There is a UK-released compilation CD, *A Dub Experience/*

Reggae Greats (Mango RRCD29), that has the bonus of a series of dub tracks as well as a Various Artists set from the label. (No tracklisting was available at time of writing.) Also there is *Time Warp Dub Clash (Old School vs New School)* (Mango CDIM1105), the first ten tracks of which are Sly and Robbie's 1981 *Raiders Of the Lost Dub* album, while the other nine are dubs by such young pups as Alpha and Omega, JAH SHAKA, MAD PROFESSOR and Dub Syndicate.

Steel Pulse

(David Hinds, lead vocals/guitar; Basil Gabbidon, Lead guitar/ vocals; Alphonso Martin, vocals/percussion; Selwyn Brown, keyboards/vocals/percussion; Ronnie McQueen, bass/percussion; Michael Riley, vocals/percussion; Steve Nesbitt, drums; all born late 1950s; Handsworth, Birmingham, UK)

Steel Pulse's 1978 album *Handsworth Revolution* is one of the best reggae albums ever made. *Fact*. In terms of tone, tunes and content, nothing so deftly summed up reggae in the UK in the uneasy late 1970s, as we moved from the riots of the Notting Hill Carnival to the inner-city disturbances at the beginning of the 1980s. The tracks dealt with what was perceived as police occupation of certain areas and spoke of sound system culture; of the beginnings of Rastafari; of the emergent bad man attitude; and of specifically British racial injustice. Musically, it was just as intelligent. Approaching their songs as ensemble pieces – seven writing credits weren't unusual – and adding depth to reggae arrangements by playing with the tempos, they stirred unusual keyboard and guitar sounds into the almost ethereal vocal and percussive layers. Like the rest of the best of British reggae bands at the time, they had a fantastic stage show to go with it too. Sadly, line-up changes almost directly after the recording meant they never did it again.

But the real problem Steel Pulse faced was virtually regulation among UK reggae acts. See Aswad. Their potential and their success came about because, initially, they were doing exactly what their market wanted – broad-based, witty music that acknowledged its environment while remaining true to the cause, the bassline and the late-night blues. Hell, since they'd formed at school in Handsworth – one of Birmingham's less salubrious ghettoes – they'd remained in the area, thus were as much a part of their market as anybody buying the stuff. And left alone they were bright enough and skilful enough to turn out genuinely heartfelt music of such a calibre that it got the mainstream buyers interested. Which virtually guaranteed outside interference: 'If you just tweak it that way then it'll get play-listed . . .'

To give them their credit, Steel Pulse never fell for it and changed record companies more or less like other people change socks, gaining a reputation for being 'difficult' along the way. But it also meant a series of brilliant albums, as each time they moved labels they were initially left alone and came up with something special: at Elektra it was *Earth Crisis* and at MCA it was *State Of Emergency*. After these were well received, then the 'advice' started.

Finally Steel Pulse had enough and concentrated on the American market, where they had been carving out a niche for themselves on the highly lucrative college circuit. In complete contrast to the way they were treated in Britain, where lack of record company backing spells the end for any act, in the US they are so well appreciated they were the first reggae band to play at the White House when they performed at President Clinton's inauguration in 1992. It is our loss. The rare occasions they do play the UK are experiences that shouldn't be missed.

Handsworth Revolution; Mango RRCD24

That first magnificent album in glorious digital clarity. Mid-price too. So even if you already own it, it's definitely worth buying it on CD. Although discussed in detail above, it is worth mentioning again that this is one of a handful of albums that defined UK reggae and should've been enough to let the entire world know what an enormous potential there was for our own translation of the Jamaican sound.

State Of Emergency; MCA DMCF3427

The first album with MCA, cut in 1988, that showed the band acknowledging the American market by blending electronic disco-type sounds into their mix. This isn't nearly as horrible as it might seem, though, as they cleverly created a synthesis of their own thoughtful roots reggae and modern digital sounds that became the sort of dancehall reggae you'd want to take home and listen to. This is the album with 'Love This Reggae Music', 'Hijacking' and, of course, 'State Of Emergency'.

Tribute To The Martyrs; Mango RRCD17

The follow-up to *Handsworth Revolution* that very nearly scaled those same heights. The band's personal memorial to Steve Biko, George Jackson and others who have given their lives to the cause. Less instrumentally tricky but more instantly gratifying, it confirms the group's commitment to Rastafari – apparently the reason for the line-up changes – and contains 'Sound System', 'Jah Pickney' and 'Babylon Makes The Rules'.

Reggae Greats; Mango IMCD33

The best of *Handsworth* and *Tribute*. Although, in theory, this is more than perfectly acceptable, because Steel Pulse are one of the very few reggae bands to approach albums as something beyond a collection of singles, this compilation somehow isn't quite enough.

SEE ALSO:

Reggae Refreshers Volume Two; Island/Mango RRCDS102

Third World

(William 'Bunny Rugs' Clarke, born 1956, vocals/guitar/percussion; Michael 'Ibo' Cooper, 1955, keyboards/bass/vocals/percussion; Stephen 'Cat' Coore, 1959, vocals/guitar/cello; Richie Daley, 1953, bass/guitar/vocals; Willie 'Root' Stewart, 1956, drums/vocals/percussion; Irwin 'Carrot' Jarret, 1952, percussion/vocal; all born Jamaica)

In 1978, when the twelve-inch of Third World's take on The O'Jays' 'Now That We've Found Love' hit club turntables in north London, to say it 'rocked the house' would be an enormous understatement. It was a sensation. But it combined with the group's flamboyant visual presentation and their lack of ghetto history, to spark a ridiculously time-wasting debate as to whether Third World were 'really reggae' or not. The arguments are still going on, almost twenty years later, so let's put a stop to them. *Of course* Third World are a reggae group. Nobody's who's ever heard their reading of 'Satta Massa Gana' could possibly have any doubts. They're simply a shining example of what happens when you put other influences to work within a reggae framework. In this case it was a combination of classical – Coore and Cooper, the founding members, were both conservatory trained to the highest standards; and soul – Jarrett and Stewart had both been in INNER CIRCLE and the latter had worked as a musician in the US and Canada as a teenager. Jarrett had also worked in the Jamaican National Theatre and as a TV director and producer on the island, and thus understood the need for a band to look as good as they sounded. And they were all essentially good middle-class boys.

Third World had come together in 1973 with the idea of forming a self-contained reggae band with as much emphasis on touring as recording. While this meant they were never out of work on Kingston's club scene, they couldn't get a record deal in the producer-orientated studio system. The next year the group relocated to London, where they were signed almost immediately by Island Records, the company that had BOB MARLEY's signature and could therefore appreciate the value of a *proper* group. In the correct environment, it didn't take the band long to find their level – by their second album, *96 Degrees In the Shade*, they were expressing roots sentiments and political concerns over a subtle, mellow reggae background. At times it was more like high-quality Jamaican folk music than the usual idea of reggae. After touring with the likes of The Jacksons and Stevie Wonder, the group very quickly established an international reputation that was second only to Bob Marley as reggae senior statesmen around the globe.

Although it's their earlier work – *Journey To Addis*, *96 Degrees In The Shade* and *Third World* – that remains their most exciting, no Third World album should be discounted. They continue to tour, mostly in America, and will still use Jamaican producers and studios to record.

**96 Degrees In The Shade*; Mango RRCD16

The only one of those first albums still available in its entirety. But that isn't so bad, as it's by far the best of the lot. It was their second album, and as well as coming to terms with where they stood with regard to Rastafari and cultural statement in general (the debut set had been noticeably apolitical), they were becoming far more adventurous as musicians around this time. The title track, 'Human Market Place' and 'Dreamland' stand out as being the best possible examples of Third World's softly spoken roots.

**Reggae Greats*; Mango IMCD37

A selection from the early albums that may not have everything you want on it, but it's got absolutely nothing you don't: 'Cool Meditation', 'Satta', '96 Degrees In The Shade', 'Now That We've Found Love' and 'Prisoner In The Street' are all present and very correct.

**Reggae Ambassadors – 20th Anniversary*; Island CRNCD3

Thirty-one tracks across three CDs, spanning the band's entire career, and while it's got to be worth it for the full eight and a half minutes of 'Now That We've Found Love', the second disc is horribly patchy as far too much Americana creeps in.

Peter Tosh

↠ (BOB MARLEY AND THE WAILERS) When Tosh quit THE WAILERS in 1973 the prospect of him going solo and giving free rein to his talent, temperament and commitment to social justice was an exciting one. The speak softly-and-carry-a-big-stick approach favoured by MARLEY was never going to work for a man such as Tosh. Standing six foot seven inches tall, a martial arts master and given to unreasonable displays if pique – I've personally been on the end of one – Tosh was more a man of direct action. True, he was always going to be 'difficult to deal with', but his potential as a singer, songwriter and a performer would more than make up for that. Unfortunately it didn't. Although Tosh made a lot of noise about what he was going to do and how well he was going to do it, the high spots of his solo career were never anything more than a few excellent singles: 'Maga Dog', 'I Am The Toughest', 'Steppin' Razor' and the herbsman anthem 'Legalize It', which he seemed to re-release at every available opportunity. It appeared that Tosh's career was motivated more by making a quick buck than by any long-term scheme or artistic goal, as he moved from record label to record label with vastly diminishing musical returns. And the patience of his original fans was stretched beyond the limit in 1978 when he recorded the credibility-free duet with Mick Jagger (a huge reggae fan) '(You Got To Walk And) Don't Look Back'. In 1987, he fell prey to the violence that is an escalating part of the reggae industry, when he was shot dead in his house during a bungled robbery attempt.

Legalize It; Virgin VCD2061

Worth anything they want you to pay, for the title track alone. It's pure Tosh: arrogant; direct and to the point; and a very crisp performance and production. It is still a reggae classic, twenty years after it seemed as if it was every third record played at the 1976 Notting Hill Carnival.

Equal Rights; Virgin VCD2081

This has got the man's super-militant version of 'Get Up Stand Up', plus 'Stepping Razor' and 'Downpressor'.

King Tubby

(Born Osbourne Ruddock, 1941; Kingston, Jamaica; producer/ engineer/dub innovator)
If you've read the LEE PERRY, AUGUSTUS PABLO, NINEY or BUNNY LEE entries, then you'll be aware of exactly how large a shadow King Tubby cast over the entire roots reggae industry. His remixes could take a tune, deconstruct it and then reconstruct it with the original essence intact, but with everything it didn't

need stripped away. Then into the gaps he'd place perfectly timed snatches of the melody or rhythm pattern (sometimes as little as two or three notes or one chord fed through an echo chamber or filter). Or he'd drop in a sound effect. Or, more than likely, he'd fill it with nothing at all. King Tubby's dubs were all about space and making you appreciate how a tune was working by removing large bits of it to allow what mattered to shine through. Then taking those bits – bits you might not immediately appreciate as being so vital – and re-presenting them in a way that would shock you at how powerful they were. King Tubby's dubs were about rumbling over you with a steamroller and having you wait for him to do it again. The other popular theory is that the disruption to the musical space/time continuum that a Tubby special presented was about as close as you could get to the effect of Grade 1 collie weed without actually inhaling.

But one thing was certain, King Tubby enjoyed himself as he rocked back and forth, and made the mixing process as physical as possible as he hit the spring-loaded switches and manipulated the sliders. The man was always smiling too, and this good humour and sense of fun communicated itself through his work – it may have been dreader than dread, but it was going to boost you up too. This man could turn an ordinary tune into something very special. He could push the sort of music he'd get from the abovementioned quartet even further to the point at which you found it difficult to believe.

It's not that surprising that somebody as technically minded as Tubby arrived at music through engineering – it was sometimes said that he was so into the recording studio as an end in itself that he created music only as a by-product of finding out what his gadgets would do. Back in the 1950s he set up business as an electrical repair man, with the main part of his operation devoted to fixing radios. Which he did with considerable skill. So much so, that when the sound system boom came about at the beginning of the next decade, he was in enormous demand to build amplifiers and control panels of escalating power and sophistication. By 1968, he was running his own rig, Home Town HiFi, which, as a tribute to his engineering skills, was the first sound in Jamaica to utilize reverb, echo and twin-track cross-fading. And while this quickly established him as a major player, the best was yet to come.

Tubby had been getting one foot into the music production business by working as a disc cutter – making the acetates from the studio tapes – for DUKE REID at Treasure Isle, and his yen to experiment led him to start rearranging the music by dropping out instruments or vocals and by bringing other certain elements to the fore. He went as far as to cut a handful of slates of these weird mixes, specially prepared for the Home Town deejay – a chap who went under the name of U-ROY – to toast over. That night at the dance, U-Roy's toasting was hardly needed. The crowd went absolutely wild for the cuts as Tubby manipulated the controls to provide what, to all intents and purposes, were live remixes (people who were there claim the whole night was spent licking those same four records back) and the face of reggae had changed for ever. King Tubby had supplied the first dub plates.

Naturally such a sensation wasn't going to remain a secret, so pretty soon every producer was dubbing like a master. But the wiser ones went to King Tubby and had him do it for them in the studio he'd built by the early 1970s – a studio that was continually in a state of flux as he added the latest electronic equipment as soon as it was unloaded on to Kingston's docks. Originally dub plates were strictly a one-off deal, for sound system use only, but it wasn't long before characters like Bunny Lee were making them available to an eager public.

And so it continued throughout the 1970s and into the 1980s, with a peak period some time in the second half of the earlier decade. After that, his thunderous remixes and depth-charge dubs seemed merely to be marking time while other younger producers – upstarts like PRINCE JAMMY or Phillip Smart who had apprenticed at Tubby's desk – picked up on the developing new music and streaked past him. But King Tubby was biding his time rather than just marking it. He was planning, and had built, a new all digital studio, where towards the end of the 1980s he began recording the up-and-coming dancehall singers of the day, with all the verve and flair of his roots period.

He looked set to rule the roost once again. Then on 6 February 1989 he was shot dead outside his house in St Andrews, far away from the Kingston mean streets. Nobody was ever caught, and nobody's quite sure why it happened. His body wasn't robbed. But the world certainly was. Of one of the greatest, most innovative musicians, and one of the nicest, happiest human beings.

The following three albums are the obvious selection from the dozens of CDs – legitimate and otherwise – currently in the shops with King Tubby's name on them. All of these are put together by Steve Barrow and represent three very different aspects of the great man's career. They really ought to be approached as some sort of set.

King Tubby Special 1973-1976; Trojan CDTRL409

Thirty blistering examples of what King Tubby was all about, as this represents his dub style rather than somebody else's singing or playing. The first half is the 1975 Niney album *Dubbing With The Observer*, which has been unavailable for quite some time and never before seen on CD. While the second set of songs – if 'songs' is quite the right word – is a compilation of Bunny Lee productions, offering up a string of classic reggae records. Like a recut of 'Queen Of The Minstrels' involving Augustus Pablo and his melodica. Or 'Skylarking' revisited. Or a dub mix of Cornell Campbell's 'Dance In Greenwich Farm' . . . This is one of the best collections of Tubby's craft, as not only was he peaking at the time, but so many of the tunes are so well known it's easier to realize exactly what he's done with them.

If Deejay Was Your Trade – The Dreads At King Tubby's 1974-1977; Blood And Fire BAFCD001

Tubby was well to the fore of the deejay revolution, respected as one who understood how to capture the vitality of the dance in the recording studio. All the tracks were produced by Bunny Lee; the backing was done at Striker's, while the vocals put down at Tubby's. I really ought to shut up and let the tracklist speak for itself.

Big Joe, In The Ghetto; **I-Roy**, War And Friction; **Little Joe**, Tradition Skank; **Tappa Zukie**, Jah Is I Guiding Star; **Jah Stitch**, Set Up Yourself Dreadlocks; **Dr Alimantado**, Chant To Jah; **Dr Alimantado**, Mash It Up; **Dr Alimantado and Jah Stitch**, The Barber Feel It; **Jah Stitch**, Bury The Barber; **Jah Stitch**, Black Harmony Killer; **Jah Stitch**, Greedy Girl; **Dillinger**, Regular

Girl; **Dillinger**, Daylight Saving Time; **Prince Jazzbo**, Gal Boy I-Roy; **Prince Jazzbo**, Good Memories; **Prince Far-I**, Shuffle And Deal.

Dub Gone Crazy – The Evolution Of Dub At King Tubby's 1975-1979; Blood And Fire BAFCD002

Although the dates here may seem a bit late for Tubby's dub to be evolving, this set cunningly and quite brilliantly shows the evolution of dub *at* King Tubby's. But not necessarily *by* King Tubby. Two tracks here are mixed by the master himself, but the rest are handled by his pupils SCIENTIST, Prince Jammy and Phillip Smart. While they're all obviously of the same family, each has his own distinct style, and to be able to play out the evolution of this particular dub strain in one go like this is fascinating.

ALSO RECOMMENDED:

Waterdub; Lagoon LG21055
Surrounded By The Dreads At The National Arena; Studio 16 STCD003
Crossfire; Lagoon LG21050

Although none of these is quite of the calibre of those mentioned above, they are the best of the rest. Besides which, no King Tubby mixes ought to be ignored.

SEE ALSO:

The following albums, as discussed elsewhere, are all King Tubby mixes.
Augustus Pablo: *King Tubby Meets The Rockers From Uptown*; Sanachie MESSCD1007
Augustus Pablo and Various Artists: *Classic Rockers*; Mango RRCD52
Lee Perry And King Tubby; Creole REG108
Lee Perry And King Tubby Volume Two; Creole REG108
Yabby U: *King Tubby's Prophecy Of Dub*; Blood And Fire BAFCD005
Tappa Zukie In Dub; Blood And Fire BAFCD008 (There is no Tappa Zukie entry, as this is all that is available of his work on

CD and this set – containing Tubby's dubs of Tappa-produced tunes including 'MPLA', 'Rockers', 'Judgement Time', 'So Jah Seh' and 'Babylon Fall' – is really a Tubby album.)

The Twinkle Brothers

(Norman Grant, drums/vocals; Ralston Grant, guitar/vocals; Eric Barnard, piano; Carl Hyatt, percussion/vocals; Albert Green, percussion; all born 1940s, Falmouth, Jamaica)

If proof were needed that there is life after Jamaica's North Coast hotel cabaret circuit, you need look no further than The Twinkle Brothers. In fact, it was the variety of music the group had to play, on demand, from their formation in 1962 that shaped the multi-faceted reggae they performed when they began producing themselves in 1975. There can't be many devout Rasta bands who can go from the anthemic self-composition 'Rasta Pon Top' to a dread reappraisal of the lounge-crooner's favourite, 'Distant Drums', in the space of the same stage set!

But it was such versatility that meant the group could, musically, do much more with their percussion-based set-up than you might imagine. While so many of their arrangements deviated from the reggae norm, inasmuch as the delicately woven percussion provided both the rhythm and the melody, Norman Grant was shrewd enough to keep a big bass guitar in there too. This allowed flexibility by holding down a groove to let the band members spread out a bit and take it beyond the expected Rasta sounds. At the same time, the whole group would sing (Barnard and Green provided extra backing), so the harmonizing was much broader than the usual three parts.

In the second half of the 1970s, the group really hit their stride, as their innate understanding of how to please all aspects of a crowd – another hangover from the hotel days – resulted in records that could rock, swing or smoove without compromising their Rasta ideals. The group split up in 1982, and since then Norman Grant has retained the name to record dozens of albums for his loyal European following. It's worth noting that, although these post-1985 Twinkle Brothers records are better than a great deal of reggae, they're not a patch on the original group in full flow.

*_Free Africa_; Frontline CDFL9008

An amalgamation of most of the best tracks from The Twinkle Brothers' three superb Frontline albums, _Love_, _Praise Jah_ and _Countrymen_, and the sixteen tracks go far enough across their back catalogue to mean you don't miss the originals too much. Naturally the triumphant 'Never Get Burn' is present, as is 'Since I Threw The Comb Away', 'Don't Want To Be Lonely Any More', 'Love' and 'I Love You So' – lovers' rock with that little bit extra. While the full depth of what the group was capable of comes over in the delicate 'Watch The Hypocrites' , 'Free Africa' and the sublime 'Patoo'.

SEE ALSO:

Roots 'N' Culture; Music Club MCCD128
Beyond The Frontline; Frontline FRONT1
Natty Rebel Roots; Frontline CDFL9103 (This last selection features 'Jah Kingdom Come' and 'Praise Jah', both conspicuous by their absence from _Free Africa_.)

U-Roy

➻ Although by the early 1970s U-Roy was already being over-shadowed by the generation of dreadlocks deejays who had come up behind him, it is essential he takes his place in this section. While he may not have been as dynamic as, say, BIG YOUTH, or as claustrophobically righteous as PRINCE FAR-I, U-Roy put out some well dread tunes: 'The Great Psalms', 'Natty Rebel' and 'Chalice In The Palace', to name but three. And besides, the latter of that trio is a gloriously surreal toast about a Rastaman sneaking into Buckingham Palace and smoking collie weed with Her Maj. Surely U-Roy gets extra points for that.

Once U-Roy left DUKE REID in 1973 he freelanced around, but the net phase didn't really kick off until he teamed up with producer Tony Robinson in 1975 and cut a series of albums for Virgin in the UK, which totally affirmed the deejay's dread status. Although they didn't take toasting anywhere new, the two-some mixed up revisits to U-Roy's old Treasure Isle stuff – sometimes inna rockers style, sometimes just with new words –

with fresh compositions and toasts over hits of the day. His famous delivery swooped and soared around the rhythms, managing to sound enthusiastic and laid back in the same syllable, and showed the world that the man they call The Teacher could still hold class.

The relationship came to an end in 1980, and U-Roy still records and performs on a regular basis. Take note, live shows should not be missed as, at well past fifty, he can still rock the house with all the gusto he used to bring to the Treasure Isle sound system in Denham Town all those years ago.

Original DJ; Virgin CDFL9020

The very best of both worlds, as this CD's twenty-five tracks mix up such old classics as 'Wear You To The Ball' and 'On The Beach', with the Tony Robinson specials like 'Peace And Love In The Ghetto', 'Jah Jah' and 'Natty Rebel'. An ideal way to look over what is most of the man's career.

Dread In A Babylon; Virgin CDFL 9007

This has got that amazing 'Chalice In The Palace' on it, and surrounds it with such delights as 'Listen To The Teacher', 'Natty Don't Fear' and 'The Great Psalms'.

Rasta Ambassador; Virgin CDFL 9016

More rockers rhythms, including 'Control Tower', 'Small Axe', 'Mr Slave Driver' and 'No More War', plus a couple of rock steady gems – 'Wear You To The Ball' and 'The Tide Is High'.

Rastaman Skank; Virgin TPAK19

A box set of the *Version Of Wisdom* (see page 000), *Rasta Ambassador* and *Natty Rebel* albums at the bargain price of thirty quid. Not an offer you ought to refuse.

True Born African; Ariwa ARICD071

Produced by THE MAD PROFESSOR in London in 1990, the

eccentric mixing technique works brilliantly with U-Roy's delivery, to send it spiralling into new areas of manic. Stand-out tracks are 'Ghetto Youth' and 'False Prophecy'.

SEE ALSO:

Natty Rebel Roots; Virgin CDFL9013
Big Blunts – 12 Smokin' Reggae Hits; Tommy Boy TBCD1077

The Viceroys

(Wesley Tinglin, born 1947, Kingston, Jamaica; Linval Williams, born 1950, St Mary's, Jamaica; Daniel Bernard, born 1949, Westmoreland, Jamaica; vocal trio)
A vocal trio in classic Impressions-based Jamaican style, The Viceroys were one of the earliest dedicated roots groups. These guys practically pre-dated reggae when they formed in 1968 and much of what they recorded is probably best called 'roots rock steady'. And they did it at Studio One too. Although not quite chanting down Babylon, it's marvellous to hear The Viceroys praising Jah, decrying their problems, and singing about love and unity or living naturally on the beach, over the sort of rhythms more associated with rude boys or rude reggae. They continued through the 1970s and 1980s, but nothing they did ever made as much impact as when they laid down a template for groups like THE MIGHTY DIAMONDS or CULTURE.

*Ya Ho – The Viceroys At Studio One; Heartbeat CDHB133

A collection of those late 1960s DODD-produced sides, previously released as *The Best Of The Viceroys*, including the now classic title track, plus 'Maga Down', 'Fat Fish' and 'Love And Unity'. An absolutely vital link in the chain between early Jamaican music and the roots reggae that went worldwide.

Bunny Wailer

➻ (BOB MARLEY AND THE WAILERS) When Bunny left THE WAILERS it was no big surprise – he hates flying and was therefore never keen on touring. In fact, he's not even that keen on coming to Kingston these days, preferring to remain in his secluded out-of-town farm, leaving his brother to take care of business for him. But this hasn't stopped this most gentle of men from putting out some superb music. Taking a straightforward route, rather than set himself up for a complicated fall, Bunny founded his own Solomonic record label right after leaving the group and since 1974 has ridden various styles – from roots to dancehall and back – in his high clear tenor, with considerable aplomb.

It came as an enormous shock to a lot of people when this elder statesman of roots reggae started making dancehall records in the late 1980s, and an even bigger shock when many were deservedly successful. Although a quiet, devout Rastaman, he clearly enjoys what he is doing and his music is seldom overly solemn, while his rare stage shows outside Jamaica are always joyous occasions. Bunny Wailer is still recording and performing.

Blackheart Man; Mango RRCD6

The record that broke Bunny Wailer as a solo star rather than simply an ex-Wailer. An intensely personal, deep roots affair, that is as powerful a statement today as it was in 1976 when it came out. The subject matter is Rastafari, social injustice and political wrong-doing, dealt with in a frank and open manner to some serious depth-charge reggae. The tracks 'Blackheart Man', 'Rastaman' and 'Armagideon' ought to carry a government health warning.

Bunny Wailer Sings The Wailers; Mango RRCD 8

'Dancing Shoes', 'Hypocrite', 'Mellow Mood', 'I Am The Toughest' and 'Walk This Proud Land' are among the numbers he does over with such a deft touch you wonder why he didn't sing lead in the group more often.

Roots, Radics, Rockers, Reggae; Shanachie SHANCD 43013

Mid-1980s style, light, perky reggae and Bunny's last big album before he tried his luck with dancehall reggae. It skips along, veering from the love songs to the righteous without missing a beat.

Rule Dance Hall; Shanachie SHANCD 43050

The best of Bunny's early dancehall excursions, showing his enormously melodic voice to be the perfect counterbalance for the computerized rhythms. Which, in this instance, don't seem quite as harsh as they might do.

The Wailing Souls

(Winston 'Pipe' Matthews; Lloyd 'Bread' McDonald; both born early 1950s, Kingston, Jamaica; singing group)
Over the near thirty years that The Wailing Souls have been in existence, they've had almost as many names as they've had personnel changes – The Renegades, Pipe and The Pipers, Atarra, to name but three. But two things have always remained a constant: Matthews and McDonald and the sweet three– or four–part harmonizing. Whether they're singing sweet love songs or deep roots material, their light, sufferah touch – very similar in feel to the original WAILERS – is always appealing. The comparison is well-founded too: they grew up in the same Trenchtown streets as The Wailers, were taught to sing by JOE HIGGS and, when signed to Studio One, even used to stand in for Peter and Bunny when they didn't turn up for rehearsal sessions with COXSONE. As one of the groups that survived the onset of dancehall, they are now big in America and, based in Washington, their sweet roots harmonies float over modern day rhythms as if nothing at all has changed.

Wild Suspense; Mango RRCD53

A re-release of their 1976 classic, finding them very much in Wailers mode – perky beat, punchy guitar riffs and lead 'n' backing vocal arrangements. But this isn't such a bad thing, given that among the tracklisting is 'Row Fisherman Row', 'Bredda Gravalicious' and 'Feel The Spirit'. Then, add to it seven previously unavailable dub cuts taken from the original album, and you've got quite a bargain.

Stranded; Greensleeves GRELCD 73

Nearly ten years on from Wild Suspense, this is the group easing into electronic sounds and meshing their very organic singing with the taut drums and keyboards that came to dominate mid-1980s reggae. And they do it with the kind of top-ranking style that made late-model roots such a viable proposition.

ALSO RECOMMENDED:

The Very Best Of The Wailing Souls; Greensleeves GRELCD99

Relatively recent material, combining their own productions with work by Henry 'Junjo' Lawes and Linval Thompson. Although it lacks some of the continuation of *Stranded* or *Firehouse Rock*, it is a worthwhile record of the group's 1980s phase.

Yabby U

(Born Vivian Jackson, 1953; Kingston, Jamaica; singer)
The most curious thing about Yabby was that in spite of his reputation for deep, doomy, fire-and-brimstone roots reggae with an unswerving devotion to the Rasta doctrine, he in fact practises a branch of Christianity very close to the Coptics of Northern Africa. As leader of The Prophets during the first half of the 1970s, he'd been instrumental in such roots classics as 'Chant Down Babylon', 'Run Come Rally' and 'Fire In Kingston'. But in 1975 he announced his solo status with the monumental 'Conquering Lion'. This not only set the style for his relentlessly righteous roots, but also provided his new stage name, for the chorus line went 'Yabby Yabby You/Be You/ Yabby Yabby You'. He went on to cut three vital albums – *Deliver Me From Mine Enemies*, *Chant Down Babylon* and *Conquering Lion* – before turning to production and adding extra dimension to such established toasters as Trinity, Tappa Zukie,

Jah Stitch and DILLINGER, plus bringing out the roots and culture in singers like Wayne Wade, Tony Tuff and Michael Rose.

King Tubby's Prophecy Of Dub; Blood And Fire BAFCD005

Dub cuts from the best of Yabby U, bringing us Tubby-ized versions of such crucial works as 'Conquering Lion', 'Run Come Rally' and 'Jah Vengeance'. While it's a pity none of the original albums is available in any other format than ludicrously expensive second-hand vinyl, this is a fascinating glimpse at what he was capable of. There are some densely constructed backing tracks that Tubby only barely penetrates and, in most cases, leaves far more multi-layered than you'd expect. But this is a good thing, as the booming deep beat, kicked up to steppers lightness by a flying cymbal and almost jazzy, intricately interwoven melodies, leaves Yabby's visions of dread blessedly intact without recourse to his vocals. Once more, it's a tribute to Tubby's skill and understanding that the vibe is completely untouched by all the rebuilding work that's gone on around it.

SEE ALSO:

Jammin'; Mango CIDM1010
Roots 'N' Culture; Music Club MCCD128
Beyond The Frontline; Frontline FRONT1
Tougher Than Tough – The Story Of Jamaican Music; Mango IBXCD1

VARIOUS ARTISTS

All-Time Reggae Hits; Charly CPCD8028

Eric Donaldson, Oh Cherry Oh Baby; **Festival 10**, Derrick Morgan; **Junior Byles**, Da Da; **Delroy Wilson**, Let There Be Love; **Bob Marley and The Wailers**, Duppy Conqueror; **The Natural Ites**, Picture On The Wall; **Dillinger**, Cocaine In My Brain; **Gregory Isaacs**, My Time; **Michael Prophet**, Rich Man Poor Man; **U-Brown**, Tu Sheng Pen; **Tony Tuff**, Sticky Wicket; **Don Carlos**, Nice Time (Late Night Blues); **Dennis Brown**, If I

Didn't Love You; **Al Campbell**, Bad Boy; **Errol Dunkley**, Betcha By Golly Wow; **Yellowman and Peter Metro**, The Girl Is Mine.

*Beyond The Frontline; Frontline FRONT1

Keith Hudson, Civilization; **Delroy Washington**, Freedom Fighters; **The Gladiators**, Looks Is Deceiving; **Prince Far-I**, Message From The King; **The Mighty Diamonds**, The Right Time; **U-Roy**, Wear You To The Ball; **Gregory Isaacs**, If I Don't Have You; **Big Youth**, Lightning Flash And The Weak Heart Drop; **Culture**, Behold; **U-Roy**, The Great Psalms; **The Twinkle Brothers**, Never Get Burn; **Johnny Clarke**, Declaration Of Rights; **Gregory Isaacs**, Universal Tribulation; **U-Roy**, Natty Rebel.

*Blow Mr Hornsman – Instrumental Reggae 1968-1975; Trojan CDTRL257

Carl 'Cannonball' Bryan, Jumping Jack; **Lester Sterling**, Super Special; **The Hippy Boys**, Death Rides; **Carl 'Cannonball' Bryan**, Run For Your Life; **The Soulmates**, On The Move; **The Crystalites**, Undertakers Burial; **Roland Alphonso And the Upsetters**, Roll On; **Joe Gibbs All Stars**, Franco Nero Version Two; **Jo Jo Bennett With Mudie's All Stars**, Leaving Rome; **Joe Gibbs All Stars**, Ghost Capturer; **Herman's All Stars**, Nightmare; **Val Bennett**, Judgement Warrant; **Augustus Pablo and Herman's All Stars**, East Of The River Nile; **Tommy McCook and The Impact All Stars**, Harvest In The East; **Carl Masters**, Va Va Voom; **Zap-Pow**, Broken Contract, **Skin Flesh and Bones**, Butter Fe Fish; **Vin Gordon**, If You're Ready (Come Go With Me).

*Classic Reggae Volume One; Profile PCD1434

Sugar Minnott, Good Thing Going; **The Pinchers**, Agony; **Rita Marley**, One Draw; **Johnny Osbourne**, Buddy Bye; **Barrington Levy**, Murderer; **Dillinger**, Cocaine In My Brain; **Tyrone Taylor**, Cottage In Negril; **Beres Hammond**, What One Dance Can Do; **The Tamlins**, Baltimore; **Half Pint**, Greetings; **Dennis Brown**, Sitting And Watching; **Gregory Isaacs**, Soon Forward.

Crucial Reggae; Island RRCD37

Pablo Moses, Music Is My Desire; **Inner Circle**, New Age Music; **Toots and The Maytals**, Just Like That; **Third World**, Saturday Evening, **Steel Pulse**, Reggae Fever; **Aswad**, Rainbow Culture, One Love Jamdown; **Freddie McGregor**, Jogging; **Black Uhuru**, Happiness; **Junior Tucker**, Some Guys Have All The Luck.

Jammin'; Mango CIDM1010

DISC ONE: **Bob Marley and The Wailers**, Jammin'; **Third World**, Now That We've Found Love; **Toots and The Maytals**, 54-46 (That's My Number); **Aswad**, Don't Turn Around; **Jimmy Cliff**, You Can Get It If You Really Want; **Kotch**, Wonderful Tonight; **The Slickers**, Johnny Too Bad; **Marcia Griffiths**, Electric Boogie; **Desmond Dekker**, The Israelites; **The Tamlins**, Baltimore; **Black Uhuru**, Somebody's Watching You; **The Pioneers**, Long Shot Kick De Bucket.

DISC TWO: **Sheila Hylton**, The Bed's Too Big Without You; **Jacob Miller**, All Night Till Daylight; **Jimmy Lindsay**, Easy; **Lorna Bennett**, Breakfast In Bed; **Owen Grey**, Guava Jelly; **The Heptones**, Book Of Rules; **Dennis Brown**, Sitting And Watching; **Junior Tucker**, Some Guys Have All The Luck; **Janet Kay**, Silly Games; **The Mighty Diamonds**, Pass The Kouchie; **Junior Murvin**, Police And Thieves.

Natty Rebel Roots; Frontline CDFL9103

The Gladiators, Let Jah Be Praised; **Gregory Isaacs**, Tune In; **Johnny Clarke**, Cry Tough; **U-Roy**, Natty Rebel; **Prince Far-I**, Throw Away Your Gun; **Prince Far-I**, Throw Away Your Gun Dub; **Johnny Clarke**, Declaration Of Rights; **The Gladiators**, We'll Find The Blessing; **U-Roy**, Do You Remember; **The Twinkle Brothers**, Jah Kingdom Come; **Dr Alimantado**, Slavery Let I Go; **Johnny Clarke**, Crazy Baldhead; **The Gladiators**, The Best Things In Life; **The Twinkle Brothers**, Praise Jah; **Prince Far-I**, Love Devine Dub; **Althea and Donna**, Uptown Top Ranking.

Nice An' Ruff – A Crucial Brew Of Roots, Dub And Rockers;
Music Club; MCCD 092

Black Uhuru, Sun Is Shining; **K.C. White**, No No No; **Gregory Isaacs**, Village Of The Under-privileged; **Dennis Brown**, Things In My Life; **The Abyssinians**, Y Mas Gan; **Albert Griffiths and The Gladiators**, Bongo Red; **Culture**, Rasta Capture; **Mutabaruka**, Set De Prisoners Free; **Augustus Pablo**, Dub Organizer; **I-Roy**, Maggie's Breast; **Lord Creator**, Kingston Town; **The Melodians**, Swing And Dine; **Gregory Isaacs**, Love Is Overdue; **The Meditations**, Woman Is Like A Shadow; **Horace Andy**, Girl I Love You; **Sugar Minott**, Good Thing Going; **The Tamlins**, Baltimore; **Sly and Robbie**, Triplet.

On A Reggae Tip; Island CIDTV5

Chaka Demus and Pliers, Tease Me; **Shabba Ranks**, Mr Loverman; **SL 2**, On A Ragga Tip; **Apache Indian**, Chokthere; **Material featuring Shabba Ranks**, Reality; **Maxi Priest**, One More Chance; **General Levy**, Heat; **Mad Cobra**, Flex; **Bob Marley and The Wailers**, Iron Lion Zion; **Aswad**, Don't Turn Around; **Inner Circle**, Everything Is Great; **Junior Murvin**, Police And Thieves; **Sly and Robbie**, Boops (Here To Go); **Sugar Minott**, Good Thing Going; **Third World**, Dancing On The Floor; **Maxi Priest**, Close To You; **Unitone Rockers**, Children Of The Revolution.

Planet Reggae; Charly CDINS5052

Peter Tosh, Get Up Stand Up; **Culture**, Good Things; **Black Uhuru**, Positive; **Yellowman**, Zungguzungguzungguzeng; **Dillinger**, Cocaine In My Brain; **Lee Perry and Prince Jazzbo**, The Prophet Live; **Peter Tosh**, Legalize It; **The Abyssinians**, Satta Massa Gana; **Gregory Isaacs**, Private Beach Party; **Third World**, Love Is Out To Get You; **The Itals**, Hallelujah; **Jimmy Cliff**, Reggae Night; **Bob Marley**, Soul Rebel; **Lucky Dube**, Slave; **LKJ**, Forces Of Victory; **Dennis Brown**, Money In My Pocket, **Burning Spear**, Money In My Pocket.

Pure Reggae; Island CIDTB8

DISC ONE: **Dawn Penn**, No No No; **Red Dragon with Brian and Tony Gold**, Compliments On Your Kiss; **David Morales and The Bad Yard Club featuring Papa San**, The Program; **Aswad**, Shine; **Born Jamericans**, Boom Shack-a-Tack; **Chaka Demus and Pliers and The Taxi Gang**, Twist And Shout; **C.J. Lewis**, Sweets For My Sweet; **Bitty McLean**, Dedicated To The One I Love; **Daddy Screw and Donovan Style, Lloyd Brown and Tipper Irie**, Stress (Miserable Woman); **Beenie Man**, No Mama No Cry; **General Saint featuring Don Campbell**, Oh Carol!; **Inner Circle**, Sweat (A La La La La Long); **Snow**, Informer; **Apache Indian**, Boom Shack A Lack; **General Grant**, Call Me.

DISC TWO: **Aswad**, Don't Turn Around; **Third World**, Now That We've Found Love; **Toots and The Maytals**, 54-46 (That's My Number); **Desmond Dekker and The Aces**, The Israelites; **The Slickers**, Johnny Too Bad; **Jimmy Cliff**, You Can Get It If You Really Want; **The Skatalites**, Guns Of Navarone; **The Melodians**, Rivers Of Babylon; **The Pioneers**, Long Shot Kick De Bucket; **The Heptones**, Book Of Rules; **Lorna Bennett**, Breakfast In Bed; **Owen Grey**, Guava Jelly; **Junior Murvin**, Police And Thieves; **Janet Kay**, Silly Games; **Black Uhuru**, Somebody's Watching You; **Sheila Hylton**, The Bed's Too Big Without You; **Dennis Brown**, Sitting And Watching; **Gregory Isaacs**, Night Nurse.

Reggae Classics – Serious Selection Volume One; Rewind Selecta CDREG2

The Royal Rasses, Love It The Way It Should Be; **The In Crowd**, Back A Yard; **Prince Allah**, Bucket Bottom; **Dennis Brown**, Here I Come; **Junior Byles**, Fade Away; **Motion**, No Man Is An Island; **Freddie McGregor**, Natural Collie; **John Holt**, Time Is The Master; **Jimmy Lindsay**, East; **Delroy Wilson**, I'm Still Waiting; **Matumbi**, The Man In Me; **Alton Ellis**, Mr Ska Beena.

Reggae Refreshers Volume Two; Island/Mango RRCDS102

The Wailing Souls, Very Well; **Fabienne Miranda**, Prophecy; **Michael Prophet**, Gates Of Zion; **The Heptones**, Mr President;

Black Uhuru, Botanical Roots; **Steel Pulse**, Handsworth Revolution; **Ijahman**, Heavy Load; **Max Romeo**, One Step Forward; **The Upsetters featuring Prince Jazzbo**, Croaking Lizard; **Burning Spear**, Invasion; **Junior Byles**, Fade Away; **Linton Kwesi Johnson**, Independent Intavenshan; **Gregory Isaacs**, The Border (live version); **Sly and Robbie featuring Junior Delgado**, Jail Break; **Aswad**, Dub Fire; **Jah Lion**, Sata.

*Roots and Culture – Serious Selection Volume One; Rewind Selecta CDREG3

Fred Locks, True Rastaman (So Jah Seh); **Dennis Brown**, Wolf And Leopards; **The Abyssinians**, Forward To Zion; **The In Crowd**, His Majesty Is Coming; **Faybienne Miranda**, Prophecy; **Ras Ibuna**, Diverse Doctrine; **Jacob Miller**, Tenement Yard; **Sugar Minott**, Rough Old Life; **The Royal Rasses**, Kingston 11, **Burning Spear**, Marcus Garvey; **Wayne Wade**, Black Is Out Colour; **Aswad**, Back To Africa.

*Roots 'N' Culture; Music Club MCCD128

The Mighty Diamonds, Right Time; **Big Youth**, Train To Rhodesia; **Peter Tosh**, Legalize It; **Johnny Clarke**, Rockers Time Now; **Culture**, International Herb; **The Twinkle Brothers**, Never Get Burn; **Gregory Isaacs**, Universal Tribulation; **The Abyssinians**, Jah Loves; **Prince Far I**, Message From The King; **The Gladiators**, Soul Rebel; **Big Youth**, The House Of Dreadlocks; **The Twinkle Brothers**, Free Africa; **The Tamlins with Sly Dunbar**, Sun Is Shining; **Johnny Clarke**, Roots Natty Roots Natty Congo; **Culture**, Behold; **Johnny Clarke**, Declaration Of Rights; **The Gladiators**, Looks Is Deceiving; **Delroy Washington**, Freedom Fighters; **The Twinkle Brothers**, Since I Threw The Comb Away; **The Mighty Diamonds**, Africa; **Linton Kwesi Johnson**, It Dread Inna Inglan.

*Roots Rockers; Attack CDAT112

Bob Marley, Soul Rebel; **Ken Boothe**, I Shot The Sheriff; **Linval Thompson**, Negrea African Dub; **Charlie Chaplin**, Skanky Producer; **John Holt**, The Time Is High; **Marie Pierre**, Walk

Away; **Mickey Dread**, Dread Combination; **Prince Far-I**, The Chosen One; **Jimmy Cliff**, Miss Jamaica; **Ras Michael**, Unity; **Susan Cadogan**, Nice And Easy; **Barrington Levy**, Don't Give Up; **Greyhound**, Funky Jamaica; **Barry Brown**, Jah Jah Fire; **The Upsetters**, The Return Of Django; **Horace Faith**, Black Pearl.

The Stars Of Reggae Sunsplash; Charley CPCD8025

Chalice, Vital Love; **Bunny Wailer**, Sound Clash; **Aswad**, I Need Your Loving (Need Your Love); **U-Roy**, Rule The Nation; **Gregory Isaacs**, What A Feeling; **Pat Kelly**, Talk About Love; **Eric Donaldson**, Sweet Jamaica; **Alton Ellis**, I'm Still In Love; **Blood Fire Posse**, Do You Feel Like Dancing; **Shinehead**, The Real Rock; **Josey Wales**, Let Off; **Dennis Brown**, It's Magic; **Dennis Brown and John Holt**, Wild Fire; **Shabba Ranks**, Hardcore Reggae, Going To A Fair; **Inner Circle**, Bad Boys.

Time Warp Dub Clash – Old School vs New School; Mango CIDM1105

The Paragons, Indiana James (The Man Next Door); **Ijahman**, Whip That Tarantula (Moulding); **Black Uhuru**, The Monkey Is A Spy (Sensimilla); **Burning Spear**, Pit Of Snakes (Social Living); **Wailing Souls**, Well Of Souls (Feel The Spirit); **The Viceroys**, Dub Of Gold (Heart Made Of Stone); **Black Uhuru**, Convoy Hijack (Sponji Reggae); **Junior Delgado**, Bazooka Blast (Fort Augustus); **Black Uhuru**, Fire and Brimstone (Journey); **Mad Professor**, Dub So Hard; **Manesseh**, Absentee; **Jah Shaka**, Smiling Dub; **Alpha and Omega**, One Prayer; **Mixman**, Zulu Warrior; **Mixman**, Warrior Dance; **Alpha and Omega**, Rastafari; **Dub Syndicate**, What Happened?

Tougher Than Tough – The Story Of Jamaican Music; Mango IBXCD1

•→ DISC THREE: *Natty Sing Hit Songs 1975–1981*
The Heptones, Country Boy; **I-Roy**, Welding; **Burning Spear**, Marcus Garvey; **The Mighty Diamonds**, Right Time; **Roman Stewart**, Natty Sing Hit Songs; **Leroy Smart**, Ballistic Affair; **Jacob Miller**, Tenement Yard; **Max Romeo**, War Inna Babylon;

Junior Murvin, Police and Thieves; **Culture**, Two Sevens Clash; **Delroy Wilson**, I'm Still Waiting; **Bob Marley and The Wailers**, No Woman No Cry; **Althea and Donna**, Uptown Top Ranking; **Gregory Isaacs**, Number One; **The Wailing Souls**, Bredda Grevalicious; **Sugar Minott**, River Jordan; **Willie Williams**, Armagideon Time; **Black Uhuru**, Guess Who's Coming To Dinner; **Junior Delgado**, Fort Augustus; **Freddie McGregor**, Joggin', **Dennis Brown**, Sitting and Watching. ↔

This four-CD set has yet to put a foot wrong.

4

DANCEHALL TAKE-OVER

After the death of Bob Marley in 1981 reggae was thrown into something of a tailspin. The major labels lost the interest they'd had in the 1970s, and gradually abandoned their searches for 'the new Bob Marley'.

But at grass roots level a revolution was taking place, as the musical ideas from the 1970s sounded increasingly tired. Subject matter was shifting from Jah Rastafari to prowess between the sheets. Production values were changing as computers were given far greater prominence in the studio. And deejays began taking over from the singers as the new, faster digital rhythms created a generation of toasters with machine gun-rapid diction.

But essentially, it could still be related to 'real' reggae – the musical structures were the same and the computers were doing little more than imitating 'regular' instruments. Until 'Under Mi Sleng Teng' in 1985. A catchy little tune, recorded by Wayne Smith and produced by Prince Jammy, it changed the face of reggae. It didn't have a bassline. The basic riff was played out on a cheap Casio keyboard, and it was this riff with a drum track that drove the song. It was the move the post-roots reggae industry had been looking for – now they had something that was theirs alone. (Interestingly, unlike the previous three sections, very few performers or producers cross over into this era.)

The song was versioned countless times, until the new breed began to use it as a starting point for digital adventures that became so far removed from the traditional reggae bloodline it was difficult to see (or hear) any connection other than geographical. The studio became a playground for self-sufficient computer-literate producers who would bring a deejay in to voice a track once it was finished. This was not unlike the very early days of the Jamaican music business, with artists recording stupid numbers of tracks for almost as many labels. Only this time technology meant space and cost were far less crucial, so tiny (literally) studios sprang up all over Kingston. And, once again, this created a singles-oriented market, with the sound systems ruling supreme as the ideal showcase for these deejay recordings.

But unlike that bygone era, subject matter was diametrically removed from any notions of roots and culture or peace and love. As the 1980s progressed into the 1990s, the music underwent name changes from digital (for obvious reasons), through ragga (an abbreviation of 'raggamuffin', in recognition of the latter-day rude boys that followed the sounds), to dancehall (because it was a style for the sound systems rather than the concert stages), while the lyrics evolved into two categories. Slackness took the traditional good-humoured bawdiness to quite unpleasant levels; while 'gun lyrics' were exactly that, songs written glorifying the artillery that had flooded the Kingston ghettos in the late 1980s.

Many linked this new outlook with the rise of crack cocaine and prominence of gangsta rap in the USA, but the truth is probably closer to the turnaround of the sociopolitical situation during the previous ten years. Steady economic decline since the end of the 1960s had created ever-worsening poverty. The underlying optimism of the roots era was a thing of the past. The political gunmen of the 1970s – the posses – were now surplus to requirements, and those who hadn't travelled to New York to set up in the drugs business looked on armed confrontation as a way of life (drastically reduced police budgets for West Kingston's slums didn't help matters). And the music of the ghettoes reflected this grim reality. It should be remembered, when passing judgement on even the most unpleasant dancehall records, that these are of-the-moment singles, created for instant gratification within a certain context.

Not that any of this excuses some of the crimes committed against music. As dancehall progressed, it became more and more extreme. As the computerization was not shackled by human capabilities, the speeds and structures of the tracks could be pushed to limits that were way beyond what most people considered to be reggae. In fact, the music on this side of the Sleng Teng Divide had become unrecognizable as having anything to do with, say, Duke Reid. And as this evolution took place at a staggering pace, styles, singles and artists were being confined to the dumper as soon as something, or someone, new came along – which was often merely a week or two.

Curiously, while this ensured ragga stayed as a singles-only, sound system-orientated form, the major US record companies began taking an interest in reggae more than ever before. Largely, this was because hip hop acts (notably East Coast groups) had started to incorporate dancehall rhythms into their repertoires (a duet with a Jamaican toaster wasn't unusual on an American rap album in 1992 or 1993), and in turn Jamaican producers were using many of the same sounds and samples as the rappers. But this was never a particularly easy union, and too often the albums culture of the New York record companies – with its inbuilt lengthy gestations – worked against the string of quick singles that reggae acts were geared up to. In several high-profile cases, what made the act special was sacrificed as lumbering schedules removed any immediacy the records might have had.

However, everything was about to change once more. In 1994, in answer to the rising tide of urban violence, Kingston's new police chief began closing down sound systems that played gun records. At the same time the prospect of big-bucks US recording contracts meant the slackness and general misogyny was toned down. But as far as the music was concerned it had taken itself up a blind alley. Computerization and beats per minute had gone so far they had distanced the music from the people it was supposed to be impressing, and the only way forwards was backwards.

Halfway through the 1990s, amid a growing resurgence of 1970s reggae, 'new roots music' began to be produced. Rasta was returning in a big way – presumably as some sort of spiritual backlash to the nihilism of previous years – and while the computers began to turn out 'proper' tunes, so session musicians began to find their diaries filling up again. This seems to be opening reggae up wide again, with more accessible music and mainstream record company support as artists begin making albums once more.

Where it will go is anybody's guess. But you can bet if Duke Reid is watching he's probably rocking to the rhythms of guys like Luciano, the reconstructed Buju Banton and Brian and Tony Gold.

NOTE:
Because of the nature of this most recent development in reggae, there is actually far more music from previous ages available on CD. Dancehall was such a singles-orientated form that much of it either never got as far as CD or only made it on a compilation album. Quite rightly too in many cases, as entire albums of the same deejay with the same producer are often more than even their mothers would want. Also, because the artist turnover is so rapid, the number of acts that have made a lasting contribution to the development of the music or simply achieved something beyond a couple of hit singles are few and far between. Hence the Various Artists compilation section in this chapter seems disproportionately long. But it really is the best way to approach so much dancehall. Details of what compilations particular acts appear on are absent in all but a few cases, and this is because it's quite a small clique of artists appearing on just about all of the CDs involved, so to list them would be counter-productive.

Buju Banton

(Born Mark Myrie, 1973; Kingston, Jamaica; deejay)
At the start of the 1990s, there was no more vivid an example of the sheer, dumb nihilism that epitomized dancehall reggae than Buju Banton. The 'Boom Bye Bye' controversy of a few years ago – the record appeared to endorse the shooting of homosexuals – was just the tip of a deeply unpleasant iceberg as the deejay revealed attitudes towards society in general that made Snoop Doggy Dogg seem like the sort of guy you'd want as a babysitter. But meet Buju Banton today and he's the perfect role model for how dancehall reggae can have a sense of purpose, how roots sentiment can be lyrically expressed within this medium and, perhaps most importantly, how it's possible to reclaim the harsh sounds and tempos of dancehall in the second half of the decade

and make them sound like reggae again – without losing their modern flavour.

In other words, Buju Banton is the man most likely to come through the present deejay climate with his career intact, or even as the man who brings dancehall into the international mainstream with greater effect than just a few novelty hits. Over the last couple of years he's matured at an astonishing rate – both artistically and otherwise. He's now a devout follower of Rastafari, speaks out against social injustice, he writes more love songs than sex songs, has injected his dancehall rhythms with genuine soul to make them more accessible to the world beyond Jamaica, puts on a truly dynamic stage show and has landed a large international recording contract. Did somebody say the new BOB MARLEY?

A sound system deejay since the age of thirteen, with a recording career that began soon after, Buju Banton ('Buju' is a childhood nickname meaning chubby, while 'Banton' is local slang for an accomplished story-teller) had to wait the best part of five years for success. Until his voice changed into the hoarsely expressive instrument it remains today. Once his career took off, though, there was little stopping it – tunes cut with such top producers as PHILIP BURRELL, BOBBY DIGITAL and DONOVAN GERMAIN meant he all but dominated the Jamaican charts – even the 'Boom Bye Bye' affair did little to affect his local popularity.

However, it *was* excluding him from the enormous international acclaim that seemed to be waiting as major labels began, belatedly, to sign ragga stars, and it was only after a public apology that his deal with Mercury in New York was finalized. Whether this acted as a catalyst for the Buju Banton attitude rethink is not known, but he began growing dreadlocks and reappraised his role in life with 'humble' as the hardest working adjective. Given the quality of his latest work, his obvious intelligence as to how to reach a wider audience without sacrificing his roots, and the fact that he is only twenty-four, it's very likely Buju Banton is the face of reggae's future. At this point it would be wrong not to forgive him the mistakes of a naïve seventeen-year-old who, at that time, never viewed his work as existing outside its West Kingston environment.

'Til Shiloh; Loose Cannon 524135-2

Succeeding totally as an album, this is dancehall reggae at its most mature (so far). Classy from its packaging through to its production and performance, these Donovan Germain and Dave Kelly productions rewrite the book of variety and subtlety in this genre. The sixteen tracks reintroduce the idea of a studio band (complete with horns), create a ragga beat out of Rasta-style percussion on the stunning ''Til I'm Laid To Rest', slow things down to an acoustic folk song at one point and aren't afraid of a good old dancehall tear-up. All of this while adding the most musical qualities yet to Buju's fruity growl.

Voice Of Jamaica; Mercury 518013-2

The transitionary album, recorded in 1993. By now the subject matter had matured into responsibility as the tunes deal with ghetto violence, heavy-handed authorities and Rastafari. But the music is nowhere near as three-dimensional as *'Til Shiloh*.

Beenie Man

(Born Anthony David, 1972; Kingston, Jamaica; deejay)
When Beenie Man's first album, *The Incredible Ten Year Old Wonder*, caused a dancehall sensation in 1986, it was proof that Jamaica's love of a child star was as strong as ever. Not that the diminutive deejay didn't deserve the acclaim – he'd been active on the Kingston sound system scene since the tender age of seven, as his fast, liquid, surprisingly big-voiced style had been rocking crowds at some of the largest dances. And when he started recording a year later, he'd had a Jamaican number 1, 'Too Fancy', before his ninth birthday.

But Beenie Man is also a vivid example of how 'gun lyrics' more or less took over reggae as the 1980s rolled into the 1990s. Because Beenie Man refused to write such songs, preferring instead to address social injustice, and in spite of his enormous reputation as a live sound system performer, during his teenage years his recording career never seemed to live up to that early promise.

Then he compromised his ideals and was almost immediately drawn into a war of words with up-and-coming dancehall dee-jay BOUNTY KILLER – each accused the other of stealing their style – which became the focus for dancehall reggae during 1993. Beenie Man seemed to emerge the clear winner, or as close to it as was ever likely, and by the end of 1994 he was one of the biggest stars in Jamaica.

At which point, he had the intelligence to revert back to lyrics of a far more agreeable nature: love, the dance, injustice and even the odd hymn to Rastafari. Beenie Man's current output is, like that of so many dancehall artists, astonishingly prolific but not nearly as patchy as many of his peers. While this is partly down to experience – when he released 'Veteran', he was only twenty-two but would not have been prosecuted under the Trades Descriptions Act – it's got a lot more to do with his voice. While this has retained all the lyrical dexterity of his youth, it has matured into an instrument of seductive rawness, deceptively rich both in tone and the musicalness of his delivery. Coupled with how the deejay shifts so easily from pure dancehall energy to roots to lovers' to the occasional sassy put-down of a rival, as he moves around Jamaica's better producers, Beenie Man will survive way beyond dancehall.

Blessed; Island Jamaica IMJCD3005
Guns Out; Greensleeves GRELCD

As is the nature of this style, in spite of Beenie Man's prodigious output, there are relatively few albums on release. These two are undoubtedly the best. The first is a collection of largely Shocking Vibes productions, featuring SLY DUNBAR and BRIAN AND TONY GOLD, and the tracklisting shows Beenie's full range as it veers from mild slackness ('Slam', 'Tear Off Mi Garment') to true righteousness ('Blessed', 'Freedom') and from hardcore beatbox to the vividly tuneful. *Guns Out* is a studio translation of his sound system clashes with Bounty Killer – each take six tracks, and it includes Beenie's enormous hit 'Foreign Minded'.

SEE ALSO:

It would be quicker to list the ragga compilations which Beenie Man didn't appear on, but tracks that should be looked out for are: 'No Mama No Cry' – an adaptation of the BOB MARLEY classic – on *Hail Up The Taxi* – *Sly and Robbie Present The Taxi Gang* (Island Jamaica IJCD3002); 'Dis Di Program' on *Ragga Ragga Ragga! Two* (Greensleeves GRELCD204); 'Under Mi Sensi' on *Barrington Levy's DJ Counteraction* (Greensleeves GRELCD216); and 'Praise Him' on *Conscious Ragga Volume One* (Greensleeves GRELCD216).

Bounty Killer

(Born Rodney Price, 1972; Kingston, Jamaica; deejay)
BEENIE MAN's arch rival, since the enormous similarities in style and delivery – the only noticeable difference being that Bounty Killer's voice is more on the booming side – has prompted regular accusations of plagiarism from both camps. Continuing the reggae tradition of naming deejays in the style of the glamorous badman, even at nine-years-old Bounty Killer was impressing crowds at his local Trenchtown sound system dance with his larger-than-life stage persona. He didn't start recording until nearly ten years later though, voicing his first tunes at JAMMY'S in 1990, under the name Bounty Hunter, and with Jammy's brother Trevor 'Uncle T' James at the controls rather than the King himself. That was enough, however, and as the Hunter became the Killer, he set off on a recording career that has stuck with the same studio but oscillated between 'Uncle T' and a producer called John John who, just to keep it in the family, is Jammy's son.

Naturally enough, with a name like that there were a good deal of gun lyrics on offer – Bounty's on-the-mic catchphrase is 'People dead!', and although it simply describes his mashing up the crowd and seeing off of rivals, tracks like 'Gunshot Fi Informer' and 'Gun Thirsty' were less good natured.

However, Bounty Killer has survived the clampdown on sound systems that supported gun lyrics – in 1994, Kingston's new police chief began shutting down outfits that continued to play such records or employ such deejays – because he's had no trouble going beyond such behaviour. Now, with humour, a social conscience, sheer bravado and his resonantly melodic tones, Bounty Killer is recording on his own label (still produced by John John and 'Uncle T') and starting to win acclaim beyond Jamaica and the darker part of the UK.

**Jamaica's Most Wanted*; Greensleeves GRELCD195
**Down In The Ghetto*; Greensleeves GRELCD210

The first is Bounty's debut album and comes loaded with hits – 'Man Ah Suffer', 'Roots Reality And Culture' and 'Gun Thirsty', to name but three. The last of these is Bounty in post-gun mood, and the title track, a blistering condemnation of life in the ghetto, sets the pace for some thoughtful and highly entertaining lyrics, making up some of the best-known ragga tracks of recent times.

ALSO RECOMMENDED:

*Guns Out; Greensleeves GRELCD

The sound clash album with Beenie Man, in which each deejay takes six tracks and comparisons become obvious (see also page 321).

SEE ALSO:

Any compilation involving mostly Jammy's tunes is bound to involve Bounty Killer, but some killer tracks can be found on: *Greensleeves Sampler Ten* (Greensleeves GREZ10) – 'Down In The Ghetto'; *Greensleeves Sampler Twelve* (Greensleeves GREZ12) – 'Cellular Phone'; *Ragga Ragga Ragga! Two* (Greensleeves GREL204) – 'Not Another Word' and 'Nuh Have No Heart'; *Conscious Ragga Volume One* (Greensleeves GRELCD220) – 'Book Book'.

Philip 'Fatis' Burrell

(Born 1962; Kingston, Jamaica; producer)
If you take a journey to the outer limits of reggae, you'll find Philip Burrell and his Xterminator label waiting there for you. It's an apt name too, as the rhythms coming out of his studio are the hardest, sparsest, most uncompromising beats to find their way on to record and still be called reggae. Witness his work with CAPLETON, Tiger, BUJU BANTON and COCOA TEA in

the first half of the 1990s. The most remarkable thing about Xterminator productions is how they manage to retain the idea of reggae – albeit a radical dancehall strain – while stripping the instrumentation down to two or three different percussion tracks. And this is all thanks to Burrell's handling of the vocals. Working with artists as adverse as FRANKIE PAUL and Tiger, he will pull such a performance out of the act that they can dictate the vibe of the track, while his rhythms concentrate on keeping up the sense of raw sound system dance excitement – it's not surprising Burrell is among the pioneers of live dancehall recordings. He'll manage this whether the artist concerned is singing, toasting or in combination, and whether the material is slackness, roots or simply a dancehall self-celebration, with a sense of rhythmic timing and an ability to balance the sounds so that neither infringes on the other.

When Burrell started off the studios in the early 1980s, he worked with musicians and singers as well as deejays, cutting pretty conventional digital reggae and dub mixes, and this experience he's now bringing to bear as dancehall moves into its next phase. However wild and on-the-edge an Xterminator record might be, it remains innately melodic, and therefore intriguing in the same way the dub masters of the 1970s pulled you into their work.

Xterminator; VP Records VPCD1368

Nadine Sutherland, If You Are Going To Go; **Sanchez**, Another Sad Love Song; **Marcia Griffiths**, He Will See Through You; **Luciano**, One Way Ticket; **Luckie D**, New Direction; **Sanchez**, Never Keeping Secrets; **Luciano**, Give Thanks; **Sanchez**, Forever; **Brian and Tony Gold**, Crazy; **Frankie Paul**, Ram Jam; **Beres Hammond**, Send For Me; **Singing Sweet**, Million To One; **Brian and Tony Gold**, Sitting And Waiting; **Sanchez**, Kiss Me Honey; **Freddie McGregor**; Ease Off; **Tony Rebel and Marcia Griffiths**, Treat Me Like A Lady.

The most openly tuneful side of Xterminator, only glimpsed on other albums. Put together in one compilation it almost sounds like lovers' rock. Without sacrificing any of Burrell's natural energy, though.

As well as the artists mentioned above, Philip Burrell has produced just about every modern reggae act. The following are merely a selection of the more interesting albums he has added his name to and it's best to check sleeve credits.

Frankie Paul: *Warning*; Ras RASCD307
Beres Hammond: *Full Attention*; Charm CRCD17
Capleton: *Alms House*; Greensleeves GRELCD182
Sanchez: *Boom Boom Bye Bye*; Greensleeves GRELCD186

Capleton

(Born Clifton Bailey, 1974; Kingston, Jamaica; deejay)

Back in 1992 Capleton was one of the first deejays to make an impact on the dancehall with records questioning the general state of things – i.e. that performers were getting shot with alarming regularity, and that the guns and slackness ethos was getting a little out of hand. Audiences seemed to listen too, and so this previous king of the rude rhyme appeared to reinvent himself. He even did a few records that discussed love in terms other than the purely physical. And his breathless, light style works excellently in combination, providing a counterpoint that actually works with the singers instead of merely intimidating them. Then he recorded an atrocious single called 'Buggering'.

Thankfully, Capleton is now hooked up with GUSSIE CLARKE who not only won't stand for that sort of record, but has the musical sensibilities to bring the best out of the artist.

Alms House; Greensleeves GRELCD182

Produced for Xterminator Productions, this pushes dancehall deejaying firmly back towards 'music' by introducing the notion of a bassline – albeit a very percussive bassline – to drive the rhythms. Furthermore, it employs Cat Coore, SLY DUNBAR and Robbie Lyn as studio musicians, to create tracks that go from the bouncy, deeply structured 'G.C.T.' and 'Them A Go Run', to the sparsest of numbers such as the title track. But in every instance there's a lightness of touch to Capleton's voice that sees him riding the beats rather than being dragged along by them, and it's this and his open versatility that makes him one of the most interesting dancehall deejays. This album contains the hits 'Unno No Hear', 'Make Hay' and 'Mate A Dead'.

Chaka Demus and Pliers

(Born John Taylor, 1965, Kingston, Jamaica, deejay; born Everton Banner, 1965, Kingston, Jamaica, singer)
The best known and the most endearing example of the 'combination' craze – a singer and a deejay sharing the same tune – Chaka Demus and Pliers' light touch and pop-friendly dancehall rhythms, courtesy of SLY AND ROBBIE, have seen them top charts all over the world. The curious thing about them is that neither party had a great deal of success as a solo artist, in spite of recording for several years with different producers before they decided to team up (after sharing the bill on a reggae show in Miami in 1991). They are a classic illustration of how the style works, as they obviously record together, rather than one voicing the second part on an already completed track. Whether or not they outlast the faddishness of the mainstream market with their homecrowd credibility intact remains to be seen.

At the time of writing, the duo's *Tease Me* album – featuring the hits 'Murder She Wrote', 'Tease Me' and 'Twist And Shout' – has just been taken off catalogue, but should still be possible to find. Meanwhile, the three hits crop up on numerous Mango compilations and a BOBBY DIGITAL-produced Chaka Demus solo set from 1992, *Gal Wine*, has just been reissued (Vine Yard VYCD7).

Gussie Clarke

(Born 1953; Kingston, Jamaica; producer)
Looking improbably young, given his twenty-something years in the Kingston music business, Gussie Clarke is one of the junctions where old-style roots reggae meets the modern digital variety. Growing up around the Kingston sound systems and recording studios – as a teenager his first job was as a disc-

cutter – it was only a matter of time before Clarke got involved on a more creative level. But few could have imagined he would enter at such a high level: his first production was U-ROY's 'The Higher The Mountain' single, and the first albums he cut were both works of genius – BIG YOUTH's *Screaming Target* and *Presenting I-Roy*. And this was all before he'd turned twenty-one.

But curiously, although he was highly respected as a producer of top-quality reggae, he never really exploited his skills. During the roots reggae era of the 1970s, and into the increasingly digital 1980s, he spent far more time building up his record wholesale and disc cutting businesses, pausing only to put out the occasional killer tune by the likes of AUGUSTUS PABLO, THE MIGHTY DIAMONDS, GREGORY ISAACS and DENNIS BROWN.

Then in 1988 he opened Music Works, his own fully digital, state-of-the-art studio and turned to full-time production, announcing himself with 'Rumours' by Gregory Isaacs. The record not only revived the singer's career but it – and JC Lodge's version of it, 'Telephone Love' – were such enormous hits in Jamaica, the US and the UK that suddenly Clarke was the producer everybody wanted to work with. (The 'Rumours' rhythm went on to provide the basis for one of the most successful single-rhythm albums of that era.)

Clarke was special because he had an understanding of how reggae worked that had been formed in a era when the music, on the whole, was far more subtle and complex, and required enormous attention to fine detail. And now he was applying it to his computerized set-up, with equal care and pursuit of perfection. But most importantly, it had all the soul and spine-tingling excitement of his early work with the roots deejays. Over the next three years hits flowed, by artists like Home T, SUGAR MINOTT, COCOA TEA, SHABBA RANKS, JOHNNY OSBOURNE and, of course, Gregory Isaacs.

As the 1990s got underway though, Clarke opted to drop out of production once more, concentrating on his business interests and building a new studio in Kingston. Talk is, he's now ready to get back into the frontline of music production, and should never be underestimated as a man who can bring an old-time roots vibe to the most modern of environments.

Music Works Showcase 1988 And 1989; Greensleeves GRELCD503

Lady G, Nuff Respect; **Ken Boothe**, Choice; **Dean Frazer**, Snacking; **The Mighty Diamonds**, Heavy Load; **Home T**, Single Life; **JC Lodge**, Telephone Love; **Josey Wales**, Hustling; **Robbie Lyn**, Sweet Talk; **Hopeton Lindo**, Lonely Night; **Dennis Dreary**, Ecstasy; **Shabba Ranks**, No Bother Dis; **JC Lodge**, Give A Little Love; **Sugar Minott and Little Twitch**, Funking Song; **The Mighty Diamonds**, Bad Boy Business; **Dean Frazer**, Pick Of The Past; **Gregory Isaacs and Josey Wales**, Mind You Dis; **Nadine Sutherland**, Mr Hard To Please; **Jackie Mittoo**, Space Flight; **Johnny Osbourne**, Struggle Ha Fi Gwan; **Rebel Rockers**, Keep It Coming.

A comprehensive selection of Gussie Clarke productions from this period can also be found on the early volumes of the *Greensleeves Sampler* series.

Cocoa Tea

(Born Calvin Scott, 1969; Kingston, Jamaica; singer)
Possessor of the sweetest voice on the dancehall circuit, Cocoa Tea appears to be one of the most criminally underrated singers currently recording. Other artists are well aware of his talents, as there seems no shortage of deejays cutting sides with him in combination – GUSSIE CLARKE even put together the vocal trio of Cocoa, Home T and SHABBA RANKS around the dread-locked deejay's plaintive falsetto. But even after the brilliant *Riker's Island* album, Cocoa T's solo career just doesn't seem to be able to fulfill its potential. Perhaps this is because for so long his delicate, deeply conscious approach to music has been at odds with dancehall's brashness. But with the right producer it's a real treat. Maybe now, as the tide is turning slightly and he's doing tracks like the wonderfully melodic 'Babylon Burning', Cocoa Tea will live up to expectations.

Riker's Island; Greensleeves GRELCD156
Kingston Hot; Greensleeves GRELCD174

A stunning testament to Cocoa's vocal abilities, as each set swoops between smooth roots material, soulful lovers' rock and uncompromising reality lyrics all delivered in the classiest of upper-register croons. Maybe the former just has the edge with 'Hunting In The Ghetto', 'Riker's Island', 'Bad Bwoy' and 'Fool In Love'. *Kingston Hot*, produced by HENRY 'JUNJO' LAWES, features 'Jump And Spread', 'My Girl' and 'Posse Up'.

Bobby Digital

(Born Robert Dixon, 1966; Kingston, Jamaica; producer)
For a while, back in the mid-1980s, it looked as if KING TUBBY's bloodline wasn't going to survive into the new generation of Jamaican music. Then in 1988 Bobby Digital set up Digital B, his own studio and label, and suddenly dancehall made that connection once more. It's not as if the dancehall producer built up bone-crunching, head-spinning dubs or anything like that, but his music had the same vibe as King Tubby's inasmuch as it took the current trend, pushed it a little bit further, but made sure it didn't forget what it was supposed to be – a tune. Bobby Digital's reggae was every bit as electronic as his name might suggest, but inside the hard rhythms it was never less than musical and revived the notion of a bassline as being the root from which the rest grows. Digital B was where the likes of MAD COBRA, Penny Irie and Tony Rebel started out; where GREGORY ISAACS and JOHNNY OSBOURNE gave their careers a boost; where GAR-NETT SILK got his start; and where SHABBA RANKS had his first hits after several years with other producers.

It's hardly surprising that Digital should have such a Tubby-like quality to his productions, as his heritage can be traced directly back to the late Mr Ruddock: Bobby Digital learned his craft apprenticed to KING JAMMY, who in turn did his training under King Tubby. Digital had studied electronics as a teenager and took a job as Jammy's studio engineer, but was always far more interested in the creative side of things rather than the purely technical – not that the two were that far apart in 1985. Over the next three years he learned all aspects of record production and became the operation's second-in-charge, contributing enormously to the hits that flowed from that studio. Which was when he met Shabba. Although the deejay himself wasn't too successful at that studio at that time, he struck up a close friendship with Digital, eventually talking him into leaving and setting up his own operation. And together they immediately scored hits with 'Peenie Peenie' and 'Maama Man', both recuts of songs Shabba had first recorded at Jammy's.

As Shabba Ranks went on to much greater things at Digital B, the impact he had on the dancehall scene was enormous, and enough to secure Bobby Digital as one of the genre's top three producers – COCOA TEA, Terror Fabulous, BUJU BANTON, SHAGGY and Tiger have all recorded there. But this was only part of the picture. Essentially, Bobby Digital was a music lover, and after making his name he wanted to find a singing equivalent to Shabba Ranks, to take dancehall reggae into a whole new area. In 1992 he succeeded in spectacular style when he produced the debut album for Garnett Silk, a wonderful singer and a devout young Rasta, and so precipitated one of today's reggae's strongest trends, digital roots music.

Although never as high profile as his previous employer, Bobby Digital's place in modern reggae cannot be overestimated. Today, he still turns out top-quality, exciting dancehall without losing that tuneful edge, and it is testament to his standing that even after artists have left his label for big-time US deals, they still come back to Digital B to have him produce them.

Operation D; Digital B DBTXCD2

Cocoa Tea, Holy Mount Zion; **Shabba Ranks**, Think Yuh Having It All; **Pinchers**, Indian Defenders; **Spragga Benz**, You Know She Wrong; **Admiral Tibet**, The Righteous; **Tony Rebel**, Jah See Them A Come; **Twiggy**, Lady; **Bounty Killer**, Woman Fi Pet; **Jah Mali**, Brimstone And Fire; **Terror Fabulous**, Defend; **Sanchez**, Leave Out Of Babylon; **Brian and Tony Gold and Daddy Screw**, Angel Body.

About as fine an example as you're going to get of the true versatility of the man they call Bobby Digital.

Vine Yard Revival Sampler; Vine Yard VYDCD1

Johnny Osbourne, Good Time Rock; **Gregory Isaacs**, Set Me

Free; **Sanchez**, Don't Say It's Over; **Shabba Ranks**, No To Coke; **Chaka Demus**, Get Up Stand Up; **Garnett Silk**, Bless Me; **Admiral Tibet**, Working Time; **Leroy Smart**, 100%.

This represents a good cross-section of early Bobby Digital productions (from 1989 to 1992), while later-model compilations – such as *Top Ten* and *Strictly Dancehall* – can be found on import CD. Meanwhile, other than the selected albums listed below, it's best to check for the producer's credit on recordings by the above-mentioned artists.
Admiral Tibet: *Reality Time*; Vine Yard VYCD5
Garnett Silk: *It's Growing*; Vine Yard VYCD4
Shabba Ranks: *Just Reality/Best Baby Father*; Vine Yard VYCD6

Eastwood and Saint

(Clint Eastwood, born Robert Brammer; General Saint, Born Winston Hislop; both born late 1950s, Jamaica; deejays)
If ever anybody is responsible for selling the idea of the deejay to the UK mainstream it's Eastwood and Saint. Originally produced by HENRY 'JUNJO' LAWES, their sound was early dancehall and their delivery was classic deejay duet. Their approach, however, was pure theatre – in the best possible way. Taking the idea of live performance very seriously, they figured their audience would need to have fun if they were going to get into it and they worked on an act that involved mad dancing and outrageous matching costumes. In their two-handed style, they would literally throw the lines across the stage at each other. As they sold out shows on the college circuit as well as the larger reggae club circuit, they became one of the very few post-BOB MARLEY acts genuinely to crossover.

Then they began recording in the UK, presumably in recognition of this newly found market. Although on the surface it was the same, and while musically it was technically excellent, this shift had subtly detached the duo from the root of what they were doing and the reggae crowd's perception of them became as a novelty act. And, as is the way of these things, they were never more than a passing fancy in the mainstream. Both are still recording independently of each other.

Two Bad D.J.; Greensleeves GRELCD24

It wouldn't really matter if this duo had done nothing other than this album. Along with Michigan and Smiley ('Diseases' and 'Come When Jah Call You'), Eastwood and Saint led the way in the deejay duet method that became very fashionable in early 1980s reggae, literally bouncing off Lawes's springy basslines and buoyant drums. It was all a bit exaggerated, a bit deliberately wild – in a bid to shake the music out of the doldrums it seemed to be hitting around then – and perfectly suited to Eastwood and Saint's playful style. On this set are 'Tribute To General Echo', 'Talk About Run', 'Another One Bites The Dust' and 'Can't Take Another World War'.

Eek-A-Mouse

(Born Ripton Hilton, 1957; Kingston, Jamaica; deejay)
The name came from a horse he used to back on a regular basis, and it must be said Mouse was something of a one-trick pony himself. But what a spectacular trick it was.

Mouse's forte was a highly musical, totally ridiculous scat style – 'beng beng biddy beng beng, skiddy beng biddy beng' – interspersed with his nasal singing-cum-toasting. Back in 1982, with HENRY 'JUNJO' LAWES at the controls turning out tight, slapping digital roots rhythms, Mouse exploded on to the scene, skiddy-beng-ing his way round love songs, roots material, comic numbers and pure scat sessions. It was guaranteed to vibe up any dance at a time when artists like Michigan and Smiley, EASTWOOD AND SAINT and YELLOWMAN seemed determined to exercise their senses of humour.

But Mouse seemed to have nothing else in his repertoire, or nothing else anyone was particularly interested in, and by the end of 1983 his once-soaring popularity was slipping fast as people realized if you've got one Eek-A-Mouse record you probably don't need two. Still a dynamic live performer, he tours regularly, records sporadically and has had some small acting roles.

Wa-Do-Dem; Greensleeves GRELCD31

This is the one Eek-A-Mouse album you really ought to have. Produced by Lawes, mixed by SCIENTIST and performed with much gusto, a couple of plays makes it easy to see what all the fuss was about. All the big sound system records are here: 'Ganja Smuggling', 'Operation Eradication', 'Wa-Do-Dem' and 'Long Time Ago', and it still sounds as fresh as it always did. All together now: 'beng beng biddy beng beng, skiddy beng biddy beng . . . '

The Very Best Of Eek-A-Mouse; Greensleeves GRELCD105

Not, perhaps, the most accurate title in the world, but with 'Anarexol', 'Terrorists In The City' and 'Wild Like A Tiger', it runs a reasonable second to the above.

Donovan Germain

(Born 1952; Kingston, Jamaica; producer)

Donovan Germain's Penthouse Records is an aptly named operation. The label's trademark sound – a sophisticated, melodic version of the computerized dancehall rhythms – almost single-handedly ensured the notion of smoove, shiny lovers' rock was present in the ragga-dominated late 1980s and early 1990s. And, as such, had a far greater influence on the reggae of that period than his profile might suggest.

After running a specialist reggae record shop in New York in the 1970s, Germain returned to Jamaica in 1980 to start producing records. Although he had some minor local successes during the first half of that decade, it wasn't until 1986, when he had a monster hit with Audrey Hall's 'One Dance Won't Do' – it went as far as the British pop charts – that his easy-going, late-model lovers' rock established itself. By now, with the assistance of his regular engineer Dave Kelly, the style had matured into something that was definitely dancehall originated in terms of the way it was put together and the sounds it used, but was melody – rather than rhythm – oriented, with deceptively complicated layering in its instrumentation. This music was far closer in feel to the reggae of a bygone era, and by demonstrating that 'romantic' didn't have to mean 'slushy', it owed a great deal to

American soft R&B. Maybe these two factors were the result of Germain having had his reggae tastes shaped in the days of early reggae and roots music, and of his having spent so much time in the USA.

From that point on, Penthouse became one of Jamaica's leading labels, and the sweeping, lush-by-comparison-to-what-was-going-on-around-it productions provided hits for, as well as Audrey Hall, Marcia Griffiths, BERES HAMMOND, Wayne Wonder and Carol Gonzales. A Penthouse production was always as crisp and as clean as the standards of the day demanded, but it would never be without soul, something which often didn't figure in what was being done elsewhere.

Of course, Germain didn't neglect the harder side of modern reggae either, and brought the same high standards to acts such as Tony Rebel, MAD COBRA, Cutty Ranks, Spragga Benz, Terror Fabulous and BUJU BANTON. The latter's breakthrough sessions – including 'Love Mi Browning', 'Batty Rider' and 'Bogle Dance' – were recorded for Penthouse, and a feature of Germain's productions in this deejay area was to undercut the relentless rhythms with almost subliminal melody lines, bringing a far greater sense of depth to the production.

It's now with Banton that Penthouse is spearheading dancehall's next development, for the deejay's *'Til Shiloh* album has been hailed as a masterpiece of modern roots music. In its clever combination of the sensitivity and subtlety you'd expect from righteous Rasta music, and the underlying stroppiness and hard edge of ghetto rude boy-ism, it is being compared to THE WAILERS' early work. And it's put Donovan Germain a long way ahead of his peers.

There are Penthouse compilations available on import CD, but apart from the readily available *Dancehall Old School* (detailed below) they are very hard to get hold of – most specialist shops know about them but none have any in stock! Apart from on albums by the above, Germain/Kelly productions feature heavily on Charm Records' *Just Ragga* series and the same label's *Pure Lovers* compilations.

*__Dancehall Old School__; Penthouse YYCD2835

De Vante, Fire Burn; **Spragga Benz**, The Test; **Wayne Wonder**,

Sail; **The Frisco Kid**, Chuck It; **Barrington Levy and Beenie Man**, Murderation; **Donovan Steele**, The Prayer; **Louie Culture**, Hypocrite; **Jack Radics**, Easy Money; **Terror Fabulous**, Reputation; **Donovan Steele**, S.E.X.

Brian and Tony Gold

(Born Brian Thompson, 1967, Kingston, Jamaica; born Patrick Anthony Johnson, 1968, Kingston, Jamaica; vocal duo)
A unique commodity in today's reggae climate: a close harmony duo. This pair met and teamed up while doing the rounds of the Kingston talent shows in the mid-1980s, and immediately became in demand as backing singers on all manner of records from late-model roots to early dancehall. But it's the craze for combination that really boosted the Golds – their harmonizing is so tight, it gives enormous strength to what they do but still allows all the subtleties to show through without strain. As a result they can more than hold their own against even the gruffest of deejays, who in turn can put greater muscle into their performances without fear of overbalancing anything. Their huge UK chart hit in 1994, 'Compliments On Your Kiss' (in combination with deejay Red Dragon), is a fine example of what they are capable of, while they'll also figure on tracks with artists of the calibre of CAPLETON, BUJU BANTON, SHABBA RANKS and BERES HAMMOND.

The Brian and Tony Gold CD *Green Light* is no longer on catalogue, but examples of them in combination action feature on numerous dancehall compilations. 'Compliments On Your Kiss' is on *Hail Up The Taxi – Sly and Robbie Present The Taxi Gang* (Island Jamaica IJMCD3002).

Beres Hammond

(Born 1955; Kingston, Jamaica; singer)
For years Beres Hammond seemed to be one more R&B-wannabe crooner, turning out the kind of semi-American gloop that sat well on mainstream Jamaican radio but didn't cut much ice anywhere on the sound systems. He was the sort of artist

people used to talk about as a genuine lurrrve man, while not being able to name any of his records. As if he was much better in theory than in practice. Even his big hit, 'One Dance Will Do', wasn't nearly as successful as the 'answer' records it inspired, and the duet with MAXI PRIEST, 'How Can We Ease The Pain', did much more for the British singer.

Then he fetched up at DONOVAN GERMAIN's Penthouse Records in the early 1990s and suddenly it all seemed to fall into place. Perhaps Germain understood Hammond's soul leanings and knew how to apply them to a dancehall style. Almost immediately, he started turning out hits, resulting in the spectacularly successful *A Love Affair* album in 1992, which left Hammond as one of the biggest singers in Jamaica and with a queue of producers wanting to record with him. He cut tunes with most of them, but the biggest hits came with PHILIP 'FATIS' BURRELL and the album *Full Attention*.

Following this success, Hammond signed for a major American label in 1994, and at the time of writing nothing has been heard from this union. Let's hope he doesn't go the way of so many dancehall artists who don't seem to be able to get it right away from the roots of reggae.

A Love Affair; Penthouse PHCD14

A wonderful example of digital lovers' rock. Germain's slapping rhythms, the fractured melodies and swooping, sparingly used horn parts provide the ideal framework for Hammond's voice. It's upbeat enough to keep things swinging when the singer himself might drag a wee bit, and crisp enough to give him the sheen of toughness he needs to survive in the dancehall. This set kicks off with the huge hit 'Tempted To Touch' and doesn't let up the pace with 'Falling In Love All Over Again' and 'Love Me Hafe Get', a wicked remix of 'Tempted' featuring Cutty Ranks.

ALSO RECOMMENDED:

Full Attention; Charm CRCD17

Produced by Philip 'Fatis' Burrell, overall it's not quite as smoove as *A Love Affair*, but it's still among the best digital lovers' rock on offer.

Prince Jammy (aka King Jammy or Jammy's)

(Born Lloyd James, early 1950s; Kingston, Jamaica; producer)
In 1985, Jammy had a bit of an idea. He and freelance musician/bargain-basement Casio keyboard-owner Noel Davey were fooling around with the electronic instrument. They played the pre-programmed rhythms through the studio's board, looped a section of it, slowed it down a bit and had a young singer called Wayne Smith come in and sing over the top. The result was 'Under Me Sleng Teng', the record that is universally acknowledged as the official watershed between the old and new reggae styles. It had no conventional bass and drum pattern – the one governing factor of the music up until that point – but took its rhythm from the one tinny-sounding electronic keyboard riff. The mould had been broken. But most importantly, it cleared the way for practically anybody to start making reggae without the need for studio musicians – or even a studio, come to that. The riff was immediately versioned at least 200 times, and reggae would never be the same again.

Although reggae had been standing on the brink of something dramatic for roughly the previous five years – ever since the Kingston studio-owners seriously started buying computers – it's unsurprising it took Jammy to push it over the edge. From as far back as he can remember, he was obsessed with the music, but from a technical as much as a creative point of view. As an adolescent he became involved with the sound systems, building and repairing equipment while still at school, before he set up his own Waterhouse-based system, which drew praise from the legendary KING TUBBY for its advanced electronics. Indeed Tubby never forgot his young rival, because when Jammy returned from a few years in Canada at the end of the 1970s he took him on as an engineer.

But while Jammy was learning from the master he was also building his own studio, constantly refining his equipment and experimenting to see what could be achieved – he viewed this at the time as taking the ball from Tubby and running that bit further with it. Pretty soon he was recording artists of the calibre of BLACK UHURU, Half Pint and Junior Reid, while staying in touch with what the ghetto youth actually wanted by continuing to run his Prince Jammy's sound system. Which is how he came to know that the new generation, raised on Space Invaders and beat box soul music, wanted something more. A clean break with the past. Though even he couldn't have figured on his Casio experiments having the effect they did.

Once the new style had broke, he wasn't about to let anybody usurp his leadership of it, and he promoted himself to King Jammy – deservedly so, really – and threw himself into record production on an unprecedented level. His studio was the busiest place in town as he and BOBBY DIGITAL, Jammy's son John John and his brother 'Uncle T' put out a staggering number of releases, by a range of artists that went from Tappa Zukie to Tenor Saw and from KEN BOOTHE to Pinchers. STEELY AND CLEEVIE, digital reggae's most important rhythm section established themselves at Jammy's, while of his secondary producers Bobby Digital went on to become a star in his own right.

Although Jammy slowed down considerably as he went into the 1990s, and fresh young producers began to run a bit further with his ball, he still casts an enormous shadow over the Kingston music scene. Like the ground breakers of previous eras such as DUKE REID or COXSONE or LEE PERRY, nobody can ever be sure he's not going to arrive at work one morning and change the beat again.

Sleng Teng Extravaganza; Melodie 79234-2

Wayne Smith, Under Mi Sleng Teng; **Johnny Osbourne**, Budy Bye; **Echo Minott**, Original Fat Thing; **Tenor Saw**, Pumpkin Belly; **Pad Anthony**, Cry For Me; **Hugh Griffiths**, Jamming In The Street; **Echo Minott**, Put Your Hands Pon The Key; **Woody Noble**, Ram Jam Session; **Eccleton Jarrett**, Dancehall Music; **John Wayne**, Call The Police; **Super Cat**, Trash And Ready; **Tonto Irie**, Every Posse Get Ready; **Tappa Zukie**, Big Thing; **Screechie Nice**, Understand Me Man; **Dickie Ranking**, Rap Man; **Cocoa Tea**, Hey Bobby; **Mr Lee**, Crisis; **Super Morris**, Under Me Peter Green; **Papa Faith**, Maniac; **Singie Singie**, Tell Them What They Want To Know.

King Jammy's Presents Dancehall Killers; Melodie 792909-2

Glen Ricks, Sweetie Come Brush Me; **Frankie Paul**, Boom Back

Dat; **Colin Roach and African**, Watch This Sound; **Risto Benjie, Powerman and Baby Wayne**, Never Borrow Gun Yet; **Admiral Bailey**, Do The Butterfly; **Captain Barkey**, No Gunman No Cry; **Gregory Peck**, Follow Me Go A Church; **Ken Boothe**, Sparkle; **Pinchers**, Nuh Buddah Fret; **Colin Roach and Galaxy**, Miss Goodie Goodie; **Powerman**, Work Hard; **Cornell Campbell**, Stars; **Carlton Livingston**, You Send Come Call Me.

Most artists working in digital reggae have passed through Jammy's at one time or another and credits on albums cut between 1985 and 1990 should be checked. There are numerous Jammy's compilation albums available on fairly easily obtainable import, the Greensleeves Sampler series features many of his productions, as do a large number of dancehall compilations. 'Under Mi Sleng Teng' features on *Sleng Teng Extravaganza* (see above), *Tougher Than Tough – The Story Of Jamaican Music* (Mango IBXCD1) and *Big Blunts – Twelve Smokin' Reggae Hits* (Tommy Boy TBCD1077).

Henry 'Junjo' Lawes

(Born 1958; Kingston, Jamaica; producer)
As the 1970s drew to a close, reggae seemed to be crying out for somebody to do something with it, to move it forward. One of the people who rose to that challenge was Junjo Lawes, a singer of no great success who found his niche when he produced a set of songs for BARRINGTON LEVY that made up the album Bounty Hunter. The rhythms were taut, springy and had a one drop beat that seemed to greatly exaggerate the shifts in time that the more adventurous producers were beginning to experiment with. 'Shine Eye Gal' and 'Collie Weed', from the sessions, were both Jamaican number 1s and huge sound system hits in the UK. And it's from these records that the dancehall revolution began.

Unsurprisingly, Lawes was the first down that path. With The Roots Radics as his band and with SCIENTIST as engineer, he developed a sound that was far brasher than anything that had gone before. It slapped the beat down on to the floor with big drum sounds, while an elastic bass made it bounce back up, and the percussion and lead instruments kept the tempo bubbling. He built up a stable of performers that brought the deejay back into fashion like never before – it wasn't enough just to be able to toast, Lawes's deejays were flamboyant figures, scatting, fast-talking, each with their own vocal gimmick or trademark look and performing in tandem became the thing to do. EASTWOOD AND SAINT, MICHIGAN AND SMILEY, EEK-A-MOUSE, YELLOWMAN, Josey Wales, Michael Prophet, General Echo, Little John and Billy Boyo were all Lawes's men. And, as the dancehall was their natural environment, they started using the term on record in the early 1980s.

Lawes didn't neglect the singers either. Still with The Roots Radics and with his syncopated sound in full swing, he revived the careers of artists like JOHN HOLT ('Police In Helicopter'), JOHNNY OSBOURNE ('Fally Lover') and THE WAILING SOULS ('Fire House Rock'), while kick-starting artists such as FRANKIE PAUL and COCOA TEA. Then, just when it seemed he couldn't get any bigger, in 1985 he upped and moved to New York for six years. And by the time he came back, the digital boom had happened.

Henry 'Junjo 'Lawes has re-established himself with a new studio in Kingston, and is already attracting the likes of Ninjaman. How long before a man of his innate musical sensibilities is back making hits?

Many of the albums Lawes cut with the artists mentioned above are still available on UK-released CD. The best thing to do is check under the act concerned and then read the sleeve credits. However, rest assured that the tough rubber rhythms put down by The Roots Radics are still as springy as they were over ten years ago, one of the bastions of human touch in terms of reggae instrumentation.

Barrington Levy

(Born 1962; Kingston, Jamaica; singer)
The first dancehall singer. Not just because it was Levy who HENRY 'JUNJO' LAWES took into the studio for that *Bounty Hunter* set, but because Levy has always had a dancehall attitude. His voice may be on the high side, but it's big and

powerful enough not to be intimidated by the music and his phrasing weaves in and out of the dancehall beat with a confidence and trickery that is as reminiscent of deejays as it is of singers. This is because he learned his trade singing on the Kingston sound systems as a teenager – as he was working among deejays his voice had to be strong to get across.

After his initial hits with Lawes – 'Shine Eye Gal', 'Look Youthman', 'Sister Carol' and 'Collie Weed' – for the first couple of years of the 1980s Levy was the voice of the era. He sang hits for Alvin Ranglin, George Phang and Lawes again ('Prison Oval Rock' was the big one). But it was when he hooked up with producer Jah Screw in 1984 that he really took off – 'Under Mi Sensi', 'Murderer' and 'Here I Come' were three of the biggest reggae records of the mid-1980s and they were all sung by Barrington Levy. It was the latter that propelled him to international stardom as major record companies in the UK and the US came looking for his signature. At which point he opted to broaden his appeal by trying his hand at pop and soft soul. And it all went horribly wrong.

In 1995, it remains to be seen if Barrington Levy can regain his position as one of reggae's finest, as he's lost the confidence of his original crowd. Intelligently, he's hoping to do this by reintroducing himself with updated versions of his old classics, each given a mixing desk makeover by Jah Screw and with added toasting by the current people's choices. But at the time of writing the jury is still out.

*Here I Come; Greensleeves GRELCD501

From those vintage Jah Screw sessions, featuring 'Under Mi Sensi', 'Don't Run Away', 'Vibes Is Right' and, of course, 'Here I Come'. The Barrington Levy echo has never sounded better.

With Various Artists: *Barrington Levy's DJ Interaction*; Greensleeves GRELCD216

WITH **Bounty Killer**, Living Dangerously; **Mega Banton**, Here I Come; **Beenie Man**, Under Mi Sensi; **Lady Saw**, Cool And Loving; **Daddy Screw**, Girl I Like Your Style; **Beenie Man**, Two Sounds; **Spragga Benz**, Don't Run Away; **The Frisco Kid**, Live

Good; **Cutty Ranks**, Looking For My Love; **Fragga Ranks**, Why Do You Do It; **Reggie Stepper**, Struggler.

This is the comeback album, and although it is never less than interesting, ultimately it says more about the other artists than it does about Levy.

Luciano

(Born Jepther McClymont, 1974; Davey Town, Jamaica; singer)
It had to happen sooner or later. Dancehall reggae has gone full circle and produced Luciano: a singer who writes righteous Rasta songs for a full group – drums, bass, brass, keyboards and guitar – and with 1990s sounds that owe everything to twenty years ago. In other words, reggae's bloodline has been repaired after the bassless late 1980s and early 1990s. And Luciano was always the man most likely to do this.

Coming to Kingston in the early 1990s to work as an upholsterer by day and sing on sound systems at night, Luciano's smoove tones seemed to work against him in the recording business – for he was soon in demand to sing cover versions of MOR-ish soul and mainstream reggae hits. Not exactly what he'd planned on. So when a spell with FREDDIE MCGREGOR got him noticed among the sound system crowds with his JA hit 'Shake It Up Tonight', Luciano went to work with PHILIP 'FATIS' BURRELL.

It was as if the young singer had come home. Burrell had been looking for somebody to steer into the world where dancehall met more conventional reggae, and both were keen to explore cultural themes in greater depth. The union proved to be the perfect match. Burrell provided the best musicians and production skills that recreated the roots vibe in 1990s-style, while Luciano brought his plaintive voice and a gift for songwriting that was fast maturing into a huge talent.

So far there have been four Luciano/Xterminator albums, each taking the roots approach a little further, until the current set, *Where There Is Life*, deals almost exclusively with cultural topics over the most conventionally musical backings yet. It's because Luciano's crisp rhythms succeed in ragga dances, while the roots sentiments appeal to dread audiences, that Luciano has been one of the leading figures in the present revival of cultural reggae. And it's presently doing well enough to take the singer to the very brink of international stardom. Luciano's next album will be one of the most eagerly awaited events of the reggae year.

Where There Is Life; Island Jamaica IJCD3001

Featuring players of the calibre of SLY AND ROBBIE, Robbie Lyn, DEAN FRASER and Cat Coore, this album redefines reggae to create a sound taut enough to power the songs into the dancehall, but devotes sufficient attention to sinewey melody lines to keep it from ever being abrasive. On top of that, Luciano's voice eases in and out of the gaps with an unbelievably light touch but is always strong enough to add real weight to the righteous lyrics. The album mixes up the modern lovers' of 'There's No Love In This World' with kicking ragga tones ('Where There Is Life' and 'He Is My Friend'), while the African-ish sounds of 'Just Like The Wind' recall the days of dread from twenty years ago.

ALSO RECOMMENDED:

One Way Ticket; VP Records VP1386
Moving Up; Ras RAS3129

Although these aren't quite of the same crisp, confident calibre of *Where There Is Life*, it would be wrong to assume they were merely a rehearsal. If the idea of Luciano's voice over rocking Xterminator productions hasn't convinced you, then maybe a sample of the tracklistings might help: the former features 'Poor And Simple', 'Time Is The Master' and 'Bounty Lover'; while the latter boasts 'Chant Down Babylon', 'Turn Your Life Around', 'Raggamuffin' and 'Mr Governor'.

Mad Cobra

(Born Ewart Brown, 1968; Kingston, Jamaica; deejay)
The only dancehall artist to top the US charts – mainstream

charts, that is – and only the second ever reggae artist of any sort to get that high in America, yet now recording with JAMMY'S and toasting sound systems in the ghettos of Kingston, Cobra is proof that if you've got the smarts you can really do what you want. Of course, prodigious talent helps too. Especially if you've got the kind of pop world-unfriendly approach to life that Cobra has: among his most successful home-crowd tunes were the hardcore gun lyrics 'Yush', 'Gundelero' and 'Shoot To Kill', while another big sound system hit, 'Crucifixion', endorsed homosexuality as a capital offence long before BUJU BANTON.

Then, when he had to, he went soft. Deliberately courting the kind of big US contract offered to SHABBA RANKS and SUPER-CAT, he wrote and recorded 'Love Fever' as smoove an R&B-influenced ballad as you're likely to hear. It worked, too. He signed to Columbia in 1992 and his first single topped the charts. But that was about it, and after the follow-ups fared badly he went back home – spiritually as well as physically.

Today, back in the Kingston dancehalls, Cobra is far mellower in attitude without having lost any of his original excitement and working with Jammy he would still seem to have a great deal to offer.

Hard To Wet, Easy To Dry; Columbia 472078

The American album, which neatly illustrates how close rap and reggae became a couple of years ago. The contributions from the legion of East Coast rap artists are stitched in seamlessly, while so many of the tracks have required little more than fine tuning to pitch them to the US homeboy market. Contains the number 1 hit 'Flex' and its follow-up, 'Legacy'.

Venom; Greensleeves GRELCD202

The 1994 set cut at Jammy's that reveals Mad Cobra (the name is taken from a comic book character) to have matured greatly. Alongside uncompromising reality lyrics are Rasta praises and a much more balanced world view. The rhythms, however, are as raw as ever and Cobra's voice retains its intriguing tunefulness.

An enormous amount of Cobra material never made it on to any albums – many of them UK reggae chart-toppers from 1991 and 1992 – so it's worth combing compilation sets for them.

Frankie Paul

(Born Paul Blake, early 1960s; Kingston, Jamaica; singer)
Blind since birth, and apparently once in negotiation with
Motown after a recommendation from Stevie Wonder, Frankie
Paul is one of the most recorded singers in dancehall. But he's
also one of the most reliable – unlike so many of his peers, it
doesn't matter who he's recording for and how hardcore the
rhythms are, Frankie Paul is guaranteed to turn in a wonderful,
soulful performance. He's been doing it since 1983 too.

True, there are a lot of Dennis Brown-isms in his voice, but
that's not such a bad thing, as this rolling, expressive tenor rides
just above any rhythm he's given and so automatically lightens
it on the ears, while staying far enough away from it not to take
off too much of the edge. If MAD COBRA is the link between
ragga and rap, then Frankie Paul is where dancehall meets
traditional soul singing.

Just how long he can keep it up, though, remains to be seen.
In the manner of so many reggae acts, he records for anybody,
any time, anywhere, and half a dozen albums plus countless singles a year is about par for the course. The big problem with this
is that, while it's all good, it starts to become a bit meaningless
after a while. Maybe a reduction in quantity might take the
quality to even higher levels. Or perhaps we'd just appreciate it
a bit more.

There are at least 100 Frankie Paul albums on CD at the
moment, and he features on just about every compilation worth
bothering with. The variety within the titles isn't sufficient to
pick out any as recommended – it doesn't help that the best of
the bunch, *Pass The Tu-Shung-Peng*, is on vinyl only – but if you
look for productions by either JAMMY'S or JUNJO LAWES you
won't go far wrong.

Shabba Ranks

(Born Rexton Gordon, 1965; St Ann's, Jamaica; deejay)

In 1991, when Shabba toured the UK, he couldn't go out in public without his excitable young lady fans causing serious disturbances. He's won not one but two Grammy Awards (Best Reggae Album 1991 and 1992). He signed a huge contract with Epic Records in New York in 1990. And has scored mainstream chart success on both sides of the Atlantic with songs like 'Mr Loverman'. Yet by the time he did all that, his best moments were already in his past. Shabba is a great example of how dancehall reggae could be a blind alley if you do nothing to advance what you're doing.

Toasting sound systems since the age of twelve (his family moved to Kingston when he was a child), he quickly developed a rich, luxuriously gruff voice, a way of advancing a melody even if there wasn't one in the backing track, and a stage act that didn't know the meaning of the word 'discreet' – it wasn't unheard of for him to make his entrance by helicopter at the big open-air reggae festivals. Such showmanship and an outrageous, tongue-in-cheek, ever-ready approach to the more physical aspects of lurrrve – or so his lyrics proclaimed – combined with a set of killer tunes cut for his old pal BOBBY DIGITAL in 1988/1989 to catapult him to the top of his field. As he followed up with a serious album for GUSSIE CLARKE, *Holding On*, his slackness lyrics, his raucous quick-fire delivery, his gold rope chains and his clothes that were louder than his music defined dancehall reggae for several years. Quite deservedly too.

But once in New York, although he made a point of using Jamaican producers, he'd left himself little room for manoeuvre as far as artistic advancement was concerned. He'd been bought to do what he did before and he painted himself into a corner as the prize-winning albums, *Raw As Ever* and *X-tra Naked*, were just more of what he'd done before, only slightly less so. While styles moved on, Shabba was retreading old ground and starting to look like this was all he could do. A real problem was, as so often happens with major labels, the gap between recording and release was far too long, meaning stuff was guaranteed to sound tired – and the whole point of dancehall is its immediacy.

This severely diminished his core audience. When Shabba played in Brixton just a couple of years after his personal appearance in Oxford Street had stopped traffic, the hall was only half full and the biggest audience response went to MAXI

PRIEST who came on for a combination number. Thankfully, Shabba is now back in Jamaica, working with and for his own crowd and is rapidly regaining lost ground. You get the feeling it's only a matter of time before he's back on top.

Just Reality/Best Baby Father; Vine Yard VYCD6

Both those albums were cut with Bobby Digital on the same CD. This is probably the best deal you're going to get all year. And maybe next year too. So cleverly do the sparse rhythms and driving basslines fit in with Shabba's voice that you could almost imagine the music was added after the vocals had been put down. Tracks like 'Peenie Peenie', 'Wicked Inna Bed', 'Just Reality', 'Muama Man' and 'Roots And Culture' are everything that made Shabba special in the first place. These are two of the best three albums he made.

Holding On; Greensleeves GRELCD142

This is the other one. Recorded for Gussie Clarke, and featuring combinations with Home T and COCOA TEA, this is perhaps more melodic (just) than its predecessors, but it's got all the excitement quota. Features 'Mr Loverman' (the version with Deborahe Glasgow) and 'Twice My Age'.

ALSO RECOMMENDED:

Raw As Ever; Epic 4681022

The first of the two Grammy winners, and memorable for three tunes: 'Housecall' (combination with Maxi Priest), 'Trailer Load Of Girls' (became something of a catchphrase) and 'Where Does Slackness Come From' (one of the wittiest dancehall tracks ever made).

Redrose and Malvo

(Born Anthony Cameron, 1966, Kingston, Jamaica; Anthony Malvo, born 1969, Kingston, Jamaica; vocal/production duo)
The other sweet harmony vocal duo on the dancehall scene,

these two have an astonishing amount to offer. They'll croon their own production of some righteous roots material, over an almost conventional reggae track, to come up with tunes as silky as 'Never Get'. Or they'll also produce the kind of rapid-fire percussion beats that even, say, BEENIE MAN has trouble keeping up with, the type of stripped-to-the-bone beats that originate somewhere around the point that dancehall meets jungle. Or they'll put the two together and create something really special. It's this versatility that, in the last three years, has seen artists of the calibre of CAPLETON, MAD COBRA, BRIAN AND TONY GOLD, FRANKIE PAUL, Red Dragon, Spragga Benz, Jigsy King and Jack Radics beat a path to their door. Their ability to adapt to different styles, and then adapt said style to suit them, has put them in a position to challenge the biggest production houses, and, most importantly, for us it means Redrose and Malvo records are never short of surprises.

At the time of writing there are no Redrose and Malvo compilation albums, and most of their production work is on a single-by-single basis. Therefore it's best to check Various Artist compilations, particularly the later *Greensleeves Samplers*.

Sanchez

(Born D. Thompson, 1967; Kingston, Jamaica; singer)
There's been a tradition in Jamaica to cover big pop hits in the style of the day – no matter how inappropriate the song concerned might be. And there's no reason why dancehall should be any exception to this trend. Enter Sanchez. Following in the footsteps of artists like JOHN HOLT and KEN BOOTHE, he's covered such MOR standards as 'The Lady In Red', 'The Green Green Grass Of Home', 'Won't Last A Day' and 'Let It Be Me'. He's done these for such producers of note as BOBBY DIGITAL, PHILIP 'FATIS' BURRELL and Winston Riley, though, so they don't sound half as bad as you might imagine. Indeed it's quite a welcome light relief after hours of deejay music, and if it helps get dancehall across to a wider audience than a young sound system crowd then that can't be bad either. But what really convinces me this man has a lot to offer is his and Digital's brilliant and thoughtful updating of a particular favourite of mine, THE

HEPTONES' 'Pretty Looks Isn't All'. If Sanchez can get that one right, then he can probably walk on water.

I Can't Wait; Vine Yard VYCD3

This is the album with 'Pretty Looks' on, and the whole Bobby Digital production is far warmer and with greater musical depth than might be expected, to create a crisply swinging lovers' style. But involving all the dancehall sounds. Other tracks include 'Won't Last A Day', 'Give It A Chance' and Sanchez's own composition, the woozy, high-stepping 'Rough Neck Sound'.

Garnett Silk

(Born Garnett Smith, 1966; Manchester, Jamaica; singer)
When Garnett Silk was killed in an explosion at his house in Jamaica just before Christmas 1994, reggae in general – not just dancehall – was robbed of one of its brightest stars. A devout Rasta and sweet-voiced, if untutored, singer, Silk was making an enormous impact on contemporary reggae as his 100 per cent righteousness cut a swathe through the gun culture and slackness that was dominating the music. That he did it to the tuff beats of STEELY AND CLEEVIE and BOBBY DIGITAL helped the music succeed in the dancehalls; the additional horns and lead instruments softened it sufficiently to ensure widespread radio play; and his good looks and soft-spoken charm ensured he was a huge hit with the ladies. Garnett Silk was exactly what dancehall needed, and it's very likely that it was the deep impression he made that precipitated the widespread swing back to roots by previously less-righteous performers.

But it nearly didn't happen at all. When Silk came to Kingston as a teenager, his entry into the music business wasn't as smooth as it might have been: after sessions with SUGAR MINOTT, KING TUBBY, JAMMY'S and Penthouse, he spent a long period recording with Steely and Cleevie, but only one not-too-successful single came out. It seemed nobody quite knew what to do with him, and he returned to his rural environment to write and record in Ocho Rios, away from Kingston. As he was a gentle, uncomplicated man, this change of scenery is probably highly significant, as from that point on the hits didn't stop.

After cutting singles for the local Roof International label, in 1992 he hooked up with Bobby Digital to record *It's Growing*, the most stunning example of roots music within the dancehall genre. By the end of the next year he had a contract with EastWest Records (a Warner Bros company) and was preparing to take what he did to a truly international stage, but on his own terms. In the summer of 1994 he stole the show at the annual Sunsplash reggae festival, but by Christmas he was dead. And we'll never know what he would have been capable of.

It's Growing; Vine Yard VYCD4

That first, genius album, voiced for Bobby Digital and with Silk's plaintive tenor sounding so marvellously fresh and clear as he sings of his love for Jah, mankind and life itself. Although the music isn't as richly textured as it might be, it has a very contemporary feel, making it easy to see how Silk fitted so snugly in with what was going on around him. Tunes like 'It's Growing', 'I Am Vex', 'Bless Me' and 'Place In Your Heart' carry across Garnett Silk's vibe with an unadulterated upfulness that's been missing in reggae for far too long.

Lord Watch Over Our Shoulders; Greensleeves GRELCD219

A collection of numbers that originally came out as singles, from pre-Digital sessions and thus involving the producers listed above. In some cases they have been remixed slightly, and in every case they provide a strong, rich framework – there's plenty of horns – both to cushion the beats slightly and to buoy up Silk's voice. The material is a mixture of love and roots, with the stand-out tracks being 'So Divine', 'Fill Us Up With Your Mercy' and the two versions of the title track.

Sly and Robbie

➤➤ Curiously, as the revolution Sly and Robbie did so much to set in motion got properly underway, their profile couldn't have been lower. In the reggae world anyway. During the 1980s the duo were in such demand around the world, and were so busy gathering musical styles and experimenting with the sounds of rap, electro and hip hop, that they were little more than observers in Jamaica. However, come the 1990s and it was obvious they hadn't been sleeping.

Suddenly they were back with a vengeance. Mixing Labs became the place to be as they turned the style on its head by taking the existing dancehall structures and recreating them with completely different sounds. They'd use conventional instrumentation to take the place of machines, and their knowledge of what can be done outside of computers meant they were continually moving the goalposts. Handily, this worked as a kind of job creation scheme for them – other producers began to search for that 'real' musician sound again and came looking for Sly and Robbie to play drum and bass for them. Plus they brought their pop credentials to bear on the combination scene, as their writing, production and playing for CHAKA DEMUS AND PLIERS, Red Dragon and BRIAN AND TONY GOLD topped charts all over the world.

Now, artists such as the above and of the calibre of Redrose, BEENIE MAN, Lt Stitchie and LUCIANO were queuing up at their door. The Riddim Twins, who had been so important to reggae's development since the mid-1970s, were back in the driving seat. It should be interesting getting to where they're taking us.

*Hail Up The Taxi – Sly and Robbie Present The Taxi Gang; Island Jamaica IJMCD3002

Beenie Man and Luciano, Crazy Baldhead; **Ambelique**, Going Home; **Redrose**, Money; **Prezident Brown**, People Listen; **Gina Foster and Chris Ballin**, He Said She Said; **Red Dragon**, Skin Tight; **Mykall Roze**, One A We Two A We; **Beenie Man**, No Mama No Cry; **Merciless**, Easy And Cool; **Yami Bolo**, Love My Woman; **Chaka Demus and Pliers**, Sweetie; **Lieutenant Stitchie**, The Mechanic; **Red Dragon and Brian and Tony Gold**, Compliments On Your Kiss; **Don Yute**, Freak Out.

The full spectrum of Sly and Robbie's 1990s-style productions, going from sweet lovers' to hardcore ragga, with nothing quite as straightforward as it may seem. As a statement of their intent for the coming few years, this album is a first-rate calling card.

Steely and Cleevie

(Born Wycliffe Johnson and Cleveland Brown, late 1950s; Kingston, Jamaica; rhythm section/producers)
The dancehall rhythm section – interestingly playing keyboards and drums, respectively, rather than the traditional bass and drums – as there's few people these two haven't backed, or producers they've not worked for. Their total understanding of the computerized studio environment has combined with the fact they're old enough to remember life before then – Steely was in The Roots Radics and Cleevie had been part of FREDDIE MCGREGOR's international touring band and had done sessions with BOB MARLEY. They met on a LEE PERRY session (which has to be a good sign) and got on immediately as they both complement each other's characters. In fact it's the balance of Steely's brashness with Cleevie's thoughtfulness that endows their playing with a wonderfully complete feel. Having branched into production some years ago with their own Steely and Cleevie label, they're taking a far more active part in shaping the music than if they just played for other people. Which ought to mean they'll be a force to be reckoned with for a long time yet.

There are several import CDs of Steely and Cleevie productions and their one-rhythm albums, otherwise it's best simply to check sleeve credits, as there are so few dancehall acts they haven't worked with. An involvement that is pretty much a guarantee of quality.

Supercat

(Born William Maragh, 1965; Kingston, Jamaica; deejay)
'Cat will go down in reggae history as a wasted talent: after a blistering start on the local sound systems – he was number 1

deejay on Kilamajaro at age sixteen – he signed a deal with Columbia and spent the best part of two years in New York doing nothing other than growing cold as far as the home crowd were concerned. Which probably wouldn't have mattered if, in between, he hadn't written and recorded 'Boops'. A light, jaunty number, delivered in his laconic, highly tuneful style and with a witty lyric about sugar-daddies, it was record of the year for 1985, becoming the defining sound of dancehall as an estimated 200 versions were cut within weeks of its release. It showed Supercat to be a real talent. Then . . . nothing. Still, if you're only going to leave us one tune to remember you by, it might as well be a brilliant as 'Boops'.

'Boops' is featured on *Tougher Than Tough – The Story Of Jamaican Music* (Mango IBXCD1).

Admiral Tibet

(Born Kennel Allen, 1960; Freehill, Jamaica; singer)
For reasons discussed elsewhere, conscious dancehall would seem to be where it's at as we go into the second half of the 1990s. But while it seems as if every former-ruffian deejay is sprouting dreadlocks and praising Jah, Admiral Tibet is about the only one who arrived at dancehall in a state of righteousness and has yet to deviate from that path. In fact he is far more likely to pose on an album sleeve reading the Bible than with an assault rifle or an underclothed woman. A Twelve Tribes member since his teens, although he was building a reputation for himself singing in local clubs and on sound systems, he didn't start recording until he was well into his twenties – quite simply because he didn't want to swap his peaceful rural environment for the harsher life in Kingston. But following his first Jamaican hit, 'Babylon War', in 1985, Tibet's plaintive falsetto – it's reminiscent of a young GREGORY ISAACS – and his roots and culture lyrics have graced a succession of hits. And his status beyond the Caribbean continues to grow as frequent touring presents him as a viable modern alternative to the deejays in Europe, Canada, the USA, Japan and the UK.

Reality Time; Vine Yard VYCD5
Excitement; Riddim 117502 MU761

Cut in 1991 and 1995, respectively, these two albums show how
Tibet has ridden the dancehall rhythms with practically no effect
on how he approaches his singing and his conscious songs. His
sunny falsetto is a joy to listen to on such numbers as 'Rude
Boys' (with HORACE ANDY and Linval Thompson), 'Set Me
Free', 'Dance With Me' and 'My Sound Is The Champion'.

Yellowman

(Born Winston Foster, 1959; Kingston, Jamaica; deejay)
As a six-foot-something albino black man, Yellowman is one of
the most unlikely sex symbols in the world. Let alone in the reggae world, given that albinos are shunned by Jamaican society.
But this deejay used what might have been seen as an affliction
to enormous advantage as he relentlessly marketed himself on
the notion that being an albino meant he was a *sex god*. And it
worked. Like soul music's own hardly obvious sex god, Barry
White, Yellowman got this over by sheer force of personality
and bedroom talk that knew no limits. Even in reggae's tradition
of bawdy lyrics. His outrageous rhymes and boasts of his sexual
prowess won him an enormous following among both sexes.
The term 'slackness' was coined around this time to create an
official genre of rude reggae, as this was the beginning of a
bloodline that went through SHABBA RANKS up to the likes of
CAPLETON and Lt Stitchie. However, it's worth mentioning
that although Yellowman's lyrics were seldom the sort of thing
you'd play in front of your mum, and mainstream music journalists would get up on their hind legs to denounce the 'sexism'
of it all, in context Yellow was never offensive and, with his
tongue stuck firmly in his cheek, usually very funny. Revisiting
his most outrageous moments over ten years later, it's practically easy listening compared with some of the downright nas-
tiness that makes up so many dancehall lyrics today.

Of course, none of this would have meant anything if
Yellowman hadn't been an extraordinary deejay too. His
prowess on the mic swiftly passed into reggae legend. While still

managing to sound melodic he could come to grips with the most tongue-twistingly complicated syntax, and do it at a speed that just stopped short of making listeners' ears bleed. And his frequent lapses into gloriously daft scatting made sure we knew that this was all meant to be fun.

It was Yellowman and his machine-gun delivery that made the break from the previous era's roots deejays and set up the dancehall styles that have dominated since. Likewise, JUNJO LAWES' taut obviously computerized rhythms gave Yellow an attractive springboard – in 1992 and 1993 these tunes represented the next stage of evolution towards dancehall-as-we-know-it and are the final link between traditional reggae and what happened after 'Sleng Teng'. Indeed, it was the rapid, kettle-drum-style aspect of Yellowman's delivery that provided a vivid template for the shaping of the new rhythms.

A prolific recording artist and a wonderful character, Yellowman found fame all over the world, even signing a big-style contract with CBS in New York. But by courting success around the globe, he took his eye off the ball as far as the home crowd was concerned and by the end of the decade dancehall and its new young dons had passed him by. Happily, though, as more melody creeps back into the music, Yellowman is once again on the rise, so to speak. He's slowed his patter down a bit, meaning his innate tunefulness has come to the fore, while the dread sentiments he used to express in between the slackness are now proving to be perfectly in step with the times.

There are over thirty Yellowman CDs currently released in the UK and nearly as many again on Jamaican import. However, the artistic and technical quality varies enormously and the ones to look out for were made between 1982 and 1985 and produced by Henry 'Junjo' Lawes, the best of which are detailed below.

Mister Yellowman; Greensleeves GRELCD35
Zungguzungguguzungguzeng; Greensleeves GRELCD57
Nobody Move Nobody Get Hurt; Greensleeves GRELCD71

All recorded during the same period and very similar in style and content – slackness and righteousness sitting side by side – taken in order, they show a progression both in the Lawes style and Yellow's delivery as both became harder and more rhythmic. But the most remarkable thing about coming back to these albums ten years later is that you remember more of the 'proper' tracks than you do the slackness, even though it was the latter that seemed such a big deal at the time. On the first, *Mister Yellowman*, it's 'Duppy Or A Gunman', 'Natty Sit Upon A Rock' as much as 'Yellowman Gets Married'. While 'Zungguzung-guguzungguzeng', 'Who Can Make The Dance Ram', 'Rub-A-Dub-A-Play' and 'Friday Night Jamboree' are the best on *Zungguzungguguzungguzeng*, and the title track is far and away the stand-out song on the latter.

*Kiss Me; Riddim 113862MU765

Yellow in 1995, produced by Linval Thompson and Bunny Gemini, and although not all the slackness toasts quite work – he's changed his approach to lyric writing to stay up with the pack, and much of it comes off as unpleasantly crude – the Rasta songs like 'Jordan River' and 'Give Thanks And Praise' are a treat.

SEE ALSO:

Early volumes of the *Greensleeves Sampler* series and *Tougher Than Tough – The Story Of Jamaican Music* (Mango IBXCD1).

VARIOUS ARTISTS

As with Chapter Two, when nearly every compilation album was on the same Trojan label, here Greensleeves dominates the field. This is simply because that company has been shrewd enough to license so much of the best modern reggae that an enormous proportion of reggae released in this country since the mid-1980s is on a Greensleeves-affiliated label. It would be nice to be offered a bung!

*Best Of Reggae Sunsplash; Charly CDCHARLY235

Chalice, Ital Love, Revival Time; **Sandi and The Sunsetz**, Calling You; **Bloodfire Posse**, Do You Feel Like Dancing, Can't

Stop Rocking Tonight; **Dennis Brown**, It's Magic; **Dennis Brown and John Holt**, Wildfire; **Cocoa Tea**, Botha; **Charlie Chaplin and Yellowman**, Medley; **Gregory Isaacs**, Oh What A Feeling; **Josey Wales**, Let Off; **Bunny Wailer**, Ram Jam Dance, Jolly Sessions, Sabotage.

Big Blunts – Twelve Smokin' Reggae Hits; Tommy Boy TBCD1077

Wayne Smith, Under Mi Sleng Teng (Remix); **U-Roy**, Chalice In The Palace; **Yellowman and Fathead**, Herbman Smuggling; **Lone Ranger**, Jamaican Weed; **Ninjaman**, Legalize The Herb; **Rita Marley**, One Draw; **Wayne Smith**, Under Mi Sleng Teng; **Sugar Minott**, Herbman Hustling; **Barrington Levy**, Under Mi Sensi; **Tony Rebel**, The Herb; **Frankie Paul**, Pass The Tusheng Peng; **The Mighty Diamonds**, Pass The Koutchie.

Conscious Ragga Volume One; Greensleeves GRELCD220

Luciano and Louie Culture, Real Rastaman; **Captain Barkey**, Anti-Christ; **Bunny Rugs**, Babylon Calling; **Beenie Man**, Blessed; **Frankie Paul**, Praise Him; **Simpleton**, Sick Under Rastaman Treatment; **Cocoa Tea**, Babylon Falling; **Bounty Killer**, Book Book; **Anthony Malvo**, Jah Mercy; **Simpleton**, 1/4 To 12; **Mykall Roze**, Money; **Garnett Silk**, Retreat Wicked Man; **Redrose**, Chanting Down Babylon; **Beenie Man**, Praise Him; **Luciano**, Poor And Simple.

Dancehall Style – The Best Of Reggae Dancehall Music Volume Three; Profile PCD1433

Cutty Ranks, The Stopper; **Barrington Levy**, Dancehall Rock; **Lady Patra**, Ambition; **Papa San**, Maddy Maddy Cry; **Frankie Paul**, Cassandra; **Shabba Ranks and Lovindeer**, Manhunt; **Louie Rankin**, Typewriter; **Poison Chang**, Press Up; **Capleton**, Number One Upon The Good Looks Chart; **Pinchers**, Bandelero; **Ninjaman and Flourgun**, Zig It Up; **Cocoa Tea**, Tune In.

Greensleeves Sampler; Greensleeves GREZCD1

Dennis Brown, Crazy List; **Sugar Minott**, Feel The Rydim; **Yellowman**, Zungguzungguzungguzeng; **Frankie Paul**, Pass The Tu-Sheng-Peng; **Gregory Isaacs**, Let Off Supm; **Hugh Mundell**, Africa Must Be Free By 1983; **Black Uhuru**, I Love King Selassie; **The Wailing Souls**, They Don't Know Jah; **Scientist**, Dematerialize; **Eek-A-Mouse**, Ganja Smuggling; **Clint Eastwood and General Saint**, Stop That Train; **Burning Spear**, We Are Going.

Greensleeves Sampler Volume Two; Greensleeves GREZCD2

JC Lodge, Telephone Love; **Beres Hammond**, She Loves Me Now; **Judy Mowatt**, Rock Me; **Ken Boothe**, A Man Is A Man; **Deborahe Glasgow**, Knight In Shining Armour; **Burning Spear**, Fly Me To The Moon; **Gregory Isaacs**, Rumours; **The Mighty Diamonds**, Tonight I'm Gonna Take It Easy; **Ini Kamoze**, Girl 'E'; **Dean Fraser**, Magnet and Steel; **Freddie McGregor**, Miserable Woman; **Yellowman**, Blueberry Hill.

Greensleeves Sampler Volume Three; Greensleeves GREZCD3

Ini Kamoze, Stress; **Freddie McGregor and Cynthia Schloss**, Not As Happy; **Gregory Isaacs**, Mind Yu Dis; **Deborahe Glasgow**, Champion Lover; **Clement Irie**, Kolo Ko; **Johnny Osbourne**, Trickster; **Dennis Brown and Gregory Isaacs**, Big All Round; **Sugar Minott and JC Lodge**, Since You Came Into My Life; **Carl Meeks and Daddy Lilly**, Heard About My Love; **Jimmy Cliff**, Pressure; **Thriller U**, It's Over; **The Mighty Diamonds**, Bad Boy Business.

Greensleeves Sampler Volume Four; Greensleeves GREZCD4

Shabba Ranks and Krystal, Twice My Age; **Gregory Isaacs**, Report To Me; **Tiger**, Love Me Baby; **Home T, Cocoa Tea and Shabba Ranks**, Pirate's Anthem; **Dennis Brown**, No More Walls; **Little Lenny**, Wicked and Wild; **Deborahe Glasgow and Shabba Ranks**, Mr Loverman; **Pinchers**, Blinking Something; **Papa San**, Round Table; **Cocoa Tea**, Why Turn Down The

Sound; **Dennis Brown and Tiger**, Make Up Your Mind; **Admiral Tibet**, Tell Me Which One.

*Greensleeves Sampler Volume Seven; Greensleeves GREZCD7

Shaggy, Oh Carolina; **Baja Jedd**, Bed Work Sensation; **General TK**, I Spy; **Cocoa Tea**, Getting Closer; **Buju Banton**, Yardie; **Gregory Isaacs**, Don Man Girl; **Ninjaman**, Ting A Ling A Ling A School Pickney Sing Ting; **Cocoa Tea and Shaka Shamba**, Tender Loving; **Cutty Ranks**, Wealth; **Freddie McGregor**, Playing Hard To Get; **Capleton**, After Dark; **The Mighty Diamonds**, I Need A Roof; **General TK**, Screwface; **Yellowman**, Bedroom Eyes; **Lady G**, Certain Friends; **Peter Lloyd**, Dancehall Queen.

*Greensleeves Sampler Volume Ten; Greensleeves GREZCD10

Barrington Levy and Beenie Man, Under Mi Sensi ('94 Spliff); **Lt Stitchie**, Gangster; **Dawn Penn**, Ken Boothe; **Dennis Brown and Bounty Killer**, No No No (World A Respect '94 Mix); **Yardcore Collective**, Can't Stop The Dance; **Bounty Killer**, Down In The Ghetto; **Sanchez and Stingerman**, Bumptious Girl; **Beenie Man**, Press Button (remix); **Silver Cat**, Fowl Affair; **Colin Roach**, All Over You; **Papa San**, Shoo-Be-Doo; **Redrose and Spragga Benz**, Reminiscing; **Cocoa Tea and Shaka Shemba**, One Love; **Ninjaman**, Bad Publicity; **Gregory Isaacs and Beres Hammond**, One Good Turn; **Bounty Killer and Chuck Turner**, Run Around Girl; **Dawn Penn**, No No No.

*Greensleeves Sampler Volume Eleven; Greensleeves GREZCD11

Barrington Levy and Mega Banton, She's Mine ('94 Lick); **Major Mackerel and Jennifer Lara**, Stop!; **Garnett Silk**, Lord Watch Over Our Shoulders; **Beenie Man**, World Dance; **Bounty Killer and Colin Roach**, I'll Be Back; **Lt Stitchie**, Fresh Sexy Chicken; **Mad Cobra**, Selassie I Rules; **Sanchez and Bounty Killer**, Searching; **Redrose and Malvo**, Never Get; **Buccaneer**, Set The Pace; **Bounty Killer and Junior Reid**, This World's Too Haunted; **Red Dragon**, Sweetheart; **Sanchez**, Brown Eye Girl;

Beenie Man, Name Brand; **Redrose and Merciless**, You A Mi Heart; **Louie Culture**, Ganga Lee.

Greensleeves Sampler Volume Twelve; Greensleeves GREZCD12

Beenie Man and Silver Cat, Chronic; **Marcia Griffiths and Bounty Killer**, Tell Me Now; **Merciless, Little Hero, Action Fire**, Thief In The Night; **Sattalite**, Tribute To Garnett Silk; **Bounty Killer**, Smoke The Herb; **Junior Tucker**, Properly Ride; **Bunny Rugs**, Now That We've Found Love; **Bounty Killer**, Cellular Phone; **Pinchers**, Someone's Calling; **Chevelle Franklin**, Ooh Aah; **Wayne Wonder and Don Yute**; Sensi Ride; **Leroy Gibbons**, Magic Moment ('95 Remix); **Gregory Isaacs**, Dapper Slapper; **Everton Blender**, Blen' Dem; **Little Hero**, Seek God; **Brian and Tony Gold**, Ain't Nobody.

So comprehensive is the *Greensleeves Sampler* series, it's virtually a chronology of reggae since the early 1980s. The low numbers are the buoyant, post-roots beat, the mid-range is when digital was just getting a hold, but still trying to sound like 'real' instruments, while the recent releases are dancehall in its full glory, with the computers simply being themselves. These albums are an ideal introduction to the era, and a few are missing here because they're not quite up to scratch.

Just Ragga Volume Three; Charm CRCD16

Nadine and Terror Fabulous, Action; **Dennis Brown and Lovindeer**, Hands On Lover; **Ninja Ford**, Step Aside; **Galaxy**, Protein Vitamin And Mineral; **Red Dragon**, Clap Dance; **Dead And Bury**, Powerman; **Ninja Kid**, Boom Bye Bye; **Daddy Mite**, Tickie; **Admiral Bailey**, Butterfly; **Terror Fabulous and Daddy Screw**, Broke Wine Butterfly; **Cobra**, Don't Touch The Coke; **Terror Fabulous**, No Retreat; **Major Mackerel**, Diseases; **Sweetie Irie**, Racist.

Just Ragga Volume Five; Charm CRCD25

Mega Banton and Ricky General, No Ninja No Buju; **Mega**

Banton, Decision; **Shore Line Gary**, Screem; **Ninja Kid and Jigsy King**, Skin To Skin Connection; **Buccaneer**, Flip U Flop; **Bounty Killer**, Woman A Run Mi Dung; **General Degree, Dweet Sweet**; Baby Wayne, Look How It Nice; **Lt Stitchie**, Accident; **Buju Banton**, Good Looking Gal; **Buccaneer**, Ordinary Love; **Tony Curtis and Jigsy King**, My Sound A Murder.

*Just Ragga Volume Six; Charm CRCD28

Frankie Paul and Bounty Killer, The Real Score; **Jigsy King and Tony Curtis**, Any Man Yuh Want; **Tony Curtis**, Fantasy; **Terror Fabulous**, Watch Who You Drape, **Jacki Ranks and Susan Sweet**, Got It Drop It; **Pinchers**, Bloodstain; **Tenor Saw**, John Crow; **Black Don**, Clipper; **Spragga Benz**, Dem Flap; **Bounty Killer**, Big Or Small; **Cobra**, Body Ready; **Spragga Benz**, Jump Up And Scream; **Jigsy King**, Heaven Sent; **Mega Banton**, Money Money; **Spragga Benz**, Gi Wi Di Nanny; **Red Dragon and Deborahe Glasgow**, Respect Fi Ya Body.

*Just Ragga Volume Seven; Charm CRCD34

Top Cat, Over Your Body; **Tena Fly**, Bump And Grind; **Terry Ganzie**, Ragga Ragga; **Luciano and Gold Teet**, Searching; **Brian and Tony Gold**, Sex Me; **Beenie Man**, Modelling; **Silver Cat**, Dionne; **Buju Banton**, God Of My Salvation; **General Degree**, Papa Lover; **Jigsy King**, Eenie Meenie; **Buju Banton**, Man A Look You; **Mega Banton**, Proceed Gal; **Spragga Benz**, Camouflage; **Papa San**, Problem; **Louie Culture**, Cut That Out; **Future Troubles**, Kung Fu.

*Just Ragga Volume Eight; Charm CRCD39

Buju Banton, Rampage; **Jigsy King**, Gimme The Weed; **Top Cat**, Wine Up Yuh Body; **Tad Hunter and Louie Culture**, Let Him Go; **Cocoa Tea and Shabba Ranks**, Love Me Truly; **Terror Fabulous and Luciano**, In This Together; **Chukkie Star**, Time To Go; **Michael Rose**, Hot Stick; **Beenie Man**, All The Youths; **Ricky General**, Modelling; **Beenie Man and Michael Prophet**, Gun Man; **The Frisco Kid**, Yu Man; **Tony Rebel**, Know Jah;

Cocoa Tea and Ninjaman; This Girl Is Mine; **Beres Hammond and Red Fox**, The Wise.

*Just Ragga Volume Nine; Charm CRCD47

Cobra, Slam Good; **Red Dragon**, Woman Yuh Ready; **Simpleton**, Rubber Tyre; **Alley Cat**, B.M.W.; **Little Hero**, Raw; **Beenie Man**, Bank Robber; **Daddy Screw**, Dapper Instead; **Mega Banton**, Yuh Enemy; **Mega Banton**, Them Nu Sure; **Jooxie Nice**, Healing Of The Nation; **Lady Saw**, Incline Thine ear; **Christine 16 and Ninjaman**, Demanding; **Buccaneer**, Turn Around; **Lady G.**, Money Inna Bungle; **Glamma Kid**, Nation A Gal.

Not nearly as high profile as the *Ragga Ragga Ragga* or *Greensleeves Sampler* series, but just because the albums don't simply round up the usual suspects – not exclusively, anyway – doesn't mean they should be overlooked. On the selection made above, there are any number of gems waiting to be unearthed.

*Massive Volume Three; FFRR 8281732

DISC ONE: **Peter Hunnigale and The Night Flight Band**, Ragamuffin Girl; **Anthony Malvo and Tiger**, Come Back To Me; **Phillip Leo and CJ Lewis**, Why Do Fools Fall In Love; **Trevor Hartley and Clement Irie**, No More Nine Til Five; **Tenor Fly**, Roughneck Fashion; **Junior Tucker**, Don't Test; **Barry Room**, Making Love; **Frankie Paul**, Dial My Heart; **Deborahe Glasgow**, Give Me That Touch; **Kofi and John McLean**, I'm Still In Love With You; **Gregory Isaacs**, Too Good To Be True; **Slim Baston**, Push Push.

DISC TWO: **Aswad and Sweetie Irie**, On And On; **Barrington Levy and Sasafras**, Step Up In Love; **JC Lodge**, Telephone Love; **Foxy Brown**, Fast Car; **Clement Irie**, Nice Every Time; **Pepper and Daddie Freddie**, Ickie Fashion; **Thriller U**, It's Over; **The Instigators**, We Ain't Been Getting Along; **Janet Davis**, Two-Timing Lover; **Sandra Cross**, My Best Friend's Man; **Anthony Mike**, Car Crash; **Freddie McGregor**, Smile.

**Massive Volume Four*; FFRR 8282102

DISC ONE: **Krystal and Shabba Ranks**, Twice My Age; **Janet Davis and CJ Lewis**, Worried Over You; **Gregory Peck**, Poco Man Jam; **Chaka Demus**, Chaka On The Move; **Admiral Bailey**, Holy Water; **Sweetie Irie and Joe 90**, New Talk; **Maxi Priest and Tiger**, I Know Love; **Deborahe Glasgow and Shabba Ranks**, Mr Lover Man; **Phillip Leo and CJ Lewis**, Good Thing Going; **Junior Reid**, One Blood; **Maka B and Kofi**, Proud Of Mandela; **Nerius Joseph**, Guidance.

DISC TWO: **Beats International Featuring Lindy Layton**, Dub Be Good To Me; **Frankie Paul**; I Wanna Rock; **Cocoa Tea**, First Date; **Sanchez**, Tears; **Mike Anthony**, Glide Gently; **Peter Hunningdale**, If You Want It; **Barry Boom**, Hurry Over; **Royden Foster**, Dancing With My Baby; **Winsome and Frankie Paul**, Let's Start All over; **Home-T**; Are You Going My Way; **Trevor Hartley**, Baby Don't Go Too Far; **Karen Smith**, Paradise; **Intense**, You Are The One.

The *Massive* albums concern themselves with the lighter end of dancehall and modern-day reggae. Perhaps most suitable for the beginner, or as some sort of chill-out zone for the true hard-core fan.

*Ragga Mania One; Fashion FABCD001

General Levy, Ragga Ragga; **Top Cat**, Request The Style; **Janet-Lee Davis and Tippa Irie**, Baby I've Been Missing You; **Ricky General**, Splurt; **Sweetie Irie**, Slim Body Girls; **Cutty Ranks and Tenor Levy**, Wha Dem A Watch We For; **Tenor Fly**, Bright Side Of Life; **CJ Lewis and Phillip Leo**, Why Do Fools Fall In Love; **Red Dragon**, Leave Your Man Alone; **Jack Radics**, Groovin'; **Joseph Cotton**, Rub Up Push Up; **Nerious Joseph and Tenor Fly**, My Girl; **Frankie Paul**, FP The Greatest; **Nerious Joseph**, Guidance; **Dirtsman**, Impeccable.

As a mid-priced, cross-the-board compilation, this really can't be beaten. It takes in Jamaica and the UK, hardcore and lovers', the pop and the inaccessible, and the well known and the obscure. It would be one of the perfect starting points for late-model ragga, if only it didn't have such awful packaging and an information-free sleeve. Still, it's only *Volume One*.

Ragga Ragga Ragga! One; Greensleeves GRELCD192

Jigsy King, Don't Know; **Capleton**, Husband Goody Goody; **Galaxy P**, Movie Star; **Bounty Killer and Redrose**, Intimate; **Snagga Puss**, Woman Fi Look Good; **Brian and Tony Gold and Capleton**, Living In A Dream; **Mad Cobra**, Mek Noise; **Cocoa Tea and Buju Banton**, Too Young; **Major Mackerel**, Galong So; **Spragga Benz**, Red Alert; **Jigsy King**, Work The Body Good; **Daddy Screw and Major Christie**, Sake A Yuh Body; **Snagga Puss, Redrose, Lizard, Frankie Paul, Flourgon, Malvo and Red Dragon**, Informer; **Ninjaman and Ninja Ford**, The Return – Father And Son; **Grindsman**, Rude Bwoy No Powder; **Galaxy P**, Money; **Baja Jedd**, Holy Moly; **Red Fox**, Jessica.

Ragga Ragga Ragga! Two; Greensleeves GRELCD204

Bounty Killer and Ninjaman, Bad Boy Nuh Cub Scout; **Beenie Man**, Dis De Program; **Papa San**, Sireen; **Terror Fabulous**, Run Come; **Saba Tooth**, Wap Dem Girl; **Bounty Killer**, Trespass; **Duckman**, Fat Piece Of Goose; **Ninjaman**, Hollow Point Bad Boy; **Red Dragon**, Burning Up; **Bounty Killer**, Not Another Word; **Daddy Screw**, You Must Be A Maniac; **Lt Stitchie**, Wood Fire; **Galaxy P**, Dem Bawling Out; **Tumpa Lion**, Jockey Wid Di Distance; **Daddy Lizard**, Run Gal Run; **Mad Cobra**, Hotness; **Simpleton**, Sperm Rod; **Bounty Killer**, Nuh Have No Heart.

Ragga Ragga Ragga! Three; Greensleeves GRELCD212

Beenie Man, World Dance; **Bounty Killer**, War Is Not A Nice Thing; **Turbo Belly**, Wap Dem; **Silver Cat**, Dead In Ya; **Louie Culture**, Woman No; **Jigsy King**, Every Mickle Makes A Muckle; **Pinchers**, Hey Boy Red Indian; **Mad Cobra**, Gallowas; **Ninjaman**, World Dance; **Judas**, Nozzle And Trigger; **General Degree**, Only Master God; **Red Indian**, Riding Through South; **Chuckleberry**, My Sound; **Merciless**, Joker Gangsta; **Papa San**, Bun Ting; **Mad Cobra**, More Dem Talk; **Buccaneer**, Police In A Pocket; **Daddy Squid**, You Dead Again.

The *Ragga Ragga Ragga!* series is one of the best recent ragga compilations: taking mostly Jammy's, Shocking Vibes or Redrose and Malvo productions, and with an accent on variety, the albums cut across all aspects of dancehall reggae in the mid-1990s but manage to keep the beat on the hardcore side. These are not really for the nervous.

Ram Dancehall; Mango CDIM1018

JC Lodge, Hurricane; **Cocoa Tea**, Bad Love Affair; **Lady Patra**, Lonely Am I; **Dean Fraser**, Caution; **Hugo Barrington**, True Loving; **Brian Gold and Tony**, Maniac; **Tiger**, Never Let Go; **Home-T**, Don't Throw Your Love Away; **Johnny P**, Ring A Roses; **Admiral Tibet**, Madman.

Ras Records Presents A Reggae Christmas; Ras RASCD3101

Don Carlos and Glenice Spencer, We Wish You A Merry Christmas, Jingle Bells; **June Lodge**, Joy Of The World; **Freddie McGregor**, Oh Come All Ye Faithful, Feliz Navidad; **Michigan and Smiley**, Little Drummer Boy; **Peter Broggs**, The Twelve Days Of Christmas; **Pablo Black**, Silent Night; **Eek-A-Mouse**, The Night Before Christmas.

This mildly dancehall (well, you can't have anything too violent on a belly full of Turkey and Christmas pudding!) CD isn't nearly as cheesy as you'd think it might be. In fact, if you've played your *Salsoul Christmas Album* until it's worn out, this'll make a very good alternative.

Reggae Dance Party; Ras RASCD3018

Natural Beauty, Nice Up Dance; **Barrington Levy**, Do The Dance; **Michigan and Smiley**, Reggae Ska; **Don Carlos**, Springheel Skanking; **Wayne Smith**, Teach Me To Dance; **Black Uhuru**, Great Train Robbery; **Paul Blake and The Blood Fire Posse**, Get Flat; **Sugar Minott**, Rub-A-Sound; **Horace Andy**, Elementary; **JC Lodge**, You Can Dance; **Gregory Isaacs**, Private Beach Party.

Reggae Hits Volume One; Jetstar JECD1001

Barrington Levy, Under Mi Sensi; **Sugar Minott**, Herbsman

Hustling; **Tony Tuff**, Mix Me Down; **Neville Brown**, Haul And Pull Up; **Gregory Isaacs**, Lovers Magic; **Dennis Brown**, Someone Special; **Natural Touch**, Gimme Good Loving; **Sandra Reid**, Feel So Good; **Carol Campbell**, Between You And Me; **Paulette Tajah**, Cos You Love Me baby; **Aswad**, Roots Rocking; **The Investigators**, Woman I need Your Loving.

Reggae Hits Volume Two; Jetstar JECD1002

John Holt and Dennis Brown, Wildfire; **Gregory Isaacs**, I'll Be On My Way; **The Mighty Diamonds**, Inferiority Complex, Country Living; **Junior Byles**, Curly Locks; **Horace Fergeson**, Senci Addick; **Caroll Thompson**, Baby Be True; **Sandra Reid**, Caught You In A Lie; **Sister Audrey**, I Love You; **Paula**, Jazzy; **Tinga Stewart**, I'm Gonna Fall In Love; **Horseman**, Horsemove (giddiup); **Sugar Minott**, A House Is Not A Home.

Reggae Hits Volume Three; Jetstar JECD1003

Nitty Gritty, Sweet Reggae Music; **Frankie Paul**, Shub In; **Kenny Knots**, Watch How the People Dancing; **Half Pint**, Greetings; **Pam Hall**, Dear Boopsie; **Supercat**, Boops; **Sophia George**, Girlie Girlie; **Tyrone Taylor**, Members Only; **Audrey Hall**, One Dance Won't Do; **Jack Wilson**, Sixth Street; **Tipper Irie**, Hello Darling; **Peter Hunnidale**, Be My Lady; **Sandra Cross**, It's You; **Undivided Roots**, Party Nite; **Boris Gardiner**, Guilty.

Reggae Hits Volume Six; Jetstar JECD1006

Boris Gardiner, My Commanding Wife; **Clement Irie and Robert French**, Bun And Cheese; **Kofi**, Looking Over Love; **Sanchez**, Baby Can I Hold You Tonight; **Wayne Wonder**, New Way To Say I Love You; **Bob Marley**, Stick By Me; **Manifest**, I Want To Get Next to You; **Top Cat**, Love Me Ses; **Intense**, On My Mind; **Roni**, Lovers' Affair; **Taxman** Fatal Attraction; **Madoo, U.U. and Captain Barky**, Mix Up; **Douglas, Lambert and Wayne Fire**, Sweet And Nice.

Reggae Hits Volume Eight; Jetstar JECD1008

Michael Prophet and Ricky Tough, Your Love; **Major Danger**, Know Fi Move Your Waist; **Red Dragon**, Ku Klung Klung; **Chaka Demus**, Spirit; **Nardo Ranks**, Burrp; **Sweetie Irie**, Money Honey; **Johnny P**, Body Tune Up; **Frankie Paul and Papa San**, Buck Wild; **Thriller U**, Careless Whisper; **Sammy Levi**, Mrs Jones; **Lloyd Brown**, Sharing The Night; **Leroy Mafia**, Finders Keepers; **Wayne with Brian and Tony Gold**, One Night Wonder; **Calvin**, 2AM; **Pure Silk**, Do You Ever Think About Me; **Trisha**, Ticket To Ride.

Reggae Hits Volume Thirteen; Jetstar JECD1013

Shaggy and Rayvon, Big Up; **Capleton**, Man Kind; **General TK**, I Spy; **Buju Banton**, How The World A Run; **Carol Gonzalez**, Second Class; **Terror Fabulous**, Woman A You; **Tenor Saw and Buju Banton**, Ring The Alarm Quick; **Marcia Griffiths, Tony Rebel, Cutty Ranks and Buju Banton**, Discovery; **Sanchez**, Missing You Now; **Freddie McGregor**, I Was Born A Winner; **Beres Hammond, Sugar Minott and Tony Rebel**, Where Is The Love; **Beres Hammond and Buju Banton**, Who Say Man No Cry; **Barry Boom and Cutty Ranks**, Can This Be Real; **Wayne Wade**, I Love You Too Much; **Lefty Banton**, You Are My Lady; **Frankie Paul**, End Of The Road; **Jack Rueben and The Riddle**, Go Round; **Singing Sweet**, Save The Best For Last.

This selection of *Reggae Hits* is a good cross-section of a series that mixes up the old and the new with particular success, leaving listeners in no doubt about how it all relates to each other.

This Is Dancehall; Continuum CDCTUM1

Marcia Griffiths, Sugar Wogga Man; **Anthony Haughton**, How Else Can I Ease The Pain; **Singing Melody**, Best Friends; **Frankie Paul**, My Love; **Kevin B**, Every Kind Of People; **Jerry Johnson**, Sax-A-Rock; **Reverend Badoo**, Send Down Some; **JR Demus**, Work It Out; **Ravon**, Struggle; **Shaggy**, Science; **Dollar Man**, New Talk; **Judas**, Pretty Girls; **White Mice**, The Love Is Gone; **The Livin' Crew**, Dub Dis.

Tougher Than Tough – The Story Of Jamaican Music; Mango
IBXCD1

DISC FOUR: *Dance Hall Good To We 1982-1993*
Gregory Isaacs, Night Nurse; **Yellowman**, Mad Over Me;
Michigan and Smiley, Diseases; **Johnny Osbourne**, Water
Pumpee; **Frankie Paul**, Pass The Tusheng Peng; **Barrington
Levy**, Here I Come; **Tenor Saw**, Ring The Alarm; **Wayne Smith**,
Under Me Sleng Teng; **Anthony Redrose**, Tempo; **Supercat**,
Boops; **Half Pint**, Greetings; **Admiral Bailey**, Punanny; **Red
Dragon**, Hol' A Fresh; **Gregory Isaacs**, Rumours; **Tinga Stewart
and Ninjaman**, Cover Me; **Papa San and Lady G**, Legal Rights;
Shabba Ranks, Wicked Inna Bed; **Pichers**, Bandelero; **Tiger**,
Yuh Dead Now; **Buju Banton**, Bogle Dance; **Chaka Demus and
Pliers**, Murder She Wrote; **Shaggy**, Oh Carolina.

Which brings us back nicely to where it all started and 'Oh
Carolina'. But more than just closing the circle, this last chapter
in the *Tougher Than Tough* story is ideal for those who are a bit
intimidated by the current state of play in the dancehalls. With
the exception of the last track, this is all pre-1993 and therefore –
given the speed of dancehall reggae's evolution – very early
stuff, with the computers still sounding like 'proper' instruments. All the important evolutionary tracks are there – 'Boops',
'Sleng Teng', 'Greetings', 'Bandelero' and so on – so it works
both as a bridge from one era to the next and as an enjoyable
gateway for the sceptical.